DEDICATED TO

J. F. K.

PREFACE

In this book I have attempted to provide the reader with an account of those aspects of ferromagnetism which give promise of being of outstanding interest during the next few years. Ferromagnetism as such is no longer fundamentally a mystery, and if, for this reason, the subject has lost its attractiveness for some, others will be stimulated to use it in attempts to clear up a few of the many dark corners in the theory of metals. It is in this direction, in all likelihood, that the future of the subject lies.

It is as yet too soon to tell how such applications may best be made and I have, therefore, attempted in only one or two places to indicate such applications specifically. But it has been my aim to emphasize a manner of analyzing the problem that was sufficiently rigorous to bring out the physical kernel of the phenomena involved and yet simple enough to be capable of generalization to the more complex systems which are bound to become of increasing interest as our understanding of ferromagnetism becomes more complete.

To be more precise, there are three fundamental problems which strike me as among the most interesting and important of those confronting the student of metals today, and all three of these may conveniently be approached by a study of magnetic phenomena, especially in relation to ferromagnetic media.

The first problem is the preparation of materials of accurately known chemical composition. Dr. Yensen's chapter on this subject indicates something of its importance and scope but could easily be expanded into a book of its own, a book in which considerable space should be devoted to the application of thermodynamics and physical chemistry to the reactions going on in an annealing furnace.

The second is the study of Zwicky's "cooperative phenomena" and the related structure-sensitive properties of metals which are so strikingly apparent in ferromagnetic materials. Among the simplest examples of such effects are those depending on the geometrical arrangements of atoms in an alloy, the superstructures, solubility limits, aging characteristics, etc., and the corresponding quantities related to the mutual arrangement of elementary magnets in a metal. Here, it seems to me, the important thing is to build a theory of alloys that will account for their properties about as well as the simple Weiss theory accounts for the magnetic properties of iron; I have, consequently, emphasized those methods which I hope can do this instead of going into detail about the many interesting attempts that have been made to correct the relatively minor points at which the Weiss theory is inadequate.

The third problem is that of measuring the physical condition, by which I mean the internal strains and the grain orientations, of metals. Although methods for doing this are well known, there are cases in which the magnetic approach to the problem may be of importance, and I have tried to indicate in general how a study of the symmetry properties of polycrystals may be a useful supplement to the established methods.

Since this book covers ground between physics and metallurgy, it will probably have readers of widely different training. For the sake of those who merely want a general understanding of the arguments rather than an ability to use them in original work, I have prefaced most of the mathematical sections with illustrations of how the results may be obtained in simple cases by more elementary methods.

The application of quantitative reasoning in metallurgy and the presentation of metallurgical problems to physicists should lead us to many new and fascinating discoveries. It is with the hope that my book may in some slight way be useful in bringing this about that I turn it over to its readers.

FRANCIS BITTER.

MASSACHUSETTS INSTITUTE OF TECHNOLOGY,
CAMBRIDGE, MASSACHUSETTS,
June, 1937.

ACKNOWLEDGMENTS

I take great pleasure in thanking all those who have helped me in the preparation of this book, and especially in expressing my indebtedness to Dr. T. D. Yensen of the Westinghouse Research Laboratories for contributing Chapter IV on "Magnetic Materials and Their Preparation," a subject to which he has devoted a lifetime of study; to Professor F. Zwicky of the California Institute of Technology for contributing the appendix on one of his many brilliant conceptions, "Cooperative Phenomena"; to Dr. W. C. Elmore for contributing paragraphs 33 and 34 on magnetic powders and their application to the study of magnetic structures and other problems; to Dr. F. Seitz for valuable suggestions on the application of matrix methods to the discussion of symmetry properties; to Dr. R. M. Bozorth for reading the manuscript; to L. P. Tarasov and A. R. Kaufman for helping with the proof reading; and lastly to M. A. B. for timely assistance during various stages of the work.

FRANCIS BITTER.

MASSACHUSETTS INSTITUTE OF TECHNOLOGY,
CAMBRIDGE, MASSACHUSETTS,
  June, 1937.

CONTENTS

INTRODUCTION
TO FERROMAGNETISM

CHAPTER I

GENERAL INTRODUCTION

The object of this book is to describe the outstanding properties of ferromagnetic substances and especially to correlate as many of these properties as possible. This first chapter contains a brief introduction to some of the concepts commonly used in thinking of magnetism and an outline of the main characteristics of ferromagnetic materials.

1. Ferromagnetism.—There are many properties that might be taken as criteria for the existence of ferromagnetism, or by means of which a definition might be attempted, but it would be difficult to make a definition that would be both useful and precise. In the pages to come the term will be used in a loose sense only, and will mean "magnetism similar to that of iron." Very few substances are ferromagnetic. They are iron, nickel, cobalt, some of their alloys with each other and with other elements, a few substances containing only nonferromagnetic elements, and a good many minerals. As a class, these substances are unique because of the relatively large forces they can exert on each other over macroscopic distances. It is impossible to state quite generally what the seat of these forces is, but it will often be found useful to think of them as arising from magnetic particles having atomic or subatomic dimensions and consequently to interpret changes in magnetic condition as due to changes in the elementary magnetic particles.

Ferromagnetism manifests itself as an interaction between two or more bodies, and we therefore require two or more observations to specify the conditions in any particular experiment. In other words, in describing the magnetic state of a body, we must take into consideration both the distribution of magnetism outside the body and the internal properties of the body. In order to simplify the detailed description of external conditions, the notion of a magnetic field is introduced. This field, denoted by the symbol **H,** is a function specifying for every point in space both a number and a direction. Such a function is called a vector-point function. The introduction of **H** serves to standardize external conditions. Thus, instead of specifying that in a given experiment the sample to be tested was placed so many centimeters from the pole of a magnet constructed according to such and such specifications, we say that the test piece was placed at a given point in a field **H.** In the following paragraphs certain relationships between magnetism and electricity are listed by means of which an experimenter may determine just what field is produced in his apparatus.

The second requisite for describing magnetization must involve a knowledge of the properties of materials. It turns out that we require another vector-point function **I.** This function, called the intensity of magnetization, or simply the magnetization, vanishes in empty space, as might be anticipated from the fact that it describes a condition of matter. A study of these vector fields **I** and **H** will form the chief part of this book.

It seems a pity that in attempting a description of ferromagnetic action, we should begin by making use of such a mysterious and nebulous concept as the magnetic field. As it has been introduced, the magnetic field is a *function* which is useful in describing magnetic interactions. We shall use it as such a mathematical fiction only, and the question of its physical reality and structure need not concern us.

We could now proceed to define **H** and **I** quantitatively in terms of magnets and the forces acting between them and so perhaps avoid a few assumptions that are not essential to the further development of the subject. It seems advisable, however, to follow a course more in keeping with the historical development of magnetism and, as we proceed, to point out which results obtained are most general, and which depend on special assumptions.

2. Magnetic Poles and Their Fields.—A part of our legacy from the past is a concept that has proved very useful in spite of the fact that, as far as we now know, it has no counterpart in nature. The concept is that of an isolated magnetic pole, a point in space assumed to have special properties. Like poles repel each other, unlike poles attract each other with a force that is proportional to the product of their pole strengths and inversely proportional to the square of the distance between them. This is known as Coulomb's law. Unit pole strength is so defined in the c.g.s. system of units that two like unit poles situated 1 cm. apart in a vacuum will repel each other with a force of 1 dyne. From this follows a simple definition of magnetic fields. The force that any arrangement of poles exerts on unit positive pole at any given point is equal in magnitude and direction to the magnetic field **H** at that point.[1]

Our earth is itself a permanent magnet, and we can make use of this fact in defining the difference between the unlike poles mentioned above. A positive, or north, pole is attracted to the geographic north; a negative, or south, pole to the geographic south. The unit of magnetic field is the oersted. A field of 1 oersted exerts a force of 1 dyne on a unit pole. It is sometimes convenient to express a magnetic field graphically. This is done by means of lines which are everywhere parallel to the field, and whose density is equal to the field strength. Such lines are called "maxwells," and the number of oersteds at any given point is numerically equal to the number of maxwells per square centimeter, the square centimeter being measured on a surface

---

[1] The notation used in this book is the following: A vector quantity is designated by **bold-face type**. Let **i, j, k** be unit vectors parallel to the x-, y-, and z-axes of a right-handed orthogonal coordinate system. A vector from the origin to the point (x, y, z) is written

$$\mathbf{r} = x\mathbf{i} + y\mathbf{j} + z\mathbf{k}$$

The scalar product of two vectors **a** and **b** is

$$\mathbf{a} \cdot \mathbf{b} = a_x b_x + a_y b_y + a_z b_z$$

where a_x is the x component of **a**, etc. The vector product of **a** and **b** is

$$\mathbf{a} \times \mathbf{b} = (a_y b_z - a_z b_y)\mathbf{i} + (a_z b_x - a_x b_z)\mathbf{j} + (a_x b_y - a_y b_x)\mathbf{k}$$

The operator *del* is written

$$\mathbf{\nabla} = \frac{\partial}{\partial x}\mathbf{i} + \frac{\partial}{\partial y}\mathbf{j} + \frac{\partial}{\partial z}\mathbf{k}$$

and the Laplacian

$$\mathbf{\nabla}^2 = \frac{\partial^2}{\partial x^2} + \frac{\partial^2}{\partial y^2} + \frac{\partial^2}{\partial z^2}$$

perpendicular to the field. The number of maxwells issuing from a unit pole may be calculated by remembering that at a distance of 1 cm. the field strength is 1 oersted. The total number of maxwells, therefore, is numerically equal to the surface area of a sphere of unit radius, or 4π.

According to the preceding, the field surrounding a pole may be written

$$\mathbf{H} = \frac{m}{r^2} \frac{\mathbf{r}}{r} \tag{1}$$

m being the pole strength, r the distance from the point in question to the pole, and the direction of the field being, of course, everywhere radial. Instead of this vector field, a scalar potential is sometimes used. This quantity φ is so defined that its negative gradient is the magnetic field

$$-\nabla\varphi = \mathbf{H} \tag{2}$$

The potential of an isolated pole is then

$$\varphi = \frac{m}{r} \tag{3}$$

and may be shown by integrating (1) to be equal to the work in ergs required to bring unit positive pole from infinity to a point r cm. from the pole m.

Since fields add vectorially, we may write for the resultant field due to any number of poles

$$\mathbf{H} = \sum_n \mathbf{H}_n = -\sum_n \nabla\varphi_n = -\nabla\sum_n \varphi_n \tag{4}$$

The potential due to a group of poles is equal to the sum of the potentials of the individual poles. An expression often used in the study of magnetism is that representing the potential due to equal unlike poles a fixed distance δ apart, at distances r from the poles large compared to δ. This potential, or field, is said to be that of a dipole. The strength of a dipole is called its moment $\mathbf{\mu}$, where

$$\mathbf{\mu} = m\mathbf{\delta} \tag{5}$$

$\mathbf{\delta}$ being a vector numerically equal to δ and pointing from the south to the north pole. The potential at any point due to a dipole a distance r away may be derived as follows: If r_1 and r_2 are the distances from the poles to the point in question, as shown in Fig. 1, and θ is the angle between $\mathbf{u}$ and $\mathbf{r}$, we have

$$\varphi = \varphi_1 + \varphi_2 = \frac{m}{r_1} - \frac{m}{r_2}$$

$$= \frac{m}{r - \frac{\delta}{2}\cos\theta} - \frac{m}{r + \frac{\delta}{2}\cos\theta}$$

$$= \frac{m}{r}\left(\frac{1}{1 - \frac{\delta}{2r}\cos\theta} - \frac{1}{1 + \frac{\delta}{2r}\cos\theta}\right)$$

$$= \frac{m\delta}{r^2}\cos\theta = -\mathbf{u}\cdot\nabla\frac{1}{r} \tag{6}$$

terms involving $(\delta/r)^2$ being neglected in comparison with unity. Furthermore, since $\mathbf{H} = -\nabla\varphi$, we arrive at the following expression for the field of a dipole for $r \gg \delta$:

$$\mathbf{H} = -\nabla\left(-\mathbf{u}\cdot\nabla\frac{1}{r}\right)$$

$$= -\frac{\mathbf{u}}{r^3} + \frac{3\mathbf{u}\cdot\mathbf{r}}{r^5}\mathbf{r} \tag{7}$$

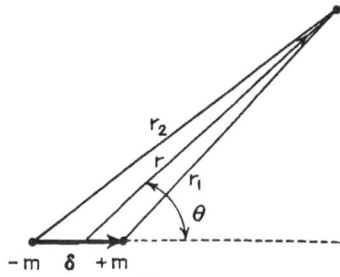

FIG. 1.

The mathematical study of the behavior of poles among which the inverse-square law holds has been a subject of much interest to mathematicians, and their work has been fundamental in the development of the theory of electricity and magnetism. Several especially important results are stated below. They follow from the inverse-square law of force.

Gauss's Theorem.—If any closed surface is taken in the magnetic field, and if H_n denotes the component of the magnetic field at any point of this surface in the direction of the outward drawn normal, then

$$\iint H_n ds = 4\pi M \tag{8}$$

where the integration extends over the whole surface, and M is the total charge enclosed by this surface.

The Equations of Laplace and Poisson.—The potential defined above satisfies Poisson's equation

$$\nabla^2 \varphi = -4\pi\rho \tag{9}$$

where ρ is the density of magnetic poles in space. When $\rho = 0$, this is called Laplace's equation.

$$\nabla^2 \varphi = 0 \tag{10}$$

Green's Theorem.—It may be shown that in any closed volume V bounded by a surface S

$$\int_V \mathbf{W} \cdot \nabla u\, dv = \int_S u\mathbf{W} \cdot \mathbf{n}\, ds - \int_V u\nabla \cdot \mathbf{W}\, dv \tag{11}$$

$\mathbf{n}$ being a unit vector normal to the surface S and pointing outward. This is a special form of Green's theorem.

3. The Magnetism of Electricity in Motion.—Somewhat over 100 years ago, in 1820, Oersted discovered that electric currents produced magnetic actions. The nature of this action may be expressed mathematically by saying that the infinitesimal field $d\mathbf{H}$ produced by an element of current di at a distance $\mathbf{r}$ is

$$d\mathbf{H} = \frac{di \times \mathbf{r}}{r^3} \tag{12}$$

This is known as the law of Biot and Savart.

In the present discussion, since $\mathbf{H}$ is already defined, we may take this equation as defining something new—an electric current. Practically, of course, the opposite procedure is more convenient, *viz.*, to define currents independently—by their electrolytic action, for instance—and from this to proceed to the concept of magnetic fields and poles. All that we have done so far, then, is to describe how hypothetical poles will be acted on by other poles or by electric currents. The rather abstract ideas with which we have been dealing are, however, made applicable to the experimental world by the introduction of a further relationship expressed in the law of electromagnetic induction, based on Faraday's discoveries of the year 1831. This law states that a changing magnetic field produces in a conductor an electromotive force (e.m.f.) proportional to the rate at which the conductor cuts lines of magnetic flux. It now becomes possible to calculate the effect of one current on another, and the magnetic field appears only as a mathematical tool to help in the calculation.

Amplified, and assuming the existence of electric charges in empty space only, the foregoing statements may be put into the following concise form:

$$\mathbf{\nabla} \cdot \mathbf{E} = 4\pi\rho$$

$$\mathbf{\nabla} \cdot \mathbf{H} = 0$$

$$\mathbf{\nabla} \times \mathbf{E} = -\frac{1}{c}\dot{\mathbf{H}}$$

$$\mathbf{\nabla} \times \mathbf{H} = \frac{1}{c}(\dot{\mathbf{E}} + 4\pi\rho\mathbf{v})$$

$$\mathbf{F} = \mathbf{E} + \frac{1}{c}\mathbf{v} \times \mathbf{H} \tag{13}$$

where ρ is the density of electric poles, $\mathbf{E}$ is the field due to these poles, $\mathbf{v}$ is their velocity, and $\mathbf{F}$ the total force acting on a pole of unit strength. When $\rho = 0$, Eqs. (13) reduce to Maxwell's equations for empty space.

As an example of the application of these ideas, we shall consider the magnetic field due to an electric charge moving in a closed circular orbit. The average effect of such a charge is equivalent to that of a circular current, and the field of such a current may be found by integrating Eq. (12):

$$\mathbf{H} = \int d\mathbf{H} = \oint \frac{d\mathbf{i} \times \mathbf{R}}{R^3} \tag{14}$$

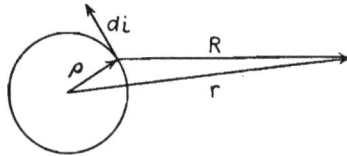

FIG. 2.

where $\mathbf{R} = \mathbf{r} - \mathbf{\rho}$, as shown in Fig. 2.
We may write

$$\frac{1}{R^2} = \frac{1}{r^2 + \rho^2 - 2r\rho \cos\theta} = \frac{1}{r^2}\frac{1}{1 - 2\frac{\mathbf{r} \cdot \mathbf{\rho}}{r^2} + \frac{\rho^2}{r^2}}$$

or, for $r >> \rho$, so that ρ^2/r^2 may be neglected in the foregoing expression,

$$\frac{1}{R^2} = \frac{1}{r^2}\left(\frac{1}{1 - 2\frac{\mathbf{r} \cdot \mathbf{\rho}}{r^2}}\right) = \frac{1}{r^2}\left(1 + 2\frac{\mathbf{r} \cdot \mathbf{\rho}}{r^2}\right)$$

$$\frac{1}{R^3} = \frac{1}{r^3}\left(1 + 2\frac{\mathbf{r} \cdot \mathbf{\rho}}{r^2}\right)^{\frac{3}{2}} = \frac{1}{r^3}\left(1 + 3\frac{\mathbf{r} \cdot \mathbf{\rho}}{r^2}\right)$$

and hence

$$\mathbf{H} = \frac{1}{r^3}\oint di \times (\mathbf{r} - \varrho)\left[1 + 3\frac{\mathbf{r} \cdot \varrho}{r^2}\right]$$

Because $\oint di \times \mathbf{r} = 0$, and because we are neglecting powers of ρ/r higher than the first, this expression reduces to

$$\mathbf{H} = -\frac{1}{r^3}\oint di \times \varrho + \frac{3}{r^5}\oint di \times \mathbf{r}\,\mathbf{r} \cdot \varrho \qquad (15)$$

It is necessary to rewrite this expression in order to see the significance of the second term on the right side of Eq. (15). If **a, b, c** are any vectors at all, then

$$\mathbf{a} \times [\mathbf{b} \times \mathbf{c}] = \mathbf{b}(\mathbf{a} \cdot \mathbf{c}) - \mathbf{c}(\mathbf{a} \cdot \mathbf{b})$$

from which it can be deduced that

$$\mathbf{a} \times [\mathbf{b} \times \{\mathbf{c} \times \mathbf{d}\}] = \mathbf{b}(\mathbf{a} \cdot \mathbf{c} \times \mathbf{d}) - \mathbf{c} \times \mathbf{d}(\mathbf{a} \cdot \mathbf{b})$$
$$= \mathbf{a} \times \mathbf{c}(\mathbf{b} \cdot \mathbf{d}) - \mathbf{a} \times \mathbf{d}(\mathbf{b} \cdot \mathbf{c}) \qquad (16)$$

The equality of the two expressions on the right side of Eq. (16) makes it possible to write, putting

$$\mathbf{a} = \varrho \qquad \mathbf{b} = \mathbf{d} = \mathbf{r} \qquad \mathbf{c} = di$$
$$\mathbf{r}(\varrho \cdot di \times \mathbf{r}) - di \times \mathbf{r}\varrho \cdot \mathbf{r} = \varrho \times di\,\mathbf{r} \cdot \mathbf{r} - \varrho \times \mathbf{r}\,\mathbf{r} \cdot di$$

or, since

$$\mathbf{a} \cdot \mathbf{b} \times \mathbf{c} = \mathbf{a} \times \mathbf{b} \cdot \mathbf{c}$$
$$\oint[\mathbf{r}(\varrho \times di \cdot \mathbf{r}) + di \times \varrho\,\mathbf{r} \cdot \mathbf{r}] = 2\oint di \times \mathbf{r}\,\varrho \cdot \mathbf{r} + \mathbf{r} \times$$
$$[\oint(di\,\varrho \cdot \mathbf{r} + \varrho\,di \cdot \mathbf{r})]$$

The last integral, upon evaluation, is found to be zero. In order to show that this is so, put

$$di = -c \sin \theta d\theta \mathbf{i} + c \cos \theta d\theta \mathbf{j}$$
$$\varrho = \rho \cos \theta \mathbf{i} + \rho \sin \theta \mathbf{j}$$
$$\mathbf{r} = r_x \mathbf{i} + r_y \mathbf{j} + r_z \mathbf{K}$$

and the integral in question reduces to expressions of the form

$$\int_0^{2\pi} (\sin^2 \theta - \cos^2 \theta)d\theta$$

which vanish.

The first integral on the right is identical with the second in Eq. (15). Noting that $\oint di \times \mathbf{r} = 0$, we obtain for H

$$\mathbf{H} = -\frac{1}{r^3}\oint di \times \varrho + \frac{1}{r^5}\frac{3r^2}{2}\oint di \times \varrho - \frac{1}{r^5}\frac{3\mathbf{r}}{2}\mathbf{r} \cdot \oint di \times \varrho$$

or, putting $\mathbf{\mu} = -\frac{1}{2}\oint di \times \varrho$, we obtain

$$\mathbf{H} = -\frac{\mathbf{\mu}}{r^3} + 3\frac{\mathbf{\mu} \cdot \mathbf{r}}{r^5}\mathbf{r} \qquad (17)$$

which is identical with Eq. (7). The field of a magnetic doublet is identical with that of a circular current at sufficiently great distances from the doublet or current. For points close to the dipole, or for distances r comparable to ρ in Fig. 2 or comparable to δ in Fig. 1, the similarity just observed disappears. If the current in the integral $\oint di \times \varrho$ is interpreted as the average effect of an electron of charge e e.s.u. moving around the circumference of a circle of area A in a time τ, then the scalar value of the magnetic moment may be written

$$\mu = \frac{eA}{c\tau} \qquad (18)$$

c being the velocity of light. This result can be shown to hold for any orbit of area A.[1]

4. The Vectors I and B.—In the last two sections some of the properties of the magnetic field were sketched, first in connection with magnetic poles, then in connection with electric currents. Especially important for our discussion of ferromagnetism are the expressions for the field of a dipole, as given in Eqs. (7) and (17). We shall use the term "magnetic dipole" to denote any system of magnets or currents from which fields arise that may satisfactorily be described by the expression

$$\mathbf{H} = \frac{\mathbf{\mu}}{r^3} - 3\frac{\mathbf{\mu} \cdot \mathbf{r}}{r^5}\mathbf{r} \qquad (19)$$

regardless of whether these fields are actually due to magnetic doublets or to currents or to a combination of both. In treating

---

[1] For further discussion, see M. ABRAHAM and R. BECKER, "The Classical Theory of Electricity and Magnetism," Blackie & Son, Ltd., London, 1932; C. E. WEATHERBURN, "Elementary Vector Analysis," George Bell & Sons, Ltd., London, 1928.

problems in which dipoles are so close together that their separation is comparable to the dimensions of the dipoles themselves, further assumptions must be made.

A particularly simple model, and one that is in many respects similar to actual matter, consists of an array of dipoles, each being free to rotate but otherwise fixed in space. The intensity of magnetization I of such a model is then defined as the average magnetic moment per unit of volume. Being an average quantity, the magnetization is not satisfactorily defined until the exact way of taking the average is specified. The difficulty of defining a suitable averaging process is illustrated in the following example.

Suppose that in a volume V there are N molecules of water. The average density of molecules is then $\rho = N/V$. What is the smallest volume v in which it is probable that a count would reveal n molecules, where $n/v = \rho$? Obviously, the answer to this question depends on the order of magnitude of the density fluctuations present. If we have a perfectly uniform arrangement of molecules, as in ice, then this smallest volume v is of the order of magnitude V/N, the average volume per molecule. If we have a random arrangement, as in water vapor, some fluctuations will occur, and we should have to measure the space occupied by a certain number of molecules in order to get a fair estimate of the average density. If we have to do with a fog, in which we have droplets as well as vapor, obviously the volume v must be large enough to determine the average number of drops per unit volume.

Returning now to the problem of magnetic intensity, we must be prepared to face the same situation. It may happen that in an aggregate of dipoles certain groups here and there have a different average orientation from their neighbors, just as drops have a different average density from the surrounding vapor. Indeed, as we shall find later on, this is precisely what happens normally even in as homogeneous a material as a single crystal. The symbol I for the intensity of magnetization at any point must therefore, in general, carry a subscript to denote how large a region in the neighborhood of that point was used in its evaluation. In the absence of a subscript, it will be assumed that the region was large enough so that the choice of a still larger one would not have altered the result.

The magnetic field due to any distribution of dipoles, and consequently also the field due to any given distribution of intensity of magnetization, may be calculated by means of Eq. (19). In terms of the potential, we have from Eqs. (4) and (6)

$$\varphi = -\sum \mathbf{\mu} \cdot \mathbf{\nabla}\frac{1}{r} = -\int \mathbf{I} \cdot \mathbf{\nabla}\frac{1}{r}dx'dy'dz'$$

$\mathbf{I}$ is the intensity of magnetization at the point x', y', z', and

$$\mathbf{\nabla}\frac{1}{r} = \left(\frac{\partial}{\partial x}\mathbf{i} + \frac{\partial}{\partial y}\mathbf{j} + \frac{\partial}{\partial z}\mathbf{k}\right)\frac{1}{\sqrt{(x-x')^2 + (y-y')^2 + (z-z')^2}}$$

It can be shown that

$$\mathbf{\nabla}\frac{1}{r} = -\nabla'\frac{1}{r}$$

where ∇' indicates differentiation with respect to x', y', and z'. We therefore have

$$\varphi = \int_v \mathbf{I} \cdot \mathbf{\nabla}'\frac{1}{r}dx'dy'dz'$$

or, using Green's theorem [Eq. (11)],

$$\varphi = \int \frac{\mathbf{I} \cdot \mathbf{n}}{r}ds - \int \frac{\mathbf{\nabla} \cdot \mathbf{I}}{r}dv$$

But we showed in Eq. (3) that the potential due to an isolated pole of strength m was m/r. It follows, therefore, that the dipoles of a magnetized body produce a field identical with that of free poles distributed inside the body with a density $\rho = -\mathbf{\nabla} \cdot \mathbf{I}$ and on its surface with a density $\sigma = \mathbf{I} \cdot \mathbf{n}$. In a uniformly magnetized body $\mathbf{\nabla} \cdot \mathbf{I} = 0$, and the external field may therefore be thought of as arising from a surface distribution of poles only.

In addition to the vectors $\mathbf{H}$ and $\mathbf{I}$, a third vector $\mathbf{B}$ is often used in describing magnetic materials. This vector, called the magnetic induction or magnetic flux density, is usually defined by the relation[1]

---

[1] An international commission has recently proposed that the unit of $\mathbf{B}$ be the gauss and that of $\mathbf{H}$ the oersted. This definition requires that Eq. (20) be written

$$\mathbf{B} = c\mathbf{H} + 4\pi\mathbf{I}$$

c being a constant with the dimensions of gauss/oersteds. For further discussion see A. E. Kennelly, *Trans. A.I.E.E.*, **50**, 737, 1931. In much of the literature both $\mathbf{B}$ and $\mathbf{H}$ are expressed in terms of gauss.

$$\mathbf{B} = \mathbf{H} + 4\pi \mathbf{I} \tag{20}$$

When all three of these vectors are parallel, it is sometimes convenient to use the quantities

$$\mu = \frac{B}{H} \tag{21}$$

$$k = \frac{I}{H} \tag{22}$$

called the permeability and susceptibility, respectively. The scalar μ above is, of course, not to be confused with the vector $\mathbf{\mu}$ used to represent the magnetic moment of a dipole.

The susceptibility and permeability are related by the equation

$$\mu = 1 + 4\pi k$$

Materials for which k is negative are called "diamagnetic." Materials for which k is positive are either paramagnetic or ferromagnetic, the latter classification being reserved for materials which, like iron, show saturation and hysteresis effects.

In order to describe changes in the magnetization of our model, certain assumptions must be made as to how a dipole may change its orientation. This last point is most important, and much confusion has arisen from a lack of understanding of its fundamental significance. For example, let us consider the two kinds of dipoles discussed in Par. 2 and 3. We shall now, of course, have to go beyond the expressions for the field at distant points and consider the mechanical properties of the dipoles them-

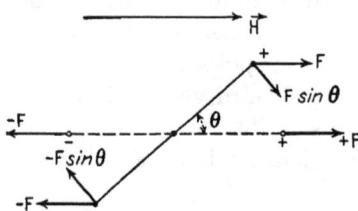

FIG. 3.

selves. For the time being we shall assume the dipoles to be sufficiently far apart so that the forces they exert on each other are negligible in comparison to the forces exerted by externally applied fields, and we shall take up first the case where the dipoles consist of magnetic poles only, the external field being uniform and equal to **H.** The conditions are illustrated in Fig. 3. From the definition of magnetic poles it follows that forces will act on the poles of the various doublets and will tend to rotate them until they are parallel to the applied field. In this position the external forces no longer exert a

torque.   The magnetization **I** plotted as a function of **H** for this
model may be represented by the curve shown in Fig. 4, called
the "magnetization curve."   In the absence of a field the dipoles
may be oriented at random.   The application of a small field
serves to render them all parallel.   The model is magnetized to
"saturation," this saturation intensity
being represented by I_0.   A further
increase of **H** cannot increase **I**.   If the
dipoles are bound to certain orientations
in the model by elastic forces of some kind,
then small fields will produce small rotations, larger fields will produce further
rotations, and the magnetization curve of
the model will be a gradually ascending

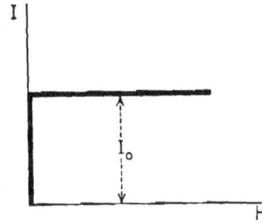

FIG. 4.

curve rather than the steep curve shown in Fig. 4.

. Magnetization proceeds very differently if we assume a model
identical in every respect with that of the previous paragraph,
except that the dipoles are electrons moving in circular orbits.
According to Larmor's theorem,[1] if an electron moving in an
elliptic or circular orbit around a nucleus is subjected to the action
of a magnetic field, the orbit is not oriented with respect to the
field but precesses around the direction of the field with a velocity
$\omega = eH/2mc$.   The magnetization of this model, unless it is
modified in some way, will therefore be unaffected by the presence
of an external field except in so far as the precession ω is concerned.
The effect of the precession is diamagnetic and will not be considered here.

Instead of proceeding from a model, as above, we might have
begun by assuming Maxwell's equations, a modified form of
Eq. (13).

$$\nabla \times \mathbf{E} = \frac{1}{c}\dot{\mathbf{B}}$$

$$\nabla \times \mathbf{H} = \frac{1}{c}(\dot{\mathbf{D}} + 4\pi\mathbf{j}) \qquad (23)$$

$$\nabla \cdot \mathbf{D} = 4\pi\rho \qquad \nabla \cdot \mathbf{B} = 0 \qquad \mathbf{D} = \epsilon\mathbf{E} \qquad \mathbf{B} = \mu\mathbf{H}$$

[1] J. LARMOR, "Aether and Matter," p. 341, The University Press,
Cambridge, Mass., 1900.   It can be shown, in fact, that the effect of a field
H on any system of particles that are affected by H according to the $\mathbf{v} \times \mathbf{H}$
law of Eq. (13) is entirely equivalent to a rotation about the direction of
H with an angular velocity $\omega = eH/2mc$.

j is the current density. These equations partially determine the behavior of matter. Some properties are left open and can be specified by suitable assumptions concerning μ and ϵ.

One of the consequences of these equations, to which we shall have occasion to refer, is that any change in the number of lines of magnetic flux linking a closed electric circuit produces an e.m.f. in that circuit. The value of this induced e.m.f. V is given by the negative time rate of change of flux linkage.

$$V = -\frac{\partial \Phi}{\partial t} \qquad (24)$$

Φ being the total flux linking the circuit.

5. Energy Relations.[1]—In considering the energy relations involved in magnetizing processes, it is convenient to make the following subdivisions:

E_1 = energy of the field-producing apparatus.

E_2 = energy of the sample being magnetized.

E_{12} = mutual energy resulting from the interaction of the sample and the field-producing apparatus.

W_{AB} = work done by external mechanical forces in moving the sample from one place A to another B.

This subdivision is perhaps arbitrary but will be found useful in following the changes produced by various types of magnetization. From these definitions and the principle of conservation of energy it follows that

$$W_{AB} = \delta E_1 + \delta E_2 + \delta E_{12} \qquad (25)$$

the symbol δ meaning the change in going from one state to another. In this section we shall consider the evaluation of the preceding quantities in two important cases.

Case 1.—The field is produced by a fixed distribution of poles. In this case E_1 = const., and therefore $\delta E_1 = 0$. The simplest example to consider is that of a permanent pole of strength m moved about in the field by external forces. The energy E_2 of the sample is constant; therefore $\delta E_2 = 0$, and (25) reduces to

$$W_{AB} = \delta E_{12}$$

If the points A and B are a distance ds apart, as shown in Fig. 5,

[1] See also E. A. Guggenheim, *Proc. Roy. Soc.*, **155**, 49, 1936.

we have from the discussion in Par. 2 for the force exerted by the field on m

$$\mathbf{F} = m\mathbf{H}$$

and, since the external force F_e required to move the pole is $-F$,

$$W_{AB} = -m\mathbf{H} \cdot \mathbf{ds} = -mHds \cos \theta$$

and the total mutual energy E_{12} is the work needed to bring the pole m from field free space to any point p

$$W_{\infty,p} = E_{12} = -m\int_p^\infty \mathbf{H} \cdot ds \tag{26}$$

The next simplest case is that of a dipole.   Again, $E_2 = $ const., or $\delta E_2 = 0$; and

$$W_{AB} = \delta E_{12} \tag{27}$$

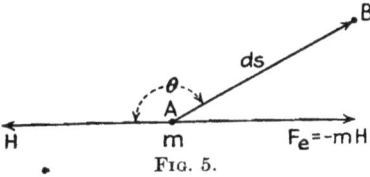

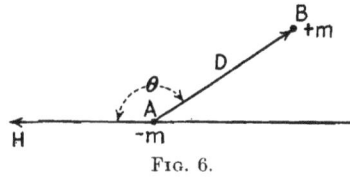

FIG. 5.   FIG. 6.

For a dipole to be brought from infinity to the position shown in Fig. 6, work equal to

$$W_{\infty,p} = E_{12} = -m\int_B^\infty \mathbf{H} \cdot ds + m\int_A^\infty \mathbf{H} \cdot ds \tag{27a}$$

$$= -m\int_B^A \mathbf{H} \cdot ds = -mHD \cos \theta = -\mathbf{\mu} \cdot \mathbf{H} = -\mu H \cos \theta$$

must be done.   Two types of forces are exerted by the field on the dipole.   A torque T given by

$$T = -\frac{\partial W}{\partial \theta} = -\mu H \sin \theta$$

and a force $\mathbf{F}$ given by

$$\mathbf{F} = -\text{grad } W = \frac{\partial \mathbf{\mu} \cdot \mathbf{H}}{\partial x}\mathbf{i} + \frac{\partial \mathbf{\mu} \cdot \mathbf{H}}{\partial y}\mathbf{j} + \frac{\partial \mathbf{\mu} \cdot \mathbf{H}}{\partial z}\mathbf{k}$$

which, if θ remains constant, and μ_H is put for $\mu \cos \theta$, reduces to

$$\mathbf{F} = \mu_H \nabla H$$

The next step is to consider an aggregate of dipoles which are rigidly connected. This is essentially a permanent magnet, whose intensity of magnetization I is given by the resultant moment per unit volume of its constituent dipoles.

$$I = \Sigma \mu \qquad \text{or} \qquad I_H = \Sigma \mu_H$$

Here, again, we have $E_2 = $ const., or $\delta E_2 = 0$. The preceding formulas for a dipole may be extended to the case of a permanent magnet by summation, giving

$$W_{\infty, p} = E_{12} = -\mathbf{I} \cdot \mathbf{H} = -I_H H \qquad (28)$$

Changes in the system brought about by moving the sample from a point A at which the field is H to another B where the field is $H + dH$ are conveniently illustrated in Fig. 7. In the position A we have

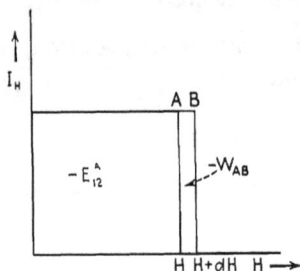

Fig. 7.

$$E_{12}^A = -I_H H$$

or the area shown in the figure. In the position B we have

$$E_{12}^B = -I_H(H + dH)$$

and from Eq. (27)

$$W_{AB} = \delta E_{12} = -I_H(H + dH) + I_H H = -I_H dH$$

as shown in the figure.

If, now, we proceed to arbitrary magnetic materials whose magnetization may change, we may no longer put $\delta E_2 = 0$. However, the mutual energy E_{12} for any given intensity of magnetization is the same as it was for the case of a permanent magnet. Consider a sample whose magnetization changes according to Fig. 8. The amount of work done in moving it into an infinitesimally larger field is $-I_H dH$, and the work done in moving it from A to B is

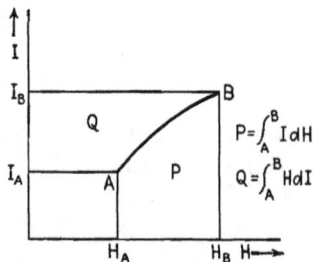

Fig. 8.

$$W_{AB} = -\int_A^B I_H dH = -P$$

P being the area shown in the figure. Also, we have

$$E_{12}^A = -I_H H_A$$
$$E_{12}^B = -I_H H_B$$

and therefore

$$\delta E_{12} = -P - Q$$

Finally, using (25), and remembering that $\delta E_1 = 0$, we have

$$-P = \delta E_2 - P - Q$$
$$\delta E_2 = Q = \int H dI_H \tag{29}$$

Our final result may be summarized by saying that the mutual potential energy per unit volume between a sample and a field produced by fixed poles is

$$-IH$$

I being assumed parallel to H. The work done in magnetizing unit volume of the sample by moving it in the field is

$$-\int I dH$$

and the resulting change in the internal energy per unit volume of the sample for an adiabatic change is

$$\int H dI$$

In Par. 4 it was stated that changes of magnetization in the presence of electrical conductors produced currents by induction. The production of such currents requires work. It is evident, therefore, that the foregoing relation can be applied only in the absence of conducting materials. The consideration of the modifications produced by the presence of conductors leads to the simple example discussed as case 2.

Case 2.—The field is produced by a solenoid. Consider a solenoid, very long compared to its diameter, having N turns per centimeter and a cross-sectional area of 1 sq. cm. A battery maintains a current i in the solenoid, giving a field

$$H = 4\pi N i$$

near its center. A piece of magnetic material may be fitted into the central portion of the solenoid. A battery delivers energy at a certain rate to maintain the current. This expenditure of energy fore, have to be fitted into the picture of crystals arrived at from other studies.   Since Laue's discovery in 1912 that crystals may be used as gratings to form X-ray spectra, much work has been done in analyzing the structure of crystals.   The information obtained deals chiefly with the geometrical arrangement of atoms to form a space lattice.   The emphasis on the atomic structure of solids resulting from these X-ray investigations naturally focused attention on what may be called the atomic structure of magnetism and is to a great extent responsible for the many attempts that have been made to explain ferromagnetism in terms of atoms having a magnetic moment.   A further step which made the atomic models very attractive was the introduction of the Bohr magneton.   This magneton was a consequence of Bohr's model of the hydrogen atom, in which an electron in performing its orbital motions could assume only certain integral multiple values of a fundamental unit of angular momentum.   From this it followed that only certain discrete orbits were allowed, and consequently only discrete magnetic moments—a different moment for each permissible orbit.   Subsequent developments of the quantum theory have modified Bohr's original theory without, however, radically altering the basic ideas involved.   Especially important was the addition of the magnetic moment of the electron, which is often spoken of as resulting from a spin.   A magneton, consequently, is not an object having a separate existence of its own but rather a property (the permanent magnetic moment) of an atom, or of a molecule, or of an electron or proton.   We therefore cannot say that the magneton has such and such properties but must describe each new manifestation of a magnetic moment in terms of the particular atomic configuration involved.   A symbol is reserved for the moment of the Bohr magneton, μ_B, which is numerically equal to

$$\mu_B = \frac{eh}{4\pi mc} = 0.92 \times 10^{-20} \qquad (36)$$

Having considered the chief arguments for the atomic model of a ferromagnetic substance, let us see what is to be said against it.   In the first place, the magnetic moment of an atom in the solid state is not a directly observable quantity, and objections might be made on that basis.   Furthermore, in the case of a molecule such as NO, for example, which has a permanent moment, it is not possible to say that either of the constituent atoms is magnetic. We speak of the molecule, *i.e.*, the combination of the two atoms, as having a moment. Another, and perhaps more graphic, way of saying the same thing is by making use of wave-mechanical concepts. According to wave mechanics, an atom is better described as a continuous distribution of electric density around a central nucleus than as discrete electrons moving in orbits. When atoms are packed close together as in a crystal, they have a tendency to coalesce and form something much like a continuum of electric density. It is not possible, in general, to say that a particular electron belongs to a particular atom. We must rather say that all the electrons, especially the outer electrons in a metallic medium, are shared among all the atoms.

7. Magnetization and Hysteresis.—In actual materials the magnetization curve is not a smooth curve. This fact is known as the "Barkhausen effect" and is interpreted by saying that when an elementary magnet is deflected through more than some critical angle, it disturbs the equilibrium of its neighbors and consequently sometimes causes a local magnetic eruption of sufficient violence to be recorded experimentally as a kink in the magnetization curve. More generally, we may say that the Barkhausen effect indicates the existence of local instability in the direction of magnetization. In addition to these abrupt changes, there are also gradual and continuous changes. There is evidence that these latter are reversible, in contradistinction to the Barkhausen jumps, which are not. Because of the existence of irreversible changes of magnetization, the magnetization curve obtained in proceeding

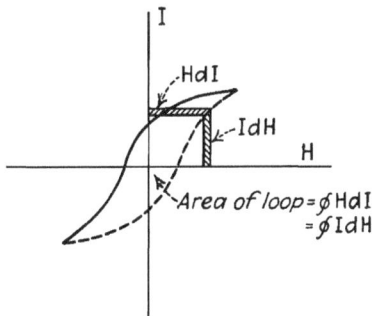

FIG. 9.

from $+H$ to $-H$ is not the same as that obtained in proceeding from $-H$ to $+H$. This is called "hysteresis." A closed magnetization curve is called a "hysteresis loop." Figures 9 and 82 show magnetization curves and hysteresis loops. Hysteresis effects in single crystals are generally slight. The typical magnetization curve has three characteristic parts. For small values of H the magnetization increases slowly, then more and more rapidly, and finally, for large values of H, increases slowly again and approaches a saturation value. The exact form of the magnetization curve depends on how it is measured. The most usual procedure is to connect the tips of a series of hysteresis loops taken by varying H between the limits $\pm H$ and having gradually changing amplitudes. Another way is to demagnetize[1] the sample after every measurement, go in one step from $H = 0$ to the desired H, and observe the corresponding I. Still another way is to proceed from $H = 0$ in steps without intermediate demagnetization. These three procedures give very similar but not identical curves. A fourth procedure which often gives an entirely different curve from the first three is to submit the sample to a demagnetizing process while it is under the influence of the field strength at which measurements are to be made. The curve so obtained is called the "ideal magnetization curve" and is further described in Chap. VI.

An interesting item in Fig. 9 is the area of the hysteresis loop. It has the dimensions of magnetic moment per unit volume times magnetic field, or, according to Eq. (28), energy per unit volume. This suggests the possibility of finding a relationship between the area of the loop and the work done in the process of magnetization. That such a relationship exists is immediately apparent from Eq. (29) or (35) when integrated around a closed loop.

The work done on unit volume of a sample in taking it around a closed hysteresis loop is equal to the area of the hysteresis loop and is also equal to the change in the internal energy of unit volume of the sample. This internal energy appears in the form of heat.

8. Ferromagnetism and Temperature.—The process of magnetization is perhaps the point of chief interest in the study of ferromagnetism, both from a physical and from a practical point of view. There are, however, a host of less striking phenomena intimately connected with magnetization which are as little understood and which need to be studied as essential parts of

---

[1] Four ways of demagnetizing a sample are (1) to heat it to a high temperature; (2) to put it in an alternating magnetic field whose amplitude is gradually reduced to zero; (3) to give it a mechanical shock or to apply some other gradually decreasing mechanical disturbance; and (4) to pass through it a gradually decreasing alternating current.

the main problem. A most important factor is the temperature.
Changes in temperature have a large influence on ferromagnetism
indirectly, through their effect on structure. Thus changes in
phase, for instance, produce radical changes in magnetic properties. But temperature has a more direct influence on ferromagnetism as well. Besides the gradual changes produced at all
temperatures, there are comparatively abrupt changes at the
magnetic transformation point, or Curie temperature, usually
designated by the letter θ. Below this temperature substances
are ferromagnetic; they exhibit saturation and hysteresis phenomena. Above it they are paramagnetic.

The magnetization of a sample depends on its previous
thermal history as well as on its previous magnetic history.
Especially in the neighborhood of critical temperatures is this
thermomagnetic hysteresis, as we might call it, very marked.
As a result, it is impossible to make any generally applicable
statements concerning the dependence of magnetization on the
temperature. Sometimes magnetization increases and sometimes it decreases with temperature. One regularity, however,
can be segregated from the large number of existing observations.
In general, the saturation intensity decreases as the temperature
increases.[1]

A very important aspect of ferromagnetism and temperature is
the question of energy content. When a sample is magnetized,
its temperature undergoes a change. That a dissipation of heat
accompanied magnetization was known for a long time. But
that a part of the corresponding temperature change was reversible was first observed by Weiss and Piccard and was called by
them the magnetocaloric phenomenon. Recently Ellwood has
shown that the dependence of the temperature of an isolated body
on its magnetization in low fields is quite complicated. These
effects, though usually very small and difficult to measure, are
fundamental to an understanding of ferromagnetism and should
be thoroughly investigated. There is not much hope of having a
satisfactory theory until the basic energy relations are quite
clear. Chapter IX contains a further discussion of this aspect
of the problem.

9. Ferromagnetism and Mechanical Deformation.—When a
ferromagnetic substance is magnetized, there occurs, in

[1] Pyrrhotite seems to be an exception (see Fig. 117).

general, a change of volume and also of shape—it may swell, stretch, and even bend or twist. Such phenomena of change of dimensions with magnetization are classified under the name "magnetostriction."

Conversely, mechanical deformations produce profound changes in the magnetic properties, especially in so far as magnetization is concerned. The effects of strains are also to be observed in other properties, *e.g.*, as changes in the electrical and mechanical properties. Furthermore, the elastic properties of a substance depend on its magnetization.

None of the phenomena just mentioned is large or easily observable, other than the dependence of magnetization on mechanical deformation. Cold working and annealing a sample can change its magnetic properties at low fields as regards order of magnitude. Those not familiar with the subject may perhaps be warned that a piece of "iron," for instance, can be one of a great number of things, having most varied electrical, magnetic, and mechanical properties. This is due not only to the presence of impurities but also to the presence of strains due to any causes whatever.

10. Various Thermal and Electrical Effects.—So far, we have spoken chiefly of magnetization and the various factors that affect it. As might be expected, magnetization has an influence on many of the various properties of a ferromagnetic substance. The change in dimensions we have already noted. Similarly, magnetization produces changes in electrical and thermal properties. These effects depend on the orientation of the magnetic field, electric field, temperature gradient, etc., with respect to each other and to the crystal axes.

The most important observations center on two kinds of experiments. In the first, electrical currents are sent through a crystal in various directions and under various conditions of magnetization, and the resulting distribution of electric (or thermal) potential observed. This is the case, for instance, in experiments on the change of resistance of ferromagnetics with magnetization; or in the Hall effect, where the electrical potential differences established in the z direction, for instance, by a magnetic field in the x direction and a current in the y direction are investigated. In the second kind of experiment, temperature gradients are set up, and the resulting flow of electricity or heat from one region to another is observed as a function of the magnetic state of the conductors used.

The complexity that can be achieved by combining and varying all these factors is quite considerable. At any rate, it is clear that magnetic, electrical, thermal, and mechanical properties are closely interwoven. Phenomena of this type are observed in most substances, but they are radically modified by ferromagnetism. A further discussion of the effects here mentioned is to be found in Chap. VIII.

11. Time.—When a magnetic field is applied to a ferromagnetic substance, the final magnetic state is not reached instantaneously. This time lag is partly due to induced eddy currents. Because ferromagnetic substances are, as a rule, good conductors, changing magnetic fields induce currents in them which, in turn, produce their own transient magnetic fields. These transient fields, of course, affect the magnetization. But the time lag in magnetization is not due entirely to eddy currents. A "permanent" magnet, for instance, if stored in a low field, such as the earth's field, will gradually lose at least some of its magnetization. This slow change may cover a period of years and seems to have nothing to do with eddy currents. In part, such changes are due to the diffusion and change of phase of impurities, but it has not yet been established that the observed peculiarities can be entirely accounted for in this way. Many experiments have been performed on ferromagnetic materials in rapidly oscillating fields, but the complicated results of these investigations will not be treated in this volume.

12. Optical Effects.—Of the great amount of work done in magneto-optics, very little concerns itself with ferromagnetic substances. Important effects are the Kerr effect, which is the rotation of the plane of polarization of a light beam reflected from a polished magnetized surface; and the Faraday effect, which is the rotation of the plane of polarization of a light beam in going through a magnetized medium. This can, of course, be observed only in very thin ferromagnetic films, as ferromagnetic substances in bulk are opaque.[1]

[1] S. R. WILLIAMS, "Magnetic Phenomena," McGraw-Hill Book Company, Inc., New York, 1930; M. VON LAUE, "Handbuch der Experimentalphysik," vol. 18; VOIGT, "Magneto- und Elektro-optik," Teubner, Leipzig, 1908.

CHAPTER II

HISTORICAL DEVELOPMENT

In this chapter an account is given of the main stages of the development of our ideas about ferromagnetism. From very early times until quite recently the subject was of interest to mankind chiefly because of its application in the construction of the mariner's compass. Aside from this, it was little more than a curiosity. With the advent of electricity, however, magnets and magnetic materials have taken on a new and ever increasing significance not only to the physicist and the metallurgist but, indeed, through the development of electrical engineering, to the man in the street. Today magnets and magnetic materials are indispensable to the comfort and economic life of a large part of the population of the globe.

13. Gilbert (1540–1603).—In Gilbert's time magnetism could hardly have been called a science. Some facts were known: that certain substances, now called ferromagnetic, had the power of strongly attracting or repelling each other over distances of the order of magnitude of centimeters; that magnetism could be communicated from natural magnets to other substances, notably iron; and that a delicately suspended magnet could be used to help find one's way by virtue of its property of pointing approximately north and south. But these facts were buried under a mountain of superstition. The loadstone, since it could be demonstrated at any time to possess a few remarkable properties not common to the rest of matter, was assumed to possess a great many more properties not so easy to demonstrate, especially supernatural and healing powers which were used in charms and medicines. William Gilbert, a physician, was interested in the loadstone and undertook an experimental investigation of its properties. His researches are described in his book "De Magnete," which is of interest chiefly as one of the first attempts to separate fact from fiction.

26

14. Coulomb[1] **(1736–1806) and Poisson**[2] **(1781–1840).**—For a long time not much was done to improve the early qualitative ideas of Gilbert. Newton's chief contribution was the introduction of the calculus, an indispensable tool in the hands of later investigators in many fields. But mathematics is applicable only to an exact science, and up to this time only qualitative information concerning magnetism was available. Coulomb remedied this deficiency. He proposed the law that now bears his name, stating that magnetic poles repel or attract each other inversely as the square of their distance apart. With this information at hand, Poisson created the science of magnetostatics. That is, assuming Coulomb's law and using in its application the method of the infinitesimal calculus, he was able to describe the interaction existing between arbitrarily distributed permanent poles.

15. Ampère[3] **(1775–1836).**—Poisson's work showed how to describe simply and accurately the forces that magnets exert on each other. The physical question as to the actual origin of these forces was, however, untouched. A great advance in this direction was due to Ampère. His work is based on the discovery by Oersted in 1820 that electric currents produce magnetic fields. Each atom is supposed to contain a circular current, now often called an Amperian current. As was shown in Par. 3, such a current is essentially equivalent to a magnetic dipole, and the magnetization of matter containing many atoms in which Amperian currents are circulating may consequently be described as being due to the reorientation of the equivalent atomic dipoles.

16. Weber[4] **(1804–1891) and Maxwell**[5] **(1831–1879).**—Ampère's ideas were extended by Weber. He assumed an interaction between elementary magnets. Maxwell further developed the theory to include hysteresis phenomena. He did this by assuming that if an elementary magnet be rotated by more than a critical amount, it is in unstable equilibrium and jumps into a new position. Both of these ideas survive in a qualitative form in our present theories.

---

[1] COULOMB, *Mém. acad. roy.*, p. 606, 1785.
[2] POISSON, *Mém. de l'Institut*, **5**, 247, 488, 1820.
[3] AMPÈRE, *Mém. de l'Institut*, **6**, 175, 1823.
[4] W. WEBER, *Pogg. Ann.*, **87**, 145, 1854.
[5] J. C. MAXWELL, "Electricity and Magnetism."

17. Atomic and Statistical Aspects of Ferromagnetism.—A most important advance in the growth of physical ideas was taking place during these years. The fundamental laws of classical physics had been established, and first attempts were being made by one group of physicists to build the science of matter on these foundations, attempts that led in the course of time to the discovery of electrons and protons and the present theories of atomic structure. Another group of physicists, however, were examining the actual mechanical, thermal, optical, magnetic, and other properties of matter, and striving to work back from these to an understanding of the operation of the fundamental laws. Between these two lines of approach was the seemingly hopeless complication of dealing with the chaos of large numbers of particles. The introduction of statistical methods led to a great simplification of the difficulties. By averaging certain properties of the individual members of large groups of particles, the behavior of matter in bulk was gradually finding a satisfactory interpretation. It was further found that in this averaging process many details of the structure of the elementary particles disappear. It is often possible to derive an average property of a group without a detailed knowledge of the elements composing the group. Thus, for instance, much of the kinetic theory of gases can be developed with the assumption that atoms behave like rigid spheres or point centers of force. The behavior of a gas can be interpreted quite satisfactorily with such simple assumptions, and it is only in matters of detail that our present knowledge of atomic structure has been necessary in completing the theory.

Similarly, the first steps in the theory of magnetism were made with only the simple assumption that each atom was a small permanent magnet. This model has proved enormously useful and is the basis for most of the considerations of the coming chapters. With a suitable statistical treatment and a few very general assumptions about the interactions of the magnetic particles with each other and with the body of a solid, a large number of properties can be satisfactorily treated. The more detailed information available about atomic structure is useful at present chiefly in helping in the physical interpretation of the interactions just mentioned and, it is to be hoped, will eventually make it possible to fill in the gaps in the present theories.

18. The Beginning of a Quantitative Theory.—By the beginning of the twentieth century the value of a thermodynamic treatment of many chemical and physical problems had been convincingly shown, and ferromagnetism, too, was attacked from this point of view. The first law of thermodynamics, stating the principle of the conservation of energy, requires for its application essentially two things: an expression for the work done on a substance when it is made to undergo a certain change, and an expression for the corresponding change in its internal energy. By using expressions for the magnetic energy derived as in Par. 5, it is possible to relate by means of the first law such phenomena as, for instance, the change in length produced by a change in magnetization with the change in magnetization produced by a change in length. Relations of this kind were tested by Honda[1] and were found to agree, in general, fairly well with experimental data. A detailed treatment of some of these phenomena, taking into account the different mechanical and magnetic properties of crystals in various directions, is to be found in Chap. VII and a treatment of the thermodynamics of magnetization (neglecting magnetostriction) is given in Chap. IX.

19. The Statistics of Dipoles. Langevin.—With Langevin's paper[2] on para- and diamagnetism we come to the first quantitative treatment of the magnetization of actual materials. Langevin considered a group of dipoles so far apart that they exerted no forces on each other. The energy of a dipole of strength $\mathbf{\mu}$ in a magnetic field $\mathbf{H}$ is then given by $-\mathbf{\mu} \cdot \mathbf{H}$, as in Eq. (27a); or, if θ is the angle between $\mathbf{\mu}$ and $\mathbf{H}$, we may write $E = -\mu H \cos \theta$. The problem was to find out how a body made up of such dipoles would become magnetized. In Par. 4 two possible magnetization curves are described. Langevin generalized these elementary considerations to include the effect of temperature agitation. The work of Maxwell and Boltzmann in statistical mechanics had paved the way for this. Their investigations had led to the result that if each of a large group of particles in equilibrium at the temperature T has a potential energy $\epsilon(x)$ depending on some coordinate x, the probability of finding any one particle between

---

[1] K. HONDA, "Magnetic Properties of Matter," Syokwabo and Company, Tokyo, 1928, contains a general description of early work and further references.

[2] P. LANGEVIN, *Ann. chim. phys.* (8), **5**, 70, 1905.

x and $x + dx$ is proportional to

$$e^{-\frac{\epsilon(x)}{kT}}$$

or that the number of particles dn between x and $x + dx$ is

$$dn = ce^{-\frac{\epsilon(x)}{kT}} dx \tag{37}$$

where c is a constant determined by the total number of particles.
$N = \int dn$. k is a universal constant frequently called Boltzmann's constant and equal to 1.37×10^{-16} ergs per degree.

This result was, of course, immediately applicable to Langevin's problem. The number of particles pointing in a given direction $d\omega$ (see Fig. 10) is

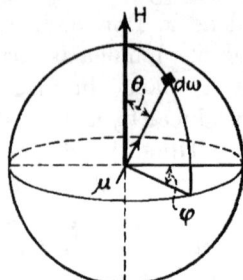

$$dn = ce^{-\frac{\mu H \cos\theta}{kT}} d\omega \tag{38}$$

where $d\omega = \sin\theta d\theta d\varphi$.

Fig. 10.

Substituting $\mu H/kT = a$, $\cos\theta = x$, from which it follows that $\sin\theta d\theta = -d\cos\theta = -dx$, we have

$$dn = -ce^{ax}dxd\varphi$$

To evaluate c we perform the integration over all possible values of θ and φ, with the result that

$$N = \int dn = -c\int_0^{2\pi} d\varphi \int_1^{-1} e^{ax}dx$$
$$= -\frac{2\pi c}{a}e^{ax}\Big]_1^{-1} = \frac{4\pi c}{a}\sinh a \tag{39}$$

or

$$c = \frac{Na}{4\pi \sinh a} \tag{40}$$

Just as we found the total number of magnets by integrating the number dn pointing in a direction $d\omega$, so we can find the total intensity of magnetization by integrating the expression for the intensity dI of those magnets pointing in the direction $d\omega$. Thus, since $dI = \mu \cos\theta dn$, we have

$$I = \int dI \doteq -c\mu\int \cos \theta e^{a\cos\theta} d\omega$$

$$= \frac{\mu N a}{4\pi \sinh a} \int_0^{2\pi} d\varphi \int_1^{-1} x e^{ax} dx$$

$$= \mu N\left(\coth a - \frac{1}{a}\right) = \mu N L(a). \tag{41}$$

The function $\left(\coth a - \dfrac{1}{a}\right)$ is sometimes written $L(a)$, after Langevin, who first performed the derivation that led to it. For large or small values of a more convenient approximate expressions may be given, as follows:

for $a \gg 1$

$$L(a) = 1 - \frac{1}{a} + 2e^{-2a} + \cdots$$

for $a \ll 1$

$$L(a) = \frac{a}{3} - \frac{a^3}{45} + \cdots \tag{42}$$

Remembering that $a = \mu H/kT$, it is possible to plot magnetization curves and to show their dependence on both H and T, as has been done in Fig. 11.

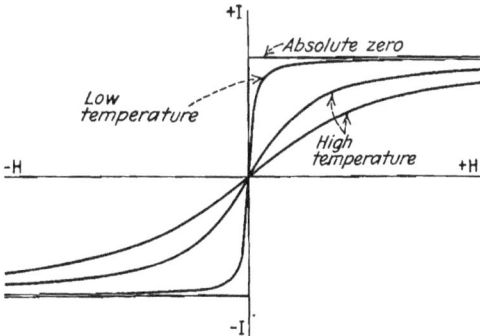

FIG. 11.

If the elementary magnetic particle can assume only certain orientations with respect to the magnetic field, the results just obtained must be modified. "Spatial quantization," as this is called, is a more recent discovery, but its effect on the statistics of dipoles may conveniently be discussed here in connection with Langevin's earlier contributions.

If the moment of the elementary particle can assume only $2y + 1$ different orientations such that the component of the magnetic moment in the direction of the field has the values

$$\frac{y}{y}\mu, \frac{y-1}{y}\mu, \cdots, -\frac{y-1}{y}\mu, -\frac{y}{y}\mu, \text{ as}$$

shown in Fig. 12, we have for the number of particles having a component $\frac{m}{y}\mu$ in the direction of the field

$$ce^{\frac{m\mu H}{y k T}} \equiv ce^{\frac{m}{y}a}$$

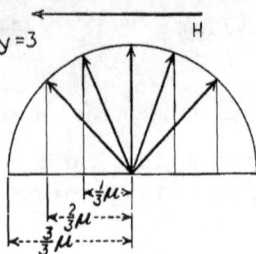

Fig. 12.

and hence for the magnetization

$$I = \mu N\frac{\dfrac{y}{y}e^{\frac{y}{y}a} + \dfrac{y-1}{y}e^{\frac{y-1}{y}a} + \cdots - \dfrac{y}{y}e^{-\frac{y}{y}a}}{e^{\frac{y}{y}a} + e^{\frac{y-1}{y}a} + \cdots + e^{-\frac{y}{y}a}} = \mu N\frac{m\displaystyle\sum_{-y}^{y}\frac{m}{y}e^{\frac{m}{y}a}}{m\displaystyle\sum_{-y}^{y}e^{\frac{m}{y}a}}$$

which reduces, for the special case of only two possible orientations, parallel and antiparallel to the field, $y = 1$, to

$$I = \mu N \tanh a = \mu N\frac{e^a - e^{-a}}{e^a + e^{-a}} \tag{43}$$

and for the case of all possible orientations $y = \infty$ to Eq. (41), as may be seen by putting

$$\lim_{y\to\infty}\frac{m\displaystyle\sum_{-y}^{y}\frac{m}{y}e^{\frac{m}{y}a}}{m\displaystyle\sum_{-y}^{y}e^{\frac{m}{y}a}} = \frac{\displaystyle\int_{-1}^{1}xe^{ax}dx}{\displaystyle\int_{-1}^{1}e^{ax}dx} = \frac{\left[\dfrac{e^{ax}(ax-1)}{a^2}\right]_{-1}^{+1}}{\left[\dfrac{e^{ax}}{a}\right]_{-1}^{+1}} = \coth a - \frac{1}{a}$$

These equations are further discussed in Par. 50, and their contents illustrated in Fig. 70.

Langevin's theory was successful in explaining many of the properties of paramagnetic substances, and in Par. 21 we shall apply it to ferromagnetism.

20. Ewing's Model of a Ferromagnetic Substance.—Langevin approximated a magnetic substance by means of a group of dipoles in thermal equilibrium so far apart that they exerted no forces on each other.   The absence of internal couplings, and the consequent simple energy expressions, made the calculations of the previous section possible.   Ewing proceeded in just the opposite way.   His approximation consisted of a group of dipoles near enough together to exert considerable forces on each other but devoid of thermal agitation.   This model was not easy to treat mathematically except in very special cases but could be built experimentally in the laboratory, and its properties observed directly.   The qualitative resemblance between the properties of Ewing's models and those of actual ferromagnetic substance is striking.   The models consist essentially of large groups of little magnets supported on pivots near each other.   In the absence of an external field they orient themselves in such a way as to reduce their mutual magnetic energy as in Fig. 13, for instance, which is taken from Ewing's book "Magnetic Induction in Iron and Other Metals."   If, now, a magnetic field is applied in some arbitrary direction, the little magnets turn, at first only a little; then the groups become unstable, and abrupt changes in orientation occur; and finally for large fields the model is saturated—all the little elements are parallel to the external field.

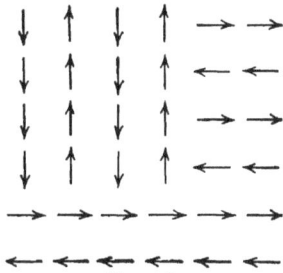

Fig. 13.

Magnetization curves and hysteresis loops obtained with such a model are shown in Fig. 14.   The similarity to actual hysteresis curves, as we have said, is striking, and more extended investigations showed that it was possible to include in the comparison such factors as the effect of strains and vibration and such details as a time lag, accommodation,[1] etc.

The feature of Ewing's model responsible for its success is that the orientation of any element is determined not only by the

---

[1] When a ferromagnetic substance is subjected to a periodically varying *H*, the hysteresis loop is, in general, not a closed curve.   Only after the cycle has been traversed many times do the magnetic changes become truly cyclic.   Accommodation refers to the establishing of a state in which a periodically varying *H* produces identical hysteresis loops in every cycle.

externally applied field but by an internal field as well. The internal fields responsible for ferromagnetism, however, cannot possibly be of magnetic origin, as we shall see farther on.

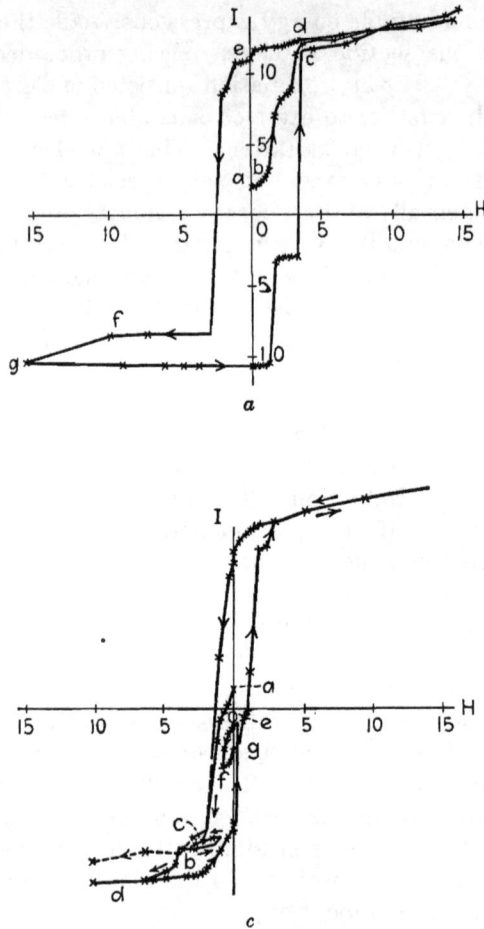

Fig. 14.—Magnetization curves and hysteresis loops obtained from a Ewing observations by J. W. Capstick and is reproduced from Ewing's book " Magnetic

21. The Weiss Molecular Field.[1]—Following Ewing's qualitative introduction of internal fields into the description of ferro-

---

[1] For further discussion see, for instance; P. WEISS and G. FOEX, "Le Magnétisme," Colin, Paris, 1926; E. C. STONER, "Magnetism and Matter," Methuen & Company, Ltd., London, 1934.

magnetism came Weiss's attempt to do this quantitatively, using at the same time Langevin's results on the effect of temperature. It was shown in Par. 19 that the intensity of magnetization of a

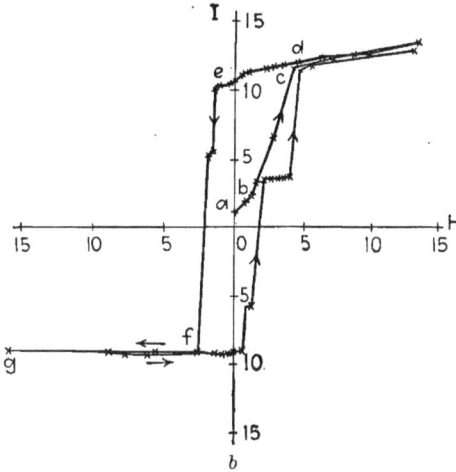

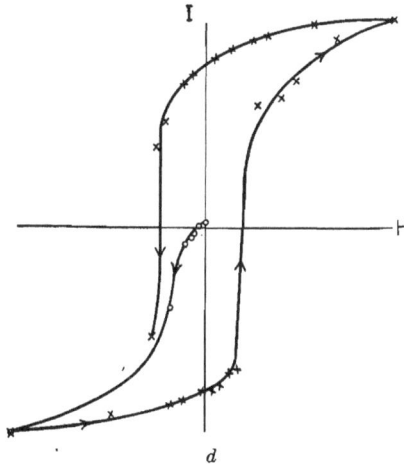

model.   (*a*, *b*, *c* are taken from A. Hoopes, *Electrician*, **27**, 99, 1891; *d* represents Induction in Iron and Other Metals.")

group of magnets having only thermal interaction is given by

$$\frac{I}{I_0} = L(a)$$

where $a = \mu H/kT$ (44)

and I_0, the saturation intensity obtained when all the elementary magnets point in the same direction, is written for μN. Weiss proceeded to modify this equation by taking into consideration the interaction between elementary magnets. The mathematical description of a situation as complex as that which exists in the Ewing model was quite out of the question, and the natural simplification was to average out the fluctuations arising from the atomic nature of the material. Suppose that a magnetic field H produces a magnetization I parallel to itself. The total field H_T acting on an elementary particle will be the magnetic field H plus another local field H_l which, as an approximation, Weiss assumed parallel and proportional to I. This may be expressed mathematically by putting

$$H_T = H + H_l$$
$$H_l = N_w I$$

where N_w is a constant. Very beautiful consequences follow from this simple assumption and its substitution in Eq. (44). This substitution gives for the magnetic equation of state

$$\frac{I_w}{I_0} = L(a); \qquad a = \frac{\mu}{kT}(H + N_w I_w) \qquad (45)$$

in which I_w is used to denote that value of I which satisfies Weiss's equation. We shall see presently that I_w need not be equal to the observed intensity I.

Let us begin an examination of Eq. (45) by considering the simple case $H = 0$. I_w is then determined by the simultaneous equations

$$\frac{I_w}{I_0} = L(a) \qquad \text{and} \qquad \frac{I_w}{I_0} = \frac{kT}{\mu N_w I_0} a \qquad (46)$$

which are plotted in Fig. 15. $L(a)$ is a universal function whose slope at the origin is $\frac{1}{3}$. The second equation in (46) is represented by a straight line, whose slope is $kT/\mu N_w I_0$, passing through the origin. If this slope is greater than $\frac{1}{3}$, as in case A, Eqs. (44) have only one solution, *viz.*, $I_w = 0$. In other words, if

$$\frac{kT}{\mu N_w I_0} > \frac{1}{3} \qquad (47a)$$

the material has no magnetic moment in the absence of an external field. If, on the other hand,

$$\frac{kT}{\mu N_w I_0} < \frac{1}{3} \tag{47b}$$

the curves intersect at another point as well, as in case B, and this point determines another value of I_w which will satisfy Eqs. (46). This I_w is called the "spontaneous magnetization," because it represents a magnetization produced by the material itself without the intervention of any external field at all. $I_w = 0$, which according to Fig. 15 is always a solution, may be shown to be stable only if $(47a)$ is satisfied and hence need not be considered in case B.

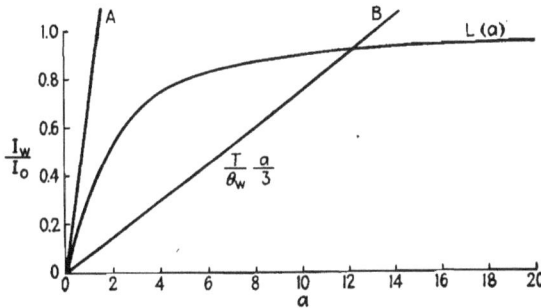

FIG. 15.—The Weiss equations (46). *A* for temperatures above and *B* below the Curie temperature.

From this discussion it is clear that spontaneous magnetization will disappear when

$$\frac{kT}{\mu N_w I_0} = \frac{1}{3} \quad \text{or} \quad T = \frac{\mu N_w I_0}{3k} \equiv \theta_w \tag{48}$$

The critical temperature θ_w is called the Curie temperature, or Curie point, after Pierre Curie who did much of the pioneering experimental work on which magnetic theories are based.   Just how to interpret the foregoing results is not quite clear, because ferromagnetic substances can, as a rule, retain a wide range of magnetizations in zero field, depending on their previous history. In other words, the experimental residual magnetization is not a simple definite quantity, as these equations indicate.   It is possible to get around this difficulty by assuming that I_w, the magnetization given by Eq. (45), is the actual magnetization in a small region of a sample but that various regions need not be magnetized in the same direction and hence that the observed magnetization I is, as a rule, less than I_w. This assumption is quite in accord with the simple notions of the molecular field so far developed. It follows that I_w is not a directly observable quantity, but its value may be estimated at high fields, when all the regions are magnetized in nearly the same direction. The existence of regions of spontaneous magnetization cannot be deduced from Weiss's equation, and in the present discussion they constitute an added assumption necessary to produce some sort of agreement between theory and experiment. In Table I are given experimental values of θ_w for various substances, together with values of N_w and $N_w I_0$, the molecular field, as derived from Eq. (48). μ is taken as one Bohr magneton,[1] 0.9×10^{-20} erg per oersted.

TABLE I.—ESTIMATES OF THE WEISS MOLECULAR FIELD $N_w I_0$ AS
CALCULATED FROM EQ. (48)
The values of θ_w are experimental Curie temperatures.

Substance	$\theta_w{}^\circ$ abs. (approx.)	N_w	I_0	$N_w I_0$, oersteds
Iron.	1060	2×10^4	1700	3.4×10^7
Cobalt. . .	1385	4×10^4	1400	5.6×10^7
Nickel.	630	5×10^4	500	2.5×10^7

It seems impossible that magnetic fields of the order of 10 million oersteds exist in a ferromagnetic substance. The theory does, however, quantitatively express certain aspects of ferromagnetism, as we shall see in the next section. In Chap. V the origin of the internal fields is more fully discussed.

22. Weiss's Magnetic Equation of State.—For a closer inspection of Eq. (45) it is convenient to rewrite it. From Eq. (48) it follows that

$$\frac{\mu}{k} = \frac{3\theta_w}{N_w I_0}$$

and consequently we may put

$$\frac{I_w}{I_0} = L(a); \qquad a = \frac{3\theta_w}{T}\left(\frac{H}{N_w I_0} + \frac{I_w}{I_0}\right) \tag{49}$$

[1] See Par. 47.

which, for $H = 0$, may be written in the simple form

$$\frac{I_w}{I_0} = L\left(\frac{3\theta_w}{T}\frac{I_w}{I_0}\right) \qquad (50)$$

Considering the ratios I_w/I_0 and T/θ_w as variables, Eq. (50) contains no constant depending on the properties of the material; it is a universal equation and is graphically represented in Fig. 16. At the absolute zero, $I_w = I_0$; as the temperature increases, I_w decreases, at first slowly and then more rapidly, until at the Curie temperature $T = \theta_w$, $I_w = 0$. The experimental evidence bearing on the correctness of Eq. (50) will be discussed in Chap. VI when the problem of estimating I_w from the observed I has received some attention. We shall find the experimental evidence in fair agreement with a modified form of Weiss's equation.

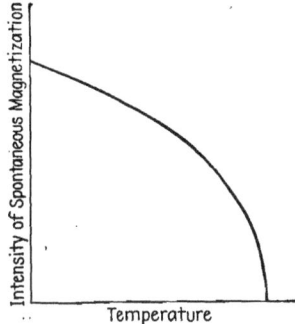

FIG. 16.—Spontaneous magnetization according to the Weiss theory.

The dependence of magnetization on H may be derived from Eq. (49). Putting for the initial susceptibility per unit volume

$$\frac{\partial I_w}{\partial H}\Bigg]_{H=0} = \chi_0 \qquad (51)$$

we have

$$\chi_0 = I_0 L'(a)\frac{3\theta_w}{T}\left(\frac{1}{N_w I_0} + \frac{\chi_0}{I_0}\right)$$

or, solving for χ_0,

$$N_w\chi_0 = \frac{L'(a)}{\dfrac{T}{3\theta_w} - L'(a)}; \qquad a = \frac{3\theta_w}{T}\frac{I_w}{I_0} \qquad (52)$$

$N_w\chi_0$ is also a universal function of T/θ_w and is plotted in Fig. 17. As has already been pointed out, I_w, and consequently χ_0, cannot be observed directly below the Curie temperature, and as yet our knowledge of the magnetization process is not, in general, sufficient to determine to what extent magnetization in small fields is due to an increase in the spontaneous magnetization I_w. Above the Curie point, however, χ_0 is directly observable, and experimental data are qualitatively in agreement with Eq. (51) which, since $L'(a) = \frac{1}{3}$ for $a = 0$, reduces to the modified Curie equation

$$\chi_0 = \frac{\theta_w/N_w}{T - \theta_w} \tag{53}$$

In order to get some idea of the magnetizability predicted by Eq. (52) for a ferromagnetic substance consider such material

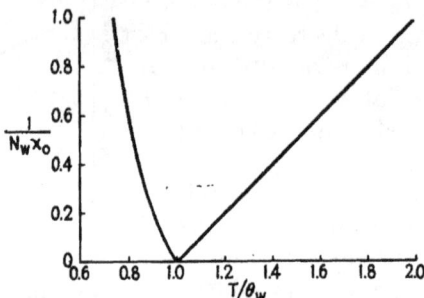

FIG. 17.—The inverse initial susceptibility as a function of temperature according to the Weiss theory.

at a point on Fig. 17 for which $T/\theta_w = 0.95$, *i.e.*, below but near the Curie point. From the graph we see that

$$\frac{1}{N_w\chi_0} = 0.1 \qquad \text{or} \qquad \chi_0 = \frac{10}{N_w} \sim 2 \times 10^{-4}$$

using for N_w an average value of 5×10^4. For lower temperatures this initial susceptibility decreases rapidly. Such values are negligible compared to the actual observed susceptibilities, and we are forced to conclude that other processes are responsible. This is, moreover, just what might have been expected on the basis of the hypothesis suggested in Par. 21 that spontaneous magnetization does not include an entire sample. The action of the magnetic field would be to turn the direction of magnetization of the various spontaneously magnetized regions into the direction of the applied field, or to make some grow large at the expense of others, and consequently the observed change in magnetization would be much greater than the change in intensity of any particular region.

23. Further Development of the Ideas of Ewing and Weiss.— Although the work of Ewing and Weiss was clearly on the right track, it needed considerable modification. Ewing's model, translated to atomic dimensions, led to quantitatively incorrect results. Weiss's theory needed to be modified to take into account a possible randomness in the orientation of the molecular field and a possible relationship between the orientation of this field and crystal structure. Honda and Okubo,[1] Gans,[2] and Frivold[3] attacked these questions, and although their results are not directly used in the interpretation of ferromagnetism developed in subsequent chapters, their work foreshadowed the more recent and successful attacks on the difficulties involved.

Honda and Okubo undertook what amounted to a mathematical treatment of the Ewing model. They considered a group of nine parallel magnets, arranged as in Fig. 18, and calculated the energy of the group as a function of the direction of magnetization. The result was

$$E_\theta = \text{const.} - A \cos 4\theta \quad (54)$$

A is a constant depending on the size and spacing of the elements. Equation (54) states that if $A > 0$, the energy of the group is least when the magnetization is in the direction of a side of the square in Fig. 18 and greatest in the direction of a diagonal. This

FIG. 18.

expression is of great interest and will crop up again in our later discussions. The important step forward in these considerations was the introduction of the symmetry of the atomic lattice into the interaction between the magnetic elements.

Other interesting contributions were made by Gans, who attempted to formulate mathematically the fluctuation of the magnetic field within a magnetic substance. He, and subsequently Frivold, obtained results that have not yet been made use of in the general theory. A discussion of fluctuations has also been given by Néel.[4]

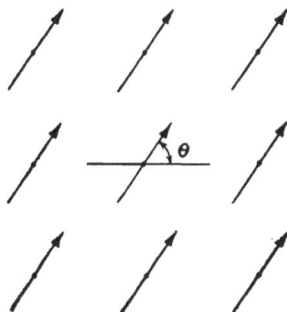

[1] K. HONDA and J. OKUBO, *Sci. Rep. Tôhoku Imp. Univ.*, **5**, 153, 1916.

[2] R. GANS, *Göttingen Nach.*, p. 197, 1910; p. 118, 1911.

[3] O. FRIVOLD, *Ann. Physik*, **65**, 1, 1921.

[4] L. NÉEL, thesis, Strasbourg, 1932.

24. The Present Importance of Ferromagnetism.—Today ferromagnetism is of interest in various fields, especially physics, metallurgy, and engineering. Some of the physicists who in the past have been concerned chiefly with the development of atomic theory have turned their attention to the problem of how atoms are combined to form molecules and the more complex aggregates in liquids and solids. Large groups of atoms have properties that individual atoms do not possess. Among the most interesting of these properties are the so-called "structure-sensitive" properties which depend very much on the presence of impurities and on other structural details. Certain aspects of ferromagnetism are outstandingly structure sensitive and are therefore important as examples of the subtle balance of conflicting tendencies shown in many ways by great varieties of substances. It is not yet clear how such phenomena may be described, but even if no essentially new ideas are required, there are at any rate new ways of applying the old ones to be discovered.

In Chap. V we shall describe the present theories of ferromagnetism and show that they are capable of accounting for many of the properties of ferromagnetic materials. The magnetization of the earth's core is, however, not included, and the theories in their present form do not account for its existence at the high temperatures of the earth's interior.

Ferromagnetism also promises to be of importance as a tool in the investigation of the structure of metals. For instance, by investigating the field on the surface of a magnetized piece of iron it is possible to detect holes, cracks, or other imperfections near a surface. Such experiments are still in their infancy, and it is to be expected that further work in this direction will have important results. Furthermore, in Chap. VII we shall show that the magnetization curve of a crystal depends on its elastic deformation and that different types of deformation give rise to different magnetization curves. It should therefore be possible to infer the strain in a crystal from observations of its magnetic properties and so obtain information on the internal state of a piece of metal in various stages of plastic deformation or softening by annealing.

And finally there is the enormous commercial importance of ferromagnetic materials. They form an essential part of almost every electrical machine and every electric circuit. More efficient and cheaper materials are wanted, with the most varied properties.   What is ideal for a telephone cable is useless for a transformer.   Up till now the physicist has been of little help to the engineer in developing magnetic materials.   Those now in use have been developed by more or less blind trials, and radical improvements are surely still to be made.

CHAPTER III

ABOUT METALS AND ALLOYS

So far we have approached the problem of ferromagnetism from the theoretical and historical points of view. The material in Chaps. I and II constitutes the background with which the physicist is equipped to proceed in his investigations. Many workers in this field, however, are metallurgists concerned with the production and development of materials to fill the various needs of industry. These workers base their ideas and criticize their results from a different point of view. To them a piece of iron is not the simple thing Fe, or even Fe plus impurities. The properties of their product depend on exactly how the material is treated; how it is hammered, rolled, heated, and cooled; and on how the impurities are distributed. It is the purpose of this and the next chapter to outline some of the outstanding properties of metals and the problems facing the physicist in preparing samples for experimental research. A reasonably complete treatment of these matters would require a whole book, and one which the author is not competent to write. The scanty material presented should, however, make clear the importance of the metallurgical aspects of ferromagnetism.

25. Single Crystals.—In discussing single crystals it will be convenient to take up first the geometrical arrangement of the atoms; second, the structure of the atomic cores consisting of the inner electrons; and, third, the properties of the outer electrons.

As regards the geometry of crystal lattices, we shall consider here only a few items of nomenclature. The types of crystals with which we shall have to do are illustrated in Fig. 19. The shaded planes are of particular interest in discussing the magnetic properties. The numbers (100), (110), etc., are called "Miller indices" and refer to the reciprocal intercepts $(1/x, 1/y, 1/z)$ of a given plane with coordinate axes as indicated. In cubic crystals a $[1/x, 1/y, 1/z]$ axis is perpendicular to a $(1/x, 1/y, 1/z)$ plane. A negative intercept is written $(1, 1, \bar{1})$, for instance, meaning

$(+1, +1, -1)$. In the cubic system the axes normal to the planes illustrated in Fig. 19 are sometimes designated as follows:

[100], [010], etc.........................Tetragonal
[110], [011], etc.........................Digonal
[111], [11Ī], etc.........................Trigonal

In general, crystals are not mathematically perfect. In addition to accidental distortions due to impurities, inclusions, external stresses, etc., there are certain other distortions due to the nature of the substance itself. In the latter category may be

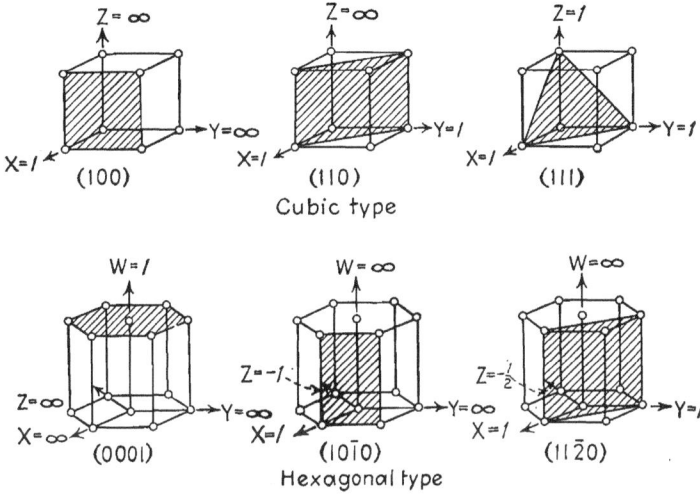

FIG. 19.—Designation of the principal planes in cubic and hexagonal lattices.

included magnetostrictive strains, for instance, which vary with the degree of magnetization. Various deviations from geometrical perfection will be taken up in subsequent sections of this chapter.

The atomic cores, which determine the crystal symmetry mentioned above, are composed of heavy nuclei and a group of bound electrons circulating about them. The nuclei vibrate about their mean position, and this vibration is more violent at high than at low temperatures. At sufficiently high temperatures the nuclei move through the crystal by changing places with each other. The motion of the bound electrons is not directly influenced by the temperature. These inner electrons may be regarded as forming an electric fluid arranged in layers about the nuclei. The inner layers are probably spherically symmetrical and have no resultant angular momentum. The shape of the outer layers may be affected by the crystal symmetry and will, in general, have a further symmetry of their own. The angles at which X rays are reflected from crystals are determined by the relative positions of the atoms,.but the relative intensities of reflections from various planes and in various orders are determined by the distribution of the electric fluid surrounding the nuclei. This method of measuring the distribution of electricity in a crystal is very tedious but has been carried out for a few crystals, and the results support the preceding assumption of the existence of layers. If the cores have not the same symmetry as the crystal itself various orientations of the cores with respect to each other are to be expected with corresponding changes in the physical properties of the crystal. Such changes are to be expected upon heating the crystal, especially in the presence of external perturbing forces, such as magnetic fields. Very little work has been done on the atomic cores in crystals. Peculiar effects resulting from heating in a magnetic field have been reported for bismuth by Goetz and Hasler,[1] for steel by Pender and Jones,[2] and for pyrrhotite by Weiss and Kunz,[3] but the observations require further study for their interpretation. More recent observations by Bozorth and Dillinger are discussed in Par. 72.

Metals are characterized by a further group of electrons surrounding the cores and relatively free to circulate from one part of a crystal to another. These electrons are responsible for electrical conductivity.

26. The Deformation of Crystals.[4]—The deformations produced in a crystal by sufficiently small external forces are usually approximately reversible, or elastic. When the force is removed, the crystal will again assume its original shape if the deformation has been within the elastic limit. Deformations beyond the plastic limit, on the other hand, produce lasting changes and are called "plastic deformations." Single crystals of metals are generally very soft, and very small forces produce plastic deforma-

---

[1] A. Goetz and M. Hasler, *Phys. Rev.*, **36**, 1752, 1930.

[2] H. Pender and R. L. Jones, *Phys. Rev.*, **1**, 259, 1913.

[3] P. Weiss and J. Kunz, *J. phys.*, **4**, 847, 1905.

[4] "Handbuch der Physik," vol. 6, Chap. 5 by J. W. Geckeler, and Chap. 6 by A. Nádai; "Handbuch der Experimentalphysik," vol. 5, pt. 1, by G. Sachs.

tions. It has even been suggested that perfect crystals with no impurities have no elastic limit at all but flow plastically with the application of even infinitesimal forces. There is unquestionably a tendency in the direction of low elastic limits for pure crystals, but the experimental evidence as yet available is hardly sufficient to warrant quite such a sweeping generalization. In most materials the elastic limit is raised by the addition of impurities, by mechanically working the material (hammering, rolling, stretching, etc.), or by lowering the temperature.

Within the range of elastic deformations, the deformation is approximately proportional to the force producing it. A statement of this fact is embodied in Hooke's law. In Chap. VII we shall find that Hooke's law must be modified for ferromagnetic materials. Single crystals are not elastically isotropic; i.e., a given force will produce different deformations if applied in different directions to a crystal.

Small deformations within the elastic limit are not accurately reversible and are accompanied by an evolution of heat. This is often spoken of as being due to "internal friction," or "elastic hysteresis." Although small deformations within the elastic limit may be repeatedly applied without producing observable changes in the structure of a metal, they do, in fact, weaken it and, if applied sufficiently often, may break the material. This weakening of the metal by elastic deformation is called "fatigue."

Plastic deformations are not homogeneous but result from a breaking up of crystal grains into pieces which supposedly slip over each other, sometimes along certain crystallographic planes, called "slip planes." Often slip planes are spaced at fairly regular intervals.

As deformation proceeds, each crystal is more and more broken up until finally only submicroscopic grains remain. Each such little grain has stored up in it a certain amount of energy, part of which is in the form of elastic energy due to the forces exerted by neighboring grains, part in the form of a surface energy due to the local disturbances at the grain boundaries.

As crystals are broken up by plastic deformation, the resulting small grains tend to orient themselves with respect to the direction in which flow takes place. Every kind of flow produces a typical orientation of the grains, or fiber structure. Fiber structures resulting from a single process repeated over and over, as, for instance, in the rolling of sheets or the drawing of wires, are typified by one or more preponderant grain orientations. The crystal axes of the grains are not accurately parallel to each other but are distributed around these predominant average orientations, the amount of deviation from the mean depending on many factors, such as the extent of the plastic deformation, the temperature at which it was carried out, the purity of the material, etc.

Fiber structures may be determined by means of X rays. If X rays are passed through a thin piece of metal on to a photo-

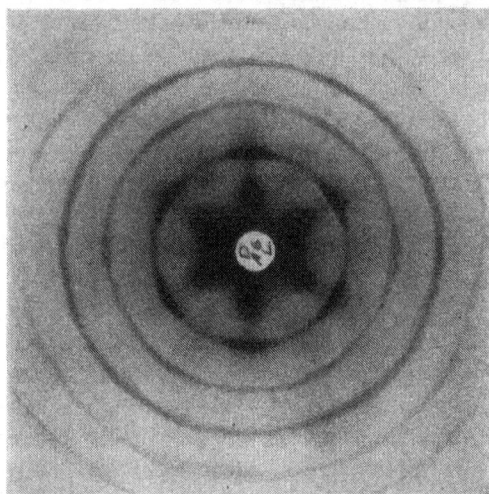

FIG. 20.—X ray fiber diagram of a drawn iron wire by J. T. Norton.

graphic film, they produce blackening in spots, and from the position of these spots the orientation of the crystal planes from which they were reflected can be inferred. Figure 20 shows such a photograph. If all grain orientations had been present in equal numbers, there would have been on the film only a central spot surrounded by a series of rings each uniformly blackened. The fact that the rings are spotty, however, shows that a random grain orientation was not present in the material; and from the positions of the spots on such photographs taken with X rays passing through the material in several directions the distribution of grain orientations may be calculated. Grain orientations may be measured magnetically (see Par. 64).

27. Recrystallization.[1]—As the temperature of a crystal is increased, the atoms begin to move about in the crystal more and more. The diffusion coefficient changes very rapidly with the temperature, so that the diffusion appears to set in abruptly at elevated temperatures, although· it actually exists at low temperatures as well. Such effects are easily detected in alloys, where changes in concentration with the time can be observed; and since we know that a foreign atom can move about in a crystal, we may assume that all the atoms of a crystal do so as well.

The various physical properties change in different ways when stresses are relieved by annealing. Continued heating may produce recrystallization, which, as the name implies, means the formation and growth of new crystal grains. The most important factor in determining the extent and nature of recrystallization in material of given chemical composition seems to be the potential energy stored up in the strained grains. For instance, similar·samples having undergone different amounts of similar plastic deformation will recrystallize quite differently when heated. Some sequences of treatments will result in the appearance of large grains; some will result in small grains. When recrystallization sets in, the new grains may have quite different orientations from the old ones, but the new distribution of orientations is not at all necessarily a random one.

28. Solid Solutions.—Small amounts of a foreign substance may influence the behavior of ferromagnetic crystals enormously, especially if present in the form of separate atoms in solution. Atoms in solution may be present as substitution atoms, as in Fig. 21, or as interstitial atoms crowded between the atoms of the crystal. In either case they will disturb the lattice in their immediate vicinity. In the absence of definite information, we may assume this distortion to be due to a repulsion, as in Fig. 21a, or an attraction, as in Fig. 21b, which the foreign atom exerts on its immediate neighbors.

It is of interest to know something of the distribution of atoms in solution in a lattice. If their concentration is sufficiently small, the forces that they exert on each other may be neglected, and

---

[1] C. F. ELAM, "Distortion of Metal Crystals," Clarendon Press, Oxford, 1935; E. SCHMID and W. BOAS, "Kristallplastizität," Julius Springer, Berlin, 1935; G. TAMMANN, *Z. Metallkunde*, **26**, 97, 1934.

their distribution will be a random one.   The most convenient way of expressing a distribution is to consider a large quantity of substance in which there are N atoms of impurity.   Divide the substance into n equal parts, or cells.   Let $N/n = \xi$ be the average number of impurity atoms per cell, and let $f(a)$ be the

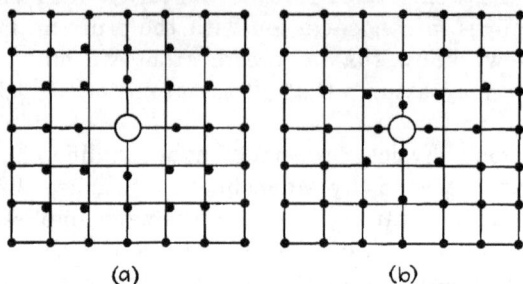

(a)   (b)

Fig. 21.—Two possible deformations produced by a substitution atom in a lattice.

probability of finding a such atoms in a cell chosen at random. If the distribution is a random one, it can be shown that[1]

$$f(a) = \frac{N!(n-1)^{N-a}}{a!(N-a)!n^N} \qquad (55)$$

which for large values of N, n and ξ reduces to the approximate expression

$$f(a) = \frac{e^{-\frac{(\xi-a)^2}{2\xi}}}{\sqrt{2\pi\xi}} \qquad (56)$$

Curves for various values of ξ are plotted in Figs. 22 and 23. As an example consider a crystal in which there is 0.1 per cent of impurity in solution, the crystal being divided into little cubes containing 1000 atoms each.   An atom in the center of such a group will be 10 atomic diameters removed from an atom at the center of a neighboring group.   On the average, each such group of 1000 will contain 1 atom of impurity.   From the curve for $\xi = 1$ in Fig. 23 it follows that about $\frac{1}{3}$ of the groups will contain no impurity atom; about $\frac{1}{3}$ will contain 1; and the remaining $\frac{1}{3}$ will contain 2 or more.   If the atoms in solution attract each other, they will tend to cluster together, and therefore the distribution

[1] F. Bitter, *Phys. Rev.*, **37**, 1527, 1931.

will be less uniform and will depend on the temperature. If repulsive forces exist, the distribution will be more uniform.

29. Superstructures.—The distributions found in the preceding section will, in general, apply only to dilute solutions.

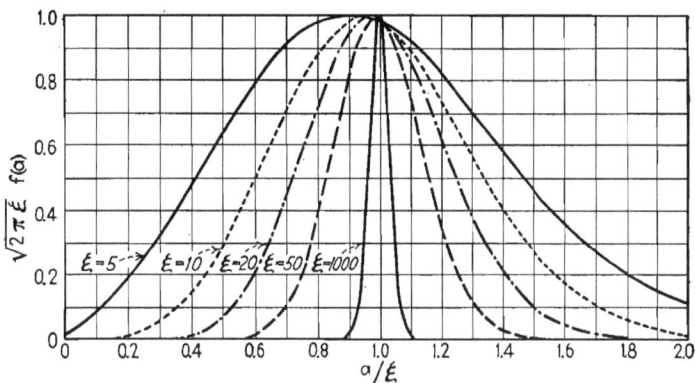

FIG. 22.—$f(a)$ is the probability of finding a particles in any one of a large number of cells among which particles have been distributed with an average density ξ.

As the concentration is increased, the atoms of the solute may tend to condense and so form a new phase, or their distribution in the solvent may tend to become more uniform. These more

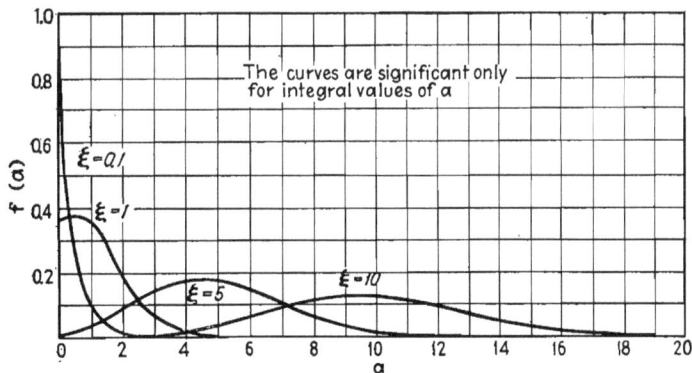

FIG. 23.—$f(a)$ is the same function as in Fig. 22 but is here plotted for small values of ξ.

uniform distributions are sometimes called "superstructures." For certain concentrations and temperatures, foreign atoms may tend to arrange themselves at regular intervals in a crystal, and such regular arrangements can be detected by means of X rays.[1]

30. Inclusions.—When the concentration of a foreign substance has reached the limit of solubility, precipitation takes place, and the new phase appears in the form of inclusions. At room temperature, however, diffusion in solids proceeds very slowly, and it is therefore possible to maintain a supersaturated solution at room temperatures for long times.

Precipitation in a supersaturated solution can be accelerated by plastic deformation. The inclusions produced by such treatments are small and have been observed only in special cases.[2]

The shapes of inclusions vary greatly, from randomly distributed masses of irregular shape and size to the beautifully regular striations found, for instance, in pearlite.

31. Critical Temperatures.—The outstanding critical temperatures in pure metals are those associated with phase changes, involving a rearrangement of atoms. These changes generally occur at very sharply defined temperatures and are accompanied by the evolution or absorption of heat. If, for instance, a body is heated and then allowed to cool very slowly so that all its parts are at sensibly the same temperature, the resulting cooling curve, in which the temperature is plotted as a function of the time, will, in general, be a smooth one. Wherever phase changes occur, however, anomalies will appear in the cooling or heating curves. There are many ways in which phase changes can be detected, as most of the physical properties of a body alter abruptly with a change of phase. The temperatures at which changes of phase take place can be altered by the application of pressure.

At high temperatures, where the atoms because of their large kinetic energies are relatively free to move about in each others' fields of force, changes in atomic arrangement can take place quickly. At low temperatures such rearrangements take place very much more slowly. Cobalt, for instance, has a face-centered cubic lattice structure at high temperatures and, if cooled slowly so that the atoms have time to take up their most stable positions,

---

[1] For further discussion see W. L. Bragg and E. J. Williams, *Proc. Roy. Soc.*, A, **145**, 699, 1934; H. A. Bethe, *Proc. Roy. Soc.*, A, **150**, 552, 1935.

[2] A. Kussmann and H. J. Seemann, *Z. Physik*, **77**, 567, 1932. For further discussion of inclusions and their bearing on magnetic properties, see Chap. IV.

appears at room temperature in the form of hexagonal close-packed crystals. If quenched (cooled rapidly by immersion in a liquid) so that the atoms do not have time to rearrange themselves, the face-centered cubic structure persists at room temperature, the atoms being "frozen" in this configuration.

Less clearly defined anomalies than these discussed above occur in the heating curves of plastically deformed material. The work necessary to produce such deformation is, in part, stored up as potential energy in the material and reappears in the form of heat when the temperature is high enough for recrystallization to proceed. The recrystallization temperature is, however, not so sharply defined as the critical temperatures at which phase changes take place.

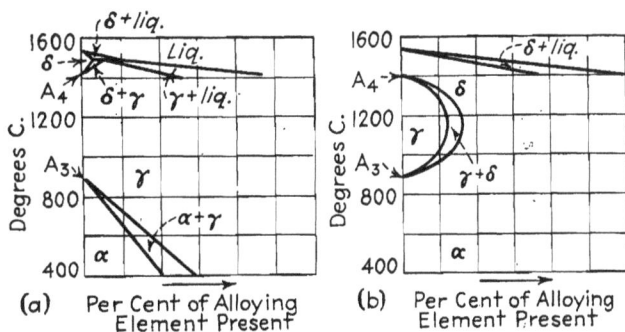

FIG. 24.—Two characteristic types of phase diagrams for iron alloys.

Critical temperatures may be due to electronic as well as atomic rearrangements, as in the case of the Curie temperature, for instance, at which ferromagnetism goes over into paramagnetism. There are, it is true, changes in the shape of a ferromagnetic sample at the Curie temperature which must necessarily involve changes in the interatomic spacing, but these changes in atomic spacing do not involve a change in lattice type and are of secondary importance as compared with the electronic changes.

In alloys the critical temperatures already discussed are less sharp than in pure metals. There is, in general, a range of temperatures in which a mixture of two phases may occur as shown in Fig. 24. Furthermore, an alloy that is homogeneous at high temperatures in one phase will no longer be so after being cooled through a critical temperature to another phase unless very special precautions are taken. For instance, an ingot made by pouring a well-mixed molten alloy into a mold will not necessarily have the same composition on its surface, which solidified first, as in its interior, which solidified last.

The presence of an alloying element also changes the temperature at which phase changes take place. Two typical phase diagrams of iron alloys are shown in Figs. 24a and b. α refers to the body-centered cubic lattice structure, γ to the face-centered cubic modification, and δ to the body-centered cubic modification existing at high temperatures. These diagrams are of especial interest because of the importance of iron in ferromagnetic problems. A classification of elements according to whether they produce diagrams of type a or b is shown in the following table.[1]

Elements Producing a Diagram of Type *a*	Elements Producing a Diagram of Type *b*
Boron	Beryllium
Carbon	Aluminum
Nitrogen	Silicon
Oxygen	Phosphorus
Sulphur	Vanadium
Manganese	Chromium
Cobalt	Arsenic
Nickel	Molybdenum
Copper	Tin
Zinc	Antimony
Rhodium	Tungsten
Iridium	
Platinum	

And finally there are a whole host of temperatures which for one reason or another play an important part in the preparation of metals, temperatures determined by years of experience as suitable for the annealing, quenching, tempering, ageing, purifying, etc., to which a metal must be submitted to give it the desired properties. The physical effects of some of these heat treatments are understood. Many, and especially those used to produce special magnetic properties, are not.

32. Block Structures.—Although the theories describing crystals in terms of perfect geometrical arrays of identical atoms have had considerable success in describing certain properties, they have been entirely unsuccessful in describing other prop-

[1] F. Wever, *Stahl u. Eisen*, **49**, 839, 1929; T. D. Yensen and N. Ziegler, *A.I.M.E.*, *Iron Steel Div.*, 313, 1931, have shown that this classification has a bearing on ferromagnetic problems.

erties, especially those often referred to as "structure sensitive." Various attempts have been made to get a better interpretation of experimental data by assuming imperfect lattices, some of the work dealing with random imperfections, caused by the treatment which the crystal received during its production; other work dealing with a possible block structure, inherent in the nature of the crystal itself. The chief difficulty in the way of rapid progress in these directions is that of experimentally observing small lattice imperfections. Much qualitative evidence is available to support both types of theories, and it seems likely that both must be considered in discussing actual materials.

Fortunately, however, in ferromagnetic crystals the old magnetic-powder technique, refined and developed for microscopic observations, has been found adequate for revealing surface structures, and the observations leave no doubt that characteristic orderly substructures exist in various ferromagnetic crystals. The remainder of this chapter is given over to a description by W. C. Elmore of the magnetic-powder method and of the results achieved with it. Elmore's development of the magnetic-colloid technique, partly in collaboration with L. W. McKeehan, has put into the hands of students of ferromagnetism an important new tool.

In the appendix is a theoretical discussion of "Cooperative Phenomena" by F. Zwicky, who first proposed block structures and has done much to stimulate interest in this important aspect of the structure of matter.

33. The Use of Magnetic Powders and Suspensions (by W. C. Elmore).—Coarse magnetic powders, such as iron filings, have long been used to explore magnetic fields. The best known example is perhaps the demonstration of the distribution of poles and of lines of force around permanent magnets. The method is, however, capable of revealing much finer detail and has been used for some time as a nondestructive test for inhomogeneities in all kinds of ferromagnetic samples.[1] An illustrative example is discussed below.

---

[1] Representative photographs of the kinds of results to be obtained and further references may be found in A. V. DeForest, *Iron Age*, **127**, 1594, 1934; *Proc. Am. Petroleum Inst.*, **15M**, Sec. IV, 37, 1934; *J. Applied Mechanics*, **3**, A-23, 1936; T. R. Watts, *J. Am. Welding Soc.*, **9**, 49, September, 1930; F. Bitter, *Mech. Eng.*, **55**, 287, 1933.

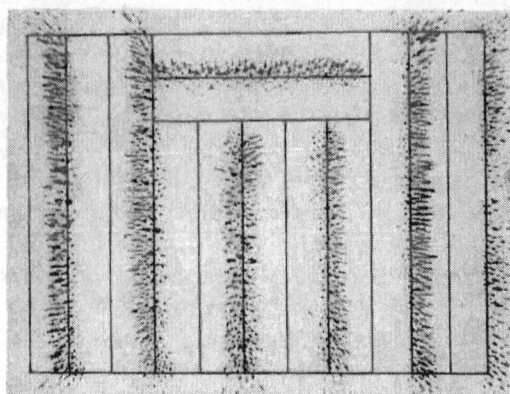

(A)

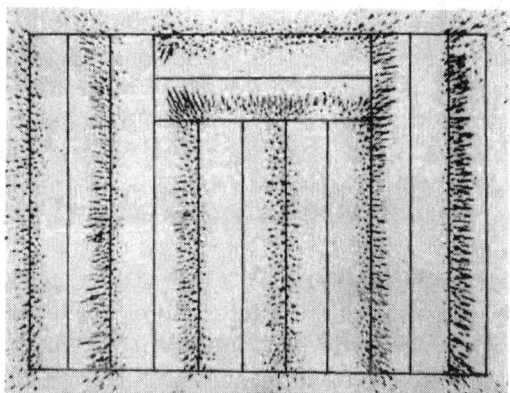

(B)

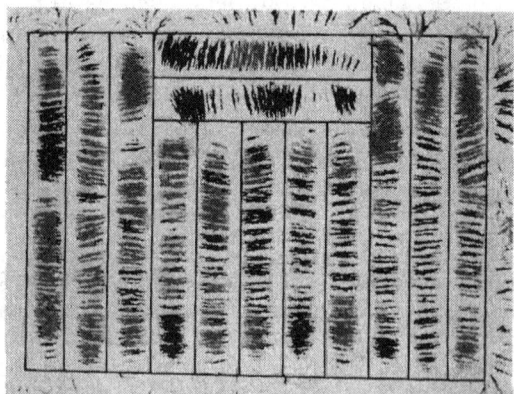

(C)

Fig. 25.—Patterns made by sprinkling iron filings onto a card held above an array of permanently magnetized steel strips. (*A*) Normal applied field positive; (*B*) negative; (*C*) zero.

Figure 25 shows a set of patterns made by sprinkling iron filings onto a piece of cardboard mounted above a number of permanently magnetized strips of steel. The strips were magnetized across their length and arranged as the lines in the figure indicate, with adjacent edges having the same polarity. Two of the patterns were made with an applied external field superposed on that of the strips. This field was approximately normal to their plane and differed in direction for the two patterns. The other pattern was made with only the field of the strips present. These patterns are shown here, since they suggest the distribution of magnetization giving rise to some of the patterns found on iron, to be described later.

The powder technique was first applied on a microscopic scale by von Hamos and Thiessen,[1] and independently by Bitter.[2] The former attempted to reveal the connection between strain and local magnetization of a nickel wire. The latter discovered by this method the magnetic patterns on the surface of iron, cobalt, and nickel crystals.

Since the experimental details of the powder technique are not generally known, it seems worth

FIG. 26.—Apparatus used for observing magnetic structures.

while to present them here. The specimen with a smooth plane horizontal is mounted either between the poles of a horizontal electromagnet (H parallel to the surface) or upon the pole of a vertical electromagnet (H normal to surface). An arrangement that permits the application of both fields, as, for instance, in the apparatus shown in Fig. 26, is perhaps most useful. The smooth surface of the specimen may be a naturally occurring one or one

[1] L. VON HAMOS and P. A. THIESSEN, *Z. Physik*, **71**, 442, 1931.

[2] F. BITTER, *Phys. Rev.*, **38**, 1903, 1931; **41**, 507, 1932.

that has been prepared by suitable metallurgical polishing. Since distortion in the polished layer may influence the magnetization of the surface, a method for producing a mirror surface on a metal with as little damage as possible is much to be desired.

With the specimen magnetized in a definite manner, a small quantity of a fine magnetic powder suspended in liquid is placed on its surface. After a few minutes the resulting distribution of the powder is examined with a microscope. Since each particle of the powder becomes a small magnetic dipole in the presence of a magnetic field, the powder will collect in regions where the local concentration of magnetic lines of force near the surface is a maximum.[1] If a volatile liquid is used, such as alcohol or ethyl acetate, the liquid may be allowed to evaporate before examination. If water is used with the powder in a truly colloidal state, it is usually necessary to rinse away the excess colloid not concentrated near the surface and to employ a microscope coverglass, particularly at higher magnifications.

Various magnetic powders have been tried, including Fe_2O_3, Fe_3O_4, pyrophoric iron, and iron particles produced by sublimation or by sparking iron electrodes in alcohol. Gamma (ferromagnetic) Fe_2O_3 (siderac) is particularly suitable.

The magnetic powder may be used in two ways. If the particle size is approximately 1 micron or larger, the powder tends to settle out by gravity; magnetic field gradients hasten the settling and pull the particles into regions where the field is most intense. However, if the particles are so small (less than 0.1 micron) that they exhibit a violent Brownian movement (form a true colloid), they will not settle out but will be merely concentrated in certain regions near the surface by the highly nonuniform field existing there.[2] If, in the latter case, the field distribution is changed by some means, the local swarms of particles immediately migrate to new regions of highly nonuniform H. To prevent the colloid particles, which are always electrically charged, from touching

---

[1] Mathematically, if M is the magnetic moment per particle and H is the magnetic field near the surface of the specimen, then the force on each particle will be $F = M \cdot \nabla H$. Now, $M = M(H)H$ where $M(H)$ is essentially positive (if each particle has a permanent moment M_0 then $M(H) = M_0/H$); hence we may write $F = M(H)H \cdot \nabla H = \frac{1}{2}M(H)\nabla H^2$. The magnetic particles will collect in regions into which the forces F converge, i.e., in regions where H^2 is greater than in near-by regions.

[2] L. W. McKEEHAN and W. C. ELMORE, *Phys. Rev.*, **46**, 226, 1934.

the metallic surface and coagulating, it is found necessary to leave an invisible film of grease on the surface or, much better, to coat the surface with a very thin lacquer. The lacquer, in addition, will prevent rust from forming on iron specimens. Suitable colloids will reveal magnetic structure so sharply that the full resolving power of the microscope may be used to advantage.

34. Magnetic Structures (by W. C. Elmore).—The description of the patterns to be found on ferromagnetic crystals is complicated because of the many different observations that have been made. The results cannot as yet be systematized, as the

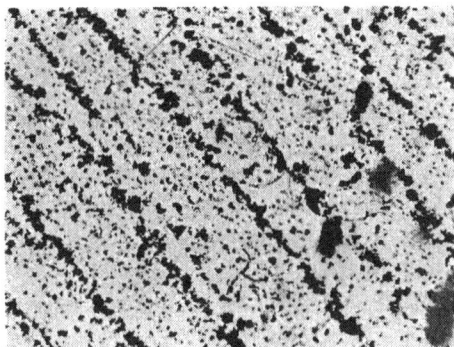

FIG. 27.—Lines of fairly coarse magnetic powder found on a large crystal grain in an unpolished sample of hydrogenized iron. Magnetization transverse and nearly perpendicular to pattern lines. (50 ×.)

relevant factors in most of these observations are not yet established beyond a doubt. Only a brief survey of those observations which seem fairly definitely settled will, therefore, be given, it being understood that these comments, and even the original papers on which they are based, give only special results on the basis of which one must generalize with great caution.

Iron.—Bitter[1] first showed that a regular magnetic structure in iron crystals could be revealed by depositing a magnetic powder on them. The powder formed sets of parallel lines on the natural faces of crystals occurring in iron or iron-silicon ingots, or on strips annealed in hydrogen, when they were magnetized parallel to a surface. The pattern shown in Fig. 27 is typical of structures revealed in this manner. The spacing of the lines on unpolished

[1] See footnote, Par. 33.

specimens ranges from around 40 to 100 microns and seems, in general, not to be fixed in the specimen.

Other workers have used the powder technique to investigate polished iron crystals magnetized parallel to their surface. In general, patterns with smaller line spacings often containing two sets of parallel lines were found. Akulov and Degtiar[1] succeeded in getting such a pattern with no applied H, and in a later paper Akulov and Raewsky[2] reported a periodic change in the direction of the powder lines as an iron crystal is plastically deformed. Becker and Freundlich[3] followed the appearance of the line deposits as an iron crystal was magnetized to saturation. As magnetic saturation was approached, the pattern lines became broken and always occurred perpendicular to the direction of magnetization regardless of the crystal orientation. Kaya[4] in two papers investigated the appearance of the line patterns on simple atomic planes as a function of magnetization and polish. Along the steep part of the magnetization curve, lines were observed only after polishing, and these were parallel to the intersection of (100) planes with the surface. A "maze-type" pattern was obtained for samples polished by rubbing in all directions. This type of pattern is fixed in the surface of the crystal. For higher magnetizations, where rotational processes are involved (see Chap. VI) lines parallel to the intersection of (110) planes with the surface were obtained. This type of pattern is not fixed in the surface but can be shifted by changes of magnetization. The foregoing results have been confirmed by Sixtus[5] in as yet unpublished work.

Using the true colloid and magnetizing a single crystal of silicon iron normal to the surface, McKeehan and Elmore[6] discovered an interesting shift of colloid lines when the field was reversed. The crystal surface was approximately (100), and a maze-type pattern was formed consisting of two sets of lines along the traces of the (100) planes most nearly perpendicular to the surface. Upon reversing the field all of the pattern lines were found to shift

---

[1] N. Akulov and M. Degtiar, *Ann. Physik*, **15**, 750, 1932.

[2] N. Akulov and S. Raewsky, *Ann. Physik*, **20**, 113, 1934.

[3] R. Becker and W. Freundlich, *Z. Physik*, **80**, 292, 1933.

[4] S. Kaya, *Z. Physik*, **89**, 1934; **90**, 551, 1934.

[5] K. J. Sixtus, *Phys. Rev.*, **45**, 565, 1934.

[6] See footnote, Par. 33.

into the middle of the spaces. The shifting was completely reversible. The average spacing of lines in these patterns was about 4 microns. With no applied field a double pattern was obtained with lines spaced 2 microns apart. Although the no-field pattern was at first considered to consist of the two single patterns occurring simultaneously (and so reported), closer observation has shown definitely that the no-field pattern lines come halfway between the pattern to be obtained by superposing the other two patterns. Figure 28 illustrates the three patterns. These patterns were found on a polished silicon-iron single crystal containing about 3 per cent silicon. Crystals of more nearly pure iron also yield very similar patterns differing chiefly in the average line spacing. The deposits of iron filings shown in the preceding section behave in an analogous manner and thus suggest the arrangement on the crystal surface of the magnetization which will account for the observed patterns and the shifting effect.

In a later paper Elmore and McKeehan[1] extended their study of the silicon-iron patterns. Their experiments revealed a remarkable stability of the patterns and uniformity of the line spacings in patterns made on various cuts of the same crystal, provided the angles which the cuts made to the (100) planes in question were taken into account. They found, however, that different crystals from similar stock showed different average line spacings.

If the specimen was momentarily magnetized parallel to its surface, and then a pattern deposited on it by means of a normal field alone, a new line pattern at places differing from the old was formed, but the lines of it all lay on portions of a mesh that could be assigned from previous patterns. A fairly heavy etch does not apparently alter the patterns here described.

On some silicon-iron specimens having naturally smooth surfaces, the finely spaced maze pattern has not been found, although polishing will produce such a pattern. There are some indications from the behavior of the colloid, however, that a magnetic structure exists on these unpolished surfaces at a scale below or very near to the revolving power of the microscope. It would seem that polishing strains or the application of fairly large

[1] W. C. ELMORE and L. W. McKEEHAN, *Trans. A.I.M.E.*, **120**, 236, 1936.

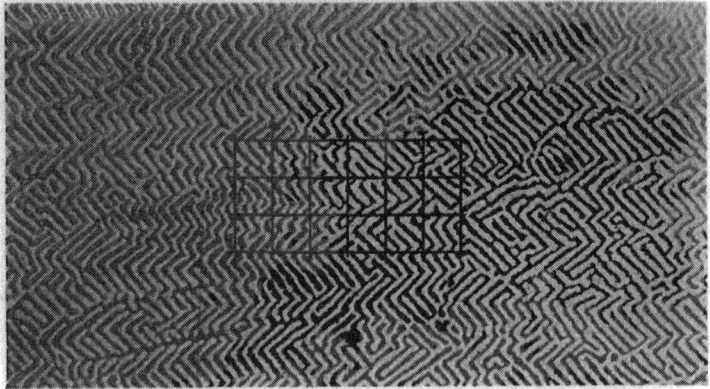

(A)

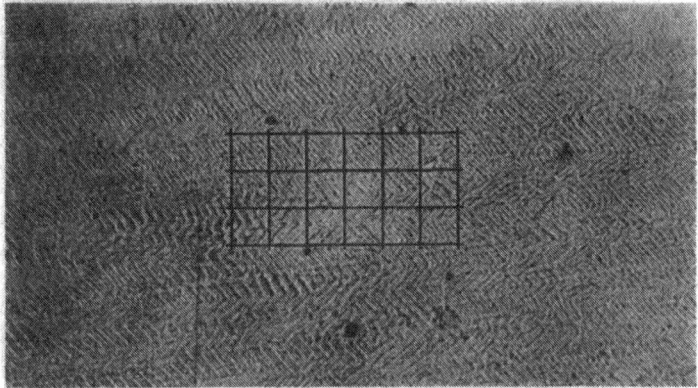

(B)

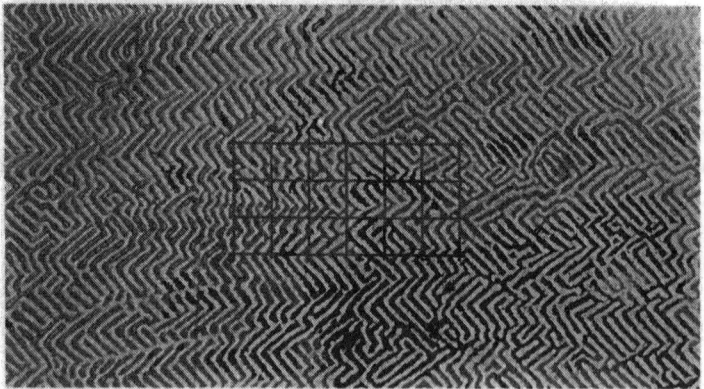

(C)

FIG. 28.—Maze patterns of colloidal Fe_2O_3 found on an approximately (100) face of a polished silicon-iron single crystal.   Grille $41\mu \times 82\mu$.   (A) Normal applied field positive; (B) zero; (C) negative.

external fields causes a coarser magnetic structure which can then be revealed in detail by magnetic powder or colloid.

Nickel.—The magnetic deposits which von Hamos and Thiessen[1] obtained on a stretched nickel wire did not show the characteristic line patterns that Bitter[1] found upon small unpolished ingots of nickel when suitably magnetized. By gradually increasing the magnetization parallel to the surface and making successive deposits of powder, Bitter discovered that in some cases each of the original lines would split into several parallel components. One of these patterns is shown in Fig. 29. These lines were shown not to be fixed in the crystal but could be shifted by successively magnetizing and demagnetizing the sample.

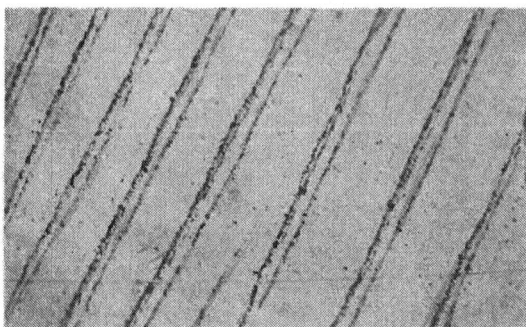

FIG. 29.—Powder pattern on an unpolished nickel crystal. The splitting of lines here in evidence increases as the transverse magnetization is increased. (75 ×.)

Sixtus[2] studied patterns on a polycrystalline nickel-iron wire which could be subjected to torsion. The line deposits that he found do not seem to be connected with the more regular patterns of Bitter. Kaya and Sekiya,[3] however, obtained a series of regular line patterns on various simple crystal planes of single nickel crystals. These lines appeared only at higher magnetization and could be formed along either (100) or (110) planes. The spacing of the lines on nickel is relatively great; in fact, on some crystals the lines may be seen with the naked eye.

Müller and Steinberg[4] deposited powder on a compressed nickel plate and discovered that short line deposits appeared perpendic-

[1] See footnote, Par. 33.
[2] K. J. SIXTUS, *Phys. Rev.*, **44**, 46, 1933.
[3] S. KAYA and J. SEKIYA, *Z. Physik*, **96**, 53, 1935.
[4] N. MÜLLER and D. STEINBERG, *Tech. Phys. U. S. S. R.*, **1**, 205, 1934.

ular to the direction of compression.   They magnetized the nickel normal to its surface.

McKeehan and Elmore[1] used colloid to form a pattern on a polished (100) face of a single nickel crystal magnetized normally. Instead of a line pattern they found a "dot" pattern which showed to some extent a characteristic shifting upon reversing the field.   The closest spacing of the dots was about 0.6 micron.   It was impossible to find a connection between the dot pattern and the orientation of the nickel crystal.   A pair of these patterns is shown in Fig. 30 for the two directions of the normal field.

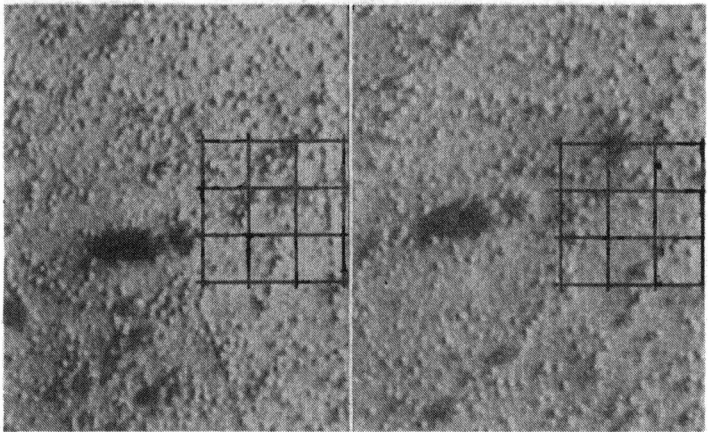

Fig. 30.—Dot patterns of colloid on a (100) face of a polished nickel crystal for the two directions of normal applied field.   Grille 12μ × 12μ.

Cobalt.—Bitter[2] has been the only one to study the magnetic structure of cobalt.   He found that the pattern on the (0001) plane consists of a lacelike network having a somewhat imperfect hexagonal symmetry, as the pattern in Fig. 31 shows.   On planes approximately perpendicular to the basal plane he found patterns of parallel lines.   Patterns on cobalt were easily obtained with no external field.

The present writer has made a few colloid patterns on a polished cobalt ingot which contained large grains.   The patterns on individual grains were essentially the same as Bitter found but of a smaller scale.   When a normal magnetizing field was reversed, a pronounced shifting effect of the pattern was observed,

[1] McKeehan and Elmore, *Phys. Rev.*, **46**, 529, 1934.
[2] See footnote, Par. 33.

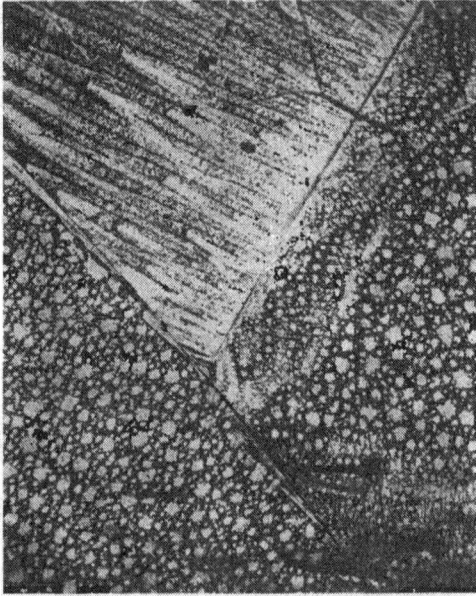

Fig. 31.—Lacelike pattern found on (0001) plane of cobalt.   (75 ×.)

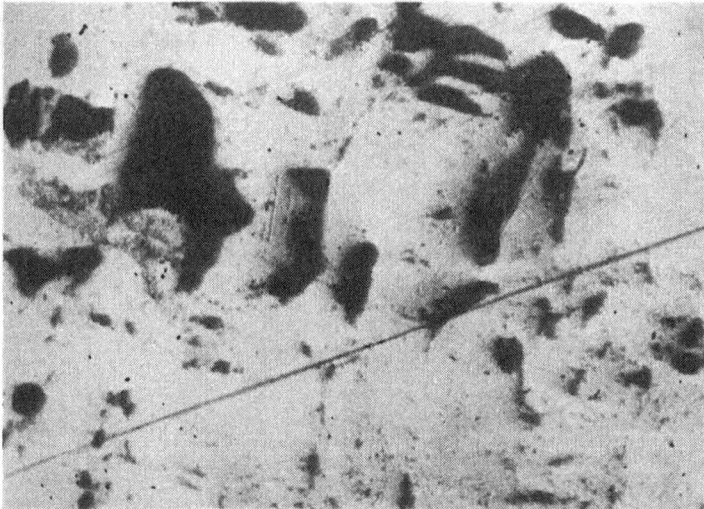

Fig. 32.—Segregations of colloid on a polished sample of 18–8 stainless steel which has been severely cold worked.

similar to that of the pattern on iron crystals.   Cobalt seems to have a stray field near its surface greater than that of the other ferromagnetic crystals.

Magnetite.—Müller and Steinberg[1] found a'pattern of crooked lines on magnetite.   They used a normal field and discovered that the lines and spaces interchanged upon reversing the field and depositing a new pattern.   The spacing of the lines varied from 30 to 300 microns.   This particular magnetic structure seemed to be located rather permanently in the crystal.

The colloid technique has proved itself useful as an adjunct to etching.   The line patterns on iron or silicon steel will show any marked preferential grain orientation.   As a further example we may mention its use to detect the presence of ferrite in an austenitic phase such as 18–8 stainless steel.   The colloid deposit on a piece of this steel, which has been cold worked by rolling, is shown in Fig. 32.   The colloid, in general, may be used to detect the presence of a ferromagnetic phase in one that is not ferromagnetic, or vice versa.

[1] See footnote, page 63.

CHAPTER IV

MAGNETIC MATERIALS AND THEIR PREPARATION

By

T. D. YENSEN

The purpose of this chapter is twofold. First, it is intended to serve as an aid to those who are contemplating research work in ferromagnetism without having had experience in the preparation of materials and in the treatment of samples for this purpose. Second, it is hoped that by considering the points brought out in this and the previous chapter, the reader may acquire an understanding of the difficulties involved in interpreting observational data. One cannot speak of the properties of steel, or even of iron, as one speaks of the properties of oxygen. For instance, before attempting an interpretation of their properties, one must know both the chemical composition and the physical condition of ferromagnetic materials. When this can be explicitly given, it is of course best to do so. In other cases, we must know the relevant factors in the preparation of samples and so arrive at least at a well-defined and repeatable state and infer from this as best we can those items which have not been observed.

The problem involved in the preparation of materials is, necessarily, to a large extent metallurgical but in some particulars goes much beyond what is usually dealt with in textbooks on metallurgy. This is due to the fact, now well established, that ferromagnetic properties are greatly affected by factors that until recently have been regarded as unimportant from both a scientific and a practical point of view. It has often been pointed out that ferromagnetism is a function of the regularity and orientation of the atomic arrangement in the crystal lattice and of the interaction between the electrons of neighboring atoms. It therefore has become obvious why it is that any factor that has a tendency to disturb this regularity and orientation and this free interaction will seriously affect the ferromagnetic properties. A single atom of some foreign element entering the crystal lattice of the ferromagnetic material will produce a local distortion the effect of which may spread to thousands of atoms in the neighborhood. The realization of this situation has consequently made it highly desirable to find ways and means of controlling impurities in amounts previously regarded as traces. Furthermore, there are other factors that produce similar effects, such as strains caused by precipitates (inclusions) and grain boundaries in general as well as by unequal cooling or heating of various parts of the sample, all of which must be taken into account and kept under control in order to make an intelligent study of ferromagnetic materials. And, finally, there is the lattice orientation factor which has been shown to be of great importance, particularly at high flux densities. This chapter should therefore be regarded as a supplement to a general treatise on metallurgy[1] to cover such points as are of particular importance in connection with the subject of ferromagnetism.

35. Commercial Iron.—The purest iron commercially made during the past twenty years has a composition somewhat as follows:

[1] *Ferrous Metallurgy:*

GUERTLER and LEITGEBEL, Vom Erz zum metallischen Werkstoffe, Akademische Verlagsgesellschaft, vol. 23, Leipzig, 1929.

JEFFRIES and ARCHER, "The Science of Metals," McGraw-Hill Book Company, Inc., New York, 1924.

OBERHOFFER, "Das technische Eisen," 3d ed., Julius Springer, Berlin, 1936.

SMITHELLS, "Impurities in Metals," Chapman and Hall, Ltd., London, 1928.

STOUGHTON, "The Metallurgy of Iron and Steel," 4th ed., McGraw-Hill Book Company, Inc., New York, 1934.

Metallography:

BULLENS, "Steel and Its Heat Treatment," 3d ed., John Wiley & Sons, Inc., New York, 1927.

GUERTLER, "Metallographie," Bornträger, Berlin, 1925.

HOYT, "Metallography," McGraw-Hill Book Company, Inc., New York, 1920–1921.

SAUVEUR, "Metallography and Heat-treatment of Iron and Steel," 9th ed., McGraw-Hill Book Company, Inc., New York, 1935.

TAMMANN, "Lehrbuch der Metallkunde," 4th ed., L. Voss, Leipzig, 1932.

TAMMANN, "A Text Book of Metallography," trans. from 3d German ed. by Dean and Swenson, Chemical Catalog Company, Inc., New York, 1925.

	Per Cent
C...	0.02
S...	0.02
P...	0.02
Mn...	0.02
Si..	0.01
O...	0.06
Fe..	99.85

Such iron is made in basic open-hearth furnaces by an intensive refining process, the carbon, manganese, and silicon being removed by means of oxidizing slags and the sulphur and phosphorus by means of reducing slags.   In pouring the molten iron from the furnace into a ladle and in "teeming" it from the ladle into the ingot molds, considerable oxidation takes place, and it is common practice to add some deoxidizer such as Al, Si, or Mn or alloys or some of these with Ca or Fe to the iron during both operations, with the expectation that the resulting oxide will float to the surface and not become embedded in the iron.   However, most oxides are quite viscous at the melting point of iron and on this account are difficult to remove completely.   Furthermore, during the subsequent rolling or forging operations the metal is subjected to oxidizing conditions which tend to saturate it with oxygen in solution.   As the metal cools to room temperature, the solid solubility of oxygen in iron decreases, with the result that it is precipitated as an oxide of iron or of some of the other elements present.   As the oxide cannot escape, it remains in the iron as inclusions either in the grain boundaries or inside the grains.   As a result of these two as well as other incidental processes, most commercial iron products contain oxide inclusions in addition to other precipitates like Fe_3C, FeS, and MnS, in which form C, S, and Mn usually are precipitated from solution during cooling.   Furthermore, from purely theoretical considerations, it is obvious that the presence of these precipitates is clear evidence that the iron still contains certain amounts of O, C, S, Mn, and P in solution, as the precipitates have been formed by reactions such as

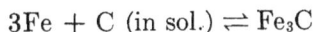

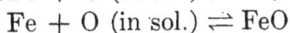

$$3Fe + C \text{ (in sol.)} \rightleftharpoons Fe_3C$$
$$Fe + O \text{ (in sol.)} \rightleftharpoons FeO$$
$$\text{Etc.}$$

The reactions tend toward completion from left to right only when the Fe_3C and FeO are completely removed.   The fact that the solubility of C, O, and S in iron at room temperature is less than 0.01 per cent has caused metallurgists in general to ignore them and to concentrate their attention on the visible precipitated inclusions. While the latter are of great importance, we can no longer ignore the former, particularly in connection with ferromagnetism. The reason for this conclusion will be briefly considered in the next section.

36. The Importance of Small Amounts of Impurities. *a. Carbon and Other Interstitial Impurities.*—An important type of impurity is one whose atoms, because of their nonsimilarity to the parent metal, do not substitute for the atoms of the parent metal in the crystal lattice but either combine with them to form compounds or occupy, more or less temporarily, the interstitial spaces in the crystal lattice of the parent metal. Such elements are C, O, N, S, P.[1]

In amounts less than 0.01 per cent, carbon has usually been regarded as a trace and so reported by chemical laboratories. The ordinary method of analysis for carbon in iron has been incapable of a greater degree of accuracy than ± 0.01 per cent, and the ordinary method of preparing iron invariably introduced more than this amount of carbon even if the iron contained less than this amount to begin with, such as electrolytic iron.[2] With the advent of vacuum furnaces, however, this situation changed radically, as by melting in vacuum it was possible to make the reaction

$$C + O \rightleftharpoons CO$$

go from left to right to a degree depending only on the limiting CO pressure that could be maintained. Without knowing the actual carbon content, the author, in 1914–1915, obtained magnetic properties that surpassed any previously obtained[3] by melting electrolytic iron in a vacuum furnace. The result of several years of research revealed the fact that carbon in amounts less than 0.01 per cent has proportionately much greater effect on the magnetic properties than carbon in larger amounts.[4] A new

[1] T. D. Yensen, *Phys. Rev.*, **39**, 358, 1932.

[2] T. D. Yensen, *Univ. Illinois, Eng. Exp. Sta., Bull.* 72, 1914.

[3] T. D. Yensen, *Gen. Elec. Rev.*, **18**, 881, 1915; *Univ. Illinois, Eng. Exp. Sta., Bull.* 83, 1915; *Trans. A.I.E.E.*, **34**, 2601, 1915; *Bull. A.I.M.E.*, 1916, p. 483; *Met. Chem. Eng.*, **14**, 585, 1916.

[4] T. D. Yensen, *Trans. A.I.E.E.*, **43**, 145, 1924.

method of determining carbon in metals, described in Par. 45, improved the accuracy to ± 0.0001 per cent,[1] making it possible to obtain reliable relationships between carbon contents and magnetic properties down to a few thousandths of a per cent carbon. By extrapolation to zero carbon, these results indicated that perfectly pure iron should have zero hysteresis loss and exceedingly high permeability. Subsequent investigations have served to confirm this conclusion.[2] The preceding investigations

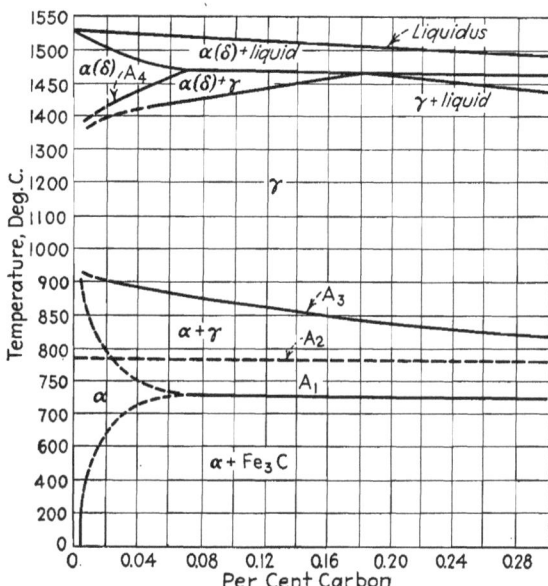

FIG. 33.—Constitutional diagram of the Fe-C system.

also showed the possible cause of these new results; for carbon contents less than 0.006 per cent no carbon precipitate (Fe_3C) appears in iron at room temperature, whereas amounts greater than this, but less than about 0.05 per cent, precipitates as Fe_3C ("cementite") during cooling from 700°C. When the carbon content exceeds 0.05 per cent the excess precipitates at the eutectoid temperature (700°C.) in layers of Fe_3C alternating with layers of Fe ("ferrite") giving a pearly appearance as seen under the microscope and therefore named "pearlite." The agreement between these results and the iron-carbon equilibrium diagram

---

[1] T. D. YENSEN, *Trans. Am. Electrochem. Soc.*, **37**, 227, 1920.

[2] P. P. CIOFFI, *Nature*, **126**, 200, 1930; *Phys. Rev.*, **39**, 363, 1932.

is apparent from Fig. 33. Other impurities such as sulphur[1] and oxygen[2] act similarly and have similar effect on the magnetic properties of iron and iron alloys.

b. Solubility and Colloidal Precipitates.—The foregoing evidence at first led to the conclusion that the solubility of carbon in iron at room temperature, based on the apparent absence of precipitates in iron with less than 0.006 per cent C, lies between 0.005 and 0.01 per cent. Recent considerations, however, tend to show that either this and all other conclusions in regard to solubility based on microanalysis should be modified or our definition of crystalline solubility should be changed.

In the first place, the fact that no precipitates can be seen at a magnification of even 5000 diameters is no proof that precipitates are not present. The smallest particle that can be seen at such magnification contains at least 1 million atoms, and there must exist particles of all sizes even down to the smallest crystalline units containing a few atoms. Such particles cannot diffuse through the lattice, but thermal agitation will cause them to dissociate into atoms or ions that are capable of diffusing and recombining with other atoms or ions.[3] If we define true solubility on the basis of diffusion, then clearly the part of the impurities in solution comprise only the atoms or ions that at any one instant are in a state of transition. All other atoms are in chemical combination either with the solvent atoms or with each other. In either case they constitute a separate phase, or a compound may *by itself* be regarded as a solid solution[4] but not as dissolved in the parent metal. (See also Gottschalk and Dean, "The Solubility of Gases in Metals."[5])

On the basis of the preceding consideration, impurities in a metal may consequently exist in two states:

1. In true solution; separate atoms or ions in a state of diffusion.

2. As precipitates in the form of chemical compounds (inclusions). These may be gaseous (in blowholes), liquid, or solid.

The second state may be divided into two arbitrary classes:

[1] T. D. Yensen, *Trans. A.I.E.E.*, **43**, 145, 1924.
[2] T. D. Yensen and N. A. Zeigler, *Trans. Am. Soc. Metals*, **23**, 556, 1935.
[3] R. T. Phelps and W. P. Davey, *Trans. A.I.M.E.*, **99**, 234, 1932.
[4] T. D. Yensen, *Trans. A.I.M.E.*, **99**, 248, 1932.
[5] V. H. Gottschalk and R. S. Dean, *Trans. A.I.M.E.*, **104**, 133, 1933.

   a. Colloidal particles, smaller than 10^{-16} cm.^{3}

   b. Ordinary inclusions, larger than 10^{-16} cm.^{3}

   As far as the effect on the magnetic properties is concerned, however, n atoms of impurity in the form of colloidal precipitates may be just as harmful as these same n atoms in true solution. On this account, it is more logical, as far as magnetic properties are concerned, to combine impurities in solution with colloidal precipitates. In this class we must consequently include all impurities in true solution (C, S, P, O, N, H, etc.); all colloidal crystalline and amorphous particles from whatever source, such as C (as graphite), Fe_3C, Fe_3P, FeO, Fe_4N, Mn_3C, MnS, MnO, SiO, Al_2O_3, Cr_2O_5, and combinations of these; and, finally, colloidal liquid and gaseous globules such as H_2, O_2, H_2O, CO, CO_2, CH_4, N_2. In short, we must include in the first class all foreign matter that cannot be detected by means of a 5000-magnification microscope and call it "dissolved or colloidal impurities" and place in the second class all other foreign matter and call it "inclusions."

   37. The Electrolytic Refining of Metals.—The first process used by investigators in their attempt to obtain a purer product than that obtainable by commercial means (see Par. 35) was the electrolytic process. Burgess[1] and Terry[2] in the United States and Müller[3] and Fisher[4] in Germany were among the first to use this process for refining iron. The various methods developed for refining iron, nickel, and cobalt electrolytically are briefly described in Hughes, "Modern Electroplating," 1923;[5] and more fully in Engelhardt, "Handbuch der technischen Elektrochemie," 1931;[6] in Pfanhauser, "Die Elektrolytischen Metallniederschläge, 1928,"[7] and in Cleaves and Thompson, "The Metal

[1] C. F. Burgess and C. Hambuecken, *Iron and Steel Mag.*, **8**, 48, 1904. C. F. Burgess and A. H. Taylor, *Trans. A.I.E.E.*, **25**, 459, 1906. C. F. Burgess and A. H. Taylor, *Trans. Am. Electrochem. Soc.*, **15**, 369, 1909. C. F. Burgess and J. Aston, *Electrochem. Met. Ind.*, **7**, 403, 1909; *Met. Chem. Eng.*, **8**, 23, 79, 131, 191, 452, 1910.

[2] E. M. Terry, *Phys. Rev.*, **30**, 133, 1910.

[3] A. Müller, *Stahl u. Eisen*, **29**, 919, 1909.

[4] F. Fisher, *ETZ*, **31**, 621, 1910.

[5] W. E. Hughes, "Modern Electroplating," H. Frowde and Hodder and Stoughton, London, 1923.

[6] V. Engelhardt, "Handbuch der technischen Elektrochemie," vol. I, part I, Akad. Verlagsges., Leipzig, 1931.

[7] W. Pfanhauser, "Die Elektrolytischen Metallniederschlage," Julius Springer, Berlin, 1928.

—Iron,"[1] Chaps. I and II. As these texts give all the technical information necessary for producing electrolytic metals, it will only be mentioned here that at present (1936) there are no commercial plants in operation in the United States producing electrolytic iron and cobalt regularly,[2] so that anyone wishing to use such materials to any large extent may either have to set up

Average Composition of Electrolytic Deposits

Iron	Per Cent
C (in solution or combined)	0.005 to 0.007
C (as occluded gas)	0.005 to 0.007
S (depending on electrolyte and thoroughness of cleaning)	0.002 to 0.005
P	0.002 to 0.005
Mn	0.002 to 0.005
Si	0.002 to 0.010
Cu (depending on Cu in anode)	0.002 to 0.020
Fe (exclusive of oxygen)	99.98 to 99.93

Nickel	
C	0.005 to 0.010
S (depending on electrolyte and thoroughness of cleaning)	0.002 to 0.015
P	0.001 to 0.002
Mn	0.001 to 0.002
Si	0.010 to 0.020
Fe	0.240 to 0.250
Co	0.300 to 0.500
Cu	0.050 to 0.200
Ni	99.35 to 99.00

Cobalt	
C	0.005 to 0.010
S (depending on electrolyte and thoroughness of cleaning)	0.002 to 0.015
P	0.001 to 0.002
Mn	0.001 to 0.002
Si	0.001 to 0.002
Fe	0.070 to 0.100
Ni	0.010 to 0.020
Cu	0.020 to 0.040
Co	99.90 to 99.80

[1] H. E. Cleaves and J. G. Thompson, "The Metal—Iron," McGraw-Hill Book Company, Inc., New York, 1935 (Alloys of Iron Research Series).

[2] They can probably be procured in small amounts from scientific supply houses and from research laboratories, which either have small plants in operation for their own use or have supplies on hand for experimental purposes.

his own plant or purchase them from Europe (see references in texts listed on p. 73).[1]

We thus have at our disposal iron, nickel, and cobalt of high degree of purity as far as absence of ordinary impurities is concerned. To get rid of Fe, Co, and Cu in Ni is a very difficult task on account of the electrode potentials; and if these elements are objectionable, other methods must be resorted to, such as reduction of pure compounds with hydrogen at high temperatures.

But even if the foregoing elements are not objectionable, the electrodeposited metals may usually be regarded merely as melting stock for the preparation of samples for magnetic research work even if unalloyed samples are wanted. This is due to the fact that the deposit usually is irregular, contains gas holes (hydrogen bubbles), and often is too brittle to forge or roll without some preliminary special treatment. Furthermore, on account of the usual porosity of the deposits they are subject to oxidation. This is particularly true of iron. Some investigations have been made on electrolytic iron as deposited and after annealing, but the results are unreliable and cannot be regarded as representing tests on pure iron. The electrolytic metals may therefore be considered as starting materials from which pure metals and alloys can be made.

38. The Chemical Refining of Metals. Carbonyl Iron.—The most successful of the various methods so far tried is the one known as the carbonyl process, whereby iron, nickel, cobalt, and even combinations of these can be obtained in the form of powder of great purity. As the process is similar for the various products, only the one for producing iron will be described.[2]

Carbonyl iron is the product of the thermal disintegration of iron carbonyl during which metallic iron is formed under the development of carbon monoxide. The liquid carbonyl, $Fe_2(CO)_9$, is first made by treating iron with CO at a low temperature. By heating this at 100°C. the carbonyl vapor is decomposed:

$$2Fe_2(CO)_9 \rightleftharpoons 3Fe(CO)_2 + Fe + 300 \text{ cal.}$$

[1] Since the manuscript was written, the author has found that National Radiator Company, Johnstown, Pa., has a plant in operation for producing electrolytic iron sheet of very good quality.

[2] SCHLECHT, W. SCHUBARDT and F. DUFTSCHMID, *Z. Elektrochem.*, **37**, 485, 1931. H. E. CLEAVES and J. G. THOMPSON, "The Metal—Iron," Chap. III, McGraw-Hill Book Company, Inc., New York, 1935.

The iron falls out in the form of globules 10^{-3} to 10^{-4} cm. in diameter, containing less than 0.005 per cent S and P. By heating these globules above 700°C. they may easily be sintered into a compact mass which can be forged or rolled into any desired shape.

Composition.—From statements made by the manufacturer and from analyses made by the author, the composition of carbonyl iron powder may be expected to fall within the following range:

	Per Cent
Fe.	99.9 to 99.3
C.	0.02 to 0.10
O.	0.10 to 0.60
S.	0.005 to 0.007
P.	0.005 to 0.007
Si.	0.04 to 0.05
Mn.	0.08 to 0.10
Ni.	nil
N.	0.005

Carbonyl iron can therefore not be regarded as a purer product than carefully prepared electrolytic iron. On the contrary, as far as carbon and oxygen are concerned, it is not nearly so pure. The same statement that was made in regard to electrolytic iron also applies to carbonyl iron, *viz.*, that it can be considered only as a starting material from which pure metal and alloys can be made.

39. Refining and Alloying by Melting.—The higher the temperature the more rapid reactions between elements take place, and it is, therefore, necessary in preparing base metals like iron, nickel, cobalt, and alloys in which these elements predominate to isolate the molten metal from the ordinary atmosphere and, in general, to avoid gases that react with metals. In melting electrolytic iron, for example, under atmospheric pressure, in magnesia crucibles placed in a furnace lined with carbon resistor plates the furnace atmosphere will consist largely of CO which will react with the iron and contaminate it with both oxygen and carbon, with the result that the final product will contain up to 0.1 per cent C and 0.1 per cent O and have very poor magnetic properties. This difficulty may be avoided by a number of methods.

a. Melting in a Vacuum Furnace.—With C and O present in the molten iron and CO present in the furnace atmosphere the following reaction takes place:

$$C + O \rightleftharpoons CO$$

As long as the CO is removed by the pumps the reaction goes from left to right, and C and O are eliminated to the point where the limit of the vacuum pump has been reached. If this is of the order of 10^{-3} mm. Hg or less, the C or O content of the iron will be of the order of 0.001 per cent. Excess of either can be removed by the addition of the other, but this is usually a difficult adjustment to make. A preferable procedure is to adjust for a slight excess of carbon in the final charge and then to remove this from the finished solid material by annealing either in vacuum with a slight amount of O or in H, as will be described in Par. 40.

Only two types of vacuum furnaces will be mentioned:

1. The *Arsem type*[1] consisting essentially of a graphite helix resistor held between water-cooled terminals, screened by a graphite cylinder and enclosed in a water-cooled metal tank. A pressure of 0.01 mm. Hg can be maintained with the furnace cold; but when hot, the gases given off by the graphite parts prevent the pressure from going much below 1 mm., with the result that the C or O content will be of the order of 0.01 per cent. As the heating has to be transferred from the graphite helix to the charge through the crucible, the latter has to be made from a refractory material which does not weaken at a temperature several hundred degrees above the melting point of the charge. As this is a severe order to fill, the usual practice is to use fused MgO crucibles[2] supported inside a graphite crucible. There is a slight reduction of MgO in contact with graphite at temperature of 1600 to 1800°C.; but as Mg does not alloy with the iron group, it will evaporate and condense on the cold part of the furnaces.

2. In the *high-frequency induction* furnace developed by Northrup the heat is generated inside the metal charge, and the crucible consequently does not have to stand such a high temperature as in the case of the Arsem type. Refractory materials of lower softening points which are easier to make into crucibles can

[1] W. C. ARSEM, *Trans. Am. Electrochem. Soc.*, **9**, 153, 1906. T. D. YENSEN, *Univ. Illinois Eng. Exp. Sta. Bull.* 72, Mar. 1, 1914.

[2] T. D. YENSEN, *Trans. Am. Electrochem. Soc.*, **32**, 165, 1917.

consequently be used, such as alumina (alundum) and zirconium silicate (zircon).   The latter is particularly satisfactory.

In order to employ the high-frequency principle for vacuum melting, the coil can be either placed outside the vacuum tube or enclosed in the vacuum chamber.   In the former method the

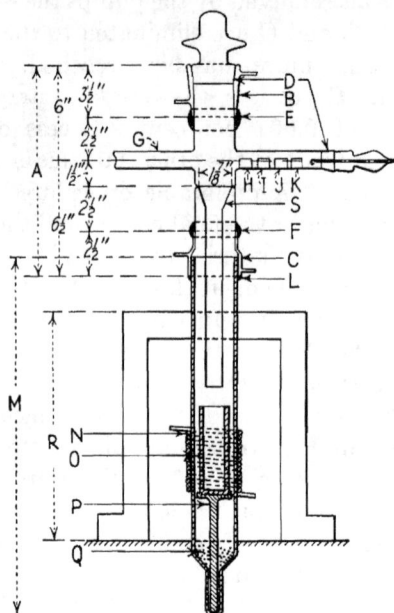

Fig. 34.—High-frequency vacuum furnace used for the analysis of the total oxygen.

A. Glass attachment.
B. C, water jackets.
D. Ground-glass joints.
E. F, rubber water seals.
G. Glass connection to the mercury pumps.
H. I, J, K, samples.
L. Vacuum cement joints.
M. Silica tube (furnace proper): 30½ in. length; 2⅜ in. outside diameter; 2¼ in. inside diameter; 3½ in. length

at one end narrowed to 1 in. outside diameter and sealed.
N. High-frequency coil.
O. Graphite crucible: 1¾ in. outside diameter, 1¼ in. inside diameter, 5 in. high, ⅜ in. bottom.
P. Graphite support.
Q. Coarse alundum sands.
R. Asbestos lumber stand.
S. Removable glass funnel.

vacuum tube must be capable of withstanding fairly high temperatures and rapid changes in temperature, and these requirements, coupled with the necessity that it be impervious to gases, nonferromagnetic, and of high electrical resistivity, practically limit the available material to quartz and to water-cooled glass. Even with quartz the high-frequency coil has to be water cooled in order to keep the temperature of the tube and coil within satisfactory limits.   The expense and characteristics of quartz tubes limit such furnaces to small sizes, and it is particularly suitable for use in connection with apparatus for determination of gases given off by heated or molten metals. Figure 34 shows such a furnace constructed by N. A. Ziegler,[1] in which a graphite

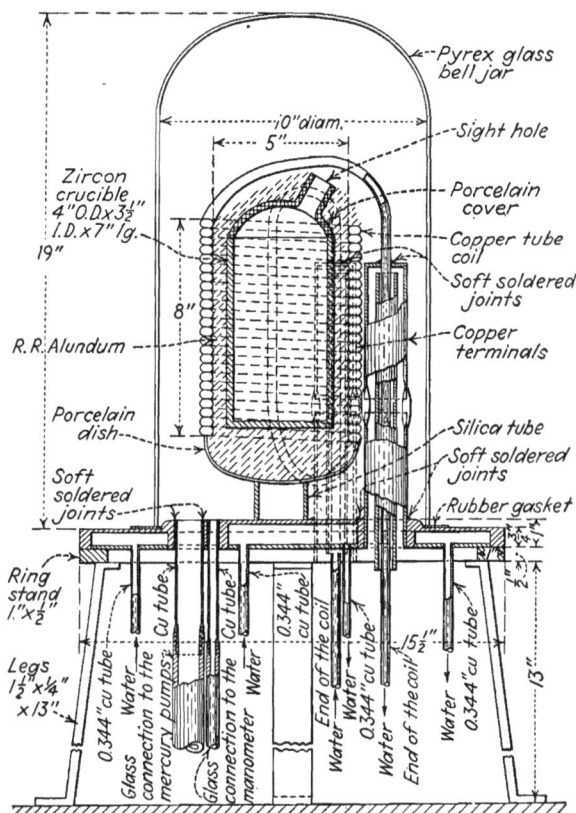

FIG. 35.—Bell-jar high-vacuum induction furnace.

crucible is used as heating element, which is used for determining oxygen in alloys. Slightly modified and using a MgO, Al_2O_3, or zircon crucible, it can also be used for the purpose of making small samples of metals and alloys.

The second type of high-frequency vacuum furnace is illustrated in Fig. 35, a furnace of about 5-kg. capacity constructed

[1] N. A. ZIEGLER, *Trans. Am. Soc. Steel Treating*, **18**, 76, 1932.

by Brace and Ziegler[1] in 1927 and used for the purpose of preparing pure alloys for research work. In this type the whole furnace is enclosed in an inverted glass bell jar (whence its name "bell-jar furnace"), and a pressure of less than 0.001 mm. Hg can be reached under the bell jar with 5 kg. of molten alloy in the zircon crucible. This, to date, is the most satisfactory type of vacuum furnace for research work, as there are no voluminous parts to give off gases continuously at a high temperature, as in the case of the Arsem furnace.

b. Melting in a Neutral-gas Atmosphere.—If no refining is required, it is conceivable that a metal or alloy can be satisfactorily melted in a furnace in which a chemically neutral atmosphere is maintained, such as argon, neon, or perhaps even nitrogen. The difficulty in this method is primarily the purification of the gases, particularly as far as oxygen is concerned, as a very small amount of oxygen will ruin the alloy for magnetic and most other purposes. Theoretically, CO and CO_2 can be used in combination to give an oxidizing, neutral, or reducing atmosphere, and this is the method used in practice in open-hearth furnaces; but the composition for a certain reaction, or for neutrality, changes with the temperature, and it is very difficult, if not impossible, to control it so as not to contaminate the charge with carbon, oxygen, or both, particularly in small-scale operations such as exist in research laboratories. Without the use of vacuum it is also impossible to replace completely the original air in the furnace with the neutral gas and thus to avoid oxidation. For all these reasons, and perhaps others, this method is not recommended for research work.

c. Melting in Hydrogen.—Hydrogen has for many years been regarded as the ideal gas for use in the preparation and heat treatment of base metals. Not only does hydrogen reduce oxides, but it also eliminates many other impurities and gaseous compounds, *e.g.*, sulphur (H_2S), phosphorus (PH_3), and carbon (CH_4). The rate of reduction of oxides at 1000 to 1200°C. is slow when the oxygen content is reduced below 1 per cent; and while complete reduction at these temperatures is improbable,[2] the rate increases

[1] P. H. Brace and N. A. Ziegler, *Trans. A.I.M.E., Proc. Inst. Metal Div.*, **78**, 544, 1928.

[2] The Ledebur process of oxygen determination depends upon the reducing power of hydrogen at these temperatures and is consequently now regarded

as the melting point of iron is approached. At 1400°C. and above, reduction complete to within a few thousandths of a per cent of O_2 takes place in a relatively short time. While there is still some question as to the merits of bubbling hydrogen through molten metals, it is safe to state that iron, nickel, and cobalt that have been heated in a stream of pure hydrogen up to and beyond the melting points and then protected from oxidation during the cooling-down period in a similar manner will contain not over 0.002 per cent O_2 and will also be free from C, S, and P to the same extent. The necessary precautions to take in order to make the process a success consist in the following:

1. Use crucibles made from refractories that are not readily reduced by H_2 at the temperatures involved, such as MgO, Al_2O_3, ZrO_2, and zircon.

2. Use pure H_2, the H_2O content having been reduced to a small fraction of a per cent. It is sometimes stated that for removing carbon it is necessary to use moist hydrogen. While the H_2O present may hasten the removal of carbon by the formation of a film of oxide on the surface of the metal, it is not regarded as essential, and it is believed to be safer to use dry hydrogen at least during the finishing operation, as absence of H_2O is necessary for the complete removal of oxygen.

The melting can be made in high-frequency induction furnaces, passing the hydrogen through an iron or quartz pipe to the bottom of the charge and withdrawing it, as the metal melts. Sufficient hydrogen must be used to prevent the entering of air into the crucible chamber. A steady flame burning from a small opening in the cover will insure this.

40. Refining by Annealing.—Annealing is generally defined as heating a solid metal for some time at a relatively high temperature, followed by slow cooling. Refining under such conditions will consequently be the result of a diffusion process.

a. Annealing in Vacuum.—Even with the lowest pressures obtainable in the laboratory under ideal conditions—10^{-8} mm. Hg—the residual gas is probably largely oxygen, nitrogen, and water vapor. Under less favorable conditions, such as are encountered in laboratory furnaces, imperceptible leaks keep the

as unreliable, unless special precaution are taken (see B. M. LARSEN and T. E. BROWER, *Trans. A.I.M.E., Iron and Steel Div.*, vol. 100, p. 196, 1932; W. W. STEVENSON, *Industrial Chemist*, June, 1935).

pressure up to 10^{-1} to 10^{-3} mm. Unless the entire furnace chamber is enclosed in a container filled with some other gas, it is therefore safe to assume that the furnace atmosphere in a vacuum furnace is oxidizing and that there will be an oxide film on the sample annealed in such a furnace. If the sample contains carbon, there will be a tendency for this to be eliminated by diffusion to the surface, where it will combine with the oxygen of the oxide film to form CO and escape to the surrounding space. Samples very low in carbon can consequently be prepared in this way. If there is a deficiency of oxygen, more can always be supplied by admitting the required amount of air. However, in the case of

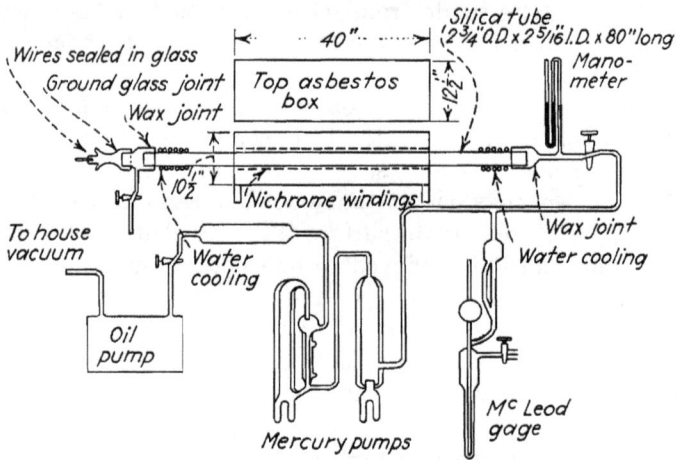

Fig. 36.—High-vacuum annealing furnace.

unalloyed iron and many alloys as well, oxygen diffuses into the metal when the temperature exceeds a certain value (for iron, 900°C.); and if held above this value for any length of time, the oxygen concentration in the interior will reach 0.10 per cent.

To decarbonize such material in a vacuum furnace is, therefore, not advisable, as the rate of carbon diffusion is very low below 900°C. On the other hand, any alloy containing a large percentage of Si or Al becomes coated with a protective oxide scale which prevents excessive oxidation during an oxidizing annealing treatment, and such alloys can be decarburized in this way provided the samples are heavy enough so that the surface film is of no importance. In no case should this process be used for thin sheets without taking special precautions.

For temperatures not exceeding 1100°C., the most convenient type of furnace is that illustrated in Fig. 36, designed by N. A. Ziegler, consisting essentially of the following elements:

1. A quartz.tube, constricted into a small tube at one end for making connection to the vacuum system and the other end fitted with a water-cooled ground-glass joint, attached to the quartz tube with vacuum cement.

2. A heating element of nichrome ribbon wound directly on the quartz tube sliding into an alundum tube.

3. The heat insulation applied in the form of two cones with their apexes at the center of the furnace to provide uniform temperature.

For higher temperature vacuum annealing a combination of porcelain and platinum may be used, but preference is now given to high-frequency induction heating, using furnaces of the type illustrated in Fig. 34. Instead of the quartz tube shown there, a water-cooled glass tube may be used, as done by Cioffi.[1]

b. Annealing in Hydrogen.—This is the best annealing process to use where a pure product is desired, as hydrogen not only reduces the ordinary oxides at temperatures of 1100 to 1500°C. but eliminates other impurities as gases (CH_4, H_2S, PH_3), as already mentioned under Par. 39c. Hydrogen also makes it possible to use high melting-point heating elements like molybdenum or tungsten with safety. A furnace of this type, constructed by A. A. Frey, is illustrated in Fig. 37. Alundum tubes are sealed into the iron shell so that hydrogen can be circulated outside as well as inside the main tube and thus protect the heating element from oxidation. Temperatures as high as 1600°C. can be obtained with this furnace, high enough to melt all the ferromagnetic elements and alloys in which they predominate.

By annealing iron in hydrogen at 1450°C. it has become possible to purify it sufficiently to reach values of permeability and hysteresis loss approaching those predicted by the author in 1924[2] for pure iron. This was done by Cioffi in 1930, who was at first inclined to think that the unusual results were due to hydrogen dissolved in the iron.[3] After two years of study on this point, the view has come to prevail that the function of the hydrogen is

---

[1] P. P. CIOFFI, *J. Franklin Inst.*, **212**, 601, 1931.

[2] T. D. YENSEN, *Trans. A.I.E.E.*, **43**, 145, 1924.

[3] P. P. CIOFFI, *Nature*, **126**, 200, 1930; *Phys. Rev.*, **38**, 363, 1932.

merely that of a purifying and protecting agent and that the remarkably high values of maximum permeability (over 300,000) are due to the purity of the iron.[1]   The latest results show that the samples contain less hydrogen than it is possible to measure accurately (0.00005 per cent by weight).

41. Heat Treatment.—The object of a heat treatment, other than refining heat treatments such as were discussed in Par. 39, is either to attain equilibrium conditions between the various constituents of a metal (normalizing) or to prevent such equilib-

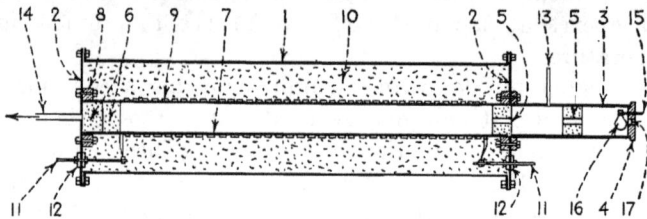

Fig. 37.—High-temperature hydrogen furnace.

DESCRIPTION AND MATERIAL

1. Steel shell 12 in. inside diameter by 44 in. long; $\frac{1}{4}$-in. wall with $1\frac{1}{2}$ by $\frac{3}{4}$ in. flanges each having 12 $\frac{5}{8}$-in. diameter bolt holes.
2. End plates $14\frac{3}{4}$-in. diameter by $\frac{1}{4}$ in. thick.
3. Forehearth 3 in. inside diameter by 12 in. long.
4. Gas-tight cover equipped with calibrated pyrometer lamp.
5. Removable refractory baffle brick with $\frac{3}{4}$-in. sight holes.
6. Refractory brick.
7. Alundum tube 3 in. inside diameter by $3\frac{3}{4}$ in. outside diameter by 44 in. long.
8. Asbestos lumber rings 3 by 6 by 1 in. for centering alundum tube.
9. Molybdenum resistor 0.005 by 1 by 34 ft.
10. Calcined aluminum oxide 99.5% Al_2O_3, 100 mesh (M3750).
11. Steel terminals $\frac{3}{4}$ in. diameter.
12. Mica and steel washers to form gas-tight insulation.
13. Hydrogen inlet, $\frac{1}{2}$-in. pipe.
14. Hydrogen outlet, $\frac{1}{2}$-in. pipe.
15. Leads to pyrometer lamp.
16. Calibrated pyrometer lamp.
17. Glass window.

rium from being reached (quenching).   Quenching in ferrous metallurgy is usually a hardening process, because it either keeps the impurities and alloying elements in a supersaturated solution, or it precipitates them in a finely divided state, in both cases producing a strained or distorted crystal structure, such as to prevent easy slipping along the lattice planes.   Such a treatment is necessary for the production of permanent magnet steels in which carbon is an essential element.   Other elements, such as tungsten or chromium, may be added because of the effect that they have on the state of the carbon when the alloy is quenched

---

[1] T. D. YENSEN, *Year Book Am. Iron Steel Inst.*, 452, 1931; *Metal Progress*, **21**, 33, 1932; Discussion of Ferromagnetism, *Phys. Rev.*, **39**, 337–378, 1932. G. W. ELMEN, *Elec. Eng.*, **54**, 1292, 1935.

and subsequently "tempered" (annealed at a low temperature).[1]
In plain Fe-C alloys the transformation from the face-centered
(gamma) structure to the body-centered (alpha) structure (see
Fig. 33) takes place even on very rapid cooling. At room
temperature, therefore, the Fe-C alloys present a structure
("martensite") composed of alpha iron with an amount of carbon
in solution depending upon the rate of cooling. This being a
supersaturated solution, there is a tendency for the carbon to
precipitate as Fe_3C (cementite). It will do so very slowly at
room temperature and more and more rapidly as the "tempering"
or "drawing" temperature is increased. The result is an alloy
containing Fe_3C in finely dispersed form to which various names
have been applied—"troostite," "osmondite," "sorbite," largely
based on appearances under the microscope. The difference is one
of degree rather than of kind, depending upon the size and distribution of the precipitate Fe_3C. The finer and more dispersed this
precipitate the harder is the alloy, as it interferes with slipping
along the lattice planes. It also prevents easy orientation of the
magnetic units or blocks and consequently is all-important in
connection with permanent magnet materials.

The limiting case as far as hardness is concerned is that in which
all the carbon remains in solution down to a low temperature and
is then precipitated as Fe_3C. This cannot be done by even the
most drastic quenching of plain Fe-C alloys, as the alpha structure cannot retain more than a small amount of carbon in solution. By the addition of tungsten or chromium, however, the
transformation from gamma to alpha can be prevented or slowed
down so that much carbon can be retained in solution down to a
temperature at which coagulation of the precipitate, when it
does form due to diffusion of carbon, does not take place to any
appreciable extent.

For the production of materials with high magnetic permeability and low hysteresis loss it is now believed that regularity of
the crystal lattice is an essential prerequisite and that any treatment that interferes with such regularity should be avoided.

With the impurities eliminated to the desired point by any of
the methods described in Par. 39 and 40, and with the material
in the shape in which it is to be used, the final operation consists

---

[1] P. H. Brace, *Elec. J.*, **26**, 111, 1929.

in annealing and cooling it to room temperature in such a way as to secure a homogeneous structure, as nearly free from lattice distortions as possible. In most cases this simply means slow cooling, slow enough to insure equal contraction throughout. For iron, iron-silicon, and similar alloys cooling at the rate of 30°C. per hour from 900°C is common practice.

In some cases there may be a tendency toward segregation of the main constituents. In the permalloy range of the Fe-Ni alloys (near 76 per cent Ni), for example, rapid cooling from about 600°C. may retain the alloy in the form of a homogeneous $FeNi_3$ structure, whereas slow cooling may cause segregation into regions of Fe_2Ni_2 and Ni_4 structures. While rapid cooling may produce some strains, this may be less of an evil than the suggested segregation. Specifications, therefore, call for rapid cooling from 625 but not so rapid as to produce strains.[1]

Different explanations have been offered to account for the permalloy phenomenon. Thus, Lichtenberger[2] is of the opinion that the most favorable composition should be the mean of the three following compositions: (1) that at which the direction of easy magnetization changes from [100] to [111] (71 per cent Ni); (2) that for which magnetostriction disappears (83 per cent Ni); and (3) that for which magnetostriction is equal along all three crystallographic axes (85.5 per cent Ni). This mean is 79.8 per cent Ni, whereas experiment gives about 78.5 per cent.

Finally, Steinhaus, Kussmann, and Scharnow[3] conclude from their studies and experiments that the most favorable composition is a compromise between that for the orderly arrangement in $FeNi_3$ (76 per cent Ni) and that for zero magnetostriction (82 per cent Ni) and that the rapid cooling is of advantage because it keeps certain impurities in solid solution instead of precipitating them as colloidal particles, thereby setting up strains that affect the permeability.

The preceding examples are typical of various heat treatments which are of importance in connection with ferromagnetic materials. In investigating alloys for this purpose, possibilities of this nature should always be kept in mind, as it may be possible to

[1] T. D. Yensen, *Year Book Am. Iron & Steel Inst.*, 452, 1931. O. Dahl, *Z. Metallkunde*, **24**, 107, 1932.

[2] F. Lichtenberger, *Ann. Physik*, **15**, 45, 1932.

[3] *Z. Instrumentkunde*, **51**, 241, 1931.

change the magnetic properties radically by the use of a special heat treatment.

42. Effect of Grain Size and the Production of Grain Growth.— As early as 1913 Ruder[1] showed qualitatively that the hysteresis loss of silicon-iron sheets decreases as the ·grain size increases. In 1924 the author[2] published the first quantitative relationship between hysteresis loss and grain size for iron and iron-silicon alloys, and this was slightly modified in 1930[3] when the following formula was proposed:

$$W_h = 100 \times \sqrt{N}$$

where W_h = Hysteresis loss in ergs per cubic centimeter per cycle for $B = 10,000$ gauss; N = number of grains per square millimeter of actual surface as seen on a polished and etched cross section under a magnification of 100 diameters.

This conclusion has been debated by a number of investigators (see bibliography in ref),[3] but it is now generally conceded that some such relationship as expressed in the preceding formula exists.[4]

The author's explanation of this effect is that it is due to lattice distortion. Where two grains meet having different lattice orientation (and they would not be separate grains unless the orientation were different) there are bound to be irregularities in the atomic arrangement. According to the theory that the magnetic properties are functions of the regularity of the lattice, we should consequently expect low permeability and high hysteresis along the grain boundaries. Assuming that the region affected has the same thickness irrespective of the grain size, we find that the volume effected is proportional to $\sqrt{N}$,[2] and the experimental results verify this conclusion. This being the case, it is very desirable to know how to control grain size. The fundamental principle in connection with grain growth is the same as

[1] W. E. RUDER, *Trans. A.I.M.E.*, **47**, 369, 1913.

[2] T. D. YENSEN, *Trans. A.I.E.E.*, **43**, 145, 1924.

[3] T. D. YENSEN, *Metals and Alloys*, **1**, 493, 1930.

[4] F. WEVER and G. HINDRICHS, *Mitt. Kaiser Wilhelm Inst. Eisenforschung zu Düsseldorff*, **13**, 273, 1931.

that governing the production of single crystals, *viz.*, a recrystallization proceeding gradually from one point to another, or, stated differently, the prevention of crystallization starting from many points simultaneously.

One of the chief factors starting crystallization is the presence of impurities, and a pure metal or a pure alloy in the form of a solid solution is, therefore, a prerequisite for ·the production of large grains.   Small particles, such as oxides, carbides, or other precipitates, constitute nuclei around which crystallization proceeds in all directions with the result that the individual grains (consisting of a continuous lattice with a definite orientation throughout) will be small.

The existence of allotropic transformations introduces difficulties in growing large grains.   If a metal is heated above the transformation temperature, it will recrystallize in cooling.   As it is next to impossible to prevent the transformation from starting in a large number of places simultaneously, the result is always grain refining in such cases.   Unalloyed iron and iron-carbon alloys can therefore not be produced readily with large grains by heating above 900°C.

The various methods of producing large grains are well summarized by Van Liempt[1] and later by Ziegler,[2] giving references to numerous original papers on the subject.   The two most successful methods so far developed are the following:

1. The cooling of a liquid metal in such a way that the crystalization starts from one point only.   The use of a conically shaped crucible is used for this purpose, the freezing starting at the apex.   In view of the statement made above, this method can obviously not be used with metals and alloys having allotropic transformations.

2. The straining of a polycrystalline material above its elastic limit followed by annealing at elevated temperatures but not above its transformation temperature if any exists.

Straining beyond the elastic limit produces lattice distortions within the grains and, therefore, a tendency toward recrystallization.   There is a definite relationship between the cold deformation and grain growth.   For unalloyed iron the greatest grain growth seems to take place after about 2.5 per cent cold deforma-

---

[1] M. VAN LIEMPT, *E.I.M.M.E.*, *Proc. Inst. Met. Div.*, **78**, 307, 1928.
[2] N. A. ZIEGLER, *Trans. A.I.M.E.*, *Iron and Steel Div.*, **90**, 209, 1930.

tion and by annealing at 880°C. for 48 to 72 hr.[1] For silicon-iron having no allotropic transformations (Si > 2 per cent) the annealing can be done at any temperature, and the higher the temperature the shorter is the time that is required for certain grain growth. Large grains are readily produced in 4 per cent silicon-iron sheets by a small amount of cold rolling and annealing at 1100°C. As a matter of fact, it is difficult to prevent grain growth in such alloys.

43. Effect of Lattice Orientation on the Magnetic Properties.— While the low-density permeability and the hysteresis loss are

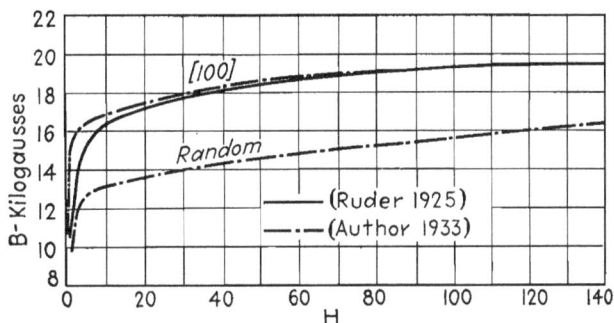

FIG. 38.—Magnetization curves for 3.25 per cent Si-Fe.

largely functions of impurities and grain size, we find that the high-density permeability is largely a function of the grain orientation, *i.e.*, the angular relationship between the magnetizing force and the lattice. Furthermore, the direction of easy magnetization relative to the cube edge is different for different ferromagnetic materials.

In Par. 62 the magnetization of single crystals of various materials is discussed in some detail, and it is shown that in iron, for instance (see Fig. 106), magnetization proceeds to saturation most readily when magnetized in a [100] direction. It therefore follows that a polycrystal can be magnetized to saturation in smaller fields if the grains are predominantly so oriented that the [100] axes of a preponderance of the grains is parallel to the applied field. This is borne out by experiment. In iron-silicon alloys the [100] axes are also directions of easy magnetization, as was shown experimentally by Ruder.[2] In Fig. 38 are curves

[1] N. A. ZIEGLER, *Trans. A.I.M.E., Iron and Steel Div.*, **90**, 209, 1930.
[2] W. E. RUDER, *Trans. Am. Soc. Steel Treating*, **8**, 23, 1925.

obtained on two polycrystalline samples[1] which show clearly the difference between material having a grain orientation with [100] axes parallel to the magnetization and material having a random orientation. For comparison, Ruder's curve for a single crystal is included. The value of $4\pi I$ at saturation for this material is about 20,000.

44. Aging.—By "aging" is meant a gradual spontaneous change in the physical properties of a metal at the temperatures at which it is used. Magnetic aging has been known ever since electrical engineers started to use iron in electrical apparatus, manifesting itself as an increase in hysteresis loss and a decrease in permeability with time under normal operating conditions. The use of silicon in iron largely eliminated aging, but the nature of the phenomenon was not understood until recently. The author has for a number of years insisted that magnetic aging, (like other types of aging) must be due to impurities, either entering the iron from the atmosphere or changing the form in which they exist in the iron. The first possibility was tested by J. M. Grzybowski at the author's suggestion in 1930,[2] with the result that no aging was found by exposing rings of unalloyed iron having a maximum permeability of the order of 20,000 to H_2, N_2, O_2, H_2O, CO_2, and vacuum for many days at temperatures ranging from 20 to 160°C. A test in a mixture of H_2O and CO_2 that would generate nascent hydrogen in contact with iron and thereby cause a solution of hydrogen in iron was planned but not carried out, as it became evident at the time that aging is due to the second alternative, *viz.*, a change in form of the impurities already existing in the iron. In the latter case the author had at first looked for impurities gradually going into solution but had not been able to reconcile this with the probability of the reverse being true after the metal had been cooled from high temperatures. The solubility of carbon in iron, for example, is higher at 900° than at 20°C. (Fig. 33), and similarly for other impurities. If there is any change, therefore, this must be due to a supersaturated solid solution and must consist of a precipitation of the impurity. At a relatively low temperature (20 to 100°C.) such precipitation must take place in the form of

---

[1] Unpublished results obtained at the Westinghouse Research Laboratories, 1933.

[2] *Westinghouse Res. Rept.* R-8435-A, Jan. 29, 1931 (unpublished).

particles containing only relatively few atoms (*i.e.*, colloids), and it must be a very slow process. Furthermore, as equilibrium is being approached, precipitation and dissociation take place simultaneously, and through the process of diffusion of the dissolved atoms (atoms in transition) there will be a tendency toward coagulation of the precipitated particles. In short, the change will be from a supersaturated solid solution through colloidal precipitates to larger inclusions. In view of the conclusions arrived at in Par. 37*b* we should, on the basis of the foregoing reasoning, expect the magnetic properties (as measured by permeability and hysteresis) at first to grow worse and then perhaps to improve, depending on the purity of the material and the previous heat treatment. Improvements following initial aging may especially be expected on this basis for materials containing a relatively large amount of impurities after rapid cooling.

Valuable contributions to the question of magnetic aging by precipitation have been given during the past few years by W. Koester,[1] W. Eilender and R. Wasmuth,[2] G. Tammann,[3] R. F. Mehl,[4] F. R. Hensel,[5] L. R. Van Wert,[6] and A. A. Bates.[7] Koester's work is especially noteworthy, notwithstanding the fact that the amounts of impurities that he used are much greater than the amounts usually present in magnetic materials. The conclusion arrived at by all these investigators is that aging is found and may be expected for iron containing one or more of the impurities whose solubility curve for α-iron is similar to that for carbon, *viz.*, nitrogen, oxygen, sulphur, and phosphorus.[8]

On the basis of these results, magnetic aging may be expected under certain circumstances in iron containing one or more of the foregoing impurities in the following amounts:

[1] W. KOESTER, *Archiv. f. Eisenhüttenwesen* **2**, 503, 1929; **3**, 553, 1930 (transl. in *Metals and Alloys*, **1**, 571, 1930); **3**, 637, 1930; **4**, 145, 389, 1930; **4**, 537, 609, 1931.

[2] *Archiv. f. Eisenhüttenwesen*, **3**, 659, 1930 (transl. in *Metals and Alloys*, **1**, 732, 1930).

[3] *Z. Metallkunde*, **22**, 365, 1930.

[4] *Iron & Steel Can.*, **13**, 265, 1930.

[5] *Trans. A.I.M.E., Iron and Steel Div.*, **93**, 255, 1931.

[6] *Trans. A.I.M.E., Iron and Steel Div.*, **93**, 230, 1931.

[7] *Trans. A.S.S.T.*, **19**, 449, 1932.

[8] T. D. YENSEN, *Phys. Rev.*, **39**, p. 358, Jan. 15, 1932.

	Per Cent
Oxygen..................................	More than 0.005
Nitrogen...............................	More than 0.001
Carbon.................................	More than 0.001
Phosphorus...........................	More than 1.20
Sulphur[1]..............................	More than 0.001

On account of its high solubility in iron (over 1 per cent at 20°C.) phosphorus cannot be the cause of aging in ordinary iron and iron alloys which invariably contain less than 0.05 per cent P. It is also doubtful whether sulphur has anything to do with aging of ordinary magnetic materials, as its solubility apparently is very low even at high temperatures. Nitrided steels are known to be subjected to aging because of the presence of nitrogen, and carbon steels because of carbon. The only data available in regard to oxygen and magnetic aging show that 0.02 to 0.04 per cent oxygen is sufficient to cause aging in unalloyed iron.[2]

The underlying principle governing the cause and remedy of aging is clear from what has already been stated. In unalloyed iron as ordinarily made, aging is caused by oxygen, carbon, and nitrogen precipitating at operating temperatures as colloidal particles of oxide (FeO), carbide (Fe_3C), and nitride (Fe_4N). The last may not be an important factor in materials that have not been nitrided by means of ammonia or subjected to the attack of nascent nitrogen in any other way, as the nitrogen content of such iron should not be more than a few thousandths of a per cent at the most. For such materials only carbon and oxygen, therefore, remain as possible aging elements. The purest commercial unalloyed iron usually contains 0.01 to 0.02 per cent C and 0.05 to 0.10 per cent O. As the solubility at room temperature is of the order of 0.001 per cent C and 0.01 per cent O, and as ten times these amounts can be retained in solution during cooling, aging of such iron is easily explained on the basis of colloidal precipitation over long periods.

When silicon is added to such iron, however, the silicon and oxygen tend to precipitate as SiO_2, a very stable compound, so

---

[1] The solubility of sulphur in α-iron is not yet determined with any degree of accuracy. It is stated to be 0.01 to 0.02 per cent at 1150°C. and 0.015 to 0.02 per cent at 940°C. and that the solubility in α-iron increases with temperature (Benedicks and Lofquist).

[2] T. D. Yensen and N. A. Ziegler, *A.I.M.E.*, *Tech. Pub.* 624, February, 1935.

that with 3 to 4 per cent Si present, practically all oxygen is removed from solution at a high temperature as SiO_2 (or as a silicate), and there is none left to precipitate during or after cooling to room temperature. In such alloys, therefore, carbon remains as the only aging constituent, and considerable evidence is available to show that 0.005 per cent C is sufficient to cause aging in Fe-Si alloys, unless precautions are taken by means of proper cooling rates and reannealing treatments.

45. Methods of Analysis.—In this section will be described only such methods of analysis as are of particular importance in connection with ferromagnetic materials and that as yet are too new or too special to have found a place in standard textbooks on analytical chemistry. These include the most accurate methods of analysis for

   a. Carbon.

   b. Oxygen, nitrogen, and hydrogen.

      1. As inclusions (*a*) gaseous, (*b*) solid.

      2. In solid solutions.

For standard methods of determining the preceding and other impurities the reader is referred to the following textbooks:

"Standard Methods of Chemical Analysis," Wilfred W. Scott, 2 vols., D. Van Nostrand Company, Inc., New York, 1927.

"Applied Inorganic Analysis," W. F. Hillerbrand and G. E. F. Lundell, John Wiley & Sons, Inc., New York, 1929.

"Chemical Analysis of Iron and Steel," G. E. F. Lundell, J. I. Hoffman, and H. A. Bright, John Wiley & Sons, Inc., New York, 1931.

a. Carbon Analysis.—In Par. 36 reference was made to a new method of determining carbon in iron and iron alloys, and the necessity and justification for this new method capable of an accuracy of ± 0.0001 per cent were pointed out.

The ordinary method of carbon analysis consists in burning 2 g. of millings of the sample in a stream of oxygen at a temperature of 900 to 1050°C., passing the gaseous mixture through $CaCl_2$ or P_2O_5 to absorb the H_2O and then through a bulb containing KOH or its equivalent [such as soda lime or $Ba(OH)_2$] to absorb the CO_2, the increase in weight of the bulb giving the weight of CO_2. This method is satisfactory for samples containing 0.1 per cent C or more.

By certain modifications and refinements an accuracy of ± 0.001 per cent is obtainable, such as the method developed by the Bureau of Standards, requiring much time and a very high temperature[1] (1525°C.); or an elaborate apparatus may be employed for determining the CO_2 by means of an electrolytic resistance method,[2] or by cumbersome filtering and igniting of the $BaCO_3$ that is sometimes used.[3]

The principles of the new method do not differ fundamentally from the ordinary combustion method except in that the CO_2 is frozen out by means of a liquid-air trap and determined volu-

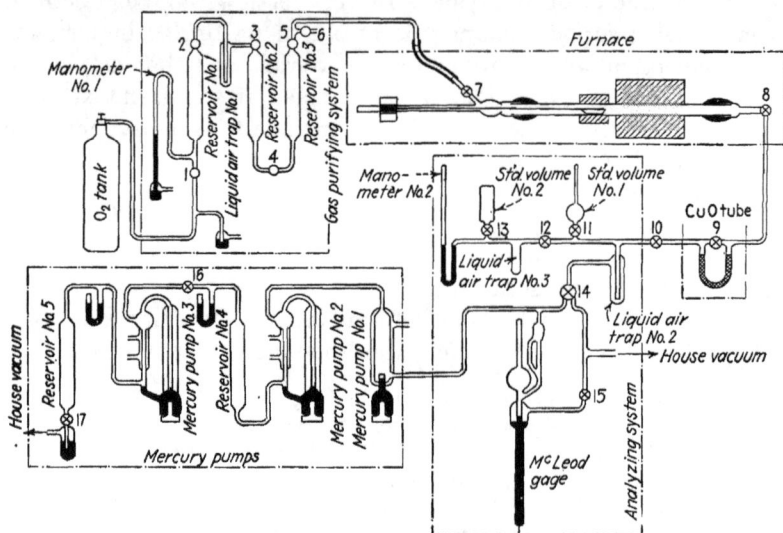

Fig. 39.—Apparatus for the determination of carbon.

metrically and in that the combustion tube is evacuated before the sample is burned. It is, therefore, usually referred to as the vacuum-liquid-air method. It was originated by the author[4] and later improved upon by him and his associates. It was recently described in detail in a paper by N. A. Ziegler,[5] and only a brief outline will be given here. A schematic diagram of the apparatus is shown in Fig. 39. A 2-g. sample thoroughly cleaned to remove surface contaminations is placed on decarbonized,

[1] F. R. Cain and H. E. Cleaves, *J. Ind. Eng. Chem.*, **8**, 321, 1916.

[2] J. R. Cain and L. C. Maxwell, *J. Ind. Eng. Chem.*, **11**, 852, 1919.

[3] "Research and Methods of Analysis of Iron and Steel," p. 83, American Rolling Mill Co., Middletown, Ohio, 1920.

[4] T. D. Yensen, *Trans. Am. Electrochem. Soc.*, **37**, 227, 1920; U. S. Patent 1,515,238, Nov. 11, 1924.

[5] N. A. Ziegler, *Trans. Am. Electrochem. Soc.*, **56**, 251, 1929.

granulated MgO in a decarbonized alundum boat which is pushed into the cold part of the combustion tube. The tube is then closed and evacuated to 0.001 mm. Hg, after which the boat is transferred to the 600°C. part of the tube, and the evacuation continued for 5 to 10 min. to eliminate the occluded gases on the surface of the sample. These may be analyzed for carbon, if desired, by the same method as described below. The boat is then transferred to the 1050°C. part of the furnace; the two-way stopcock (14) closed; and oxygen, purified by means of liquid air, passed into the tube. The oxidation of the sample can be readily followed by the pressure reading of the manometer (M-2); and as soon as this is complete, stopcock 7 is closed, and the tube slowly evacuated through the trap (L.A.T. 3) immersed in liquid air. When the pressure has been reduced to 0.001 Hg, stopcocks 10 and 14 are closed, and the CO_2 transferred from (L.A.T. 3) to (L.A.T. 2) by transferring the liquid air to (L.A.T. 2) and placing hot water on (L.A.T. 3). When the transfer of CO_2 is complete, stopcock 12 is closed, and hot water placed on (L.A.T. 2). The pressure on the manometer (M-2) then, by means of an equation, gives the amount of CO_2, and consequently of carbon, in the sample. As 1 mm. on the manometer corresponds to 0.0002 per cent C in a 2-g. sample, the limit of accuracy of the analyzing system is about ±0.0001 per cent. The reproducibility in a regular analysis is of the order of ±0.0005 per cent which with extra precautions can be improved to ±0.0001 per cent.

The only disadvantage of the method for general use is that liquid air and vacuum are required; but where these are available, it is believed that it is the most accurate and reliable method so far developed. However, it is not recommended for analysis of samples containing more than 0.1 per cent C, as in such cases the ordinary method is sufficiently accurate and requires less time and expense.

    b. Oxygen, Nitrogen, and Hydrogen.—These elements occur in metals in three states, two of which may be combined under one heading:

        1. Inclusions.

                a. Gaseous inclusions (gases in blowholes CO, CO_2, N_2, H_2, CH_4).

                b. Solid inclusions (oxides, nitrides, hydrides, etc.).

        2. Solid solutions (atomically dispersed in the lattices).

As their effect on the physical properties of the metals depends primarily on the form in which they exist (see Par. 36), it is of the utmost importance to distinguish between the forms in reporting the analysis.

An excellent treatment of the subject of gaseous elements in metals was given by W. Hessenbruch in 1929[1] in which all the various methods for analyzing and distinguishing between the various forms are given. These will be referred to only briefly, with the exception of the vacuum-fusion method (for determining total amount of oxygen, nitrogen, and hydrogen) which will be treated more at length, as this determination is of primary importance in connection with magnetic materials.

Gaseous inclusions are determined by disintegrating the sample under oil and collecting the gases liberated from the blowholes. As any kind of mechanical disintegration cannot be expected to reach most of the colloidal blowholes, only gases occurring as ordinary inclusions can consequently be determined by this method.

Gaseous and solid inclusions larger than 10^{-16} cm.[3] can be fairly accurately estimated by microscopic analysis at high magnification. Colloidal particles obviously cannot be detected by this method.

Solid oxide inclusions can be determined by the electrolytic extraction method developed at the U. S. Bureau of Mines by G. R. Fitterer.[2] Microscopic examination of the particles thus collected will give the size and character of the inclusions.

The preceding three methods in conjunction with microanalysis for grain size, X ray analysis for grain structure, accurate carbon determination (Par. 44a), and accurate determination of total oxygen, hydrogen, and nitrogen will give the information necessary to correlate the composition and grain structure of a material with its magnetic and other physical properties.

The vacuum-fusion method for determining total oxygen, nitrogen, and hydrogen was developed independently by Hessenbruch and Oberhoffer[3] in Germany and by Jordan and associates[4]

[1] W. Hessenbruch, *Z. Metallkunde*, **21**, 46, 1929.

[2] G. R. Fitterer, *Trans. A.I.M.E.*, *Iron Steel Div.*, **93**, 196, 1931.

[3] W. Hessenbruch and P. Oberhoffer, *Stahl u. Eisen*, **48**, 486, 1928.

[4] L. Jordan and J. R. Eckman, *Bur. Standards, Sci. Papers*, **20**, 445, 1925; **22**, 467, 1927. H. C. Vacher and L. Jordan, *Bur. Standards J. Res.*, **7**, 375, 1931.

in the United States. It has been modified by Ziegler,[1] who substituted volumetric determination of the extracted gases for the gravimetric methods used by the originators; as the former is probably more reliable, this will be described here.[2]

Figure 40 is a diagram of the apparatus as used by Ziegler in the Westinghouse Research Laboratories.

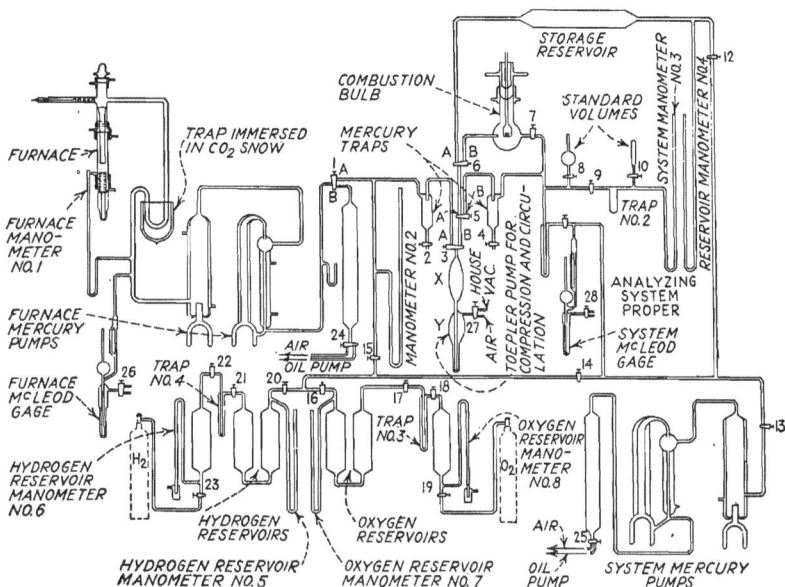

FIG. 40.—Apparatus for the analysis of oxygen, hydrogen, and nitrogen.

The vacuum furnace for melting the samples is of the high-frequency induction type, consisting of a quartz tube with a glass head sealed to it with vacuum cement. The high-frequency coil consists of water-cooled copper tubing enclosing the lower part of the quartz tube. The graphite crucible serves the double purpose of heating element and receptacle for melting the sample. It is supported on a graphite pedestal.

The samples to be analyzed are placed in the side tube of the glass head from which each in turn can be dropped into

[1] N. A. ZIEGLER, *Trans. Am. Electrochem. Soc.*, Preprint, **62**, 109, 1932.

[2] Recently, the gravimetric method of absorption and weighing has been modified by Greiner (see Scaff and Schumacher, Some Theoretical and Practical Aspects of Gases in Metals, *Metals and Alloys*, **4**, 7, 1933).

the crucible by means of a magnet outside the tube manually operated.[1]

Vacuum in the furnace is maintained by means of a set of mercury diffusion pumps backed up by oil pumps, and power is supplied by a high-frequency power-tube oscillator. A trap immersed in CO_2 snow is installed between the furnace and the mercury pumps to prevent mercury vapors from passing into the furnace.

The furnace head is connected to the analytical system by means of hard glass tubing and carefully made stopcocks. No rubber tubing is used. The operation is as follows:

After the crucible and samples have been introduced, the furnace and analytical system are evacuated to a pressure of about 0.001 mm. Hg. Current is then applied to the coil, heating the graphite crucible to about 1800°C. in a few minutes and maintaining it at this temperature for an hour to degasify it. Power is then temporarily shut off, while the first sample is dropped into the crucible. This precaution prevents too rapid evolution of gas. As soon as the sample is melted, any oxygen in it will combine with the carbon, either in the sample or in the crucible, to form CO. Hydrogen and nitrogen will also be eliminated, and all gases thus driven off are discharged into the reservoirs of the Toepler pump. When the pressure in the reservoir has reached a certain value, stopcock 3 is turned to position B, and the gases allowed to expand into the analyzing system limited by stopcocks (3, 4, 7, 8, 10, 11). A new supply of gases is then drawn into X, and the operations repeated until all gases from the furnace have been removed and stored in the preceding volume. This usually takes 15 to 20 min. The analysis proper of these gases then follows by transferring them to the volume (1-2-3-15) by means of the Toepler pump. Reading of manometer 2 is recorded from which total amount of gases is computed, composed of CO, H_2, and N_2.[2]

A known amount of purified oxygen, from the oxygen reservoir, about equal to the amount of the total gases, is added; current is

---

[1] A recent improvement consists in closing the top of the crucible by means of a graphite ball, magnetically manipulated, after the sample has been dropped in. This prevents spattering and loss of heat by radiation. (H. A. Sloman, *Iron Steel Inst. (London)*, 6th *Report of the Heterogeneity of Steel Ingots* (1935), *Secs.* 4, 71.)

[2] Experience has shown that amount of H_2O and CO_2 can be neglected.

applied to the combustion bulb, heating the filament "white hot," and CO_2 snow is applied to trap 1. The gases are then slowly circulated by the Toepler pump through the combustion bulb and trap 1. Coming in contact with the white-hot filament, H_2 and CO combine with oxygen to form H_2O and CO_2, respectively, the H_2O freezing out in trap 1. The gases are circulated back and forth by means of the Toepler pump until no further reaction takes place, as indicated by reading of manometer 2 remaining constant; they are then again transferred into volume (1-2-3-15), and reading of manometer 2 recorded. From the difference between this and the original reading the amount of H_2O can be calculated. Trap 1 now contains all this H_2O and by transferring the CO_2 snow from trap 1 to trap 2 and applying hot water to trap 1, the H_2O is transferred to trap 2. This H_2O is then allowed to evaporate, producing a certain reading of manometer 3. Then by opening different stopcocks (10, 9, 8, 7) the H_2O can be expanded sufficiently so that Boyle's law can be applied with sufficient accuracy. The final reading of manometer 3 and the known volume then give a second reading for computing the amount of H_2O and, consequently, of H_2. The H_2O is then rejected by evacuation, and the amount of CO_2 determined in a similar way by using liquid air, except that in this case the determination can be made in the smallest volumes, as CO_2 is near enough to a perfect gas to make Boyle's law applicable for all pressures.

The remainder of the gas, now in volume (1-2-3-15), contains the original nitrogen and the excess oxygen, the amount being calculated from the reading of manometer 2.

From the various readings thus obtained the amount of H_2, O_2, and N_2 in the sample can be computed. The H_2 and O_2 are determined in two ways—from direct measurement of the frozen-out H_2O and CO_2 and by computation of the original gaseous mixture at different stages of the analytical procedure. Unless the two sets check within a certain limit, the results are not considered reliable. With a 10-g. sample the accuracy of the apparatus is within ± 0.002 per cent of the true value for each element.[1]

---

[1] For the latest developments on this subject see J. G. THOMPSON, H. C. VACHER, and H. A. BRIGHT, Cooperative Study of Methods for Determination of Oxygen in Steel, *Metals Technology*, **3**, 8, Dec., 1936.

46. Ferromagnetic Materials.—At the beginning of the twentieth century, iron alloys, with the exception of iron-carbon alloys, were still in their infancy,[1] and unalloyed sheet iron was used for transformers and other alternating-current electrical apparatus.

Largely owing to the work of Curie[2] in France it had been found that carbon is essential for permanent magnets and that it is necessary to quench the alloys from definite temperatures in order to obtain the best results. The iron-carbon constitutional diagram had been established in its rough outline,[3] and the cause of the quenching effect had been assigned to the retention of carbon in solid solution in the iron.[2]

Conversely, it was appreciated that for high permeability and low hysteresis loss the carbon content should be low,[4] and this, in conjunction with the idea that sulphur and phosphorus are generally harmful, led to the adoption of Swedish charcoal iron as a standard of excellence for magnetic purposes. This or similar grades of wrought iron was the "pure iron" used by Rowland[5] in the United States in the 1870's, by Ewing[6] in Scotland in 1880, by Hadfield[7] in England, and by Gumlich[8] in Germany around 1900. Its composition may be judged by that of Hadfield's Swedish-iron samples reported as follows:

	Per Cent
C	0.028
Si	0.07
S	0.005
P	0.044
Mn	Trace

[1] R. A. Hadfield, *Proc., Inst. Civil Eng.*, **93**, 1, 61, 1888; *Trans. A.I.M.E.*, **23**, 148, 1893, *J. Iron Steel Inst.* (*London*), II, 41, 1888; I, 156, 1894. J. Hopkinson, *Phil. Trans.*, **178**, 455, 1885.

[2] See S. P. Thompson, *J. Inst. Elec. Eng.*, **50**, 80, 1913.

[3] F. Osmond, *J. Iron Steel Inst.*, I, 38, 1890. W. C. Roberts-Austen, *Proc. Inst. Mech. Eng.* (*London*), 35, 1899. H. B. Roozeboom, *Z. physik. Chem.*, **34**, 437, 1900; *J. Iron Steel Inst.* (*London*), II, 311, 1900.

[4] J. Hopkinson, *Phil. Trans.*, **176**, 455, 1885. J. A. Ewing, "Magnetic Induction in Iron and Other Metals," 3d ed., rev., p. 83, "The Electrician" Printing & Publishing Co.

[5] Henry A. Rowland, *Phil. Mag.*, **46**, 140, 1873; **48**, 321, 1874.

[6] J. A. Ewing, *Phil. Trans. Royal Soc.*, **176**, 530, 1885.

[7] W. F. Barrett, W. Brown, and R. A. Hadfield, *Proc. Royal Dublin Soc.*, **7**, 67, 1900.

[8] E. Gumlich and E. Schmidt, *Elektrotech. Z.*, **22**, 691, 1901.

Its magnetic properties are shown in Fig. 41 (see p. 100, footnote 7). Because of its low electrical resistance—about 10.5 microhms per cubic centimeter—the eddy currents were very large, when the iron, even in the form of thin sheets (0.035 cm.), was subjected to alternating currents. Its total loss was 3.5 watts per kilogram for 10,000 gauss and 60 cycles per second (2.5 hysteresis and 1.0 eddy loss).[1] Furthermore, after being placed in use, the losses would gradually increase, and it was quite common to find them doubled in the course of several months. Dismantling trans-

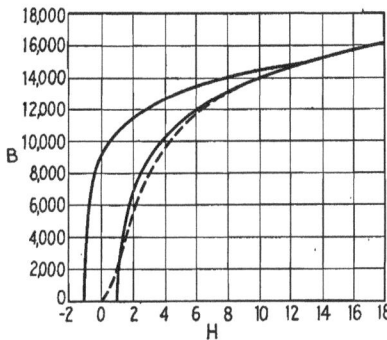

FIG. 41.—Magnetization curve and hysteresis loop of annealed Swedish charcoal-iron bar. (*Barrett, Brown, and Hadfield*, 1900.)

Electrical resistance = 10.5 microhms
μ_{max} = 2500
Hysteresis loss (for B = 15,000) = 6000 ergs per cubic centimeter per cycle
Hysteresis loss (for B = 10,000) = 3000 ergs per cubic centimeter per cycle
Total loss for 0.014-in. sheets
$\left. \begin{array}{l} B = 10,000 \\ f = 60 \text{ cycles} \end{array} \right\}$ = 3.5 watts per kilogram

formers and reannealing the iron were often resorted to in those days, and in order to prevent such occurrences "air-blast transformers" were designed,[2] but even with such precautions flux densities had to be kept very low to prevent heating above 50°C. and consequent aging.

Efforts were made to discover the factors that determine hysteresis and aging, but the conclusions were conflicting and were stated in the most general terms. One investigator[3] states "that the hysteresis constant . . . is not so much dependent upon the chemical composition as upon the physical structure due to the method of working." Another investigator (see p. 87, footnote 2) concludes "that aging may be prevented . . . if the

[1] Calculated on the basis of information obtained from references.
[2] General Electric Co., *Pamphlet* 9081, p. 8, Oct. 1, 1900.
[3] A. H. FORD, *Trans. A.I.E.E.*, **17**, 207, 1900.

sheets are of the proper chemical constitution and subjected to proper heat treatment and are not subsequently exposed to temperatures higher than 75°C. . . . ''

These statements undoubtedly represent the common views and the common experiences both in Europe and in the United States at the opening of the century. But great changes were already pending. In his laboratory in Sheffield, Hadfield had been investigating iron alloys since 1882,[1] largely for the purpose of finding better materials for structural uses. He had experi-

FIG. 42.—Magnetization curve and hysteresis loop for $2\frac{1}{2}$ per cent iron-silicon alloy. (*Barret, Brown, and Hadfield*, 1900.)

Electrical resistance = 40 microhms
μ_{max} = 5000
Hysteresis loss (for B = 15,000) = 4700 ergs
Hysteresis loss (for B = 10,000) = 2200 ergs
Total loss for 0.014-in. sheets }
            B = 10,000   } 2.2 watts per kilogram
            f = 60 cycles }

mented with a large number of alloying elements, chiefly tungsten, cobalt, nickel, chromium, carbon, manganese, silicon, and aluminum.[2] Among his acquaintances he counted men connected with the electrical industry as well as those devoted to iron and steel. A cooperative research was started, and the first important results were published in 1900 in a paper by Barrett, Brown, and Hadfield.[3] The significance of the results is shown in Fig. 42 by comparison with Fig. 41. By alloying his iron with

[1] R. A. HADFIELD, "The Work and Position of the Metallurgical Science," p. 45, Charles Griffin & Company, Ltd., London, 1921.

[2] R. A. HADFIELD, *Proc. Inst. Civil Eng.*, **93**, 1, 1888; *J. Iron Steel Inst.* (*London*), II, 222, 1889.

[3] F. BARRETT, W. BROWN, and R. A. HADFIELD, *Proc. Royal Soc., Dublin*, **7**, 67, 1900.

$2\frac{1}{2}$ per cent silicon (or $2\frac{1}{4}$ per cent aluminum) he doubled the maximum permeability, decreased the hysteresis loss by 25 per cent, and quadrupled the electrical resistance. The great importance of the last was at first not fully appreciated until Gumlich called attention to it.[1] Because of the higher resistance the eddy-current losses were decreased to one-fourth those of unalloyed iron, making the total loss 2.2 instead of 3.5 watts per kilogram, a decrease of 37 per cent, and aging troubles practically disappeared. Using 4 per cent silicon, the losses were decreased to 2 watts per kilogram. The electrical industry received the news with enthusiasm, but because of metallurgical difficulties several years passed before the new alloys were produced commercially. By 1903, however, they were used on a small scale in England and Germany, and by 1907 in the United States. Since that time they have been universally adopted the world over not only for transformers but also to a large extent for rotating machines. But before we continue with our consideration of alloys, it is desirable to study the element that is the basis of all useful magnetic materials, *viz.*, iron. By so doing we shall be able to remove certain confusing factors, whose removal will make it easier to comprehend the subject as a whole.

The Magnetic Properties of Iron.—During the period since 1912, taking advantage of the experiences of Burgess and Aston[2] with electrolytic iron, constant efforts have been made to remove as much as possible of the last traces of impurities in iron for the purpose of determining its real magnetic properties.[3] By using electrolytic iron and vacuum furnaces for melting and annealing, great improvements were obtained at the University of Illinois in 1914–1915.[4] Later, approximate relationships were worked out at the Westinghouse Research Laboratories between impurities (C, S, P, Mn) and the magnetic properties as well as between the grain size and the magnetic properties.[5] These have recently[6]

---

[1] E. Gumlich and E. Schmidt, *Elektrotech. Z.*, **22**, 691, 1901. E. Gumlich and P. Goerens, *Trans. Faraday Soc.*, **8**, 98, 1912.

[2] C. F. Burgess and J. Aston, *Met. Chem. Eng.*, **8**, 191, 1910.

[3] T. D. Yensen, *J. Franklin Inst.*, **206**, 503, 1928.

[4] T. D. Yensen, *Univ. Illinois, Eng. Exp. Sta., Bulls.* 72, 83, 1914, 1915, *Trans. A.I.E.E.*, **33**, 451, 1914; **34**, 2601, 1915.

[5] T. D. Yensen, *Trans. A.I.E.E.*, **43**, 145, 1924; *Metals and Alloys*, **1**, 493, 1930. N. A. Ziegler, *A.I.M.E.*, *Tech. Pub.* 273, 1930.

[6] T. D. Yensen and N. A. Ziegler, *Trans. Am. Soc. Metals*, **33**, 556, 1935.

been superseded by more accurate ones, including oxygen, and some of them are reproduced here (Figs. 43 and 44).   Special

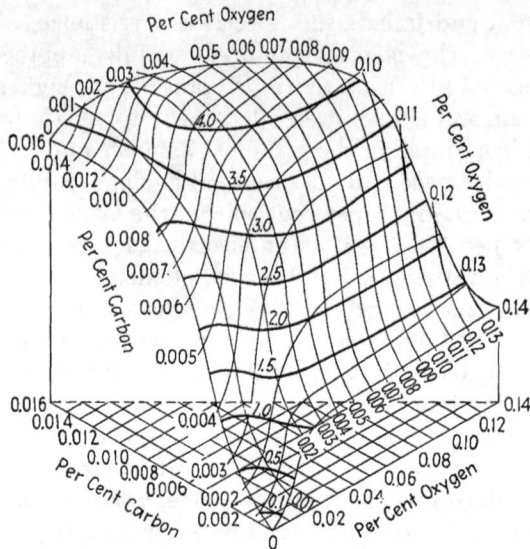

Fig. 43.—Effect of carbon and oxygen on the magnetic properties of iron.

Numbers on surface are minimum reluctivity (ρ_{min}) $\times 10^5$.   To get coercive force (oersteds) for $B = 10,000$ multiply numbers by 0.054.

To get hysteresis loss (ergs per cubic centimeter) for $B = 10,000$ multiply numbers by 164.

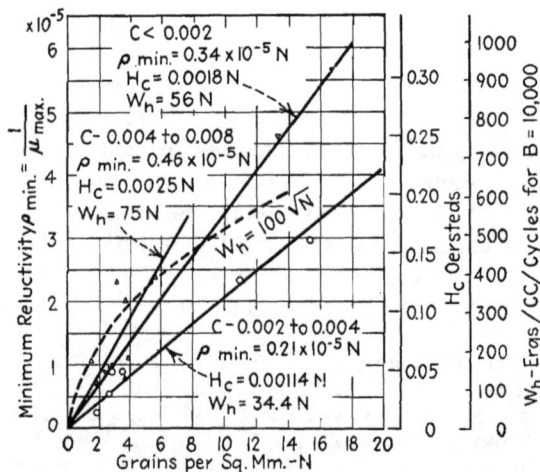

Fig. 44.—Net effect of grain size on ρ_{min}, H_c and W_h.

methods were used for determining carbon and oxygen (Par. 45a and b).   The large effect of carbon in amounts less than 0.01 per

cent is explainable on the basis of lattice distortion due to carbon
atoms or colloidal Fe_3C particles in the iron lattice.[1]

The importance of removing impurities from iron, particularly
carbon and oxygen, being fully appreciated, the next problem
was to remove the two elements simultaneously, and this is where

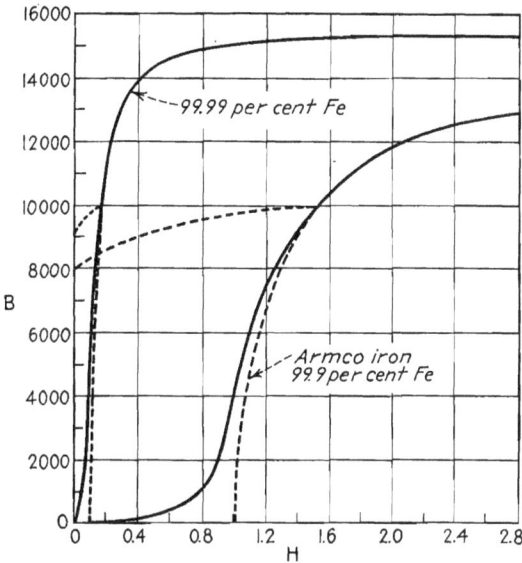

FIG. 45.—Hysteresis loops and *B-H* curves for nearly pure iron.

the high-frequency induction furnace has served, and is serving,
a very good purpose. With the charge in contact only with
pure refractories, it is possible to control the refining processes
either by means of a good vacuum or by introducing purified
gases, such as hydrogen. By balancing the oxygen in the charge
with a corresponding amount of carbon added, both elements
can be effectively removed as CO by maintaining a good vacuum
in the furnace chamber:

$$C + O \rightleftharpoons CO.$$

Iron with only a few thousandths of a per cent oxygen and carbon
has been produced in this way,[2] having magnetic properties as
shown in Fig. 45. The two samples there represented can be
definitely distinguished only by the special methods of chemical

[1] T. D. YENSEN, *Phys. Rev.*, **39**, 358, 1932.

[2] T. D. YENSEN, *Trans. Am. Electrochem. Soc.*, **56**, 215, 1929. N. A.
ZIEGLER, *A.I.M.E. Tech. Pub.* 273, 1930.

analysis referred to above, and yet the one has ten times the maximum permeability and one-twentieth the hysteresis loss of the other. As already mentioned in Par. 40b, even better results have been obtained during the last few years by annealing iron rings in an atmosphere of hydrogen at 1450°C. for many

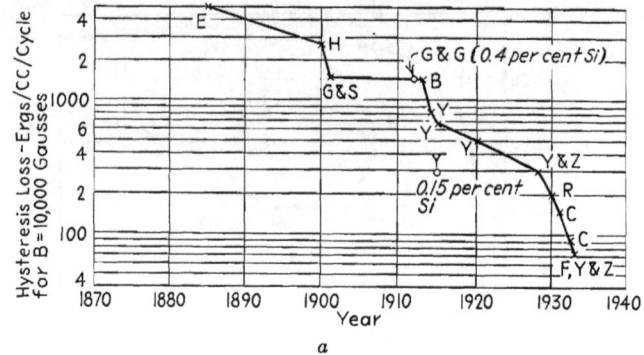

a

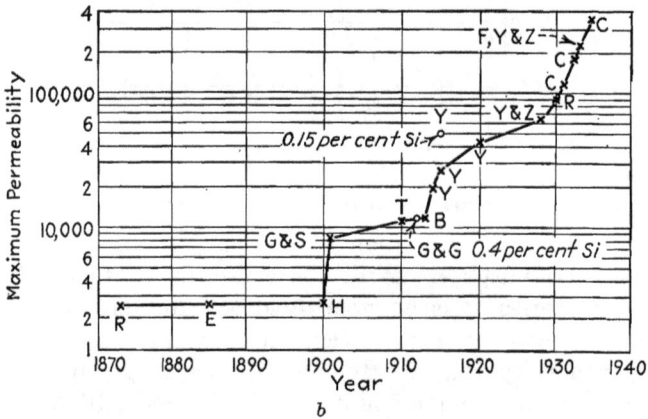

b

Fig. 46.—Improvement in magnetic properties of "pure iron."

hours.[1] By this process carbon, oxygen, sulphur, and phosphorus are largely removed.

The development in this phase of magnetic research is shown in Fig. 46. The last values shown here—$\mu_{max} = 340,000$ and $W_h = 70$—are rapidly approaching those predicted in 1924[2]

[1] P. P. Cioffi, *Nature*, **126**, 200, 1930; *Phys. Rev.*, **38**, 363, 1932. Elmen, *Elec. Eng.*, **54**, 1292, 1935.

[2] T. D. Yensen, *Trans. A.I.E.E.*, **43**, 145, 1924.

and by the Langevin-Weiss theory. This is especially true if the effect of grain orientation is taken into account.

The conclusion that we can draw from the preceding results and considerations is that *pure iron* is a perfect ferromagnetic material in the sense that it has a maximum permeability approaching infinity (its saturation value being limited by the number of magnetons) and hysteresis loss approaching zero. This, it will be noted, is. quite contrary to statements repeatedly made during the past thirty years that such and such an alloy has better magnetic properties than iron.

There are, however, several reasons for not using pure iron in practice, the chief ones being high cost and the necessity of using it in very thin sections to keep eddy currents down; also, to date no one has succeeded in obtaining the foregoing good magnetic properties with iron in sheet or wire form, because of its susceptibility to contaminating influences[1] and recrystallization at a relatively low temperature (900 to 950°C). For these various reasons iron alloys are now universally used where good magnetic properties are desired. But it should be emphasized that the benefit to be derived from alloying elements is not due to changing the magnetic properties of iron but to factors that enable us to approach these properties and to retain them as far as possible and at the same time to increase the electrical resistance.

The Iron-silicon Type of Alloys.—As already mentioned, the use of silicon helped in all the preceding respects. Hadfield's 4 per cent silicon-iron in 1903 had twice the maximum permeability, 75 per cent of the hysteresis loss, and 25 per cent of the eddy loss of the best contemporary unalloyed iron, and it exhibited no appreciable aging at 100°C.

Since that time these alloys have been subjected to a thorough study[2] and have been improved to such an extent that the mag-

---

[1] Attention should be called to recent attempts to produce iron electrolytically in the form of very thin sheets, coating these with some nonconducting film and pressing these sheets together into heavier sheets for economy in handling. Excellent results have been reported, but not yet confirmed, using such methods. ERNST KELSEN, Austrian Patents 109695, 117444, 118818, 1928–1930.

[2] See list of references in papers by T. D. YENSEN, *Trans. A.I.E.E.*, 33, I, 451, 1914; 34, 2601, 1915; and the following papers: E. GUMLICH, *Wissensch. Abh. der Reichsanstalt*, 4, No. 3, 1918. E. GUMLICH and P. GOERENS,

netic properties of the commercial product of today are much better than the original alloy in 1903. On the basis of these studies it is concluded that silicon has no direct beneficial effect on the magnetic properties of iron. Its effect, in addition to increasing the electrical resistance of iron, may be stated as follows: Silicon is very soluble in iron, even at room temperature up to 15 per cent, the silicon atoms taking the place of iron atoms in the space lattice. Dissolved in iron, silicon has a tendency to make carbon precipitate as graphite in which form it has a much smaller effect on the magnetic properties than it has when it combines with iron to form cementite (Fe_3C). Furthermore, silicon has great affinity for oxygen, forming with it the very stable compound SiO_2. This, coupled with the readiness with which it can diffuse through iron, even at relatively low temperatures, makes silicon a powerful scavenger for ridding iron of oxygen in solution. But, while SiO_2 (or silicates) can be removed as slag from molten metal, this is not the case when it is trapped or formed after solidification even as submicroscopic or colloidal particles. Once these are formed inside the iron-silicon grains, they are there to stay, as no known metallurgical process is capable of eliminating these inclusions except melting or perhaps prolonged annealing under reducing conditions at very high temperatures (1300 to 1400°C.).[1] This is one of the serious difficulties connected with the use of silicon or similar elements (like aluminum or vanadium)

ETZ, **40**, 312, 325, 334, 348, 361, 1919. G. H. Cole, *Elec. J.*, **21**, 17, 55, 1924. T. D. Yensen, *Trans. A.I.E.E.*, **43**, 145, 1924. K. Daeves, *Stahl u. Eisen*, **44**, 1283, 1924; *Z. Elektrochem.*, **32**, 479, 1926. O. von Auwers, *Z. tech. Physik*, 6, 528, 1925. W. E. Ruder, *Trans. A.S.S.T.*, **8**, 23, 1925. G. Eichenberg and W. Oertel, *Stahl u. Eisen*, **47**, 262, 1927. P. Oberhoffer, M. von Moos, and W. Oertel, *Stahl u. Eisen*, **48**, 393, 1928. M. von Moos, W. Oertel, and R. Schener, *Stahl u. Eisen*, **48**, 477, 1928. T. D. Yensen, *J. Iron Steel Inst. (London)*, **120**, 187, 1929. F. Wever and G. Hindrichs, *Mitt. Kaiser Wilhelm Inst. Eisenforschung*, **13**, 273, 1931. W. S. Messkin and J. M. Margolin, *Arch. Eisenhüttenwesen*, 6, 399, 1933. A. Winmer and P. Werthebach, *Stahl u. Eisen*, **54**, 385, 1934. W. Eilender and W. Oertel, *Stahl u. Eisen*, **54**, 409, 1934. F. L. Prentiss, *Iron Age*, **132**, 18, 1933. W. E. Ruder, *Trans. Am. Soc. Metals*, **22**, 1120, 1934.

[1] Ruder, as early as 1912, used hydrogen in annealing silicon-iron sheet (U. S. Patents 1,110,010, 1914; and 1,201,633, 1916), but the temperatures employed were probably not high enough and other conditions not ideal to effect complete reduction, judging from the results obtained.

and partly accounts for the relatively poor magnetic properties
that we still have with ordinary silicon-iron in sheet form.   How-

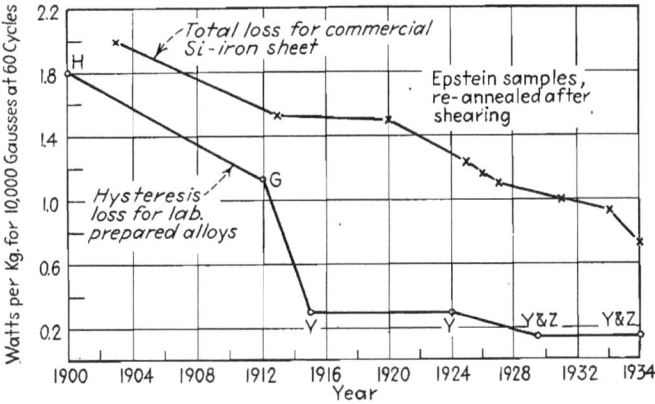

FIG. 47.—Improvement in silicon-iron, 1900–1932.

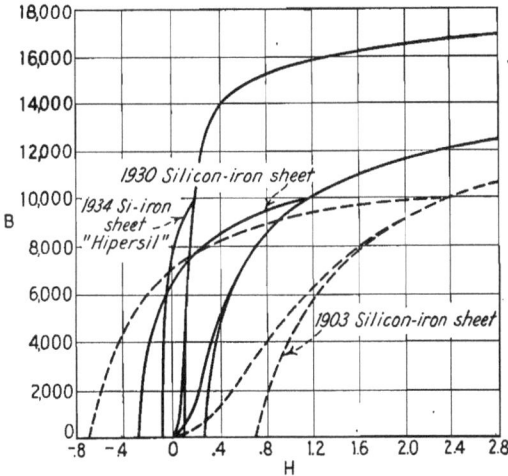

FIG. 48.—1903 vs. 1934 commercial silicon-iron sheets.

1903 *sheet:*
μ_{max} = 5000
Hysteresis loss = 2000 ergs = 1.7 watts per kilogram for f = 60, B = 10,000
Total loss = 2.0 watts per kilogram for f = 60, B = 10,000
1930 *sheet:*
μ_{max} = 12,000
Hysteresis loss = 760 ergs. = 0.6 watt per kilogram for f = 60, B = 10,000
Total loss = 1.0 watt per kilogram for f = 60, B = 10,000
1934 *sheet* "*Hipersil*":
μ_{max} = 60,000
Hysteresis loss = 200 ergs = 0.16 watt per kilogram for f = 60, B = 10,000
Total loss = 0.70 watt per kilogram for f = 60, B = 10,000

ever, in spite of these difficulties, great advances have taken place
by improved refining, rolling, and heat-treating processes, so

that, as shown in Fig. 47, the present commercial product has a total loss only about one-third that of its first ancestor. Figure 48 shows the hysteresis loops of the 1903, 1930, and 1934 commercial product.

Approximate relationships have been worked out between the impurities and the magnetic properties of iron-silicon alloys,[1] similar to those for unalloyed iron. Those for carbon are shown in Fig. 49.[2]

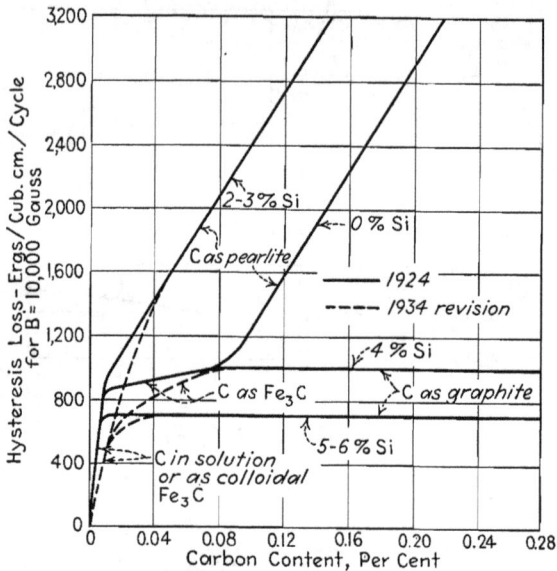

FIG. 49.—Effect of carbon on the magnetic properties of iron-silicon alloys.

Since the first appearance of these curves in 1924, alloys have been obtained with maximum permeabilities higher than 80,000 and hysteresis losses less than 200 ergs. In Fig. 50 is shown the hysteresis loop for such samples in comparison with that for high-grade silicon-iron sheet.

The last improvement shown in Fig. 48 has been accomplished by making use of the facts presented in Par. 43 in regard to the effect of lattice orientation. By special rolling and annealing processes it has been found possible to produce polycrystalline

[1] T. D. YENSEN, *Trans. A.I.E.E.*, **43**, 145, 1924.

[2] T. D. YENSEN, and N. A. ZIEGLER, *Trans. Am. Soc. Metals*, **24**, 337, 1936.

iron-silicon alloys in the form of thin sheets or strip with preferred lattice orientation ("fibering") having *B-H* curves closely

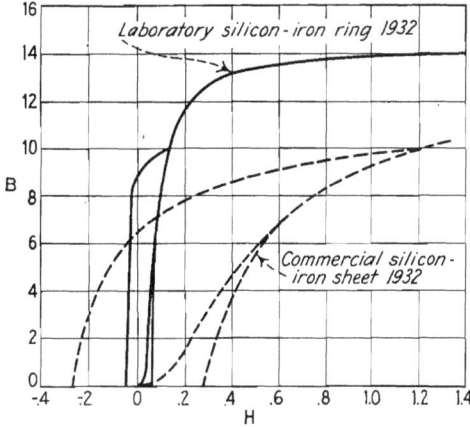

FIG. 50.—Silicon-iron 1932 commercial sheet vs. laboratory-ring samples.

Commercial sheet:
  μ_{max} = 12,000
    Hysteresis loss = 760 ergs = 0.6 watt per kilogram for f = 60, B = 10,000
      Total loss = 1.0 watt per kilogram for f = 60, B = 10,000
Laboratory ring:
  μ_{max} = 83,100
    Hysteresis loss = 163 ergs = 0.14 watt per kilogram for f = 60, B = 10,000

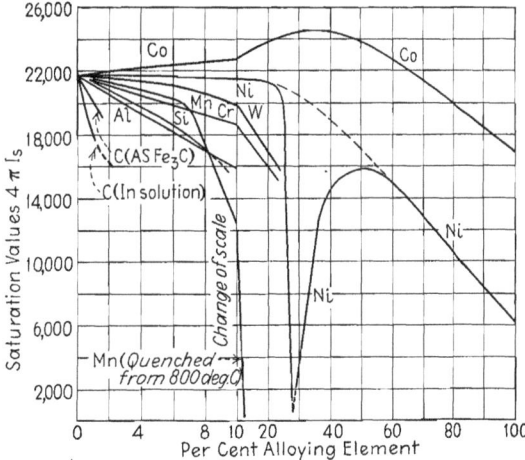

FIG. 51.—Effect of elements on the saturation value of iron.

resembling those for single crystals (Fig. 38).[1] By combined fibering and purification, sheets and strip have been produced

[1] F. BITTER, patent pending. N. P. Goss, *Trans. Am. Soc. Metals*, **23**, 511, 1935; U. S. Patent 1,965,559, 1934. K. J. SIXTUS, *Physics*, **6**, 105, 1935. R. M. BOZORTH, *Trans. Am. Soc. Metals*, **23**, 1107, 1935.

with very low losses and high permeabilities at both low and high flux densities. This new product has been named "hipersil."[1]

The effect of silicon and other elements on the magnetic saturation value of iron is shown in Fig. 51, based partly on a paper by Stäblein,[2] while the disadvantage due to brittleness imparted by silicon above 3 per cent can only be mentioned.[3]

What has been stated in regard to silicon alloys holds, in general, for the iron-aluminum,[4] iron-vanadium,[5] iron-arsenic,[6] and iron-tin[7] alloys and combinations of these.[8] Aluminum can be added in larger quantities than silicon without producing brittleness (up to 6 per cent). Vanadium also can be added in larger quantities without producing brittleness, and good magnetic properties have been obtained for ring samples, the best results being practically the same as those shown for silicon iron in Fig. 50. However, vanadium does not increase the electrical resistance nearly so much as does silicon or aluminum (see Fig. 52). This is also true of arsenic and tin and constitutes the chief reason for the main emphasis being laid on the iron-silicon and iron-aluminum alloys.

The latest contribution to this class of alloys is the Fe-Si-Al alloy containing 8 to 11 per cent silicon plus 5 to 6.5 per cent aluminum, discovered by Masumoto and called "sendust."[9] After having investigated the entire range of alloys up to 15 per cent Si and 14 per cent Al, Masumoto found that with pure alloys in the above range the permeability is exceptionally high (initial permeability up to 35,000 and max. permeability up to 162,000) and the hysteresis loss exceptionally low (28 ergs for $B = 5000$). With such high silicon and aluminum contents the

[1] *Elec. J.*, **33**, 40, 1936.

[2] F. STÄBLEIN, *Kruppsche Monatshefte*, **9**, 181, 1928.

[3] N. B. PILLING, *Trans. A.I.M.E.*, **69**, 780, 1923.

[4] T. D. YENSEN and W. A. GATWARD, *Univ. Illinois, Eng. Exp. Sta., Bull.* 95, 1917.

[5] N. A. ZIEGLER, unpublished results.

[6] C. F. BURGESS and J. ASTON, *Trans. Am. Electrochem. Soc.*, **15**, 369, 1909.

G. H. COLE and A. A. FREY, unpublished results.

[7] C. F. BURGESS and J. ASTON, *Electrochem. Met. Ind.*, **7**, 403, 1909.

[8] A. A. FREY, U. S. Patent 1,845,493, 1932 (Fe-Al-As).

[9] HAKAR MASUMOTO, Anniversary volume of *Science Repts. Tôhoku. Imp. Univ.*, Ser. I (dedicated to Prof. K. Honda), Sendai, Japan, 1936.

saturation value is necessarily low ($4\pi I_{sat} = 11{,}000$) and the alloys must be very brittle, but as powdered core material for loading coils the alloy should be very good and cost much less than permalloy (see next paragraph).

Iron-nickel Alloys.—Since the first systematic investigation by Burgess and Aston in 1910[1] these alloys have been subjected to

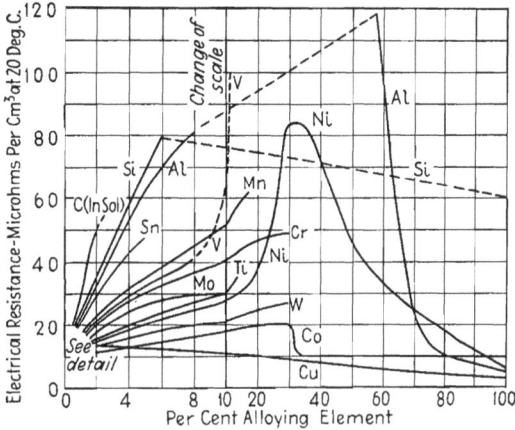

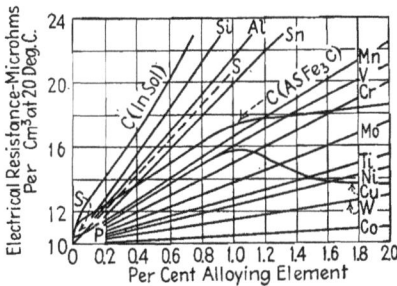

FIG. 52.—Effect of elements on the electrical resistance of iron.

repeated and thorough study by many investigators. The point that attracted most attention was the indication that alloys containing more than 30 per cent Ni had higher permeabilities at low inductions than the purest iron available at the time.

The magnetic properties of the iron-nickel alloys after ordinary heat treatment are indicated in Fig. 53. Two regions imme-

[1] C. F. BURGESS and J. ASTON, *Met. Chem. Eng.*, **8**, 191, 1910.

diately arrest attention: the cusp just below 30 per cent Ni and the maximum around 50 per cent Ni. While we have no evidence of the formation of compounds in these regions, it is quite evident

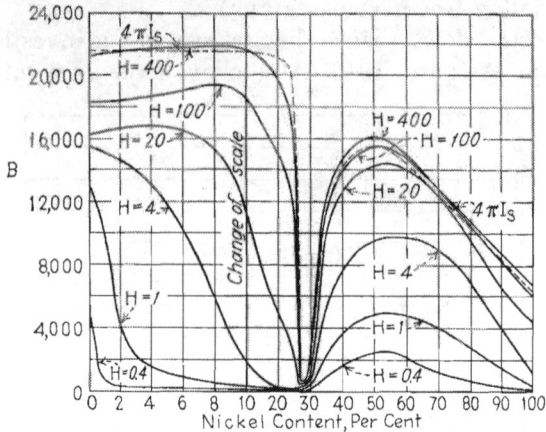

Fig. 53.—Saturation intensity $(4\pi I_s)$ and flux density for various magnetizing forces in iron-nickel alloys.

that some critical condition prevails. Now, it is possible to obtain a homogeneous structure at 26 per cent Ni, corresponding to the formula Fe_3Ni, if at this point the body-centered structure changes to the face-centered structure with the nickel atoms at the

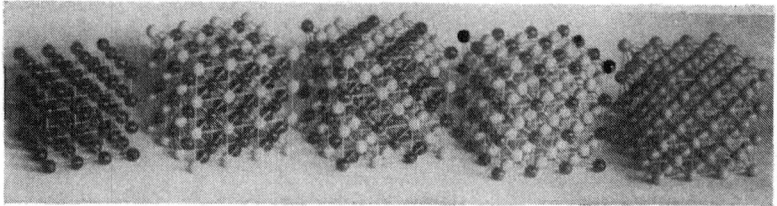

Fig. 54.—Proposed models for certain iron-nickel alloys. The models, reading from left to right, represent Fe_2 (iron); Fe_3Ni, Fe_2Ni_2 (hipernik); $FeNi_3$ (permalloy); and Ni_4 (nickel).

corners and the iron atoms at the face centers (Fig. 54). X-ray analysis shows that a change to the face-centered cubic structure actually does take place between 25 and 30 per cent Ni.[1] We may, therefore, assume that the change takes place at 26 per cent

[1] R. M. Andrews, *Phys. Rev.*, **17**, 261, 1921; **18**, 245, 1921. F. Kirchner, *Ann. Physik*, **69**, 59, 1922. H. S. Rawdon and F. Sillers, Jr., *Phys. Rev.*, **25**, 898, 1925. A. Osawa, *Science Rept. Tôhoku Imp. Univ.*, **15**, 387, 619, 1926; *J. Iron Steel Inst. (London)*, **113**, 447, 1926.

Ni and that the resulting homogeneous structure is nonferro-magnetic and may be regarded as the end point of the 0 to 26 per cent alloys and the starting point of the next division.

Similarly, the maximum point lies very close to and may coin-cide with the composition 51 per cent Ni, corresponding to the formula Fe_2Ni_2 and a homogeneous structure composed of alter-nate layers of Fe and Ni atoms parallel to the (111) plane (see Fig. 54). This is the composition that forms the basis for the

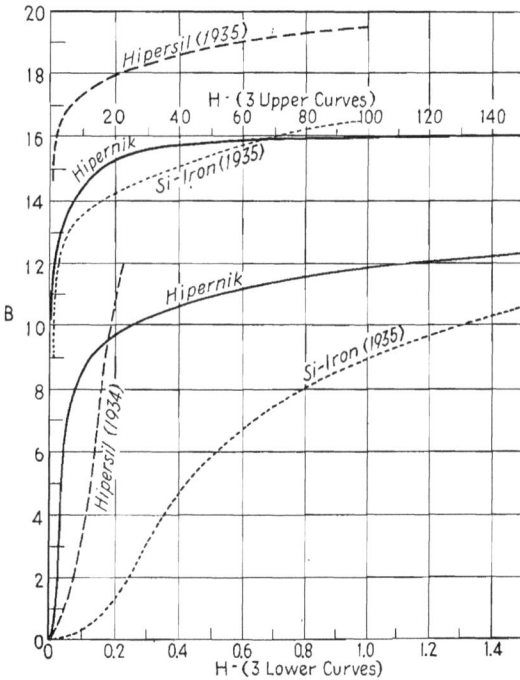

FIG. 55.—*B-H* curves for hipernik and high-silicon iron.

now well-known alloy hipernik. As ordinarily made, the 50 per cent alloy exhibits nothing remarkable; except that its saturation value is the highest of all Fe-Ni alloys above 30 per cent Ni. Some years ago, however, it was discovered that its magnetic properties could be greatly improved by annealing sheets of this alloy in hydrogen at a temperature of 1000 to 1200°C. for several hours.[1] This treatment eliminated carbon, sulphur, and other

[1] T. D. YENSEN, *J. Franklin Inst.*, **199**, 323, 1925.

impurities, but particularly oxygen, and resulted in the new alloy hipernik (from high-permeability nickel). In this case, also, the difference between the ordinary 50 per cent alloy and hipernik is

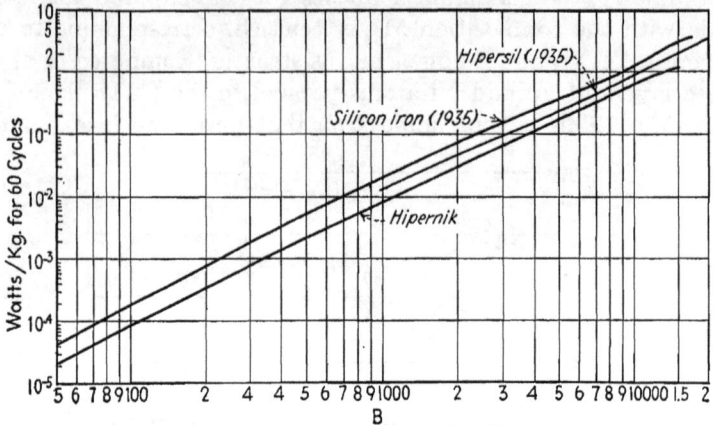

Fig. 56.—Core loss for hipernik and high-silicon iron.

of the order of 0.01 per cent of impurities, and yet hipernik sheet as commercially manufactured has a maximum permeability that has reached a value of over 150,000[1] as compared with

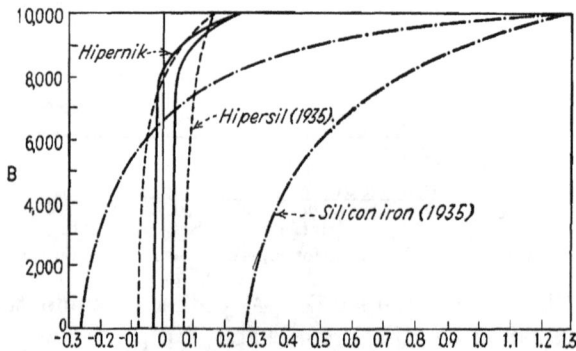

Fig. 57.—Hysteresis loops for hipernik and high-silicon iron.

less than 5,000 for the alloy as ordinarily made. Figures 55, 56, and 57 show the difference in magnetic properties between hipernik, the highest grade of hot-rolled 4 per cent silicon-iron of

[1] T. D. Yensen, *Elec. J.*, **28**, 386, 1931.

1935, and hipersil,[1] all rolled to 14-mils (0.035-cm.).   While the saturation value of hipernik (about 16,000) is lower than that for silicon-iron (19,600), its low-density permeability is much higher, and its total energy loss at all flux densities is much lower.   The base is now made in commercial quantities in electric furnaces.

The other remarkable alloy in this series is permalloy, the best composition for which appears to be 78½ per cent Ni or very close to that corresponding to the formula $FeNi_3$ (76 per cent Ni) shown in Fig. 54.   Here, again, a special heat treatment, discovered by Elmen[2] and consisting in air quenching from the

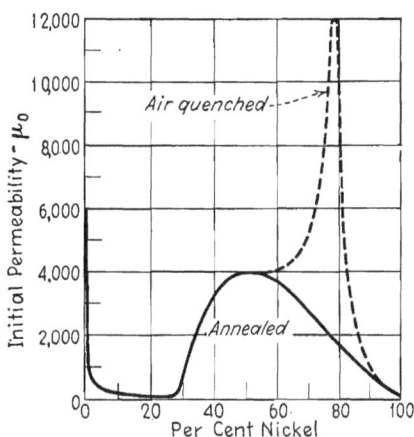

FIG. 58.—Initial permeabilities for iron-nickel alloys.

magnetic transformation temperature, produced the exceptional properties.   Figure 58 shows the effect on the initial permeability, and maximum permeabilities above 100,000 are readily obtainable, but the saturation value is low (11,000), and its electrical resistance is only about double that of iron.   However, this can be remedied by the addition of chromium or molybdenum, which help to increase the initial permeability to over 20,000[3] but at a further sacrifice of saturation value.

Numerous other modifications have been made in these alloys by the addition of other elements and by variations in the heat

[1] See pp. 110–112.

[2] H. D. ARNOLD and G. W. ELMEN, *J. Franklin Inst.*, **195**, 621, 1923.

[3] G. W. ELMEN, Bell Laboratories *Rec.*, **10**, 2, 1931; U. S. Patent 1,768,443, 1930; *Elec. Eng.*, **54**, 1292, 1935.

treatment, but no radical improvements have been made.   Modified alloys are made by various companies and are sold under various trade names, the most important of which are:

1. Mumetal, 76 per cent Ni + 17 per cent Fe + 5 per cent Cu + 2 per cent (Cr or Mn), having a maximum permeability of 45,000 to 100,000, initial permeability of 12,000 to 30,000, resistivity of 43 microhms per cubic centimeter (patented by Telegraph Construction and Maintenance Co., London, and made by Heraeus Vacuum Schmelze, Hanau-am-Main, Germany).[1]

2. Alloy "1040," made by Siemens and Halske,[2] has the following percentage composition: 72 Ni + 11 Fe + 14 Cu + 3 Mo, has a resistivity of 56 microhms, initial permeability up to 50,000, maximum permeability of 100,000, hysteresis loss of 50 ergs for $B = 10,000$, 0.04 watt per kilogram for $B = 5000$ and 50 cycles; and a saturation value $(4\pi I_s)$ about 6000.

Other alloys are rhometal (same as mumetal but with higher resistivity), megaperm (Fe-Ni-Mn), and permenorm (48 per cent Ni + 52 per cent Fe), having constant permeability of over 2000 for $H < 0.06$, $\mu_{max} = 20,000$, and electrical resistivity = 58.[1]

By cooling some of these alloys in a magnetic field through the magnetic transformation point, great improvements were obtained by the Bell Laboratories.[3]   Particularly good results were obtained with 65 per cent Ni and with 45 per cent Ni, 30 per cent Fe, 25 per cent Co (perminvar composition).   A maximum permeability of over 600,000 was reported for the 65 per cent Ni alloy.   The cause of the improvement is explained on the basis of elimination of strains due to magnetostriction.[4]

In Fig. 59 have been plotted for comparison B-H curves for iron (Fe_2), 26 per cent Ni (Fe_3Ni), hipernik (Fe_2Ni_2), permalloy ($FeNi_3$) and nickel (Ni_4).   Comparing the curve for Armco iron with that for iron, and noting that similar differences exist for the two high-permeability alloys and the corresponding alloys as known ten years ago, it is not improbable that we shall find a corresponding difference in the case of nickel after we have

[1] G. Keinath, *Archiv für Tech. Messen*, Sec. Z913-1, 2, 1931; Z913-3, 1932.

[2] H. Neumann, *Archiv für Tech. Messen*, Sec. Z913-5, 1934.

[3] J. F. Dillinger and R. M. Bozorth, *Physics*, **6**, 279,285, 1935.   G. A. Kelsall, *Physics*, **5**, 169, 1934.

[4] For details, see Chaps. VI and VII.

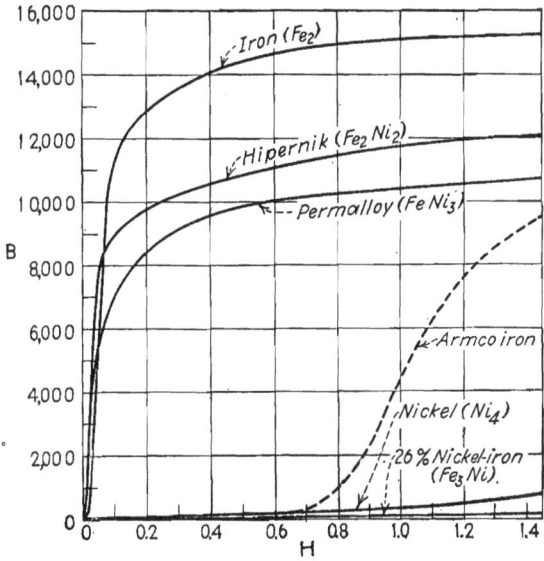

FIG. 59.—*B-H* curves for the five iron-nickel alloys Fe₂, Fe₃Ni, Fe₂Ni₂ (hipernik), FeNi₃ (permalloy), and Ni₄ with Armco iron for comparison.

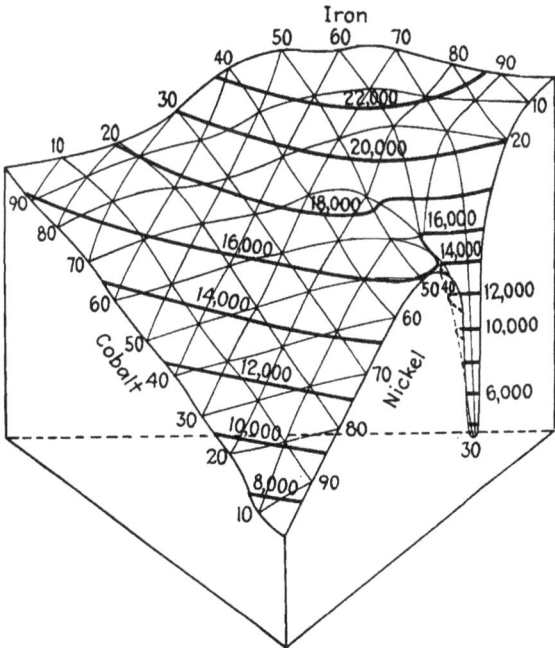

FIG. 60.—Fe-Ni-Co saturation values (Elmen).

subjected it to the same thorough study as we have iron and the 50 per cent and 78½ per cent iron-nickel alloys.

Materials with High Magnetic Saturation Value.—Iron has a saturation value of 21,600 ($4\pi I_s$). In order to exceed this value it is necessary, as far as our present knowledge goes, to alloy iron with cobalt in amounts between 0 and 65 per cent. The highest value is obtained by using 34.5 per cent Co. This was discovered by P. Weiss[1] in 1912, who obtained a 10 per cent

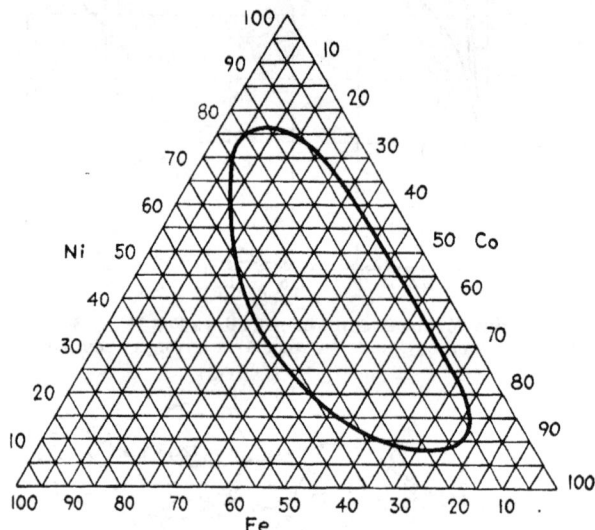

FIG. 61.—Composition diagram of the Ni-Fe-Co series. The area enclosed by the curve shows compositions with marked perminvar characteristics. (*Elmen*)

increase in the saturation value, and it was confirmed in 1915 by the author,[2] who got a 13 per cent increase. The entire series of Fe-Co-Ni alloys has since been thoroughly investigated by Elmen[3] (Fig. 60), and F. Stäblein[4] has collected curves for a number of iron alloys, as shown, slightly modified, in Fig. 51. The value 24,200 may thus be regarded as well established for 34.5 per cent cobalt-iron, corresponding to Fe_2Co.

Materials with Constant Permeability.—At the Bell Laboratories were developed certain Fe-Ni-Co alloys[5] having a constant

[1] P. WEISS, *Compt. rend.*, **156**, 1970, 1913.
[2] T. D. YENSEN, *Gen. Elec. Rev.*, **18**, 881, 1915.
[3] G. W. ELMEN, *Bell Syst. Tech. J.*, **8**, 435, 1929.
[4] F. STÄBLEIN, *Kruppsche Monatshefte*, **9**, 181, 1928.
[5] G. W. ELMEN: *J. Franklin Inst.*, **206**, 317, 1928; **207**, 582, 1929.

permeability at low magnetizing forces. These, containing in the neighborhood of 30 per cent Fe, 45 per cent Ni, and 25 per cent Co, were called perminvar. They are useful wherever a constant inductance or reactance is essential such as in filter coils for radio circuits or for loading coils for telephone circuits, where air gaps are otherwise used with sheet materials or where iron

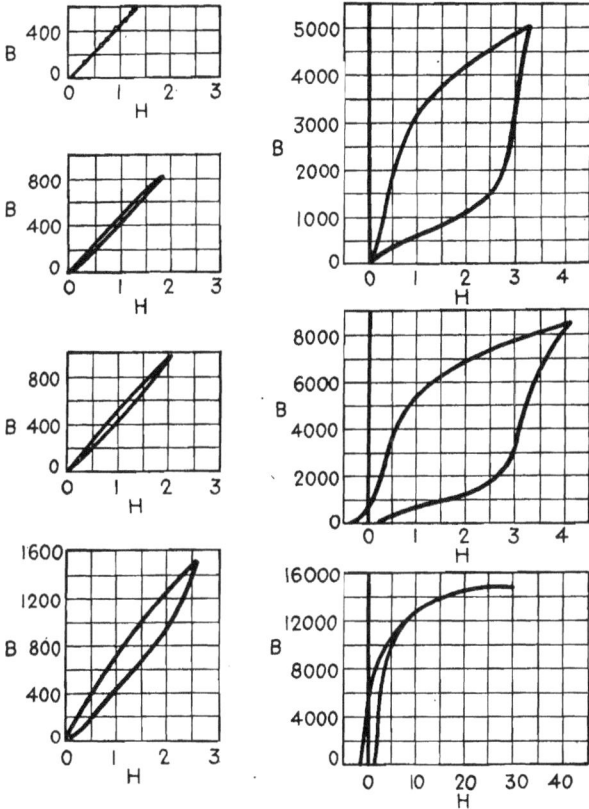

Fig. 62.—Perminvar hysteresis loops. (*Elmen*)

or permalloy is used in the form of compressed powders. Figure 61 shows the perminvar range according to Elmen, and Fig. 62 shows the hysteresis loops for the optimum composition. Similar results may be obtained with 50 per cent Fe-Ni alloys by means of a special heat treatment which, in fact, is an incomplete annealing below 800°C. Such an alloy, developed independently at the Bell Laboratories and at the Westinghouse Research Laboratories, has by the latter been called "conpernik" to distinguish it from "hipernik," as both have essentially the same composition.

A more recent development in Germany resulted in iron-nickel alloys called "isoperms" containing 35 to 55 per cent Ni with some alloying element which tends to precipitate under certain combinations of cold rolling and annealing.[1] Aluminum, copper, beryllium, manganese, and titanium have been used with varying success. The best alloy contains 40 to 45 per cent Ni, 45 to 50 per cent Fe, and 5 to 15 per cent Cu. The alloy is first drastically cold rolled, then quenched from a high temperature, further cold rolled, and finally annealed, a treatment by which the copper is precipitated in such a way as to produce a preferred arrangement of the Fe-Ni lattice, resulting in very low retentivity and constancy of permeability (50 to 60) over a wide range of H (0 to 100 oersteds).

Permanent Magnet Materials.—The characteristics desired in permanent magnet materials are just the reverse of those desired in the materials treated so far. The ideal is a material with a residual approaching saturation which remains permanently unchanged. For this reason it is essential that the coercive force be as high as possible. As all applications for permanent magnets call for an air gap, there is always present in such magnetic circuits a demagnetizing force which will decrease the true residual to some value depending on the shape of the magnet. The longer the path relative to its cross section the less the demagnetizing factor.

The principle governing the production of permanent magnets is to harden the material uniformly throughout its mass. This is most effectively done by alloying iron with some element that is much more soluble at high than at low temperatures. The treatment then consists in heating the alloy to a high temperature to bring all the alloying element into solution, then quenching it so as to retain as much of it as possible in solution, and finally allowing it to precipitate in very finely divided form (colloidal) by reheating to 100, 200, 300°C. or even higher. The phenomenon is usually referred to as disperse hardening, or precipitation

---

[1] H. SPRUNG, *Elek. Nachrichten Technik*, **10**, 317, 1933. O. DAHL and J. PFAFFENBERGER, *Z. tech. Physik*, **15**, 95, 99, 1934; *Metallwirtschaf* , **13**, 527, 543, 559, 1934; **14**, 25, 1935; M. KERSTEN, Wiss. Veröff a.d. Siemens-Konzern, **13**, 1, 1934; *Z. tech. Physik*, **15**, 250, 1934.

hardening. The hardening is due to distortion of the iron lattice by the colloidal precipitates which at the low temperature cannot be expelled to the grain boundaries or coalesce into larger particles.

The earliest permanent magnet material was carbon steel (1 to 1.5 per cent C) in which the precipitated particles are Fe_3C. The addition of tungsten (5 to 6 per cent), chromium, or molybdenum during 1910 to 1920 improved the carbon steel greatly, largely because of the effect of these elements on carbon.

. Then, some fifteen years ago, Honda[1] announced the greatly improved KS magnet steel obtained by alloying iron with 35 per cent Co, 7 to 9 per cent W or Mo, and 0.5 per cent C with or without Cr, whereby, by a special heat treatment, a coercive force of 200 oersteds was obtained. After this alloy had been firmly established in the industry[2] and further improved by the addition of titanium[3] it was found, however, that carbon is not at all essential. Good permanent alloys can be made from carbon-free binary alloys of iron with W, Mo, Be, and Ti and from ternary alloys of 65 per cent Fe + 35 per cent Co with the preceding elements.[4]

Recently, Mishima in his MK magnet steels[5] discovered that even better results can be obtained by alloying nickel (5 to 40 per cent), or nickel (5 to 30 per cent) and cobalt (0.5 to 40 per cent), with aluminum (1 to 20 per cent) and carbon (less than 1.5 per cent) with or without manganese (0.5 to 10 per cent), chromium (1 to 5 per cent), or tungsten (0.5 to 8 per cent). By the proper adjustment of the varying alloying elements it has been found possible to obtain a coercive force of over 650 oersteds with a residual of 8000 gauss. The $(B_R \times H_C)$ value for such an alloy may be as high as 2×10^6 compared with 1×10^5 for cobalt steel and 0.3×10^6 for tungsten steel. Figure 63 shows hyster-

[1] K. HONDA, *Phys. Soc. Japan*, **2**, 32, 1920; U. S. Patent 1,338,132; 133; 134, 1920.

[2] P. H. BRACE, *Elec. J.*, **26**, 111, 1929.

[3] K. HONDA, H. MASUMOTO, and Y. SHIRAKAWA, *Science Repts. Tôhoku Imp. Univ.*, **23**, 365, 1934.

[4] K. S. SELJESATER and B. A. ROGERS, *Trans. A.S.S.T.*, **19**, 554, 1932. W. KÖSTER, *Stahl u. Eisen*, **53**, 849, 1933.

[5] T. MISHIMA, *Iron Age*, Sept., 1932, p. 346.

J. A. BABBITT and T. TUJIWARA, *Aciers spéciaux, métaux, and alliages*, **8**, 84, 1933; *Ohm*, **19**, 353, 1932. K. HONDA, *Metallwirtschaft*, **13**, 425, 1934.

esis loops for cobalt and chromium magnet steels in comparison with silicon steel, and Fig. 64 shows demagnetization curves for the MK steel in comparison with that for cobalt and tungsten steels. The curves marked MK represent steels with various amounts of nickel and aluminum.

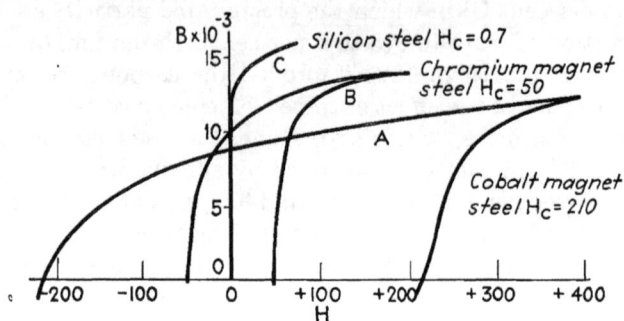

Fig. 63.—Hysteresis loops of various magnetic materials. (*Brace*)

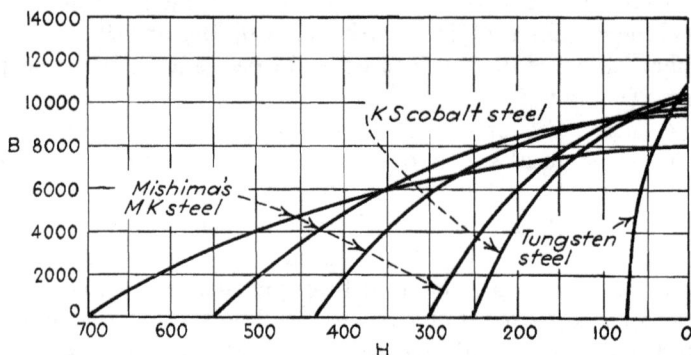

Fig. 64.—Demagnetization curves for permanent magnet materials. (*Williams*)

Finally, to complete the picture, the oxide magnets must be mentioned, developed by Kato in Japan,[1] composed of oxides of iron and cobalt, with possible addition of an oxide of Ni, Cu, Zn, Cr, or W.

For more detailed information on permanent magnet materials see also the following:

W. Köster, *Stahl u. Eisen*, **53**, 849, 1933.
W. C. Ellis and E. E. Schumacher, *Metals and Alloys*, **6**, 26, 1935.
L. Sanderson, *Heat Treating and Forging*, **21**, 13, 1935.

[1] Y. Kato and T. Takai, *J. Inst. Elec. Eng. Japan*, **53**, 408, 1933; U. S. Patent 1,976,230, Oct. 9, 1934.

R. F. EDGAR, *Gen. Elec. Rev.*, **38**, 466, 1935.
A. B. EVEREST, *Metal Treatment*, **1**, 43, 1935.
A. KUSSMANN, *Z. Ver. deut. Ing.*, **79**, 1171, 1935; *Arch. Elektrotech.*, **29**, 297, 1935.
W. S. MESSKIN and B. E. SOMIN, *Arch. Eisenhüttenw.* **8**, 315, 1935.
C. S. WILLIAMS, *Elec. Eng.*, **55**, 19, 1936.

Heusler Alloys.—Heusler alloys are as yet only of scientific interest. They furnish the proof that ferromagnetism can be obtained without the use of iron, nickel, or cobalt. Certain combinations of copper, manganese, and aluminum exhibit strong ferromagnetic properties. Thus an alloy corresponding to the composition $(Cu, Mn)_3 Al$, *e.g.*, 13 per cent Al + 30 per cent Mn + 67 per cent Cu, if quenched from a high temperature and tempered, will have a saturation value $(4\pi I_s)$ of nearly 5000 under the most favorable conditions of heat treatment. The saturation value decreases with increasing copper or decreasing manganese content, keeping the aluminum content constant at 13 per cent. It also decreases with changes in the aluminum content in both directions.

The ternary alloys of manganese-copper-tin show about the same degree of ferromagnetism as the manganese-copper-aluminum type, and both types are included in the designation Heusler alloys.

Ferromagnetism has also been observed in alloys of manganese with arsenic (Mn_3As_2); with boron (MnB); with bismuth $(MnBi)$; with carbon (Mn_3C); with nitrogen $(Mn_3N_2, Mn_5N_2,$ and $Mn_7N_2)$; with phosphorus (Mn_5P_2); with sulphur (MnS); with antimony $(Mn_2Sb, Mn_3Sb_2 MnSb)$; and with tin (Mn_4Sn).

For a more detailed account of these alloys the reader is referred to the following:

O. VON AUWERS, *Z. anorg. allgem. Chem.*, **108**, 49, 1919.
A. KUSSMANN and B. SCHARNOW, *Z. Physik*, **47**, 770, 1928.
E. PERSSON, *Naturwissenschaften*, **16**, 613, 1938; *Z. Physik*, **57**, 115, 1929.
MESSKIN-KUSSMANN, "Die Ferromagnetischen Legierungen," Julius Springer, Berlin, 1932.

CHAPTER V

INTERNAL FIELDS

The atoms of a ferromagnetic solid interact in several distinct ways which it is the purpose of this chapter to separate and formulate mathematically. The discovery that the magnetic element in ferromagnetic media is the magnetic moment of the electron due to its spin, rather than the magnetic moment resulting from the orbital motion of the electron, has made it possible to explain the molecular fields postulated by Weiss in the same terms used in accounting for atomic spectra. The quantum theory of the interaction of electronic spins assigns energies to the various possible orientations of spins with respect to each other and so can account, as we shall see, for the high intensity of magnetization that characterizes ferromagnetic materials. The mutual energy between two atoms, however, does not depend only on whether their spins are parallel or antiparallel but also on their distance apart. Atoms with parallel spins will attract or repel each other differently from atoms with antiparallel spins. In order to describe the distortion produced in a crystal by these forces it is necessary to know its elastic properties. Furthermore, in actual crystals the direction of magnetization cannot be rotated without the expenditure of a certain amount of energy. This is described by means of a crystalline field coupling the spin orientations to the body of the crystal. And finally there is the internal magnetic field. The magnetic interaction between neighboring particles is small compared with the other interactions mentioned above, but to counterbalance this the magnetic forces have much longer ranges, and because of this the total magnetic interaction between large groups of atoms is important in determining magnetic properties.

47. The Spinning Electron and the Gyromagnetic Effects.— The following considerations are based on the law of conservation of momentum of which a special case, and the one of interest here, is the conservation of angular momentum. Magnetism, as far as we can tell, is a manifestation of electricity in motion, and since

electrical particles have mass, magnetism and momentum must
be closely related. According to Eq. (18), the magnetic moment
of an electron with a charge of e e.s.u. moving around an orbit
of area A in a time τ is given by

$$\mu = \frac{eA}{c\tau} \tag{57}$$

For an electron of mass m moving in a circular orbit, we have for
the moment of momentum j

$$j = mrv$$

and since

$$v = \frac{2\pi r}{\tau} \quad \text{and} \quad A = \pi r^2$$

we obtain finally

$$\mu = \frac{e}{2mc}j$$
$$\frac{j}{\mu} = \frac{2mc}{e} \tag{58}$$

a result that can be generalized to include magnetic moments due
to orbits of any shape. From this result it immediately follows
by summation that the magnetization I due to a large number
of such magnetic elements is associated with a moment of momentum M such that

$$\frac{M}{I} = \frac{2mc}{e} \tag{59}$$

Furthermore, according to Par. 4, external magnetic fields
themselves do not reorient electronic orbits. These are reoriented
by internal forces within the magnetized body. Magnetization
should therefore proceed as follows. The presence of a magnetizable body in a magnetic field affects the energies of the various existing electronic motions. This new distribution of energy
among the atoms is not one compatible with thermal equilibrium,
and by means of collisions or other processes by which the atoms
can exchange energy a redistribution of energy with a corresponding change of magnetization from 0 to I is produced. In
this new state the electronic motions have acquired a moment of
momentum M which, according to Eq. (59), is equal to $I(2mc/e)$.

Since this was produced by an interaction with the atoms of the magnetized substance, this latter must have acquired an equal and opposite momentum $-M$. By suspending a solid body from a delicate fiber and observing the twist produced by magnetization it should therefore be possible to determine experimentally the ratio M/I.

The effect has a converse which involves the production of magnetization by rotating a body. In the part of Par. 4 dealing with the Larmor precession it was stated that the effect of a magnetic field was exactly equivalent to a rotation about the direction of the field with an angular velocity

$$\omega = \frac{eH}{2mc} \tag{60}$$

and accordingly it should be equally true that a rotation ω is equivalent to a field H. However, e/mc is 1.77×10^7, so that enormously rapid rotations are required to produce fields of even 0.001 oersted, and the effect is consequently difficult to observe.

Values of M/I differing from the foregoing can be obtained in the classical electromagnetic theory by making special assumptions about the electron and its own angular momentum, or spin. The arbitrary assumptions of the classical theory concerning the distribution of charge in electrons of various shapes have during recent years been replaced by the quantum theory which has been able to account for atomic spectra by means of a spinning electron for which the value of j/μ is mc/e, or half as great as for orbital electrons. This value is supported by a great deal of evidence but cannot be deduced from more general electromagnetic laws in the absence of a satisfactory theory of electronic structure. The magnetic moment of the spinning electron is one Bohr magneton, defined in Eq. (36).

Various attempts have been made to discover gyromagnetic effects, beginning with Maxwell in 1861, but because of experimental difficulties none were successful until 1914 and 1915 when S. J. Barnett succeeded in producing magnetization by rotation, and subsequently A. Einstein and W. J. de Haas observed the rotation produced in a delicately suspended sample by magnetization. The result of these and other investigations is, first, that ferromagnetism is due to negative electricity and, further, that M/I is very closely equal to mc/e, the value for spinning electrons, in all ferromagnetic substances[1] investigated except FeS.[2]

This result suggests that the seat of magnetism in a ferromagnetic substance is the spinning electron, a result that is confirmed by other evidence discussed further on.

48. X-ray Evidence Concerning the Magnetic Moments of Ferromagnetic Atoms.—The evidence obtained from the gyromagnetic effect leads to the conclusion that magnetization does not involve a reorientation of electron orbits but that it is the direction of the spin of the electron that is chiefly affected by external fields. This conclusion was strikingly confirmed by X-ray investigations. When light is reflected from a grating, the position of the reflected spectral lines is determined by the spacing of the grating, but the energy contained in the various orders of reflection depends on the shape of the lines in the grating. The reflection of X-rays from a crystal is determined by atomic planes in a similar way, but in this case the distribution of charge around an atom takes the place of the shape of the ruled lines. If magnetization affects the orientation of electron orbits, one would expect the intensity of X-ray lines reflected from a ferromagnetic substance to be affected by its state of magnetization. K. T. Compton and A. H. Compton and their collaborators[3] and, more recently, Yensen[4] have found no observable changes, and their results are quite consistent with the one previously arrived at, *viz.*, that magnetization is preponderantly due to a reorientation of electron spins.

49. The Quantum Theory. Equivalence Degeneracy.—The procedure prescribed by the quantum theory for solving atomic problems cannot be carried out when many particles are involved, as, for instance, in the case of a ferromagnetic solid. The development of ferromagnetic theory, however, is based on certain simple ideas which are illustrated in the theory of the hydrogen molecule. The sketch below is intended to give to those readers unfamiliar with quantum mechanics some idea of what equiva-

[1] S. J. BARNETT, *Nat. Res. Council, Bull.* **3**, 325, 1922; *Physica*, **13**, 241, 1933.

[2] F. COETERIER, *Helvetica Phys. Acta*, **6**, 483, 1933. D. INGLIS, *Phys. Rev.*, **45**, 118, 1934.

[3] K. T. COMPTON and E. A. TROUSDALE, *Phys. Rev.*, **5**, 315, 1915. A. H. COMPTON and O. ROGNLEY, *Phys. Rev.*, **16**, 464, 1920.

[4] T. D. YENSEN, *Phys. Rev.*, **31**, 714, 1928.

lence degeneracy means and of how exchange energies, which are responsible for the Weiss molecular field, are introduced into the theory.

According to the quantum theory in the form due to Schrödinger, the solution of electronic problems not involving the time is to be found in the wave equation

$$\nabla^2\psi + \frac{8\pi^2 m}{h^2}(E - V)\psi = 0 \tag{61}$$

m and h are the electronic mass and Planck's constant, respectively. V is the potential energy due to the electrostatic interaction of all the particles of the system, which, in the case of the hydrogen atom, is simply $-e^2/r$, r being the distance of the electron from the nucleus. Solutions are to consist of functions ψ which are everywhere finite and values for the undetermined constant E which together satisfy the equation. ψ may be complex, and $\overline{\psi}$ is that function obtained by replacing i by $-i$ in ψ. For any given function V, Eq. (61) has a set of solutions which correspond to the stationary states of the system described by the function V. With each of these stationary states, which we shall call ψ_n, is associated an energy E_n. If two or more states have the same energy, the system is called degenerate. The functions ψ_n have the special property of satisfying the orthogonality relations

$$\begin{aligned}\int\psi_n\overline{\psi}_m dv &= 0 \qquad n \neq m \\ \int\psi_n\overline{\psi}_n dv &= 1\end{aligned} \tag{62}$$

$\psi_n\overline{\psi}_n dv$ may be interpreted as the probability of finding an electron in the element of volume dv when the system is in the state n. The second equation above then becomes equivalent to the statement that the electron described by ψ_n is to be found in all space with a probability 1, *i.e.*, with absolute certainty. The solution of Eq. (61) for the hydrogen atom in the ground state, *i.e.*, the state having the lowest energy, is

$$\psi_0 = \frac{1}{\sqrt{\pi}}\left(\frac{1}{a_0}\right)^{\frac{3}{2}} e^{-\frac{r}{a_0}} \tag{63}$$

a_0 being a length of the order of half the atomic diameter. In this ground state the hydrogen atom has an energy E_0.

The hydrogen molecule is now to be constructed out of the solution (63) for the isolated atom by considering how two such atoms perturb each other as they are brought together from infinity. The coordinates used to describe the system are shown in Fig. 65. The two nuclei a and b are considered fixed a distance R apart. The electrons 1 and 2 are at a distance r_{12} from each other, and r_{a_1}, r_{b_1}, etc., from the nuclei. The wave equation now becomes

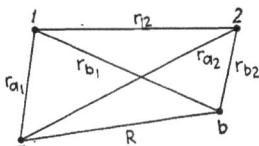

FIG. 65.

$$\frac{\partial^2\psi}{\partial x_1^2} + \frac{\partial^2\psi}{\partial y_1^2} + \frac{\partial^2\psi}{\partial z_1^2} + \frac{\partial^2\psi}{\partial x_2^2} + \frac{\partial^2\psi}{\partial y_2^2} + \frac{\partial^2\psi}{\partial z_2^2}$$
$$+ \frac{8\pi^2 m}{h^2}\left[E - \left(\frac{e^2}{R} + \frac{e^2}{r_{12}} - \frac{e^2}{r_{a_1}} - \frac{e^2}{r_{a_2}} - \frac{e^2}{r_{b_1}} - \frac{e^2}{r_{b_2}}\right)\right]\psi = 0 \quad (64)$$

Considering the nuclei at first far apart, we may assume that the atoms will not perturb each other greatly. That is, the function governing electron 1 while in atom a will be

$$\psi_0(a,1) = \frac{1}{\sqrt{\pi}}\left(\frac{1}{a_0}\right)^{\frac{3}{2}} e^{-\frac{r_{a_1}}{a_0}}$$

and while in atom b

$$\psi_0(b,1) = \frac{1}{\sqrt{\pi}}\left(\frac{1}{a_0}\right)^{\frac{3}{2}} e^{-\frac{r_{b_1}}{a_0}}$$

In other words, we should expect the equation to be satisfied by $\psi_0(a,1)\psi_0(b,2)$ or $\psi_0(a,2)\psi_0(b,1)$, *i.e.*, either with electron 1 in atom a and 2 in atom b or vice versa. Both of these states have the same energy, and the system is therefore degenerate. This particular type of degeneracy, which results from the equivalence of the electrons involved, is called equivalence degeneracy. The foregoing approximation is justified if we neglect $\frac{e^2}{R} + \frac{e^2}{r_{12}}$ in Eq. (64), which we may do for large values of R. In this approximation the solution for the ground state of the molecule is

$$\Psi_0 = c\psi_0(a,1)\psi_0(b,2) + d\psi_0(a,2)\psi_0(b,1)$$

where c and d are constants determined by the Eqs. (62).

The evaluation of c and d leads to the important result that there exist *two* linear combinations that satisfy the conditions of the problem.   That is, two normal hydrogen atoms may interact in two possible ways.   The final result is

$$\Psi_0^{(1)} = \frac{1}{\sqrt{2 + 2S}}[\psi_0(a,1)\psi_0(b,2) + \psi_0(a,2)\psi_0(b,1)]$$

$$\Psi_0^{(2)} = \frac{1}{\sqrt{2 + 2S}}[\psi_0(a,1)\psi_0(b,2) - \psi_0(a,2)\psi_0(b,1)]$$

$$S = \int \psi_0(a,1)\psi_0(a,2)\psi_0(b,1)\psi_0(b,2)dv \qquad (65)$$

If, now, the atoms are brought closer together so that

$$\frac{e^2}{R} + \frac{e^2}{r_{12}}$$

in Eq. (64) is no longer negligible, the solutions have to be modified.   The results for the energy expressions corresponding to $\Psi_0^{(1)}$ and $\Psi_0^{(2)}$ are

$$E_0^{(1)} = \frac{L + J}{1 + S}$$

$$E_0^{(2)} = \frac{L - J}{1 - S} \qquad (66)$$

where S is given in Eq. (65), and

$$L = \int \left[\left(\frac{e^2}{R} + \frac{e^2}{r_{12}} \right) \frac{\psi_0^2(a,1)\psi_0^2(b,2) + \psi_0^2(a,2)\psi_0^2(b,1)}{2} \right.$$
$$\left. - \left(\frac{e^2}{r_{a_1}} + \frac{e^2}{r_{b_2}} \right) \frac{\psi_0^2(a,2)\psi_0^2(b,1)}{2} - \left(\frac{e^2}{r_{a_2}} + \frac{e^2}{r_{b_1}} \right) \frac{\psi_0^2(a,1)\psi_0^2(b,2)}{2} \right] dv$$

$$J = \int \left(\frac{2e^2}{R} - \frac{2e^2}{r_{12}} - \frac{e^2}{r_{a_1}} - \frac{e^2}{r_{a_2}} - \frac{e^2}{r_{b_1}} - \frac{e^2}{r_{b_2}} \right)$$
$$\psi_0(a,1)\psi_0(a,2)\psi_0(b,1)\psi_0(b,2)dv$$

In words, these expressions signify the following: When two hydrogen atoms, each in its ground state, approach each other, they may interact in two ways.   The differences manifest themselves in the Ψ functions and in the energy.   The physical significance of these two interactions is that in one case, $\Psi_0^{(1)}$, the electron spins of the two electrons are antiparallel, while in the other $\Psi_0^{(2)}$, they are parallel.   This interpretation does not come directly out of the wave equation because in the preceding simple form the spin is neglected.   It can be introduced by means of an argument based on the Pauli exclusion principle.   For further information on this question the reader is referred to the original papers on the subject[1] or to the many books dealing with atomic structure.

Before leaving the subject let us examine a little more closely the nature of the solutions (65) and (66). $E_0^{(1)}$ and $E_0^{(2)}$ are functions of R, as shown in Fig. 66. In the state 2 in which the spins of the electrons are parallel, the atoms repel each other. If the spins are antiparallel, we have conditions represented by curve 1, in which a molecule with the nuclear separation R_0 is formed. This corresponds to the observed fact that the hydrogen molecule does not have a permanent magnetic moment. If we had been discussing some molecule other than hydrogen, with a different atomic wave function, we should have found other integrals

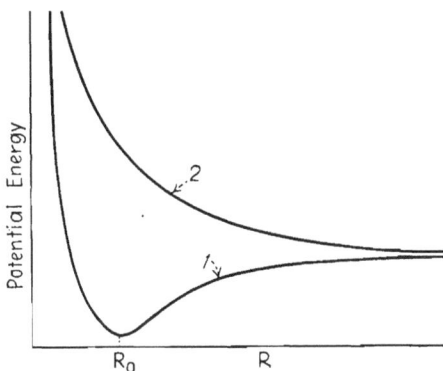

FIG. 66.—Energy as a function of atomic separation in the hydrogen molecule for the case of antiparallel and parallel spins.

L, J, and S, and hence the detail of the energy functions in Fig. 66 would have been different. In general, a group of atoms may react in various ways, and the state of lowest energy may or may not have a resultant moment, depending on the nature of the integrals L, S, and J. These integrals are different from zero only if the wave functions that they involve overlap, which they do for the hydrogen wave functions (63). The fact that there is a finite probability of finding the electron belonging to atom a in the neighborhood of atom b leads to the idea that the electrons of atoms a and b may change places. The integrals measuring this overlapping are therefore sometimes called exchange integrals, and the energies to which they give rise are called exchange

[1] W. HEITLER and F. LONDON, *Z. Physik,* **44,** 455, 1927.

energies.   Exchange energies and integrals are sometimes also called resonance energies and resonance integrals.

The spherically symmetrical wave functions of the hydrogen atoms are distorted in the hydrogen molecule.   London[1] has evaluated $\Psi\bar\Psi$ for the case of parallel and of antiparallel spins.   His results are reproduced in Fig. 67.   Since $\Psi\bar\Psi$ may be thought of for our purposes as representing an electric density, the lines in the figure represent contours of equal electric density in the molecule.   In case 1 the atoms fuse to form a molecule.   This corresponds to $E_0^{(1)}$ in Fig. 66.   In case 2 where the spins are parallel the atoms do not fuse.

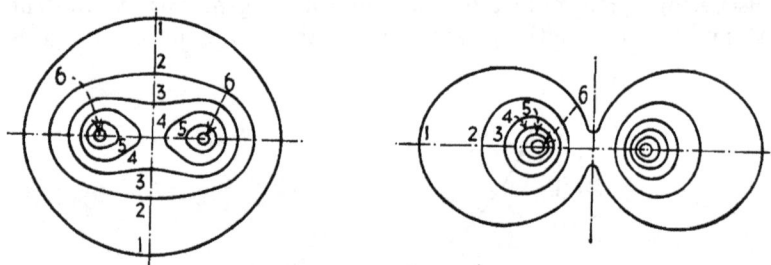

Fig. 67.—Electric density in the hydrogen molecule for antiparallel and parallel spins.

In a ferromagnetic crystal we have much the same conditions; only the state of lowest energy, as we shall see, is one in which neighboring spins are parallel.   If all the electrons in the lattice are pointing in the same direction, some particular distribution of electric density exists.   If, owing to temperature agitation, for instance, a few electron spins are reversed, the electric density will be distorted, and consequently also the potential energy curves corresponding to Fig. 66.   Changes in spin orientation will therefore change the interatomic spacings and so give rise to magnetostriction and to changes in dimensions at the magnetic transformation point where there is a great upheaval in spin orientations.

50. Heisenberg's Theory.   Molecular Fields.—In Par. 47 and 48 we saw that the magnetic elements in a ferromagnetic substance are generally spinning electrons.   The molecular field, then, is an agency tending to make the spins of electrons in adja-

[1] F. London, *Z. Physik,* **46,** 476, 1928.

cent atomic systems point in the same direction.   In Par. 49 we
saw that forces of this nature exist in a hydrogen molecule and
may be accounted for by means of equivalence degeneracy.
Electrons in neighboring atoms have a tendency to exchange
places.   The energy of this exchange depends on whether the
spins of these two electrons are parallel or antiparallel.   In the
hydrogen molecule the energy of exchange is lower when the spins
are antiparallel.   In a ferromagnetic substance we may expect
the energy of exchange to be lower when the spins are parallel.

Heisenberg[1] made the first attempts to explain ferromagnetism
in terms of exchange energies.   He pointed out that there are three
fundamentally different approaches to the problem of treating
electrons in metals.

1. Consider a gas of free electrons.   By approximation
methods introduce the effect of the fluctuating potential in an
actual lattice.

2. Consider a gas of electrons in a perfectly periodic lattice.
By approximation methods introduce the effect of irregularities.

3. Consider isolated atoms with known wave functions.   By
approximation methods calculate their interaction as they are
brought together to form a lattice.

The first two procedures were not considered to be especially
suited to the problem in question because the interactions of the
electrons among each other, which we assume to be responsible
for ferromagnetism, are not easy to calculate for such models.
The last method, which is that used in the previous paragraphs,
is, however, designed to cover just this case and was consequently
adopted by Heisenberg.   For simplicity he assumed atoms with
spherically symmetrical cores and one outer electron whose
behavior is described by hydrogen wave functions.   The total
number of atoms is $2n$.   Each atom has z neighbors, and the
perturbation energy of every pair due to exchange interaction is
given by an integral J like that used in the discussion of the
hydrogen molecule.   The exchange energy is assumed to fall off
rapidly as the interatomic distance is increased, thus justifying
the use of the nearest neighbors only for z.

Calling the resultant spin of the system $sh/2\pi$, the first part of
the problem is to find all the different possible ways in which the
individual spins can be arranged so as to produce a given resultant

[1] W. HEISENBERG, *Z. Physik*, **49**, 619, 1928.

spin s, and the energy corresponding to each of these ways.   In other words, if the resultant spin is s, this means that $2n - s$ spins are not contributing to the resultant, or that $\frac{1}{2}(2n - s)$ are antiparallel to the magnetization.   There are many ways of distributing these $\frac{1}{2}(2n - s)$ antiparallel spins among the total number $2n$.   Each way represents a certain configuration of the system and has its own energy.   The calculation of the multiplicity of the various energy levels cannot be carried out, but the most probable value of the energy E_σ for all states having a given s can be evaluated, as well as the mean square deviation from this value $\overline{\Delta E_\sigma^2}$.   The results are

$$E_\sigma = -z\frac{s^2 + n^2}{2n}J + \text{const.}$$

$$\overline{\Delta E_\sigma^2} = J^2z\frac{(n^2 - s^2)(3n^2 - s^2)}{4n^3} \tag{67}$$

The calculation of the most probable value for s under any given external conditions involves the calculation of the partition function of the system.[1]   This partition function consists of the sum over all the possible states of a system of the following function,

$$\nu(j)e^{-\frac{E(j)}{kT}}$$

where $\nu(j)$ represents the number of separate configurations of the system that have the energy $E(j)$.   This summation Heisenberg was unable to carry out because the function $\nu(j)$ is not known.   He circumvented the difficulty by assuming that the number of states between $E_\sigma + \Delta E$ and $E_\sigma + d\Delta E$ was

$$\frac{f_\sigma}{\sqrt{2\pi\overline{\Delta E_\sigma^2}}}e^{-\frac{\Delta E^2}{2\overline{\Delta E_\sigma^2}}}d\Delta E \tag{68}$$

where f_σ is the total number of states having a resultant spin s. f_σ can be calculated.   The assumption of this function is quite arbitrary, and for this reason it is difficult to determine to what extent the results arrived at by using it are reliable.   It fits the demands of Eq. (67), but so would a great many other functions that are equally plausible, and the assumption of a function

---

[1] For a discussion of partition functions, see any textbook on Statistical Mechanics, for instance that by R. H. Fowler.

differing from the Gaussian error function above would, of course, lead to different results for the magnetic and thermal properties of our model. Using Heisenberg's approximation, however, the following results are obtained:[1]

$$\frac{I_w}{I_0} = \tanh\,(a)$$

$$a = \alpha + \frac{\beta}{2}\frac{I_w}{I_0}\left[1 - \frac{\beta}{z} + \frac{\beta}{2z}\left(\frac{I_w}{I_0}\right)^2\right] \tag{69}$$

where

$$\alpha = \frac{\mu H}{kT}; \qquad \beta = \frac{zJ}{kT} \tag{70}$$

The Curie temperature is

$$\theta_w = \frac{2J}{k\left(1 - \sqrt{1 - \dfrac{8}{z}}\right)} \tag{71}$$

and the energy of magnetization is

$$E_w = -n\left\{\frac{zJ}{4}\left(\frac{I_w}{I_0}\right)^2\left(1 - \frac{2\beta}{z}\right) + \frac{J\beta}{8}\left(\frac{I_w}{I_0}\right)^4\right\} \tag{72}$$

These equations differ from the equations due to Weiss and derived in Par. 21, first, in the appearance of tanh (a) instead of the Langevin function coth $(a) - \dfrac{1}{a}$. This, as was shown in Par. 19, is a minor difference due to the assumption of only two possible orientations for the elementary particle, parallel and antiparallel to the total magnetization. The second is the appearance of the exchange energy J, or its equivalent N_w in our previous notation, in powers higher than the first. As a result, the straight lines in Fig. 15 are slightly curved. Omitting these terms, so that

$$a = \alpha + \frac{\beta}{2}\frac{I_w}{I_0}$$

---

[1] Convenient expansions for tanh (a) are

For $a \gg 1$, tanh $(a) = 1 - 2e^{-2a} + \cdots$

For $a \ll 1$, tanh $(a) = a - \dfrac{a^3}{3} + \cdots$

we get

$$\theta_w = \frac{zJ}{2k} \tag{73}$$

$$E_w = -\frac{nzJ}{4}\left(\frac{I_w}{I_0}\right)^2 \tag{74}$$

Energies J of the order of magnitude $\theta_w k$ with $\theta_w \sim 1000°$ abs. are of the right order of magnitude to be accounted for by exchange processes.

A further improvement which Heisenberg[1] was able to make was that of dropping the restriction that each atom in a ferromagnetic lattice contributes only one electron. From the saturation moments of actual substances we know that there may be more or less than one. Taking this number as y, and assuming the exchange interaction between the electrons belonging to a given atom to be large compared to the exchange interaction between the electrons of different atoms, Heisenberg calculated, with essentially the same assumptions as those used in the calculation for the case $y = 1$, the mean energy E_σ corresponding to a resultant spin s and the mean square deviation $\overline{\Delta E_\sigma^2}$. The result comes out, of course, in terms of the exchange integrals J, which enter the theory as undetermined constants. By assuming them all equal and different from zero only for adjacent atoms, he obtains

$$E_\sigma = -zy\frac{s^2 + n^2}{2n}J$$

and

$$\overline{\Delta E_\sigma^2} = J^2 zy\frac{(n^2 - s^2)(3n^2 - s^2)}{4n^3}$$

where the total number of electrons, as before, is $2n$. In order to arrive at a formula for the magnetization, it is again necessary to know the actual distribution of energy levels. Heisenberg points out that the distribution of levels at some distance from E_σ has considerable influence on the final result and that $\overline{\Delta E_\sigma^2}$ does not give the desired information. By calculating $\overline{\Delta E_\sigma^3}$, $\overline{\Delta E_\sigma^4}$, . . . , $\overline{\Delta E_\sigma^l}$ the result cannot be achieved either, because a real improve-

---

[1] W. HEISENBERG, "Probleme der modernen Physik," ed. by P. Debye, 1928.

ment on the foregoing comes only when values of $l \sim n$ are considered. The conclusion is that for the present we must give up
the idea of deriving a magnetic equation of state accurately.
Assuming a Gaussian distribution of levels, as before, Heisenberg
obtains the expression[1]

$$\frac{I_w}{I_0} = \frac{1}{y} \frac{y e^{ay} + (y-1)e^{a(y-1)} + \cdots - y e^{-ay}}{e^{ay} + e^{a(y-1)} + \cdots + e^{-ay}}$$

$$a = \alpha + \frac{y\beta}{2}\left(1 - \frac{\beta}{z}\right)\frac{I_w}{I_0} + \frac{y\beta^2}{4z}\left(\frac{I_w}{I_0}\right)^3$$

$$\alpha = \frac{\mu H}{kT} \qquad \beta = \frac{zJ}{kT} \tag{75}$$

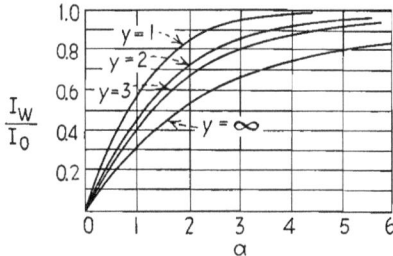

FIG. 68.—Plot of Eq. (75).

These expressions may be simplified without essentially altering
their content by omitting terms involving higher powers of J
than the first or by putting

$$a = \alpha + \frac{y\beta}{2}\frac{I_w}{I_0} = \frac{\mu H}{kT} + \frac{zJ}{2kT}\frac{I_w}{I_0} \tag{76}$$

as in the Weiss theory. Instead of the universal function $L(a)$, or
tanh (a), to represent magnetization we have

$$\frac{I_w}{I_0} = L(y,a) \tag{77}$$

where $L(y,a)$ is given by Eq. (75) and reduces[1] to the usual $L(a)$
for $y = \infty$ and to tanh (a) for $y = 1$. In Fig. 68 Eq. (75) is
plotted for various values of y, and in Fig. 69 the spontaneous
magnetization is plotted as a function of the temperature by
using both Eqs. (75) and (76). The curve for $y = \infty$ is that

[1] See Par. 19.

shown in Fig. 16, which was obtained on the basis of the Weiss theory. Figures 68 and 69 are taken from Debye's article in vol. VI of the "Handbuch der Radiologie."

Bloch,[1] on the other hand, attacked this problem in a different way and so avoided having to make the arbitrary assumption of a Gaussian distribution of energy levels. He found that at low temperatures the system should be treated with the Einstein-Bose statistics and that in this region the spontaneous magnetization can be expressed by

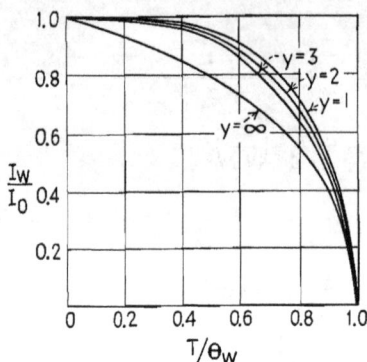

Fig. 69.—Spontaneous magnetization as a function of temperature.

$$\frac{I_w}{I_0} = 1 - \gamma\left(\frac{T}{\theta'}\right)^{\frac{3}{2}} \qquad (78)$$

where γ depends on the lattice structure, and θ' is of the order of magnitude of the Curie temperature. Heisenberg's treatment gives for this quantity, neglecting powers of J higher than the first,

$$\frac{I_w}{I_0} = 1 - 2e^{-2\frac{\theta_w}{T}} \qquad (79)$$

as can be seen from the expansion for tanh (a) given above, while the Weiss equation reduces to

$$\frac{I_w}{I_0} = 1 - \frac{T}{3\theta_w} \qquad (80)$$

which may readily be found by substituting the proper expression for a in terms of θ_w as defined in Eq. (48) into the expansions for $L(a)$ given in Eq. (42).

There is some doubt as to the validity of the assumption that the exchange energy falls off sufficiently rapidly with interatomic separation to justify the neglect of the interaction between all but the nearest neighbors in the lattice. When one considers that at distances only slightly greater than the distance from an atom to its nearest neighbors there are several times z atoms, the neglect of these others would seem a matter for further investiga-

[1] F. Bloch, *Z. Physik*, **61**, 206, 1930.

tion. Powell[1] suggests that there is evidence based on considerations involving the elastic constants that in iron the exchange energy increases with R (see Fig. 65) for small values of R.

As was pointed out in the beginning of this section, there are various possible approaches to a mathematical formulation of metallic properties, and a choice depends only on which is most convenient to handle. It is known that the electrical properties of ferromagnetic substances undergo abrupt changes at the Curie point, but this does not necessarily mean that the same electrons are responsible for both ferromagnetism and electrical conductivity. Bloch[2] has attacked the problem of the molecular

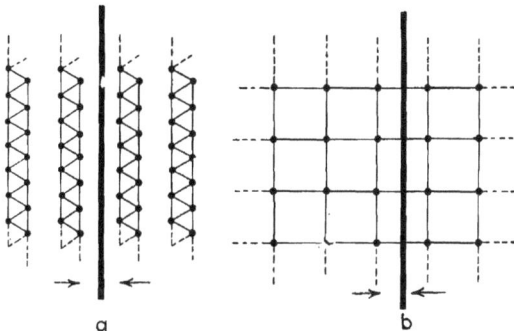

FIG. 70.

field starting with the wave functions for free electrons, rather than the hydrogen functions used by Heisenberg. Assuming an interaction between electrons, he obtained essentially similar results. An analysis by Slater[3] indicates, however, that the conduction electrons are not the ferromagnetic ones but that the incomplete next lower group in the atom is responsible.

A most interesting problem is that of determining what makes a metal ferromagnetic. On Heisenberg's theory the existence of ferromagnetism depends, among other things, on the sign of the exchange integral and on the number of nearest neighbors of an atom. Bloch's work indicates that not only the number of nearest neighbors but their grouping as well is important. For

[1] F. C. POWELL, *Proc. Phys. Soc.*, **42**, 390, 1930.

[2] F. BLOCH, *Z. Physik*, **57**, 545, 1929; p. 67 of "Leipziger Vorträge," ed. by P. Debye, Hirzel, Leipzig, 1930.

[3] J. C. SLATER, *Phys. Rev.*, **35**, 509, 1930.

instance, in Fig. 70 two plane distributions of atoms are illustrated in each of which z, the number of nearest neighbors, is equal to 4. In case (a) it is possible for two parts of the array to be magnetized in different directions without affecting the energy of the crystal due to the mutual energy of nearest neighbors at all. In case (b) this is not possible. The energies of the states in which the arrays can exist would therefore in the two cases be different, and it follows that the magnetic properties of crystals will depend not only on the number of neighbors but in general also on their arrangement with respect to each other.

The definition of ferromagnetism usually adopted, *viz.*, the existence of spontaneous magnetization as given by the Weiss type of equation [(45) or (69)], is not entirely satisfactory. This difficulty of finding a definition of ferromagnetism that is both in accordance with customary usage and at the same time precise is of secondary importance. It results from the fact that substances having properties anywhere between a typical paramagnetism and a typical ferromagnetism are quite conceivable, and there is no reason for arbitrarily separating the two types at any given stage. Nevertheless, the fact remains that iron, nickel, and cobalt have very different magnetic properties from other elements, and the reason for this is not clearly understood. What is the cause of this peculiar behavior, and what other substances show similar characteristics? Accurate magnetic investigations over wide ranges of temperature may possibly reveal that ferromagnetism or some related kind of pseudo-ferromagnetism is not so rare among the elements and other substances as it is now considered.[1]

A comparison of the results obtained in the preceding pages with experiment will be undertaken in the next chapter. It should be noticed, however, that the same objections that were raised against the Weiss theory in Par. 21 are equally applicable here. The equations characterize ferromagnetism by means of a spontaneous magnetization which is not experimentally observed, and in order to reconcile theory with experiment it is necessary to assume that the spontaneous magnetization covers small

---

[1] Gd has recently been found to be ferromagnetic at low temperatures. G. Urbain, P. Weiss, and F. Trombe, *Compt. rend.*, **200**, 2132, 1935. Progress has also recently been made in specifying the conditions for ferromagnetism. J. C. Slater, *Phys. Rev.*, **49**, 537, 931, 1936.

regions in a crystal only and that the resultant observed magnetization is due to the mutual reorientation of these regions with respect to each other. The introduction of assumptions of this kind is highly undesirable. If such equations as (69) are applicable to small regions only, there ought to be something in their derivation to indicate why this is so.

These, briefly, are the results due to the quantum theory. The one definite result is that the Weiss molecular field is due to exchange forces tending to make neighboring spins parallel rather than antiparallel and that these exchange forces have a small range which we may as an approximation assume not to extend beyond the nearest neighbors of the atom from which they originate. The other results obtained are in many respects unsatisfactory. The significance of Heisenberg's treatment is obscured by the arbitrary assumption of a Gaussian distribution of energies, and Bloch's work, on the other hand, is unfortunately limited in scope. Instead of delving more deeply into the methods used by these authors in an attempt to discover which of their results are due to which of their assumptions, we shall study the properties of a few simple models and correlate the results so obtained with those of the preceding pages. A satisfactory theory of ferromagnetism would have to make possible the derivation of a magnetic equation of state essentially similar to the equation of state of ordinary matter, and the mathematical difficulties in the way of such derivations, quite apart from the physical problem, are well known. The best that we can do at present is to give an interpretation of the quantitative relations already known in terms of a model that we shall assume to have those properties which we cannot derive.

51. Ising's Treatment of the Linear Chain.—Using the information obtained from the quantum theory that molecular fields are due to short-range forces, we may set up the following model as a first approximation to a ferromagnetic crystal: Magnetic dipoles are arranged in a geometrical array in which they interact with their nearest neighbors only and in such a way that

1. All dipoles point either to the right or to the left but never in intermediate directions (dipoles pointing to the right we shall call positive; to the left, negative).

2. The energy of the array in the absence of magnetic fields is directly proportional to the number of antiparallel neighbors.

Various arrays are characterized by differences in the number of nearest neighbors, which we shall designate by z. The values of z for typical arrays are given in Table II.

Table II.—The Number of Nearest Neighbors in Several
Geometrical Arrangements

Type	z
Linear chain	2
Simple cubic lattice	6
Body-centered cubic lattice	8
Face-centered cubic lattice	12

The energy required to reverse the orientation of a single dipole in an otherwise saturated lattice we shall call 2ϵ; and consequently the energy of every pair of neighbors of which one is positive and the other negative will be $2\epsilon/z$; and the total energy of an array in which there are p such pairs will be $2p\epsilon/z$. If magnetic fields are present, a further term must be added. Calling the total number of particles in the array N, of which n_+ are pointing to the right and n_- to the left, we have

$$N = n_+ + n_- \tag{81}$$

$$\frac{I}{I_0} = \frac{\mu(n_+ - n_-)}{\mu(n_+ + n_-)} = \frac{n_+ - n_-}{N} \tag{82}$$

and for the energy of the system

$$E(n_+, n_-, p) = -\mu(n_+ - n_-)H + 2p\frac{\epsilon}{z} \tag{83}$$

or, putting $\alpha = \mu H/kT$ and $\beta = \epsilon/kT$,

$$\frac{E(n_+, n_-, p)}{kT} = (n_+ - n_-)\alpha + \frac{2p}{z}\beta$$

The problem to be solved is that of finding the magnetic and thermal properties of this system in thermodynamic equilibrium. In order to obtain a solution it is necessary to know the number of ways $\nu(n_+, n_-, p)$ that the dipoles can be arranged for any given value of the energy, *i.e.*, keeping n_+, n_-, and p fixed. If this function ν is known, the partition function Z can be calculated:

$$Z = \sum_{n_+, n_-, p} \nu(n_+, n_-, p)e^{-\frac{E(n_+, n_-, p)}{kT}}, \tag{84}$$

and the probability of finding the system in the state specified by n_+, n_-, and p is simply

$$w(n_+, n_-, p) = \frac{1}{Z}\nu(n_+, n_-, p)e^{-\frac{E(n_+,n_-,p)}{kT}} \tag{85}$$

The magnetization produced by a field H at a temperature T is

$$I = \frac{1}{Z}\sum_{n_+,n_-,p} \mu(n_+ - n_-)\nu(n_+, n_-, p)e^{-\frac{E(n_+,n_-,p)}{kT}}$$
$$= \mu\frac{\partial \log Z}{\partial \alpha} \tag{86}$$

and the internal energy in the absence of a magnetic field is

$$E = \frac{2}{Z}\sum_{n_+,n_-,p} \frac{2p\epsilon}{z}\nu(n_+, n_-, p)e^{-\frac{E(n_+,n_-,p)}{kT}}$$
$$= \frac{2\epsilon}{z}\frac{\partial \log Z}{\partial \beta} \tag{87}$$

This formulation of the problem is very similar to that due to Heisenberg, and the difficulty that we shall encounter in finding a suitable function ν is the same that Heisenberg circumvented by the arbitrary assumption of Gaussian distribution of energies.

In 1925, or before Heisenberg had given his interpretation of the molecular field in terms of exchange energies, Ising[1] attempted to explain ferromagnetism by means of the model sketched above. He was able to obtain a solution only for the case of the linear chain which did not show spontaneous magnetization, and consequently only a brief note on his work was published. Knowing as we do, however, that short-range molecular fields actually exist, his work has taken on a new importance, first, because crystals in which each atom reacts with only two neighbors, as in the case of the linear chain, may yet be found; and, second, because this is one of the only two cases in which the problem of ferromagnetism has been rigorously solved even in the preceding simplified form. The derivation given in this section has been taken from Ising's unpublished dissertation at the University of Hamburg.

The arrangement of dipoles in a linear chain may conveniently be described in terms of the number of groups within which all

[1] E. Ising, *Z. Physik*, **31**, 253, 1925.

the dipoles are either positive or negative. In Fig. 71, for instance, there are four groups. At the extremity of adjacent groups, oppositely directed dipoles meet and give rise to an energy $2\epsilon/z$, which in this case reduces simply to ϵ as $z = 2$. The number of groups is necessarily either p or $p + 1$, depending on whether groups of like or of opposite sign are to be found at the extremities of the chain.

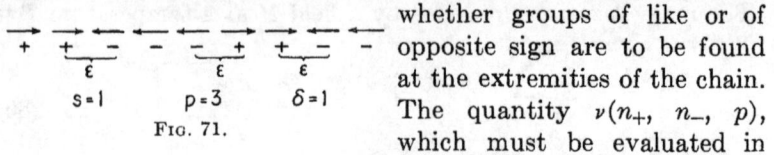

Fig. 71.

The quantity $\nu(n_+, n_-, p)$, which must be evaluated in order to make it possible to carry out the operations indicated in Eqs. (86) and (87), is in this case the number of ways in which a number N may be represented as the sum of p or $p + 1$ whole numbers $\geqslant 1$, different orders of the terms being counted separately, subject to the condition that the sum of alternate terms be either n_+ or n_-.

The evaluation of a related function $\nu_r(m)$ representing the number of ways in which a number m may be represented as the sum of r whole numbers, without reference to the sum of alternate terms, may be carried out by means of the binomial theorem. We have

$$(1 \pm x)^n = 1 \pm nx + \frac{n(n-1)}{2!}x^2 + \cdots$$

and consequently

$$\frac{x}{1-x} = i\sum_{1}^{\infty} x^i \qquad (88)$$

$$\left(\frac{x}{1-x}\right)^r = \left(i\sum_{1}^{\infty} x^i\right)^r = i_1, i_2, \cdots, i_r \sum_{1}^{\infty} x^{i_1+i_2+\cdots+i_r}$$

$$= m\sum_{r}^{\infty} \nu_r(m)x^m$$

the coefficient of x^m being just the quantity that we are looking for. Again, according to the binomial theorem, we have

$$(1-x)^{-r} = 1 + rx + \frac{r(r+1)}{2!}x^2 + \cdots = k\sum_{0}^{\infty} \frac{(r+k-1)!}{(r-1)!k!}x^k$$

and writing m for $k + r$ and with the simplified notation

$$\binom{m}{r} = \frac{m!}{(m-r)!r!}$$

we have

$$\left(\frac{x}{1-x}\right)^r = m \sum_r^{\infty} \binom{m-1}{r-1} x^m \tag{89}$$

Comparing the coefficients of x^m in (88) and (89), the desired expression is found to be

$$\nu_r(m) = \binom{m-1}{r-1} \tag{90}$$

Let us divide the arrangements of positive and negative elements in the chain into two classes: (a) those having a positive element at the left end of the chain and (b) those having a negative element at the left end of the chain; and let us consider first case a.   In this case we shall call the number of negative groups $s + \delta$, δ being either 0 or 1 depending on whether there is a positive or a negative group at the right end of the chain.   The number of positive groups consequently is $s + 1$; and s and p are related by the equation $p = 2s + \delta$.   Consider, now, the n_+ positive elements in a row and choose $s + \delta$ places at which the negative elements are to be inserted.   The n_- negative elements may be arranged in these places in

$$\binom{n_- - 1}{s + \delta - 1}$$

ways.   Likewise, the $s + 1$ places for inserting negative elements may be chosen in

$$\binom{n_+ - 1}{s}$$

ways, so that the total number of arrangements in class a is

$$\binom{n_+ - 1}{s}\binom{n_- - 1}{s + \delta - 1}$$

The total number of arrangements in class b may be found by interchanging n_+ and n_- in the preceding expression, so that the total number of arrangements in classes a and b together becomes

$$\nu(n_+,\ n_-,\ p) = \delta \sum_0^1 \binom{n_+ - 1}{s}\binom{n_- - 1}{s + \delta - 1} +$$

$$\binom{n_- - 1}{s}\binom{n_+ - 1}{s + \delta - 1} \quad (91)$$

The evaluation of Z is now reduced to carrying out the summation in Eq. 84:

$$Z = n_+,\ n_-\sum_0^N s \sum_0^\infty \nu(n_+,\ n_-,\ p)e^{(n_+ - n_-)\alpha - (2s + \delta)\beta} \quad (92)$$

The summation with respect to n_+ and n_- is to be carried out over all values satisfying Eq. (81), and the summation with respect to s can include all values up to ∞ as the binomial coefficients automatically vanish when s is too large. The summation can be carried out in a variety of ways, of which the one given below has been chosen because it is both rigorous and easy to follow, although it lacks the mathematical elegance of the methods more usually used for such problems.

The partition function Z is a function of N, the total number of particles in the system, and we may therefore use it in defining a new function $F(x)$ as follows:

$$F(x) = N\sum_0^\infty Z(N)x^N \quad (93)$$

In evaluating $F(x)$ we may sum over n_+ and n_- separately, so that with the following abbreviations we get

$$A_1 = e^\alpha \qquad A_2 = e^{-\alpha} \qquad B = e^{-\beta}$$

$$G_i = \frac{xA_i}{1 - xA_i} \qquad i = 1 \text{ or } 2$$

$$F(x) = s\sum_0^\infty \delta\sum_0^1 B^{2s + \delta}\left\{\left[n_+\sum_0^\infty \binom{n_+ - 1}{s}(A_1x)^{n_+}\right]\cdot\right.$$

$$\left[n_-\sum_0^\infty \binom{n_- - 1}{s + \delta - 1}(A_2x)^{n_-}\right] + \left[n_+\sum_0^\infty \binom{n_+ - 1}{s + \delta - 1}(A_1x)^{n_+}\right]\cdot$$

$$\left.\left[n_-\sum_0^\infty \binom{n_- - 1}{s}(A_2x)^{n_-}\right]\right\}$$

The summation with respect to n_+ and n_-, according to the first of Eqs. (88), reduces this expression to

$$F(x) = s \sum_0^\infty \delta \sum_0^1 B^{2s+\delta}(G_1G_2)^s[G_1G_2^\delta + G_2G_1^\delta]$$

and similarly the summation with respect to s and δ leaves us finally with

$$F(x) = \frac{G_1 + G_2 + 2BG_1G_2}{1 - B^2G_1G_2}$$

which is equivalent to

$$F(x) = \frac{2x[\cosh \alpha - (1 - B)x]}{1 - 2x \cosh \alpha + (1 - B^2)x^2}$$

Defining ω_1 and ω_2 in terms of the denominator of this expression as follows:

$$(1 - \omega_1x)(1 - \omega_2x) = 1 - 2x \cosh \alpha + (1 - B^2)x^2$$
$$\omega_1 = \cosh \alpha + \sqrt{\sinh^2 \alpha + B^2}$$
$$\omega_2 = \cosh \alpha - \sqrt{\sinh^2 \alpha + B^2}$$

we get

$$F(x) = \frac{2x[\cosh \alpha - (1 - B)x]}{(1 - \omega_1x)(1 - \omega_2x)}$$

or

$$F(x) = \frac{a_1x}{1 - \omega_1x} + \frac{a_2x}{1 - \omega_2x} \tag{94}$$

where

$$a_1 = \frac{2[\omega_1 \cosh \alpha - 1 + B]}{\omega_1 - \omega_2} = \omega_1 + \frac{B(1 - B)}{\sqrt{\sinh^2 \alpha + B^2}}$$

$$a_2 = \frac{2[\omega_2 \cosh \alpha - 1 + B]}{\omega_2 - \omega_1} = -\omega_2 + \frac{B(1 - B)}{\sqrt{\sinh^2 \alpha + B^2}}$$

Again, using the expansion (88), we may rewrite (94):

$$F(x) = N \sum_0^\infty \left(\frac{a_1}{\omega_1}\omega_1^N + \frac{a_2}{\omega_2}\omega_2^N\right)x^N \tag{95}$$

and, finally, comparing the coefficients of x^N in (93) and (95), we get

$$Z = \frac{a_1}{\omega_1}\omega_1^N + \frac{a_2}{\omega_2}\omega_2^N \tag{96}$$

$\omega_1 > 1$ and $\omega_2 < 1$; and consequently, for large values of N, $a_2\omega_2^{N-1}$ may be neglected in comparison with $a_1\omega_1^{N-1}$. Taking the logarithm of $Z(N)$, we get

$$\log Z = \log \frac{a_1}{\omega_1} + N \log \omega_1$$

The first term is negligible compared to the second for large N, and therefore, from Eqs. (86) and (87),

$$I = \mu N \frac{\partial \log \omega_1}{\partial \alpha} = I_0 \frac{\sinh \alpha}{\sqrt{\sinh^2 \alpha + e^{-\frac{2\epsilon}{kT}}}} \tag{97}$$

$$E = \epsilon N \frac{\partial \log \omega_1}{\partial \beta} = \frac{N\epsilon}{e^{\frac{\epsilon}{kT}} + 1} \tag{98}$$

From these expressions may be derived the atomic specific heat σ and the initial susceptibility χ_0:

$$\sigma = \frac{1}{N}\frac{\partial E}{\partial T}\bigg]_{H=0} = k\left[\frac{\dfrac{\epsilon}{2kT}}{\cosh \dfrac{\epsilon}{2kT}}\right]^2 \tag{99}$$

$$\chi_0 = \frac{\partial I}{\partial H}\bigg]_{H=0}, \qquad \frac{I_0\,\mu}{\chi_0\,\epsilon} = \frac{kT}{\epsilon}e^{-\frac{\epsilon}{kT}} \tag{100}$$

According to Eq. (97), the magnetization vanishes in zero field. This in itself is not sufficient to preclude the possibility of spontaneous magnetization. According to Eq. (86), I is defined by

$$I = n_+, \; n\sum(n_+ - n_-)\mu w(n_+ - n_-) \tag{101}$$

where $w(n_+ - n_-) =$ the probability of finding the magnetization I,

$$w(I) = w(n_+ - n_-) = p\sum w(n_+, n_-, p)$$

$w(I)$ may have either of the forms shown in **Fig. 72** and still give zero magnetization in zero field, and in order to exclude the possibility of spontaneous magnetization it is necessary to show that the conditions are those illustrated in case b. For large values of the quantities n_+, n_-, and s it is possible to simplify Eq. (91) by using Stirling's formula

$$\lim_{n \to \infty} n! = \sqrt{2\pi n}\left(\frac{n}{e}\right)^n \tag{102}$$

and consequently, neglecting small terms,

$$\log w(n_+, n_-, p) = -\log Z + n_+ \log n_+ + n_- \log n_- - (n_+ - s) \log (n_+ - s) - (n_- - s) \log (n_- - s) - 2s \log s + (n_+ - n_-)\alpha - 2s\beta$$

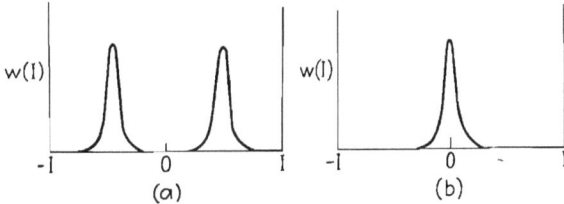

Fig. 72.

The values of n_+ and s for which this quantity has a maximum may be found by solving the equations

$$\frac{\partial \log w}{\partial s} = 0$$

$$\frac{\partial \log w}{\partial n_+} = 0$$

(noting that $n_+ + n_- = N$) which reduce to

$$\frac{(n_+ - s)(n_- - s)}{s^2} = e^{2\beta}$$

$$\frac{n_+(n_- - s)}{n_-(n_+ - s)} = e^{-2\alpha}$$

Eliminating s and solving for $(n_+ - n_-)/(n_+ + n_-)$, one gets

$$\frac{I}{I_0} = \frac{\sinh \alpha}{\sqrt{\sinh^2 \alpha + e^{-\frac{2\epsilon}{kT}}}}$$

as above, or that for $H = 0$ $w(I)$ has a maximum for $I = 0$.

This result holds only for large samples. For small values of N and at sufficiently low temperatures $w(I)$ may be expected to have two maxima, as in case a of Fig. 72, and these maxima would constitute proper evidence for the existence of regions of

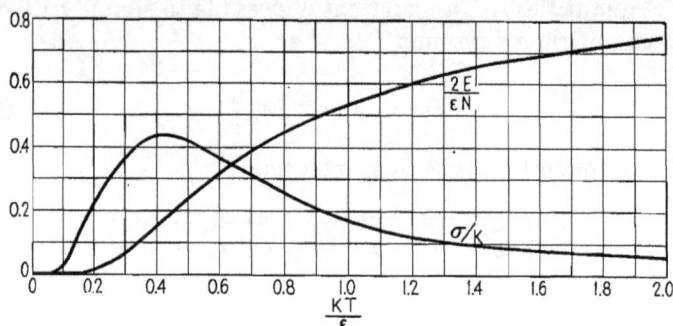

Fig. 73.—The energy and specific heat of Ising's linear chain of atoms.

spontaneous magnetization such as have been assumed to exist in actual ferromagnetic materials.

The energy and specific heat of the linear chain are plotted in Fig. 73. Materials with $z = 2$ are not known. It should, however, be observed that the anomalies in the specific heat occur at temperatures for which kT is considerably less than ϵ;

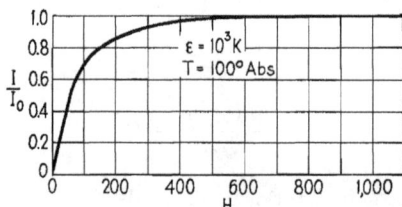

Fig. 74.—Magnetization curve of Ising's linear chain of atoms.

and consequently if ϵ is of the order of $500k$, as it is in known ferromagnetics, the anomalies are to be expected below or near room temperature.

The magnetization given by Eq. (97) is plotted in Fig. 74, assuming $\epsilon = 1000k$ and for $T = 100°$ abs. The corresponding curve for $T = 300°$ abs. would be a straight line with only a very small slope, and the behavior in the neighborhood of room temperature would be essentially that of a paramagnetic sub-

stance with a rather larger susceptibility than one is accustomed
to find in actual materials.

**52. Application of Ising's Method to Multidimensional
Crystals.**—The second type of crystal for which it is possible to
carry out calculations like those of the previous section is a multidimensional crystal in which every atom is equidistant from
every other one. Defining the energy again as in Eq. (83), it
follows that the term $2p\epsilon/z$ (p being the number of pairs of nearest
neighbors having oppositely directed magnetic moments) is in
this problem independent of the arrangement of the positive and
negative elements among each other. Each positive moment
is a member of n_- antiparallel pairs, and since there are n_+ positive moments, it follows that all told there are n_+n_- antiparallel
pairs in every arrangement of n_+ positive and n_- negative elements among each other. Replacing p by n_+n_- and z by $N - 1$
in Eq. (83), we have

$$\frac{E(n_+, n_-)}{kT} = -(n_+ - n_-)\alpha + \frac{2n_+n_-}{N-1}\beta \qquad (103)$$

The number of arrangements $\nu(n_+, n_-)$ having this energy is
simply the total possible number of arrangements of the elements
of the system. Consider the N places in our multidimensional
crystal at which the positive and negative elements are to be
placed, and let us count first the number of ways in which the
positive elements may be distributed. A place for the first positive particle can be chosen in N ways. Having chosen any one
of the N places for the first particle, there are $N - 1$ places for
the second particle, $N - 2$ for the third, etc., and $N - n_+ + 1$
places for the last. The total number of ways of distributing the
n_+ particles therefore is

$$N(N - 1)(N - 2) \cdots (N - n_+ + 1) = \frac{N!}{n_-!}$$

Having filled in the positive elements, the negative elements can
be introduced in only one way, *viz.*, by filling in the n_- empty
places. The total number of arrangements is therefore the preceding number except for the fact that in our count we have
included as distinct arrangements those obtained by interchanging positive elements among each other. For instance, we have
counted an arrangement in which the first positive element is in

a place a and the second in a place b as distinct from an arrangement in which the first element is in place b and the second in place a. The interchange of the first and second, or of any two identical elements, leaves the system unchanged, and such duplication must therefore be removed from our count. The n_+ positive elements can be interchanged in $n_+!$ ways. Dividing the number of arrangements counted by $n_+!$, we get

$$\nu(n_+, n_-) = \frac{N!}{n_+! n_-!} \tag{104}$$

and finally by the application of Stirling's theorem and substituting (103) and (104) in (85), and neglecting small quantities,

$$\log w(n_+, n_-) = -\log Z + N \log N - n_+ \log n_+ -$$
$$n_- \log n_- + (n_+ - n_-)\alpha - 2\frac{n_+ n_-}{N}\beta$$

The value of n_+ and n_- for which the foregoing expression has a maximum may be found by putting

$$\frac{\partial \log w}{\partial n_+} = 0$$

which gives

$$-\log n_+ + \log n_- + 2\alpha + \frac{2(n_+ - n_-)}{N}\beta = 0$$

$$\log \frac{n_+}{n_-} = \log \frac{I_0 + I}{I_0 - I} = 2\left(\alpha + \beta\frac{I}{I_0}\right)$$

$$I = I_0 \tanh\left(\alpha + \beta\frac{I}{I_0}\right) \tag{105}$$

This is the equation of the Weiss-Heisenberg theory of ferromagnetism. In the next section we shall discuss why our multi-dimensional crystal should have properties so similar to those of actual materials. The Curie temperature, at which spontaneous magnetization disappears, and the initial susceptibility are found from (105) to be

$$\theta = \frac{\epsilon}{k} \tag{106}$$

$$\frac{I_0 \mu}{\chi_0 \epsilon} = \frac{kT}{\epsilon} - 1 = \frac{T}{\theta} - 1 \quad \text{for} \quad T > \theta \tag{107}$$

The energy in the absence of external fields, as defined in (103), can be written in terms of the magnetization, as defined in (104):

$$E = \frac{\epsilon N}{2}\left[1 - \left(\frac{I}{I_0}\right)^2\right] \tag{108}$$

from which it follows that the atomic specific heat is

$$\sigma = k\left\{\frac{(I/I_0)^2[1 - (I/I_0)^2](T/\theta)^2}{1 - \left[1 - \left(\frac{I}{I_0}\right)^2\right]\frac{T}{\theta}}\right\} \tag{109}$$

The foregoing results are illustrated in Figs. 75 to 78. The jump in the specific heat at the Curie temperature is

$$\Delta\sigma = \tfrac{3}{2}k \tag{110}$$

53. Reversed Spins Treated as a Perfect Gas.—The results of the previous section are due to the fact that the intensity of magnetization of the z neighbors of any one atom is equal to the intensity of magnetization of the entire sample. To show this, consider any particular atom of a crystal in which each atom has z neighbors, and define ν_+ and ν_- as the number of these neighbors that are, respectively, positive and negative, and i, the local relative intensity of magnetization of these z neighbors, by

$$i = \frac{\mu(\nu_+ - \nu_-)}{\mu(\nu_+ + \nu_-)} = \frac{\nu_+ - \nu_-}{z} \tag{111}$$

where $\nu_+ + \nu_- = z$, $\nu_+/z = \tfrac{1}{2}(1 + i)$, and $\nu_-/z = \tfrac{1}{2}(1 - i)$. Defining the energy of the atom in question as in Eq. (83),

$$-\mu H + \frac{2p\epsilon}{z}$$

we find that the positive and negative orientations of the atom have energies that, divided by kT, are

$$\frac{E_+}{kT} = -\frac{\mu H}{kT} + \frac{2\nu/\epsilon}{zkT} = -\alpha + (1 + i)\beta$$

$$\frac{E_-}{kT} = +\frac{\mu H}{kT} + \frac{2\nu_+\epsilon}{zkT} = \alpha + (1 - i)\beta$$

respectively. The probability of finding the atom in either of these states is

$$ce^{-\frac{E_+}{kT}} \quad \text{or} \quad ce^{-\frac{E_-}{kT}}$$

so that we get for the contribution of the atom in question to the magnetization

$$\frac{I(i)}{\mu} = \frac{\mu c e^{-\frac{E_+}{kT}} - \mu c e^{-\frac{E_-}{kT}}}{\mu c e^{-\frac{E_+}{kT}} + \mu c e^{-\frac{E_-}{kT}}} = \tanh\,(\alpha + i\beta) \tag{112}$$

$I(i)$ being a function of the *local* intensity of magnetization. The magnetization of the entire sample will then be Eq. (112) summed over all the atoms of the system and divided by their total number N, or

$$\frac{I}{I_0} = \frac{1}{N} \sum_N \frac{I(i)}{\mu} = i \sum_{-1}^{+1} \frac{N(i)}{N} \frac{I(i)}{\mu} = i \sum_{-1}^{+1} w(i) \frac{I(i)}{\mu} \tag{113}$$

where $N(i)$ is the number of atoms for which the local intensity is i, and $w(i)$ is the probability that the local magnetization at any point be i.

Similarly, we obtain for the energy of any atom

$$E(i) = \epsilon(1 - i \tanh i\beta) \tag{114}$$

and for the total energy E of the sample

$$\frac{E}{\epsilon N} = \frac{1}{2} i \sum_{-1}^{+1} w(i) E(i) \tag{115}$$

the factor $\frac{1}{2}$ being introduced to compensate for the fact that in the sum the energy of every antiparallel pair is counted twice, once for each member of the pair.   The summations are for all values of i, which, according to (111), are

$$\frac{-z}{z}, \quad \frac{-(z-2)}{z}, \quad \cdots \quad \frac{z-2}{z}, \quad \frac{z}{z}$$

If in any model we confine our attention to states for which every atom is surrounded by a local intensity $i = I/I_0$, *i.e.*, if the local intensity is everywhere equal to the total magnetization, we have

$$w(i) = 1 \quad \text{if} \quad i = \frac{I}{I_0}$$

$$w(i) = 0 \quad \text{if} \quad i \neq \frac{I}{I_0}$$

and therefore

$$\frac{I}{I_0} = \tanh\left(\alpha + \beta\frac{I}{I_0}\right) \tag{116}$$

and

$$E = \frac{\epsilon N}{2}\left[1 - \left(\frac{I}{I_0}\right)^2\right] \tag{117}$$

as in the case of the multidimensional crystal, in confirmation of the statement made at the beginning of this section. Consequently, if for any particular values of H and T the magnetization of an actual crystal is homogeneous in the preceding sense, then it follows that under these circumstances the properties of the crystal should be those given by Eqs. (116) and (117).

In an actual crystal the local intensity will not, in general, be equal to the average total intensity for two reasons. In the first place, reversed spins will tend to cluster together because the exchange energies are equivalent to short-range attractive forces between spins of like sign. This clustering together is the same phenomenon that is found in the density fluctuations of an imperfect gas. At low temperatures and at high concentrations we have the very large fluctuations resulting from the coexistence of the liquid and vapor phases. At high temperatures and not too great concentrations the material evaporates and may be treated as a perfect gas. Even in this state, however, there are still density fluctuations from point to point in small regions of the gas, as was pointed out in Par. 28. Similarly, in the case of our ferromagnetic models, at high temperatures and for low concentrations of reversed spins, the fluctuations due to the attractive forces become insignificant, but there remain the fluctuations resulting from the fact that i is measured in a small volume comparable in extent to the interatomic spacings.

In this section we shall discuss the type of fluctuations to be expected when the attractive forces between reversed spins may be neglected. This involves the evaluation of the function $w(i)$ on the assumption that the probability that any given one of the z neighbors be positive is simply n_+/N and independent of the sign of the remaining $z - 1$ neighbors. From the foregoing it follows that the probability that any particular number ν_+ of the neighbors be positive is

$$\left(\frac{n_+}{N}\right)^{\nu_+}$$

and that the remaining ν_- be negative is

$$\left(\frac{n_-}{N}\right)^{\nu_-}$$

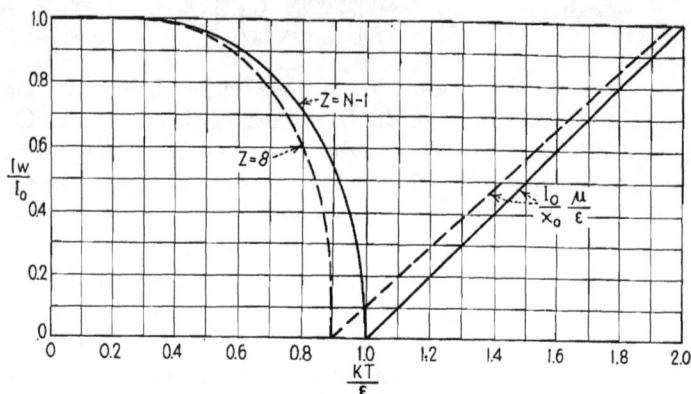

FIG. 75.

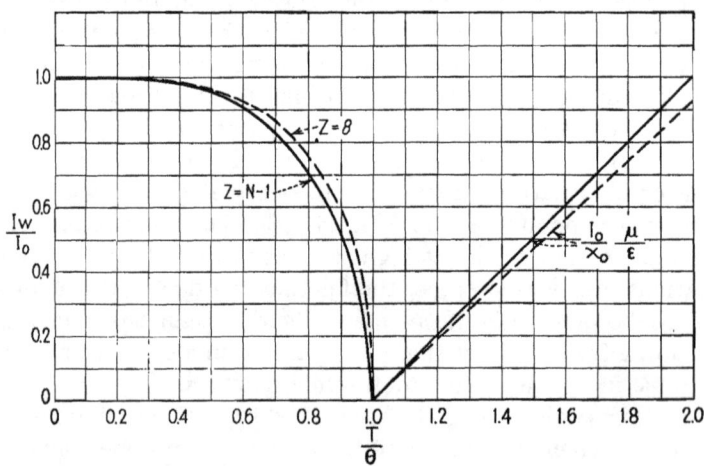

FIG. 76.

FIGS. 75, 76.—Magnetization of ferromagnetic atoms treated as a perfect gas.

The probability of finding that among the z neighbors ν_+ are positive and ν_- negative, without regard to their relative positions, is the product of the preceding two quantities multiplied by the number of possible arrangements among each other, or

$$w(i) = \frac{z!}{\nu_+!\nu_-!}\left(\frac{n_+}{N}\right)^{\nu_+}\left(\frac{n_-}{N}\right)^{\nu_-} \tag{118}$$

which can be written explicitly as a function of i by means of (111).

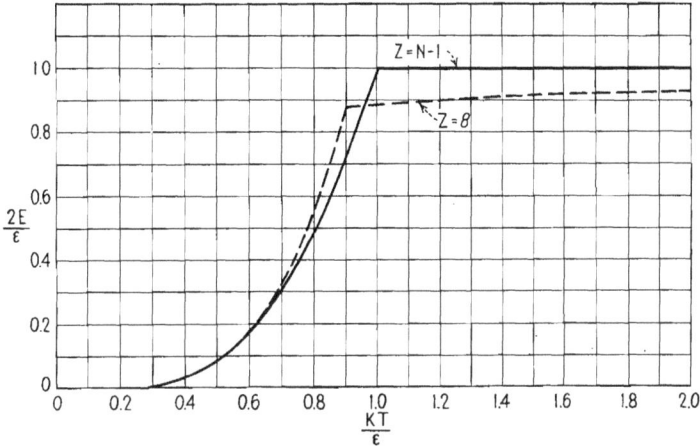

FIG. 77.

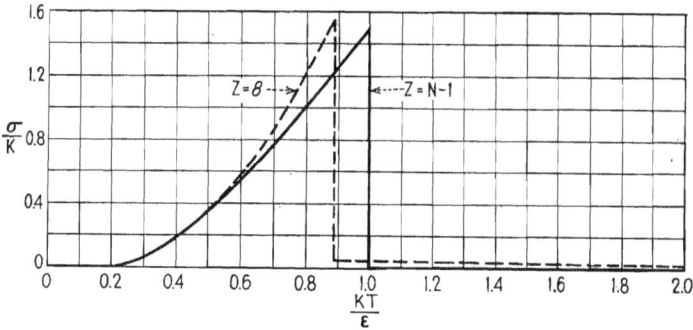

FIG. 78.

FIGS. 77, 78.—Energy and specific heat of ferromagnetic atoms treated as a perfect gas.

Equations (113) and (115) will differ more from the usual expressions of the Weiss-Heisenberg theory for small than for large values of z. In order to show what this difference amounts to, the magnetization and energy have been calculated for the lowest value of z known to occur in actual ferromagnetic materials, $z = 8$ as in iron. The specific heat and the initial susceptibility above the Curie point may be derived from the expressions for the magnetization and energy. The results obtained are plotted in Figs. 75–78 both for $z = 8$ and for $z = N - 1$, the latter being obtained from the Eqs. (116) and (117) or their equivalent as derived in the previous section. θ is the Curie temperature, and I_w is the spontaneous magnetization obtained from (113) or (116) by putting H, and therefore α, equal to zero.

Aside from the shift of the Curie temperature, the differences between the two cases are slight, and we may conclude that the effect of the fluctuations defined by Eq. (118) is relatively unimportant.

54. Crystalline Fields.—Crystals are made up of charged particles interacting with each other in a large number of ways. It is sometimes convenient to describe these interactions by means of fields, which, because of their symmetry, are called crystalline. In this section we shall discuss some of the general characteristics of crystalline fields.

The success of such an approach depends upon our eliminating from the description of a crystal the atomic and electronic complexities which we are unable to handle and retaining only certain broad features which are common to all solids. To this approximation we may regard crystals as homogeneous and describe them in terms of such quantities as temperature and density (scalar quantities), magnetization and electric polarization (vectors), and macroscopic elastic deformations (tensors). Such a description is comparable to the description of a gas in terms of pressure, density, and temperature without taking into account the atomic nature of the gas. In the case of crystals, however, such a general approach is more complicated than in the case of gases, because crystals may be divided into a number of classes according to their symmetry, and this without reference to their detailed structure, whereas all gases have the same symmetry— they are isotropic. A knowledge of crystal symmetry makes it possible to specify certain forms that the expression for the energy of a crystal must take.

By way of illustration, consider the energy of a crystal in its dependence on the direction of magnetization, the absolute value of the magnetization being constant. Let a set of three mutually perpendicular axes be fixed in the crystal, and let the directions of magnetization be given by means of the cosines of the angles between the magnetization and these axes, the so-called direction cosines α_1, α_2, α_3.   These quantities satisfy the relation

$$\alpha_1^2 + \alpha_2^2 + \alpha_3^2 = 1$$

as may be seen from Fig. 79.   The energy of the crystal in its dependence on the direction of magnetization may be expanded into a power series

$$E = c_1\alpha_1 + c_2\alpha_2 + c_3\alpha_3 + c_{11}\alpha_1^2 + c_{22}\alpha_2^2 + c_{33}\alpha_3^2 + c_{12}\alpha_1\alpha_2 + \\ c_{23}\alpha_2\alpha_3 + c_{31}\alpha_3\alpha_1 + \cdots \quad (119)$$

the c's being constants, independent of α, describing the particular crystal in question.   Suppose, now, that we are dealing with a cubic crystal and that the axes 1, 2, 3 are parallel to the cubic axes.   It is plain that magnetization along any one of these axes must yield the same energy as along any other, since all these states are indistinguishable except for our arbitrary labeling of the axes.   We may therefore put

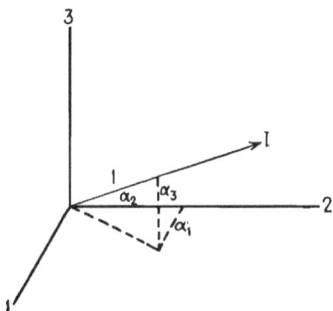

Fig. 79.

$$E(\alpha_1 = 1, \alpha_2 = 0, \alpha_3 = 0) = E(\alpha_1 = 0, \alpha_2 = 1, \alpha_3 = 0) \quad (120)$$
$$E(\alpha_1 = 1, \alpha_2 = 0, \alpha_3 = 0) = E(\alpha_1 = -1, \alpha_2 = 0, \alpha_3 = 0) \quad (121)$$

and similarly for all the other axes.   Other types of relations also exist, such as

$$E\left(\alpha_1 = \frac{1}{\sqrt{2}}, \quad \alpha_2 = \frac{1}{\sqrt{2}}, \quad \alpha_3 = 0\right) = \\ E\left(\alpha_1 = -\frac{1}{\sqrt{2}}, \quad \alpha_2 = \frac{1}{\sqrt{2}}, \quad \alpha_3 = 0\right) \quad (122)$$

as illustrated in Fig. 80.

If we were to attempt to describe a cubic crystal in terms of the first-power terms in the expansion (119), we should find from conditions similar to (121) that

$$c_1 = -c_1 \qquad c_2 = -c_2 \qquad c_3 = -c_3$$

which is possible only if all these quantities are zero.   Similarly, for second-power terms, we should find from (122) that

$$c_{12} = -c_{12} \qquad c_{23} = -c_{23} \qquad c_{31} = -c_{31}$$

and from (120) that

$$c_{11} = c_{22} = c_{33}$$

and therefore that the expression for the energy reduces to

$$E = c_{11}(\alpha_1^2 + \alpha_2^2 + \alpha_3^2) + \cdots$$
$$= c_{11} + \cdots$$

Similarly, one might go on to higher powered terms, and one would find that the first one capable of yielding a contribution having cubic symmetry was that involving fourth powers of α. The process outlined above is very laborious, especially for crys-

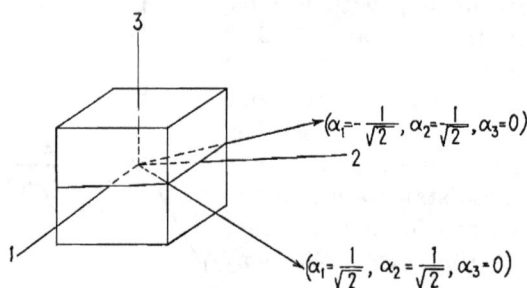

$$\left(\alpha_1 = -\frac{1}{\sqrt{2}}, \alpha_2 = \frac{1}{\sqrt{2}}, \alpha_3 = 0\right)$$

$$\left(\alpha_1 = \frac{1}{\sqrt{2}}, \alpha_2 = \frac{1}{\sqrt{2}}, \alpha_3 = 0\right)$$

FIG. 80.

tals having more complex symmetry than a cube, and we shall therefore proceed to a general method, due to F. Seitz,[1] which makes the computation of individual cases a simple matter.

The energy of any physical system belongs to a category of quantities, called scalars, which possess the important property that their magnitude is independent of any reference frame. On the other hand, vector quantities, such as the coordinates of a point relative to a Cartesian reference frame, are not invariant under a transformation of axes but obey the following law

$$x'_1 = \sigma_{11}x_1 + \sigma_{12}x_2 + \sigma_{13}x_3$$
$$x'_2 = \sigma_{21}x_1 + \sigma_{22}x_2 + \sigma_{23}x_3$$
$$x'_3 = \sigma_{31}x_1 + \sigma_{32}x_2 + \sigma_{33}x_3$$

or, more briefly,

$$x'_i = \sum_l \sigma_{il} x_l \qquad l = 1, 2, 3 \qquad i = 1, 2, 3 \qquad (123)$$

[1] F. SEITZ, Z. *Kristallographie*, (A) **88**, 433, 1934.

in which the quantities x_l are the old coordinates, the quantities x'_i are the new, and σ_{il} is the cosine of the angle between the x'- and x-axes. In order to demonstrate a useful property of the quantities σ_{il}, consider a second transformation

$$x''_i = \sum_l \rho_{il} x'_l$$

A simple calculation shows that the transformation σ followed by the transformation ρ is equivalent to a single transformation γ:

$$x''_i = \sum_l \gamma_{il} x_l$$

where

$$\gamma_{il} = \sum_k \rho_{ik} \sigma_{kl} \tag{124}$$

The expression

$$\begin{pmatrix} \sigma_{11} & \sigma_{12} & \sigma_{13} \\ \sigma_{21} & \sigma_{22} & \sigma_{23} \\ \sigma_{31} & \sigma_{32} & \sigma_{33} \end{pmatrix} \tag{125}$$

is the matrix of the transformation coefficients, and the operation (124) is called matrix multiplication. It is to be observed that in matrix multiplication $(\sigma)(\rho)$ is not, in general, equal to $(\rho)(\sigma)$. Physically this means, for instance, that a rotation of a solid through an angle ω_1 about the x-axis followed by a rotation through an angle ω_2 about the y-axis does not lead to the same position as rotation through ω_2 about the y-axis followed by rotation through ω_1 about the x-axis.

With a view to generalizing the law (123) it has been found very useful to introduce tensor quantities which consist of an aggregate of 3^m numbers $A_{l_1, l_2, \cdots, l_m}$ where $l_1, l_2, \cdots, l_m$, run from 1 to 3, which obey the transformation law

$$A'_{i_1, i_2, \cdots, i_m} = \sum_l \sigma_{i_1, l_1} \sigma_{i_2, l_2} \cdots \sigma_{i_m, l_m} A_{l_1, l_2, \cdots, l_m} \tag{126}$$

Such an ensemble is termed a tensor of the *mth* order, so that a scalar may be thought of as a tensor of zero order, and a vector one of the first order.

Tensors are said to be symmetric in two or more indices if the values of corresponding components obtained by arbitrary permutation of these indices are the same.   If components obtained by interchanging two indices have opposite signs, the tensor is said to be antisymmetric or skew symmetric in these indices.

Now, if we are concerned with a system in which the energy depends upon certain tensor quantities, such as is true for a homogeneously strained medium for which the energy depends upon the components A_{ij} of the symmetric strain tensor (to be described in detail in the next paragraph) or for a magnetized body for which it depends upon the magnetization vector, we may assume that the energy is expressible by means of an infinite series of scalar terms of the form

$$\sum_{l} c_{l_1, l_2, \cdots l_m} A_{l_1, l_2, \cdots, l_m} \tag{127}$$

where $A_{l_1, l_2, \cdots l_m}$ is one of the possible tensors derived by composition of the variable tensor quantities, and $c_{l_1, l_2, \cdots l_m}$ characterizes the medium.   It is a fortunate circumstance that in most physical problems the terms in (127) decrease in importance as the order of tensor $c_{l_1, l_2, \cdots, l_m}$ increases, and it is usually necessary to consider only a small number of terms to obtain an adequate description of facts.

When we are dealing with physical systems that possess rotational symmetry, such as crystals, we may, in general, assume that all observable quantities associated with the system will possess the corresponding symmetry.   Thus the tensors $c_{l_1, l_2, \cdots, l_m}$ in (127), which are characteristics of the medium, will be assumed to be invariant under those transformations which characterize the symmetry properties, or, more explicitly,

$$c_{i_1, i_2, \cdots, i_m} = c'_{i_1, i_2, \cdots, i_m} = \sum_{l} \sigma_{i_1, l_1}(R) \, \cdots \, \sigma_{i_m, l_m}(R) c_{l_1, \cdots, l_m} \tag{128}$$

where the primed and unprimed c's have their usual significance, and $\sigma_{i,l}(R)$ is associated with the Rth symmetry operator.   The symmetry operations met with can be divided into two large categories, viz., those which correspond to actual rotations of the crystal into itself (proper rotations) and those operations, such as reflections in a plane which passes through the crystal, which may be imagined to be performed but may not actually be carried out (improper rotations).

From the standpoint of transformation theory, both of these types belong to the category of orthogonal transformations of the form (123), any point of the crystal being taken as origin. The matrix of the transformation coefficients (125) is a quantity that is of fundamental importance from the algebraic standpoint, and for orthogonal transformations these possess the following properties:

The determinant of a transformation is always either $+1$ or -1.

It is possible to choose a particular coordinate system so that any one of the matrices of determinant ± 1 may be taken in the respective forms

$$\begin{pmatrix} \pm 1 & 0 & 0 \\ 0 & \cos\varphi & -\sin\varphi \\ 0 & \sin\varphi & \cos\varphi \end{pmatrix} \tag{129}$$

For the case of positive sign, this corresponds to a proper rotation of angle φ about the x_1-axis, while the other corresponds to a rotation of φ about x_1 followed by a reflection in a plane passing through the x_2- and x_3-axes, so that the latter represent improper rotations.

From this descriptive basis, the laws of large-scale crystal symmetry assume a simple form. They are as follows:

In all transformations of type (129) only those angles are allowable which are of the form $\varphi = 2m\pi/n$ in which m and n are integers such that $m \leq n$, and n may have no values other than 1, 2, 3, 4, 6. The exact significance of these laws is revealed only by an investigation of the lattice-structure theory of crystals.[1]

Part of the large-scale theory of symmetry is concerned with the derivation of those ensembles of rotations (129) which satisfy the crystallographic laws and may exist in the same crystal. To appreciate this point fully, it must be realized that if a crystal is invariant under two rotations of the form (129), it will also be invariant under the product of the two in the matrix sense, so that the product matrix must satisfy the symmetry laws. At any rate, the theory yields 32 groups of this sort which are generally referred to as the crystal classes and correspond to degrees of symmetry varying from that of completely anisotropic homogeneous media to media that possess the full symmetry prop-

---

[1] F. SEITZ, *loc. cit.*

erties of a cube. There are seven natural categories into which these classes fall, and these are listed below with the corresponding classes in each. These classes are represented by the generating matrix elements of the groups, which possess the property that their products and powers lead to all elements of the group, so that they alone yield all of the relations (128) that are independent.

THE GENERATING MATRICES OF THE 32 CRYSTAL CLASSES

1. C_1
$$\begin{pmatrix} 1 & 0 & 0 \\ 0 & 1 & 0 \\ 0 & 0 & 1 \end{pmatrix}$$

2. $S_1 = C_1^h = C_s$
$$\begin{pmatrix} -1 & 0 & 0 \\ 0 & 1 & 0 \\ 0 & 0 & 1 \end{pmatrix}$$

3. C_2
$$\begin{pmatrix} 1 & 0 & 0 \\ 0 & -1 & 0 \\ 0 & 0 & -1 \end{pmatrix}$$

4. S_2
$$\begin{pmatrix} -1 & 0 & 0 \\ 0 & -1 & 0 \\ 0 & 0 & -1 \end{pmatrix}$$

5. C_2^v
$$\begin{pmatrix} 1 & 0 & 0 \\ 0 & -1 & 0 \\ 0 & 0 & -1 \end{pmatrix}\begin{pmatrix} 1 & 0 & 0 \\ 0 & -1 & 0 \\ 0 & 0 & 1 \end{pmatrix}$$

6. C_2^h
$$\begin{pmatrix} -1 & 0 & 0 \\ 0 & -1 & 0 \\ 0 & 0 & -1 \end{pmatrix}\begin{pmatrix} -1 & 0 & 0 \\ 0 & 1 & 0 \\ 0 & 0 & 1 \end{pmatrix}$$

7. V
$$\begin{pmatrix} 1 & 0 & 0 \\ 0 & -1 & 0 \\ 0 & 0 & -1 \end{pmatrix}\begin{pmatrix} -1 & 0 & 0 \\ 0 & 1 & 0 \\ 0 & 0 & -1 \end{pmatrix}$$

8. V^h
$$\begin{pmatrix} 1 & 0 & 0 \\ 0 & -1 & 0 \\ 0 & 0 & -1 \end{pmatrix}\begin{pmatrix} -1 & 0 & 0 \\ 0 & 1 & 0 \\ 0 & 0 & -1 \end{pmatrix}\begin{pmatrix} -1 & 0 & 0 \\ 0 & -1 & 0 \\ 0 & 0 & -1 \end{pmatrix}$$

9. C_3
$$\begin{pmatrix} 1 & 0 & 0 \\ 0 & -\frac{1}{2} & -\sqrt{\frac{3}{2}} \\ 0 & \sqrt{\frac{3}{2}} & -\frac{1}{2} \end{pmatrix}$$

10. $C_3^h = S_3$
$$\begin{pmatrix} -1 & 0 & 0 \\ 0 & -\frac{1}{2} & -\sqrt{\frac{3}{2}} \\ 0 & \sqrt{\frac{3}{2}} & -\frac{1}{2} \end{pmatrix}$$

11. C_3^v
$$\begin{pmatrix} 1 & 0 & 0 \\ 0 & -\frac{1}{2} & -\sqrt{\frac{3}{2}} \\ 0 & \sqrt{\frac{3}{2}} & -\frac{1}{2} \end{pmatrix}\begin{pmatrix} 1 & 0 & 0 \\ 0 & -1 & 0 \\ 0 & 0 & 1 \end{pmatrix}$$

THE GENERATING MATRICES OF THE 32 CRYSTAL CLASSES.—(*Continued*)

12. $D_3 \begin{pmatrix} 1 & 0 & 0 \\ 0 & -\frac{1}{2} & -\sqrt{\frac{3}{2}} \\ 0 & \sqrt{\frac{3}{2}} & -\frac{1}{2} \end{pmatrix} \begin{pmatrix} -1 & 0 & 0 \\ 0 & 1 & 0 \\ 0 & 0 & -1 \end{pmatrix}$

13. $D_3^h \begin{pmatrix} -1 & 0 & 0 \\ 0 & -\frac{1}{2} & -\sqrt{\frac{3}{2}} \\ 0 & \sqrt{\frac{3}{2}} & -\frac{1}{2} \end{pmatrix} \begin{pmatrix} -1 & 0 & 0 \\ 0 & 1 & 0 \\ 0 & 0 & -1 \end{pmatrix}$

14. $C_4 \begin{pmatrix} 1 & 0 & 0 \\ 0 & 0 & -1 \\ 0 & 1 & 0 \end{pmatrix}$

15. $S_4 \begin{pmatrix} -1 & 0 & 0 \\ 0 & 0 & -1 \\ 0 & 1 & 0 \end{pmatrix}$

16. $C_4^h \begin{pmatrix} 1 & 0 & 0 \\ 0 & 0 & -1 \\ 0 & 1 & 0 \end{pmatrix} \begin{pmatrix} -1 & 0 & 0 \\ 0 & 1 & 0 \\ 0 & 0 & 1 \end{pmatrix}$

17. $C_4^v \begin{pmatrix} 1 & 0 & 0 \\ 0 & 0 & -1 \\ 0 & 1 & 0 \end{pmatrix} \begin{pmatrix} 1 & 0 & 0 \\ 0 & -1 & 0 \\ 0 & 0 & 1 \end{pmatrix}$

18. $V^d \begin{pmatrix} -1 & 0 & 0 \\ 0 & 0 & -1 \\ 0 & 1 & 0 \end{pmatrix} \begin{pmatrix} 1 & 0 & 0 \\ 0 & -1 & 0 \\ 0 & 0 & 1 \end{pmatrix}$

19. $D_4 \begin{pmatrix} 1 & 0 & 0 \\ 0 & 0 & -1 \\ 0 & 1 & 0 \end{pmatrix} \begin{pmatrix} -1 & 0 & 0 \\ 0 & -1 & 0 \\ 0 & 0 & 1 \end{pmatrix}$

20. $D_4^h \begin{pmatrix} 1 & 0 & 0 \\ 0 & 0 & -1 \\ 0 & 1 & 0 \end{pmatrix} \begin{pmatrix} -1 & 0 & 0 \\ 0 & -1 & 0 \\ 0 & 0 & -1 \end{pmatrix} \begin{pmatrix} -1 & 0 & 0 \\ 0 & -1 & 0 \\ 0 & 0 & +1 \end{pmatrix}$

21. $C_6 \begin{pmatrix} 1 & 0 & 0 \\ 0 & \frac{1}{2} & -\sqrt{\frac{3}{2}} \\ 0 & \sqrt{\frac{3}{2}} & \frac{1}{2} \end{pmatrix}$

22. $S_6 = C_3^i \begin{pmatrix} -1 & 0 & 0 \\ 0 & \frac{1}{2} & -\sqrt{\frac{3}{2}} \\ 0 & \sqrt{\frac{3}{2}} & \frac{1}{2} \end{pmatrix}$

23. $C_6^h \begin{pmatrix} 1 & 0 & 0 \\ 0 & \frac{1}{2} & -\sqrt{\frac{3}{2}} \\ 0 & \sqrt{\frac{3}{2}} & \frac{1}{2} \end{pmatrix} \begin{pmatrix} -1 & 0 & 0 \\ 0 & 1 & 0 \\ 0 & 0 & 1 \end{pmatrix}$

24. $C_6^v \begin{pmatrix} 1 & 0 & 0 \\ 0 & \frac{1}{2} & -\sqrt{\frac{3}{2}} \\ 0 & \sqrt{\frac{3}{2}} & \frac{1}{2} \end{pmatrix} \begin{pmatrix} 1 & 0 & 0 \\ 0 & -1 & 0 \\ 0 & 0 & 1 \end{pmatrix}$

25. $D_3^i \begin{pmatrix} -1 & 0 & 0 \\ 0 & \frac{1}{2} & -\sqrt{\frac{3}{2}} \\ 0 & \sqrt{\frac{3}{2}} & \frac{1}{2} \end{pmatrix} \begin{pmatrix} 1 & 0 & 0 \\ 0 & -1 & 0 \\ 0 & 0 & 1 \end{pmatrix}$

The Generating Matrices of the 32 Crystal Classes.—(*Continued*)

26. D_6^h
$$\begin{pmatrix} 1 & 0 & 0 \\ 0 & \frac{1}{2} & -\sqrt{\frac{3}{2}} \\ 0 & \sqrt{\frac{3}{2}} & \frac{1}{2} \end{pmatrix} \begin{pmatrix} -1 & 0 & 0 \\ 0 & 1 & 0 \\ 0 & 0 & 1 \end{pmatrix} \begin{pmatrix} 1 & 0 & 0 \\ 0 & -1 & 0 \\ 0 & 0 & 1 \end{pmatrix}$$

27. D_6
$$\begin{pmatrix} 1 & 0 & 0 \\ 0 & \frac{1}{2} & -\sqrt{\frac{3}{2}} \\ 0 & \sqrt{\frac{3}{2}} & \frac{1}{2} \end{pmatrix} \begin{pmatrix} -1 & 0 & 0 \\ 0 & -1 & 0 \\ 0 & 0 & 1 \end{pmatrix}$$

28. T
$$\begin{pmatrix} 1 & 0 & 0 \\ 0 & -1 & 0 \\ 0 & 0 & -1 \end{pmatrix} \begin{pmatrix} 0 & 0 & 1 \\ 1 & 0 & 0 \\ 0 & 1 & 0 \end{pmatrix}$$

29. O
$$\begin{pmatrix} 1 & 0 & 0 \\ 0 & 0 & 1 \\ 0 & -1 & 0 \end{pmatrix} \begin{pmatrix} 0 & 0 & 1 \\ 1 & 0 & 0 \\ 0 & 1 & 0 \end{pmatrix}$$

30. T^h
$$\begin{pmatrix} -1 & 0 & 0 \\ 0 & 1 & 0 \\ 0 & 0 & 1 \end{pmatrix} \begin{pmatrix} 1 & 0 & 0 \\ 0 & -1 & 0 \\ 0 & 0 & -1 \end{pmatrix} \begin{pmatrix} 0 & 0 & 1 \\ 1 & 0 & 0 \\ 0 & 1 & 0 \end{pmatrix}$$

31. T^d
$$\begin{pmatrix} 1 & 0 & 0 \\ 0 & 0 & -1 \\ 0 & -1 & 0 \end{pmatrix} \begin{pmatrix} 1 & 0 & 0 \\ 0 & -1 & 0 \\ 0 & 0 & -1 \end{pmatrix} \begin{pmatrix} 0 & 0 & 1 \\ 1 & 0 & 0 \\ 0 & 1 & 0 \end{pmatrix}$$

32. O^h
$$\begin{pmatrix} 1 & 0 & 0 \\ 0 & 0 & 1 \\ 0 & -1 & 0 \end{pmatrix} \begin{pmatrix} 0 & 0 & 1 \\ 1 & 0 & 0 \\ 0 & 1 & 0 \end{pmatrix} \begin{pmatrix} -1 & 0 & 0 \\ 0 & -1 & 0 \\ 0 & 0 & -1 \end{pmatrix}$$

55. The Mathematical Description of the Deformation of Crystals.—In this section we shall illustrate the application of the procedure described in Par. 54 to the elasticity of crystals. The results, of course, are not new and may be found, for instance, in Voigt's book "Lehrbuch der Kristallphysik."

Experience teaches that elastic energies may be described by a sum of terms of the form

$$c_{ijkl} A_{ij} A_{kl} \tag{130}$$

where A_{ij} are components of the strain tensor. The strain tensor defines the displacement at any point (x,y,z), the components u, v, w of the displacement along the x-, y-, and z-axes, respectively, being defined in terms of the strain tensor by the expressions

$$u = A_{11}x + A_{12}y + A_{13}z$$
$$v = A_{21}x + A_{22}y + A_{23}z$$
$$w = A_{31}x + A_{32}y + A_{33}z \tag{131}$$

This strain tensor is symmetric; *i.e.*, $A_{ij} = A_{ji}$. In much of the literature one finds quantities

$$e_{xx} = \frac{\partial u}{\partial x} = A_{11}$$

$$e_{xy} = \frac{\partial v}{\partial x} + \frac{\partial u}{\partial y} = A_{21} + A_{12} = 2A_{12}$$

which give expressions for the energy of deformed crystal differing slightly from those derived here. The more fundamental quantities A_{ij} are used hereafter, as they may be transformed by the simple procedure outlined in Par. 54.

The problem proposed is to show how the number of constants of the form c_{ijkl} in (130) may be limited for any given crystal class. Consider, by way of illustration, the case of cobalt, which belongs to the class D_6^h associated with the symmetry operators

$$\begin{pmatrix} 1 & 0 & 0 \\ 0 & \frac{1}{2} & -\sqrt{\frac{3}{2}} \\ 0 & \sqrt{\frac{3}{2}} & \frac{1}{2} \end{pmatrix} \begin{pmatrix} -1 & 0 & 0 \\ 0 & 1 & 0 \\ 0 & 0 & 1 \end{pmatrix} \begin{pmatrix} 1 & 0 & 0 \\ 0 & -1 & 0 \\ 0 & 0 & 1 \end{pmatrix} \quad (132)$$

According to (128), the relations to be satisfied are

$$c_{ijkl} = \sum_{pqrs} \sigma_{ip}\sigma_{jq}\sigma_{kr}\sigma_{ls} c_{pqrs} \quad (133)$$

the σ's being any one of the three matrices (132). For the second of these operators, for instance, the quantities σ in (133) are 0 if $i \neq p, j \neq q$, etc., and ± 1 if $i = p, j = q$, etc., so that (133) can give us only relations of the form

$$c_{ijkl} = \pm c_{ijkl}$$

the minus sign being used only if the subscript 1 appears an odd number of times. From this it follows that from the application of the second operator we can deduce

$$c_{1222} = -c_{1222} = 0$$

or that all the coefficients in which the subscript 1 appears an odd number of times must vanish. Similarly, from the third operator in (132) we deduce that all coefficients in which the subscript 2 appears an odd number of times vanish, so that we are left with an energy expression that may be written in the form

$$2E_{el} = \begin{array}{c|cccccc} & A_{11} & A_{22} & A_{33} & A_{23} & A_{31} & A_{12} \\ \hline A_{11} & c_{1111} & c_{1122} & c_{1133} & 0 & 0 & 0 \\ A_{22} & c_{2211} & c_{2222} & c_{2233} & 0 & 0 & 0 \\ A_{33} & c_{3311} & c_{3322} & c_{3333} & 0 & 0 & 0 \\ A_{23} & 0 & 0 & 0 & c_{2323} & 0 & 0 \\ A_{31} & 0 & 0 & 0 & 0 & c_{3131} & 0 \\ A_{12} & 0 & 0 & 0 & 0 & 0 & c_{1212} \end{array} \;=\; c_{1111}A_{11}^2 + c_{1122}A_{11}A_{22} + \cdots$$

This expression may be further reduced. From the first operator in (132) we get

$$c_{2222} = c_{2222}/16 + 3(c_{2233} + c_{3322} + c_{2323})/16 + 9c_{3333}/16 \qquad (134)$$
$$c_{3333} = 9c_{2222}/16 + 3(c_{2233} + c_{3322} + c_{2323})/16 + c_{3333}/16$$

By subtraction one finds

$$c_{2222} - c_{3333} = -(c_{2222} - c_{3333})/2$$

which is possible only if

$$c_{2222} = c_{3333}$$

Similarly,

$$c_{2233} = 3c_{2222}/16 + c_{2233}/16 + 9c_{3322}/16 - 3c_{2323}/16 + 3c_{3333}/16 \qquad (135)$$
$$c_{3322} = 3c_{2222}/16 + 9c_{2233}/16 + c_{3322}/16 - 3c_{2323}/16 + 3c_{3333}/16$$

and, again, by subtraction

$$c_{2233} - c_{3322} = -(c_{2233} - c_{3322})/2$$

which is possible only if

$$c_{2233} = c_{3322}$$

Further substituting these results into (134) or (135), one finds

$$c_{2323} = 2(c_{2222} - c_{2233})$$

And finally, from the first operator in (132), one finds

$$c_{1122} = c_{1122}/4 + 3c_{1133}/4$$
$$c_{2211} = c_{2211}/4 + 3c_{3311}/4$$

or $c_{1122} = c_{1133}$ and $c_{2211} = c_{3311}$
In the final calculation one finds that

$$c'_{3131} = c_{3131}/4$$
$$c'_{1313} = 3c_{1212}/4$$
$$c'_{1212} = c_{1212}/4$$
$$c'_{2121} = 3c_{3131}/4 \qquad (136)$$

where the coefficients of the transformed expressions are primed. This serves to illustrate a drawback in the notation, but one that can be overcome with a little care. The foregoing expressions mean that the transformed energy expression contains terms

$$c'_{3131}A_{31}A_{31} + c'_{1313}A_{13}A_{13}$$

for instance, which, because $A_{13} = A_{31}$, may be written

$$(c'_{3131} + c'_{1313})A_{13}^2$$

and it is this expression that becomes

$$c_{3131}A_{13}^2$$

so that (136) leads to

$$c_{3131} = c_{3131}/4 + 3c_{1212}/4$$

or

$$c_{3131} = c_{1212}$$

The result to this point gives for twice the elastic energy

	A_{11}	A_{22}	A_{33}	A_{23}	A_{31}	A_{12}
A_{11}	c_{1111}	c_{1122}	c_{1122}	0	0	0
A_{22}	c_{2211}	c_{2222}	c_{2233}	0	0	0
A_{33}	c_{2211}	c_{2233}	c_{2222}	0	0	0
A_{23}	0	0	0	$2(c_{2222}-c_{2233})$	0	0
A_{31}	0	0	0	0	c_{1212}	0
A_{12}	0	0	0	0	0	c_{1212}

(137)

These six constants may further be reduced to five in this particular case by putting

$$c_{1122} = c_{2211}$$

since

$$c_{1122}A_{11}A_{22} + c_{2211}A_{22}A_{11} = \text{const. } A_{11}A_{22}$$

The same results apply to pyrrhotite crystals Fe_7S_8, which belong to the crystal class C_6^v.

The ferromagnetic crystals Fe, Ni, Fe_3O_4 belong to the crystal class designated by O^h, and the same type of reasoning as that used above leads to the following expression

$$2E_{el} =$$

	A_{11}	A_{22}	A_{33}	A_{23}	A_{31}	A_{12}
A_{11}	c_{11}	c_{12}	c_{12}	0	0	0
A_{22}	c_{12}	c_{11}	c_{12}	0	0	0
A_{33}	c_{12}	c_{12}	c_{11}	0	0	0
A_{23}	0	0	0	$4c_{44}$	0	0
A_{31}	0	0	0	0	$4c_{44}$	0
A_{12}	0	0	0	0	0	$4c_{44}$

$$(138)$$

For many crystals of this class the elastic constants have been measured, and the symbols used in (138) are those usually used in the literature.

From the expressions like (137) or (138) for the energy of a distorted crystal it is possible to derive expressions for the stress components required to produce any given strain.

$$F_{ij} = \frac{\partial E_{el}}{\partial A_{ij}} \tag{139}$$

In using (139) care must be taken that the complete expression for E is used in which all the strain components, such as A_{ij} and A_{ji}, for instance, appear explicitly.

The preceding expression for the energy is a homogeneous quadratic function of the strain components, and the coefficients c_{11}, c_{12}, etc., are the symbols most commonly used to describe the elasticity of crystals. It is, however, equally possible to express the energy as a homogeneous quadratic function of the stress components. In this form the coefficients are generally designated by the symbols s_{11}, s_{12}, . . . , etc., where, for cubic crystals.

$$s_{11} = \frac{c_{11} + c_{12}}{(c_{11} + 2c_{12})(c_{11} - c_{12})}$$

$$s_{12} = \frac{-c_{12}}{(c_{11} + 2c_{12})(c_{11} - c_{12})}$$

$$s_{44} = \frac{1}{c_{44}} \tag{140}$$

The following expressions for Young's modulus E and the torsional modulus G in cubic crystals are useful:

$$\frac{1}{E} = s_{11} - \left[(s_{11} - s_{12}) - \frac{1}{2}s_{44} \right] \sum' \gamma_i^2 \gamma_j^2 \qquad (141)$$

$$\frac{1}{G} = s_{44} + 2\left[(s_{11} - s_{12}) - \frac{1}{2}s_{44} \right] \sum' \gamma_i^2 \gamma_j^2 \qquad (142)$$

γ_i, etc., are the direction cosines giving the direction in which the measurements are made with respect to the cubic axes of the crystal. Σ' means summation over all values of i and j other than $i = j$, or simply

$$\Sigma' \gamma_i^2 \gamma_j^2 = \gamma_1^2\gamma_2^2 + \gamma_2^2\gamma_1^2 + \gamma_2^2\gamma_3^2 + \gamma_3^2\gamma_2^2 + \gamma_3^2\gamma_1^2 + \gamma_1^2\gamma_3^2$$

which, because $\Sigma\gamma_i^2 = 1$, may also be written

$$\Sigma'\gamma_i^2\gamma_j^2 = 1 - \Sigma\gamma_i^4 \qquad (143)$$

In isotropic materials $s_{11} - s_{12} = s_{44}/2$, and the expression for the energy reduces to

$$2E_{el} = (\lambda + 2\mu)\Sigma A_{ii}^2 + \lambda\Sigma' A_{ii}A_{jj} + 2\mu\Sigma' A_{ij}^2 \qquad (144)$$

the constants having the following significance:
Modulus of compression:

$$\lambda + \tfrac{2}{3}\mu \qquad (145)$$

Young's modulus:

$$\frac{\mu(3\lambda + 2\mu)}{\lambda + \mu}$$

Poisson's ratio:

$$\frac{\lambda}{2(\lambda + \mu)}$$

Rigidity:

$$\mu$$

56. Crystalline Fields in Rigid Solids.—In this section we shall discuss the dependence of the energy of magnetized crystals on the direction of magnetization. The intensity of magnetization will be assumed constant, and its orientation given by the direction cosines α_i, as in Par. 54. For the sake of generality we shall assume that the crystals may be distorted in any manner as given by the strain tensor A_{ij} defined in Eq. (131) but that A_{ij} is independent of the direction of magnetization.

The expression for the energy of a crystal may be expanded in a series of terms of the form

$$a_i \alpha_i$$
$$a_{ij} \alpha_i \alpha_j \qquad\qquad b_{ij} A_{ij}$$
$$a_{ijk} \alpha_i \alpha_j \alpha_k \qquad\qquad b_{ijk} \alpha_i A_{jk}$$
$$a_{ijkl} \alpha_i \alpha_j \alpha_k \alpha_l \qquad b_{ijkl} \alpha_i \alpha_j A_{kl} \qquad c_{ijkl} A_{ij} A_{kl} \qquad (146)$$

and similarly for higher order terms. Those terms involving only the strains A_{ij} have been discussed in Par. 55 and give rise to the usual theory of elasticity.

As in the previous section, we shall illustrate the procedure by carrying out the calculations for cobalt. From the symmetry operators (132) we have found in the last section that coefficients involving 1 or 2 an odd number of times vanish. Of the coefficients of the first two types of terms in (146) we have left, therefore, a_3, a_{11}, a_{22}, a_{33}. Using, now, the first of the operators in (132), we have

$$a_3 = \tfrac{1}{2} a_3$$
$$a_{11} = a_{11}$$
$$a_{22} = \tfrac{1}{4} a_{22} + \tfrac{3}{4} a_{33}$$

or $a_3 = 0$, $a_{22} = a_{33}$, so that the first approximation to the energy will have the form

$$a_{11} \alpha_1^2 + a_{22}(\alpha_2^2 + \alpha_3^2) = a \alpha_1^2 + \text{const.} \qquad (147)$$

since $\alpha_1^2 + \alpha_2^2 + \alpha_3^2 = 1$.

Similarly, it can be shown that third-order terms vanish. The derivations of the fourth-order terms will be identical with those of Par. 55, giving the energy expression,[1] as far as terms of the form $b_{ijkl} \alpha_i \alpha_j A_{kl}$ are concerned,

	A_{11}	A_{22}	A_{33}	A_{23}	A_{31}	A_{12}
α_1^2	b_{1111}	b_{1122}	b_{1122}	0	0	0
α_2^2	b_{2211}	b_{2222}	b_{2233}	0	0	0
α_3^2	b_{2211}	b_{2233}	b_{2222}	0	0	0
$\alpha_2\alpha_3$	0	0	0	$2(b_{2222}-b_{2233})$	0	0
$\alpha_3\alpha_1$	0	0	0	0	b_{1212}	0
$\alpha_1\alpha_2$	0	0	0	0	0	b_{1212}

$$(148)$$

[1] This expression was first derived by P. Kapitza, *Proc. Roy. Soc.*, (A) **135**, 537, 1932.

In this case, however, we may not put $b_{1122} = b_{2211}$ because $\alpha_1^2 A_{22}$ and $\alpha_2^2 A_{11}$ cannot be contracted into one term. On the other hand, the first three terms in the left-hand column of (148) may be contracted, since

$$b_{1111}A_{11}\alpha_1^2 + b_{2211}A_{11}\alpha_2^2 + b_{2211}A_{11}\alpha_3^2$$
$$= b_{1111}A_{11}\alpha_1^2 + b_{2211}A_{11}(\alpha_2^2 + \alpha_3^2)$$
$$= b_{1111}A_{11}\alpha_1^2 + b_{2211}A_{11}(1 - \alpha_1^2)$$
$$= \text{const. } A_{11}\alpha_1^2 + \text{const.}$$

which, disregarding the term independent of α, since it is not of the form here under consideration, is equivalent to putting $b_{2211} = 0$ in Eq. (148). These constants, as will be shown later, determine the magnetostriction, or change in shape of a crystal with magnetization under constant applied forces, and they are consequently called magnetostriction constants. Five magnetostriction constants and five elastic constants are needed to describe the behavior of this type of crystal.

If (147) is not adequate to describe the behavior of an undistorted cobalt crystal, we may proceed to higher order terms, e.g., of the form a_{ijkl}. These coefficients again may be discussed with the same results as for b_{ijkl} and c_{jkl}. In this case, however, terms like $\alpha_1^2\alpha_2^2$ and $\alpha_2^2\alpha_1^2$ and $\alpha_1\alpha_2\alpha_1\alpha_2$ may be combined, and the expression may be reduced to

$$a_{1111}\alpha_1^4 + a_{2222}(\alpha_2^4 + 2\alpha_2^2\alpha_3^2 + \alpha_3^4) + a_{1122}(\alpha_1^2\alpha_2^2 + \alpha_1^2\alpha_3^2)$$

or simply

$$a'\alpha_1^4 + a\alpha_1^2 + \text{const.} \tag{149}$$

It is to be noticed that (147) and (149) are independent of α_2 and α_3. This means that to this approximation cobalt is isotropic in the plane perpendicular to the hexagonal axis. If in fact this is not true, we shall have to proceed to expressions of higher order, involving terms of the form $a_{ijklmn}\alpha_i\alpha_j\alpha_k\alpha_l\alpha_m\alpha_n$.

Similar considerations for cubic crystals give the following results for terms involving the direction of magnetization only:

$$a \, \Sigma'\alpha_i^2\alpha_j^2 \tag{150}$$

and for terms involving the strain tensor

$$b_1 \Sigma\alpha_i^2 A_{ii} + b_2 \Sigma'\alpha_i\alpha_j A_{ij} \tag{151}$$

57. Crystalline Fields in Elastic Solids.   Magnetostriction.—
In the last section we have discussed the variation of the energy
of a perfectly rigid ferromagnetic crystal when the direction of
magnetization is changed.   In actual fact, although the dimensions of materials change only little with magnetization, they
do nevertheless change, unless prevented from doing so by externally applied forces.   It is of considerable interest, therefore, to
discover how expressions like (150)
and (151) are to be modified when
the conditions of the problem are
not constant shape but constant
external force.

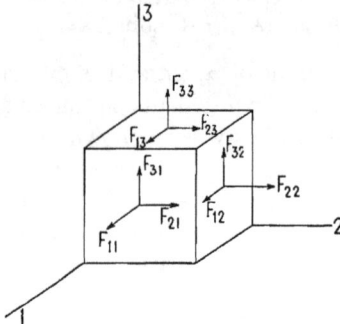

The surface forces acting on any
element of volume such as the cube
in Fig. 81 may be represented by
means of a tensor, having the
components shown.   As we are
concerned with homogeneous
states, the forces on opposite faces
of the cube may be considered equal and opposite.   From the
above and the definition of the strain tensor A_{ij} it is clear that
the work done by the component F_{ij} in producing a small
distortion A_{ij} is

$$F_{ij}A_{ij}$$

and, therefore, if W represents the total work done on the crystal
by elastic deformation,[1] and E the total potential energy stored in
the crystal by the strain, we have

$$W = \Sigma A_{ij}F_{ij} \tag{152}$$

$$F_{ij} = \frac{\partial W}{\partial A_{ij}} = \frac{\partial E}{\partial A_{ij}} \tag{153}$$

which results from the fact that for a fixed direction of magnetization the work done by the external forces is stored up as potential
energy in the crystal.

Using (153) and the suitable expression for E as derived from
(146), one gets expressions for F in terms of α and A.   These

---

[1] A function W exists for both adiabatic and isothermal processes but is,
of course, different for the two cases.   For further discussion see any
treatise on elasticity, *e.g.*, A. E. H. Love, "The Mathematical Theory of
Elasticity," Chap. III, The University Press, Cambridge, 1927.

Fig. 81.

may be solved for A in terms of α and F, and the results substituted back into (146), giving an expression for the energy of a crystal as a function of the direction of magnetization for any set of forces F.

To illustrate this we shall carry out the calculation for the case of a cubic crystal. In this case we have found, in (138), (150), and (151),

$$E = \frac{c_{11}}{2}\sum A_{ii}^2 + \frac{c_{12}}{2}{\sum}' A_{ii}A_{jj} + c_{44}{\sum}' A_{ij}^2 + a{\sum}' \alpha_i^2\alpha_j^2$$
$$+ b_1 \sum \alpha_i^2 A_{ii} + b_2 {\sum}' \alpha_i\alpha_j A_{ij} \quad (154)$$

To this expression may be added an arbitrary constant. From (153) we find

$$F_{ii} = c_{11}A_{ii} + c_{12}A_{jj} + c_{12}A_{kk} + b_1\alpha_i^2$$
$$F_{ij} = 2c_{44}A_{ij} + b_2\alpha_i\alpha_j$$

The first of these expressions may be written

$$F_{ii} - b_1\alpha_i^2 = (c_{11} - c_{12})A_{ii} + c_{12}\Sigma A_{ii}$$

By adding the three expressions found by putting $i = 1, 2, 3$, we get

$$\Sigma(F_{ii} - b_1\alpha_i^2) = (c_{11} + 2c_{12})\Sigma A_{ii}$$

and finally, using this value for ΣA_{ii} and (140),

$$A_{ii} = (s_{11} - s_{12})(F_{ii} - b_1\alpha_i^2) + s_{12}(\Sigma F_{ii} - b_1)$$
$$A_{ij} = \frac{s_{44}}{2}(F_{ij} - b_2\alpha_i\alpha_j) \quad (155)$$

Upon substituting (155) into (154), one obtains

$$E = \frac{s_{11}}{2}\sum F_{ii}^2 + \frac{s_{12}}{2}{\sum}' F_{ii}F_{jj} + \frac{s_{44}}{4}{\sum}' F_{ij}^2$$
$$+ \left(a + \frac{b_1^2}{2(c_{11} - c_{12})} - \frac{b_2^2}{4c_{44}}\right){\sum}' \alpha_i^2\alpha_j^2 \quad (156)$$

For some problems it is convenient to consider the potential energy of the crystal and of the externally applied forces together. This is simply $E - W$, and from (152) and (155) we have

$$W = \sum A_{ii}F_{ii} = -\frac{b_1}{c_{11} - c_{12}}\sum F_{ii}\alpha_i^2 - \frac{b_2}{2c_{44}}{\sum}' F_{ij}\alpha_i\alpha_j +$$
$$\text{terms independent of } \alpha \quad (157)$$

For future reference it is convenient to introduce the function E_θ giving the dependence of the energy of a crystal on the direction of magnetization. For a rigid cubic crystal this is

$$E_\theta = a\Sigma'\alpha_i^2\alpha_j^2 + b_1\Sigma A_{ii}\alpha_i^2 + b_2\Sigma'A_{ij}\alpha_i\alpha_j \qquad (158)$$

For an elastic crystal under constant external forces there is a similar expression

$$E_\theta - W = a_F\Sigma'\alpha_i^2\alpha_j^2 - \kappa_1\Sigma F_{ii}\alpha_i^2 - \kappa_2\Sigma'F_{ij}\alpha_i\alpha_j \qquad (159)$$

where

$$a_F = a + \frac{b_1^2}{2(c_{11}-c_{12})} - \frac{b_2^2}{4c_{44}} = a - \frac{b_1\kappa_1}{2} + \frac{b_2\kappa_2}{2}$$

$$\kappa_1 = \frac{-b_1}{c_{11}-c_{12}}$$

$$\kappa_2 = \frac{-b_2}{2c_{44}} \qquad (160)$$

From (155) it follows that the elastic distortion of a crystal as measured by the strain tensor components A_{ij} is a function of the direction of magnetization. This phenomenon is actually found in nature and is called magnetostriction. We shall have occasion to examine it more in detail in a later chapter. The constants κ_1 and κ_2 are called magnetostriction constants. If $\kappa_1 = \kappa_2$, the material is isotropic with respect to magnetostriction. If $c_{11} - c_{12} = 2c_{44}$, the material is elastically isotropic. If both of these conditions are met, $a = a_F$, and $b_1 = b_2$.

58. Internal Magnetic Fields.—A particular example of internal fields is the magnetic field within a substance arising from the magnetic elements of which the substance is built up. These magnetic fields are often small compared with other fields and may legitimately be neglected in some problems. They have a much longer range than, for instance, the internal fields giving rise to spontaneous magnetization, and it may therefore happen that a very large number of atoms combine to produce a considerable magnetic disturbance.

Our knowledge of the detailed structure of magnetic fields in solids is very meager, from both the theoretical and the experimental points of view. McKeehan[1] has calculated the distribution of field intensity within various geometrical arrangements of dipoles, but his results have not as yet been made use of in the interpretation of ferromagnetism.

[1] L. W. McKEEHAN, *Phys. Rev.*, **43**, 913, 924, 1022, 1025; **44**, 38, 582, 1933.

For many purposes only the average field due to the surface distribution of poles on a magnetized substance is important. Of special interest is the case, first discussed by Poisson, of an ellipsoid in a magnetic field. In this case the magnetization produced by a homogeneous field will be homogeneous. If the major axes of the ellipsoid a, b, and c are parallel to the x-, y-, and z-axes, respectively, and if the applied field has the components H_x, H_y, H_z, and the magnetization has the components I_x, I_y, I_z, then the total field acting on any point of the ellipsoid has the components

$$H_x - LI_x$$
$$H_y - MI_y$$
$$H_z - NI_z \tag{161}$$

L, M, and N being factors determined by the shape of the ellipsoid.[1]

If the ellipsoid is of rotation and flattened in the x-direction, we have, if e is the eccentricity,

$$a = \sqrt{1 - e^2}\,b \qquad b = c$$

and

$$L = 4\pi\left(\frac{1}{e^2} - \frac{\sqrt{1 - e^2}}{e^3} \sin^{-1} e\right)$$
$$M = N = 2\pi\left(\frac{\sqrt{1 - e^2}}{e^3} \sin^{-1} e - \frac{1 - e^2}{e^2}\right) \tag{162}$$

If the ellipsoid is of rotation and elongated in the direction of the z-axis,

$$a = b = c\sqrt{1 - e^2}$$
$$L = M = 2\pi\left(\frac{1}{e^2} - \frac{\sqrt{1 - e^2}}{2e^3} \log_e \frac{1 + e}{1 - e}\right)$$
$$N = 4\pi\left(\frac{1}{e^2} - 1\right)\left(\frac{1}{2e} \log_e \frac{1 + e}{1 - e} - 1\right) \tag{163}$$

For the case of a sphere,

$$a = b = c$$
$$L = M = N = \frac{4\pi}{3} \tag{164}$$

---

[1] For a fuller discussion, see MAXWELL, "Electricity and Magnetism," 3d. ed., vol. 2, p. 69, The Clarendon Press, Oxford, 1892.

CHAPTER VI

MAGNETIZATION

Before proceeding to an analysis of magnetization, let us briefly summarize a few general properties found to some degree in all ferromagnetic substances and define the symbols by means of which these properties may be expressed mathematically.

According to what has been said in Chaps. II and V, a ferromagnetic substance below its magnetic transformation point is never completely demagnetized—there are always regions of

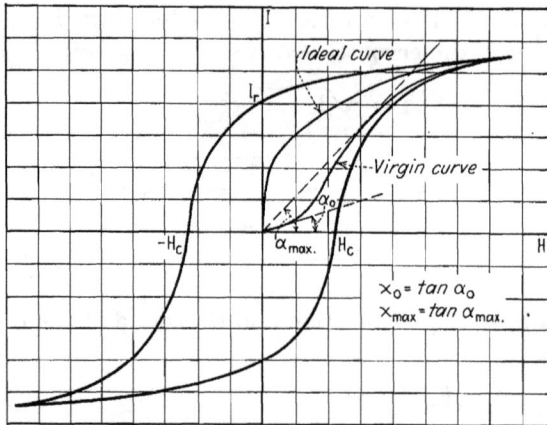

spontaneous magnetization whose intensity we have designated by I_w, while the observed magnetization of a large sample comprising many such regions has been designated by I. This latter will be called the macroscopic magnetization. A sample may be macroscopically demagnetized by reorienting the regions of spontaneous magnetization in such a way that their resultant fields cannot be observed with the usual equipment, such as magnetometers, search coils, etc. Starting with a macroscopically demagnetized sample ($I = 0$), the magnetization proceeds first

180

slowly, then more rapidly, and finally approaches saturation as shown in Fig. 82. The quantities χ_0 and χ_{max} are the initial and the maximum susceptibility respectively. More usually, the permeabilities μ_0 and μ_{max} are used, which refer to the corresponding quantities on the B vs. H curve. If the magnetic field is decreased from some large value to zero, the intensity will not vanish but merely diminish to some value I_r, called the "remanent intensity," or "remanence." In order to reduce I to zero, it is necessary to apply a negative field $-H_c$, which is called the coercive force. These are the magnetic constants most usually referred to.

In addition, the ideal susceptibility and the reversible susceptibility should be mentioned. The first of these quantities is the susceptibility as measured on the ideal magnetization curve in Fig. 82, which is the locus of points obtained by applying a demagnetizing process to a sample before determining I at each field strength. In single crystals, where there is relatively little or no hysteresis, the ideal curve approaches the virgin curve. The reversible susceptibility[1] is obtained by varying H between small limits H and $H + \delta H$ and so causing I to vary between I and $I + \delta I$. The reversible susceptibility

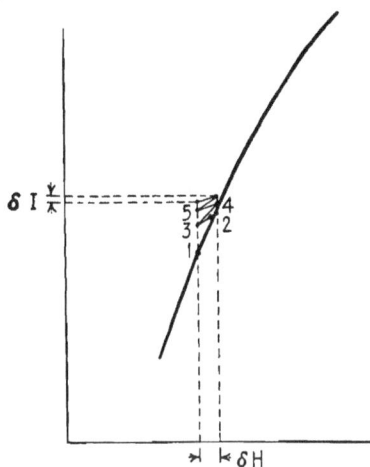

FIG. 83.

---

[1] For a further discussion of reversible magnetization the reader is referred to

R. GANS, *Phys. Zeit.*, **11**, 988, 1910; **12**, 1053, 1911; *Verhand. deut. phys. Ges.*, **12**, 20, 802, 1910; *Ann. Physik*, **64**, 621, 1921; *Z. Physik*, **29**, 270, 1924. M. SAMUEL, *Ann. Physik*, **86**, 798, 1928. G. SIZOO, *Ann. Physik*, **3**, 270, 1929. E. SPUHRMANN, *Z. Physik*, **39**, 332, 1926.
and for ideal magnetization to

E. WARBURG, *Pogg. Ann.*, **139**, 499, 1870. W. STEINHAUS and E. GUMLICH, *Verhand. deut. phys. Ges.*, **17**, 369, 1915. J. WURSCHMIDT, *Z. Physik*, **12**, 128, 1922. M. SAMUEL, *loc. cit.*

χ_r is then defined as $\lim\limits_{\delta H \to 0} \dfrac{\delta I}{\delta H}$. This is, in general, not equal to the slope of the magnetization curve $\delta I/\delta H$. To make this situation quite clear, consider Fig. 83. As H oscillates to and fro, both I and the slope $\delta I/\delta H$ change until a steady state is reached. It is the limit of this slope as $\delta H \to 0$ that determines χ_r. The term "reversible" implies that such a small cyclic process involves no dissipation of energy and is therefore truly reversible. This seems to be borne out by experiment.

In this chapter we shall be concerned chiefly with magnetization in so far as hysteresis effects may be neglected. Hysteresis will be considered separately in a later chapter. The effects of the mechanical deformation of crystals on their magnetic properties will also be considered in a separate chapter.

59. A Qualitative Discussion of Magnetization.—In Chap. V we have discussed the mechanism producing ferromagnetism, *viz.*, the internal fields tending to make neighboring magnetic moments point in the same direction, and the thermal agitation tending to counteract this alinement. The essential result of this discussion was that the statistical treatment of even the simplest three-dimensional model could not be carried through without introducing arbitrary assumptions. It is certain, nevertheless, that a correct treatment would give one of the following two types of solution for temperatures below the Curie point:

1. Spontaneous magnetization of the complete system, as given by the Weiss (Par. 21) or the Heisenberg approximation (Par. 50).

2. Spontaneous magnetization in small regions within a sample only, the regions perhaps being produced by thermal agitation, as in the special case of the linear chain of atoms (Par. 51).

In order to explain the fact that in general it is possible to demagnetize a ferromagnetic sample, it is customary to assume the existence of regions of spontaneous magnetization without specifying how they are produced. By so doing it is possible to describe many features of the magnetization process, as we shall show in the following sections. It must be borne in mind, however, that these regions of spontaneous magnetization are assumed and have not been derived from any theory, and until we know more about their constitution and origin we cannot hope to give a complete and satisfactory interpretation of the magnetization process. A particular case which we shall discuss in Par.

61 is that in which the boundary between two regions involves a
continuous change in direction of magnetization from one region
to the other.   Such a magnetization is really continuous throughout a sample (or a crystal grain) and may conveniently be thought
of as an elastically deformed spontaneous magnetization, in contradistinction to the broken-up magnetization in which regions
with definite boundaries are present, the magnetization being
zero at such boundaries.

Confining our attention for the present to the case where
definite regions are present, we may
assume a demagnetized sample to look
something like Fig. 84.   The size and
shape of the regions are for the present
quite arbitrary.   Each region is supposed
to be magnetized spontaneously to an
intensity I_w as given by such an expression as (69), the various regions differing
in direction of magnetization only.   The
energy per unit volume of any region
depends on its direction of magnetization.   This energy E_θ was discussed in
Par. 56 and 57, and a particular case for
magnetization in a plane only is illustrated in Fig. 84.   The directions of
magnetization of the regions will be those
for which E_θ has a minimum.   In general, there will be several
such possible directions.   Consider two adjacent regions A and
B magnetized as shown and in the presence of a magnetic field.
The energy per unit volume of A and B in the field is

$$E_A = -I_w H \cos \theta_A$$
$$E_B = -I_w H \cos \theta_B \tag{165}$$

where θ is the angle between H and I_w

If the magnetic field is more nearly parallel to the magnetiza-
tion of B than of A, $\theta_B < \theta_A$ and $E_B < E_A$.   The magnetic elements of A at the boundary will therefore change their direction
of magnetization from A to B and will so become part of B, with
a resultant shift of the boundary.   This will continue until A
has disappeared.   This process can go on with no change in the
energy, since the difference between E_B and E_A above may be

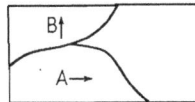

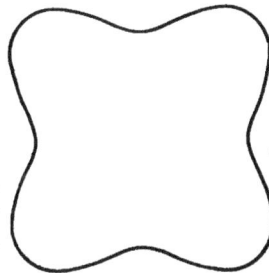

FIG. 84.—E_θ in a (100) plane.

arbitrarily small.   The growth of B at the expense of A changes
the total magnetization of the sample.   Magnetization of this
type will be called translational magnetization because it involves
a translation of the boundaries between regions or a general
shifting of the magnetic structure.   In the German literature such a change in magnetization is sometimes called a
"Schrumpfprozess."

In contradistinction to translational magnetization we have
rotational magnetization, involving the rotation of the direction
of magnetization of the different regions.   If, for instance, in

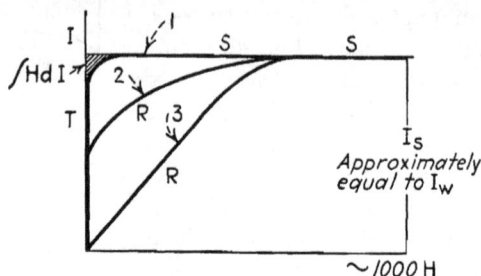

Fig. 85.

Eq. (165) $\theta_A = \theta_B$, then $E_A = E_B$, and no movement of the
boundary is to be expected.   A change in magnetization will
nevertheless take place when H is changed because the external
field will rotate the magnetization of both A and B.   The amount
of rotation may be calculated by finding the orientation of the
magnetization for which the torque exerted by the external field
H is exactly balanced by the torque exerted by the internal field,
or, what amounts to the same thing, the position for which the
total energy

$$E_\theta - I_w H \cos \theta \qquad\qquad (166)$$

is a minimum.

60. Analysis of a Magnetization Curve.—It will be sufficient,
at this point, to consider the magnetization curves typical of
single crystals.   If these are plotted on a scale sufficiently small
to show the complete curves up to saturation, much of the detail
found in the neighborhood of $H = 0$ and illustrated in Fig. 82 is
lost.   Those characteristics to be discussed in the present chapter, on the other hand, are clearly brought out.   In Fig. 85 are
shown typical curves, the scale of H being of the order of 1000

oersteds.   Referring to Fig. 84, if a field is applied to a crystal in one of the directions for which E_θ has a minimum, we may expect to find translational magnetization taking place until the whole crystal consists of only one region magnetized parallel to the field. In this condition the crystal is magnetically saturated.   Magnetization of this kind gives rise to a curve similar to 1 (Fig. 85), and the directions for which such curves are found are called directions of easy magnetization. · The change in internal energy produced by magnetization. $\int H dI$ is in this case small.   According to our model, it should be zero, since processes like the growth of A at the expense of B in Fig. 84 do not involve energy changes.

If a field is applied to a crystal in some direction other than one of easy magnetization, we may expect translational magnetization to take place first, without any change in the internal energy.   When the field is sufficiently large to produce rotational magnetization, the internal energy of the sample is increased, and we get curves similar to 2 (Fig. 85).   It may happen in special cases that there is no translational magnetization, and in such cases the curve obtained will resemble 3 (Fig. 85).

Finally, in very large fields there is very little change in magnetization.   This is called the saturation part of the curve, and the intensity of magnetization of the entire crystal is approximately that of the individual regions in both magnitude and direction.   The nomenclature governing this part of the magnetization process is not very definite.   For many purposes the magnetization is considered constant and equal to I_s, the saturation intensity.   Actually, it is not quite constant, and this variation will be further considered in Par. 65.

The parts of the magnetization curves involving translation, rotation, and approach to saturation are labeled T, R, and S, respectively, in Fig. 85.

61. Magnetization in Small Fields.   Magnetic Structures.— It is customary to speak of fields of one or two oersteds or less as small fields.   These are the fields giving rise to the steep part of the magnetization curve, Fig. 85, in which the translational processes take place.   In Fig. 86 are plotted both a function representing a possible E_θ in a plane and

$$E_{\theta+H} = E_\theta - I_w \cdot H \qquad (167)$$

$E_{\theta+H}$ being the energy of magnetization due to both the crystalline and external fields.   Small fields, as we have defined them, alter the orientations of minimum energy hardly at all, but they do produce a difference in the depth of the minima and, consequently, the translational processes previously discussed. Ideally, magnetization should proceed to a definite limit in infinitesimal fields and then break off sharply when the rotational or saturation part of the curve sets in.   In actual materials such behavior, if it exists, is obscured by hysteresis effects. These are generally ascribed to inhomogeneities in the magnetized medium which prevent the boundary between regions from moving freely.   As will be shown in a subsequent section,

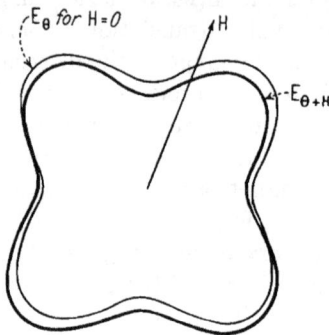

Fig. 86.

local mechanical distortions have a further effect tending to round off the corners of the theoretical curves for perfect crystals, and the rounded curves probably indicate that even carefully prepared single crystals are not geometrically perfect.

In Par. 59 it was pointed out that demagnetization of spontaneously magnetized material could be accounted for by assuming either that this magnetization was broken up into many small regions or that

an elastic distortion of the magnetization had occurred. .We shall discuss briefly the magnetic properties in small fields of such an elastically distorted magnetization.   Qualitatively, the conditions are these: Elastic deformation of a vector field can be maintained only by the application of forces, just as in the case of the elastic deformation of a solid.   Such forces may very well be present at the surfaces of crystals where the lattice spacing is somewhat changed, and an added crystalline field is therefore present.   Such a crystalline field would prevent the free rotation of the magnetic elements near the surface and could, therefore, prevent the disappearance of the elastic deformation of the magnetization in the bulk of a crystal.   The surface forces, however, could not produce the deformation.   For the purposes of the present discussion we may assume that such deformation is formed at the Curie temperature during the last heating of the sample.

The object of this discussion is to find out what types of elastic deformation are possible in a vector field; to show that these may give rise to regularly spaced inhomogeneities such as are actually found in magnetized crystals (Par. 34); and finally to show that elastic deformations, or magnetic structures, as we might call them, comparable to those actually found, lead to magnetization curves that are not inconsistent with those observed. While such evidence as is now available does not establish the correctness of these ideas, it does show that there is an interesting field for further experimental and theoretical work in this direction.

We shall derive the equations governing the elasticity of a vector field for the case of a simple cubic lattice of dipoles without thermal agitation in which only nearest neighbors interact. Consider a typical dipole at some point x,y,z of the lattice, interacting with its six neighbors located at $(x + \Delta x, y, z)$, $(x - \Delta x, y, z)$, $(x, y + \Delta y, z)$, $\cdots$, etc., as shown in Fig. 87. The distances $\Delta x, \Delta y, \Delta z$ are all equal and equal to the lattice constant δ. $\mathbf{A}(x,y,z)$ is a unit vector pointing in the direction of the magnetic moment of the dipole at (x,y,z). We shall assume that the interaction between neighboring dipoles is such that the mutual energy between any two having the orientation $\mathbf{A}$ and $\mathbf{A}'$, respectively, is

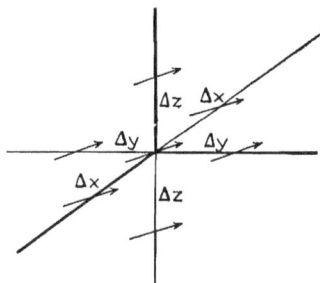

FIG. 87.

$$E = -c\mathbf{A} \cdot \mathbf{A}' \tag{168}$$

This is a minimum when $\mathbf{A}$ and $\mathbf{A}'$ are parallel. The torque $\mathbf{T}_{AA'}$ which $\mathbf{A}'$ exerts on $\mathbf{A}$ is then

$$\mathbf{T}_{AA'} = c\mathbf{A} \times \mathbf{A}' \tag{169}$$

or if

$$\mathbf{A} = \alpha_i i + \alpha_j j + \alpha_k k$$
$$\mathbf{A}' = \alpha'_i i + \alpha'_j j + \alpha'_k k$$

i, j, k being unit vectors parallel to the x-, y-, and z-axes, respectively, (169) may be written

$$\mathbf{T}_{AA'} = c[(\alpha_j \alpha'_k - \alpha_k \alpha'_j)i + (\alpha_k \alpha'_i - \alpha_i \alpha'_k)j + (\alpha_i \alpha'_j - \alpha_j \alpha'_i)k]$$

In the undistorted state all the dipoles will be parallel. If an elastic deformation of the magnetization is present, $\mathbf{A}$ will vary from point to point, and we may put for small deformations

$$\mathbf{A}(x + \Delta x, y + \Delta y, z + \Delta z) = \mathbf{A}(x,y,z) + \left(\Delta x \frac{\partial \mathbf{A}}{\partial x} + \Delta y \frac{\partial \mathbf{A}}{\partial y} \right.$$

$$+ \Delta z \frac{\partial \mathbf{A}}{\partial z} \right) + \frac{1}{2} \left(\Delta x^2 \frac{\partial^2 \mathbf{A}}{\partial x^2} + \Delta y^2 \frac{\partial^2 \mathbf{A}}{\partial y^2} + \Delta z^2 \frac{\partial^2 \mathbf{A}}{\partial z^2} + 2\Delta x \Delta y \frac{\partial^2 \mathbf{A}}{\partial x \partial y} \right.$$

$$\left. + 2\Delta y \Delta z \frac{\partial^2 \mathbf{A}}{\partial y \partial z} + 2\Delta z \Delta x \frac{\partial^2 \mathbf{A}}{\partial z \partial x} \right) + \cdots \quad (170)$$

By substituting (170) in (169) we may express the torque exerted by any neighbor on the dipole at x,y,z in terms of the derivatives of $\mathbf{A}$. For equilibrium the sum of all these torques must vanish, or if an external magnetic or internal crystalline field exerts a torque $\mathbf{T}$, the sum of the torques $\mathbf{T}_{AA'}$ must be equal and opposite to $\mathbf{T}$. Carrying out the indicated summation, the equation

$$-\mathbf{T} = c\delta^2 \sum_{x,y,z} \sum_{i,j,k} \left(\alpha_i \frac{\partial^2 \alpha_k}{\partial x^9} - \alpha_k \frac{\partial^2 \alpha_j}{\partial x^2} \right) i \quad (171)$$

is obtained. This equation may be transformed into polar coordinates θ and φ, shown in Fig. 88, by substituting the following:

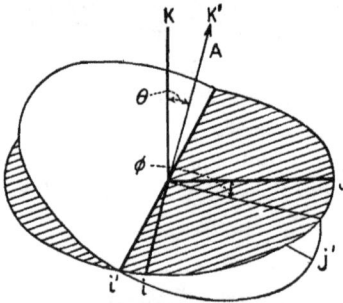

Fig. 88.

$$\alpha_i = \sin \theta \sin \varphi$$
$$\alpha_j = \sin \theta \cos \varphi$$
$$\alpha_k = \cos \theta$$

In this notation Eq. (171) becomes a rather complicated expression which may, however, be simplified by expressing the torque not in terms of its components along the i-, j-, k-axes but in terms of its components along a new set of axes i', j', k', shown in Fig. 88. k' is chosen parallel to A, i' perpendicular to k and k', and j' perpendicular to i' and k'. The result is

$$\frac{-T_{i'}}{c\delta^2} = \frac{T_\theta}{c\delta^2} = -\nabla^2\theta + \sin \theta \cos \theta (\nabla\varphi)^2$$

$$\frac{-T_{j'}}{c\delta^2} = \frac{T_\varphi}{c\delta^2} = \sin \theta \nabla^2\varphi + 2 \cos \theta (\nabla\theta) \cdot (\nabla\varphi)$$

$$\frac{-T_k}{c\delta^2} = 0 \quad (172)$$

For the sake of simplifying the notation the expressions T_θ and T_φ are introduced. T_θ is a torque tending to increase θ, and T_φ a torque tending to increase φ.

A particular case which can be solved is that in which φ is constant and θ depends on x only.   Equation (172) then reduces to

$$T_\theta = -c\delta^2\frac{d^2\theta}{dx^2} \tag{173}$$

In the absence of any fields $T_\theta = 0$, and the solution of (173) is simply

$$\theta = Bx + C$$

or the component of magnetization parallel to x

$$I_x = I_w \cos \theta = I_w \cos (Bx + C) \tag{174}$$

a periodic function of arbitrary period and phase.   This solution satisfies Eq. (173) at every point except at the boundaries of the magnetized medium.   In the absence of forces at the boundary the only permissible value of B is zero, and (174) becomes a uniform magnetization of arbitrary orientation.   If boundary forces are present, however, other values of B are permissible. Let us assume boundary conditions such that $I_x = \pm I_w$ for $x = 0$ and $x = S$.   Then (174) may be written

$$I_x = \pm I_w \cos \frac{\pi x}{L}$$

where L is any length that will go into S an integral number of times.

The effect of an external field on the foregoing solution may be found by putting $T_\theta = -\mu H \sin \theta$ (see Par. 5).   Equation (173) then becomes

$$\frac{d^2\theta}{dx^2} = \frac{\mu H}{c\delta^2} \sin \theta \tag{175}$$

whose solution involves elliptic integrals.[1]   The solution may be put in the form

---

[1] The notation here used, *e.g.*, $F(\alpha,\varphi)$, $K(\alpha)$, $E(\alpha)$, is that found in "Tables of Functions" by E. Jahnke and F. Emde, Teubner, Leipzig and Berlin, 1933.

$$H = \sin^2\alpha \, \frac{c}{\mu}\left(\frac{\delta}{L}\right)^2 F^2\left(\alpha, \frac{\pi}{2}\right)$$

$$\frac{x}{L} = \frac{F(\alpha, \varphi)}{F\left(\alpha, \frac{\pi}{2}\right)}$$

$2L$ = length of the period of the magnetization

$I = I_w \cos\theta$

$\theta = 2\varphi + \pi$ \hfill (176)

The solution is plotted in Fig. 89 in the form of I_x as a function of x for $H = 0$ and for a positive and a negative value of H. In

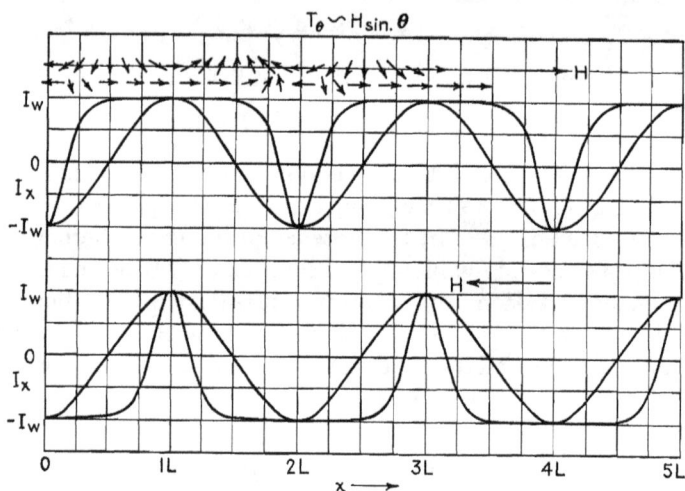

Fig. 89.—Distribution of magnetization in a medium in which the magnetization is "elastically twisted" in the x-direction.

the absence of a field there is as much positive as negative magnetization. A positive field increases the extent of the positively magnetized regions at the expense of the negative regions. Inhomogeneities of magnetization are especially marked near the points $x = 0, 2L, 4L$, etc., in positive fields and near the points $x = 1L, 3L, 5L$, etc., in negative fields.

Another case has been calculated, *viz.*, that of an internal field giving a torque

$$T_\theta = -2F \sin 2\theta$$

Such might be produced in a material by compression or elongation of the lattice. The results are plotted in Fig. 90. Although the period is the same, inhomogeneities in magnetization occur at distances L rather than $2L$, as in the case of an external magnetic field.

There is a certain similarity between the behavior of this model and the magnetic patterns actually observed in crystals.

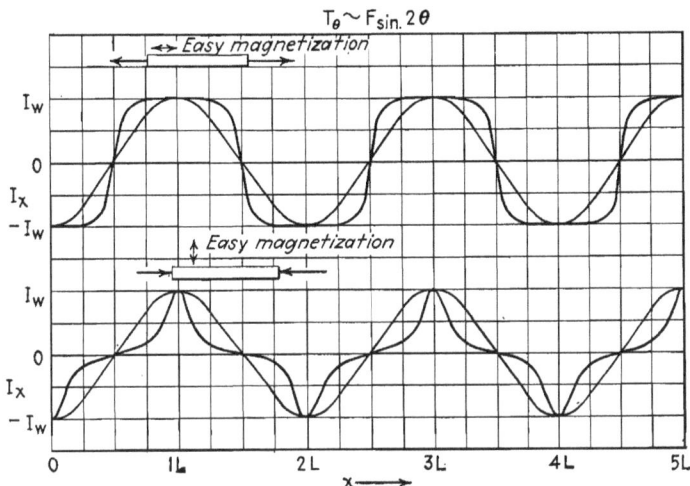

FIG. 90.—Distribution of magnetization in a medium in which the magnetization is "elastically twisted" in the x-direction.

It remains to calculate the magnetization curve of the preceding model. The average magnetization of a sample is simply the sum of the contributions of its various parts, or

$$I = \int_0^L I_x \frac{dx}{L} .$$

which, using (176), is

$$I = -I_w\left[1 - 2\frac{K(\alpha) - E(\alpha)}{\sin^2\alpha\, K(\alpha)}\right]$$

$$H = \frac{c}{\mu}\left(\frac{\delta}{L}\right)^2 \sin^2\alpha\, K^2(\alpha) \tag{177}$$

For large fields this reduces to

$$I = I_w\left[1 - \frac{a}{\sqrt{H}}\right]$$

$$a = 2\frac{\delta}{L}\sqrt{\frac{c}{\mu}} \tag{178}$$

The constant c is a measure of the energy needed to reverse a magnetic moment with respect to its neighbors and is, therefore, comparable to the quantity ϵ in Par. 52 which, in turn, is related to the Curie temperature θ (not to be confused with the angle θ used in the preceding discussion) according to Eq. (106):

$$\epsilon = k\theta$$

A reasonable order of magnitude of c may be found by putting $\theta = 10^3$, and since $k = 1.37 \times 10^{-16}$, we have $c \sim 10^{-13}$. The

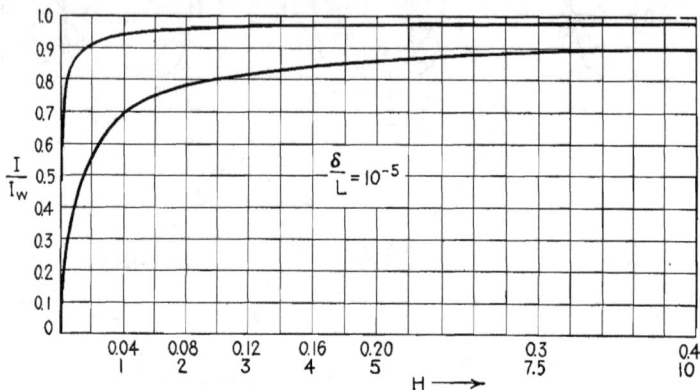

FIG. 91.—Magnetization curve corresponding to the conditions shown in Fig. 89.

constant L may be chosen arbitrarily. The spacing of actual magnetic inhomogeneities is found to be of the order of 10^{-3} cm.; and if we choose this for L, and $\delta \sim 10^{-8}$ cm., we have $\delta/L \sim 10^{-5}$. With these values and $\mu = 10^{-20}$, or 1 Bohr magneton, we get the curve in Fig. 91. Because of the roughness of our assumption no close agreement with any experimental curve is to be expected. Few if any measurements so far made show as high magnetizations in small fields as indicated in the figure. But the approximation is at least as satisfactory as that obtained by assuming separate regions of spontaneous magnetization, in which I approaches I_w in arbitrarily small fields.

These considerations may be more useful in the future when we know more about magnetization both theoretically and experimentally. Before leaving the subject, however, a few words might be said on experimental determinations of the variation of the initial susceptibility χ_0 (see Fig. 82) with tem-

perature.   Representative results are shown in Fig. 92.   Here θ
represents the Curie temperature.   Typically we have a small
initial susceptibility at temperatures well below the Curie temperature, decreasing with decreasing temperature.   As the Curie
temperature is approached from below, χ_0 rises to a maximum
and then falls rapidly to a very small value, which above the Curie
temperature becomes comparable to ordinary paramagnetic
susceptibilities.   That is roughly the behavior of both iron and
nickel, as shown in curve 1 (Fig. 92).   In iron there is, according
to Renger,[1] a small kink in the curve at $-11°C.$, as shown in
curve 2.   This is rather striking,
as no transformation at this temperature is known.   The anomaly
seems to be related to a time lag
and to a magnetic aging.   That is,
at $-11°C.$ the time required for a
steady value of I to set in after a
change in H is much greater than
either above or below this temperature.   Furthermore, the exact
shape of the kink depends on how
long the material was kept at a temperature near 120°C. during
its previous heating.

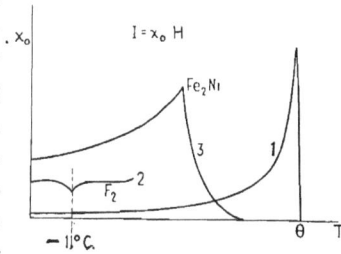

FIG. 92.—Initial susceptibility as a
function of temperature.

Besides irregularities of this type, most materials show a considerable sensitiveness to purity and to their previous history.
Thus the initial susceptibility of "iron" at room temperature,
according to Renger's early measurements, varies between 6 and
60 roughly, depending chiefly on the thermal treatment of the
sample.   In 1928 with vacuum-fused electrolytic iron Yensen and
Ziegler[2] obtained an initial susceptibility of 92, and more recently
still Cioffi[3] has obtained values of from 500 to 1600.   Work by
Becker and Kersten on the influence of deformation is mentioned
in Par. 73.

In alloys the susceptibility *vs.* temperature curves are often
quite different.   Curve 3 in Fig. 92 is for an alloy[4] having a
composition corresponding to Fe_2Ni.   The maximum is con-

---

[1] K. RENGER, thesis, Zurich, 1911.

[2] See article by T. D. YENSEN, *J. Franklin Inst.*, **206**, 503, 1928; Chap. IV.

[3] P. P. CIOFFI, *Nature*, **126**, 200, 1930; *Phys. Rev.*, **45**, 742, 1934.

[4] P. WEISS and J. DE FREUDENREICH, *Arch. sci. phys. nat.*, **39**, 125, 1915.

siderably below the Curie temperature, and the curve falls off much more gradually. In some iron-cobalt alloys there are at least two maxima according to Weiss and Freudenreich[1] and several regions in which no accurate readings were possible because of the dependence of the magnetization on the time during which the sample was exposed to the magnetic field.

62. Rotational Magnetization as a Function of H.—Rotational magnetization, as has been pointed out, results from the rotation of the regions of spontaneous magnetization. If a region is magnetized in such a direction as to make an angle ψ with the applied field, its component parallel to the field I_p, or simply I, will be

$$I = I_p = I_w \cos \psi \qquad (179)$$

and its component normal to the field

$$I_n = I_w \sin \psi \qquad (180)$$

where I_w is the intensity of the spontaneous magnetization of the region itself. The direction in which the spontaneous magnetization will orient itself will be such as to make the energy $E_\theta - \mathbf{I}_w \cdot \mathbf{H}$ a minimum, or such that

$$\delta(E_\theta - I_w H \cos \psi) = 0 \qquad (181)$$

where δ represents any variation of the orientation of I_w. In order to proceed, it is necessary to make use of the functions E_θ derived in Chap. V.

In cubic crystals the simplest function E_θ for undistorted crystals ($F_{ij} = 0$) was, according to Eq. (159),

$$E_\theta = a_F \Sigma' \alpha_i^2 \alpha_j^2 \qquad (182)$$

As we shall see, this function is satisfactory for our purposes, but in some cases better agreement with experiment may be obtained by including terms involving higher powers of α. α_i, α_j, α_k are the direction cosines of the spontaneous magnetization with respect to the cubic axes of the crystal, and a_F is a constant describing the material of which the crystal is made. Two cases are to be distinguished, *viz.*, that in which $a_F < 0$, as in nickel, or that in which $a_F > 0$, as in iron. Figures 93 and 94 show plaster models

[1] P. Weiss and J. de Freudenreich, *Arch. sci. phys. nat.*, **42**, 5, 1916; **42**, 449, 1916.

of E_θ for these two cases.   The energy of magnetization in any direction in the crystal model in the figures is given by the length

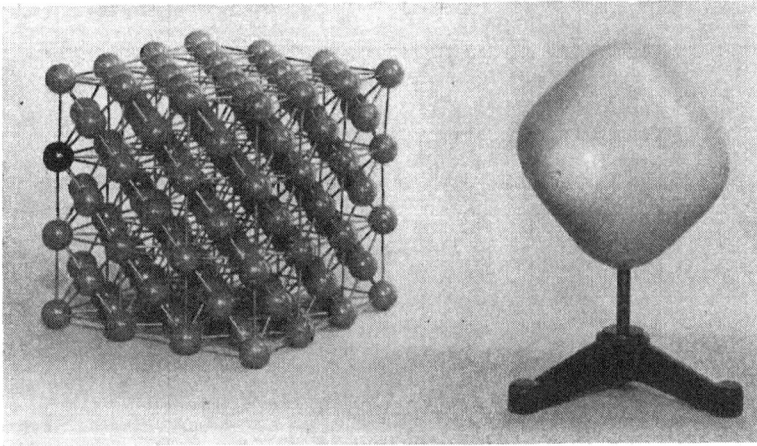

FIG. 93.—E_θ in nickel.

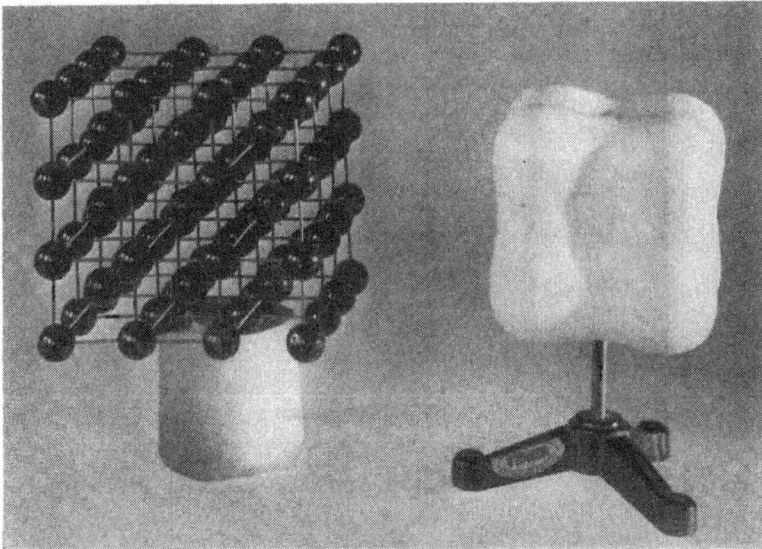

FIG. 94.—E_θ in iron.

of a line parallel to such magnetization from the center of the plaster model to its surface.   For $a_F < 0$ the energies are least parallel to the volume diagonals, or trigonal axes; these are the

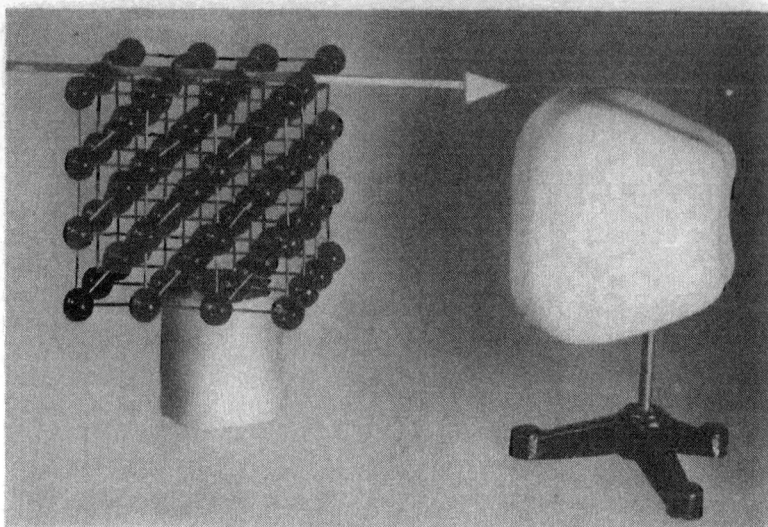

Fig. 95.—$E_{\theta+H}$ in iron.

Fig. 96.—$E_{\theta+H}$ in iron.

directions of easy magnetization; the energies are greatest parallel to the cube edges, or tetragonal axes.   For $a_F > 0$ the opposite is true, and the directions of easy magnetization are the cubic axes.

In the presence of a magnetic field we are concerned with the function

$$E_{\theta+H} = E_\theta - \mathbf{I}_w \cdot \mathbf{H}$$

This function is similarly illustrated for $a_F > 0$ and H parallel to a tetragonal, a digonal, and a trigonal axis, in Figs. 95, 96 and 97,

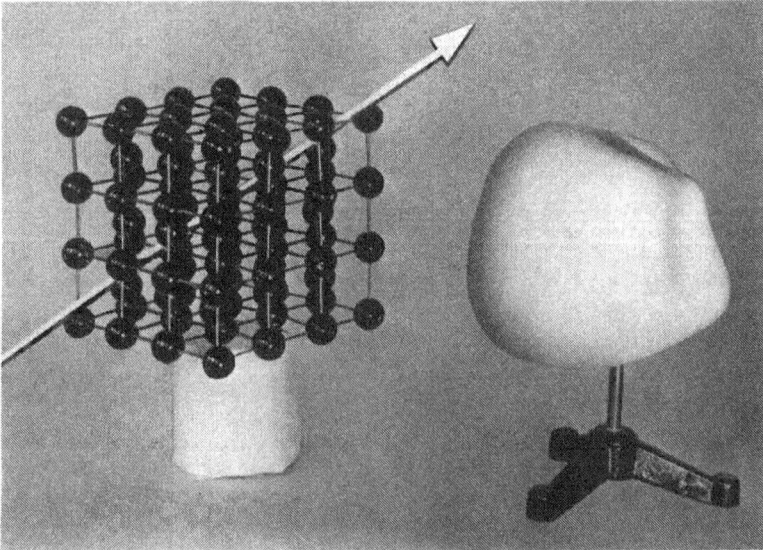

Fig. 97.—$E_{\theta+H}$ in iron.

respectively.   The shape of these models depends not only on the orientation of H but also on its magnitude.   The models in the figures were made to describe an iron crystal in a field of 100 oersteds.   They are intended to illustrate qualitatively the relative changes of depth and angular position of the various minima of $E_{\theta+H}$.

More detailed information may be obtained by examining the cross sections of these plaster models.   To do this it is convenient to replace the direction cosines by angular coordinates by putting

$$\alpha_i = \sin\theta \sin\varphi$$
$$\alpha_j = \sin\theta \cos\varphi$$
$$\alpha_k = \cos\theta$$

as shown in Fig. 98.   This gives

$$E_{\theta+H} = 2a_F\{\sin^4\theta \sin^2\varphi \cos^2\varphi + \sin^2\theta \cos^2\theta\} - \mathbf{I}_w \cdot \mathbf{H}$$

$$= \frac{a_F}{4}\left\{\frac{1}{2}\left(\frac{3}{4} - \cos 2\theta + \frac{1}{4}\cos 4\theta\right)(1 - \cos 4\varphi) + (1 - \cos 4\theta)\right\}$$
$$- \mathbf{I}_w \cdot \mathbf{H} \quad (183)$$

Putting $\varphi = 0$ restricts the magnetization to a (100) plane; and if α represents the angle between H and a cubic axis, as shown in

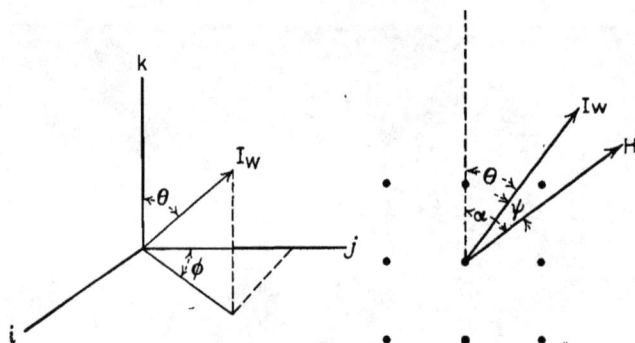

Fig. 98.   Fig. 99.

Fig. 99, we have $\psi = \alpha - \theta$, and Eq. (183) reduces to

$$E_{\theta+H} = \frac{a_F}{4}(1 - \cos 4\theta) - I_w H \cos(\alpha - \theta) \quad (184)$$

or, expressing $E_{\theta+H}$ in arbitrary units, we may divide by $a_F/4$ and obtain, for the terms containing θ,

$$E_{\theta+H} = -\cos 4\theta - 8h \cos(\alpha - \theta) \quad (185)$$

h being proportional to the external field

$$h = \frac{I_w H}{2a_F} \quad (186)$$

The properties of any given material determine the scale of h. Using Eq. (185) it is possible to calculate how $E_{\theta+H}$ varies in a (100) plane with the magnitude and orientation of the magnetic field.   Such results are plotted in Figs. 100, 101, and 102, a_F having been chosen positive, as in iron.   In Fig. 100 the magnetic field is applied in a [100] direction.   The minimum for $\theta = 0$, which in the absence of an external field ($h = 0$) has the same

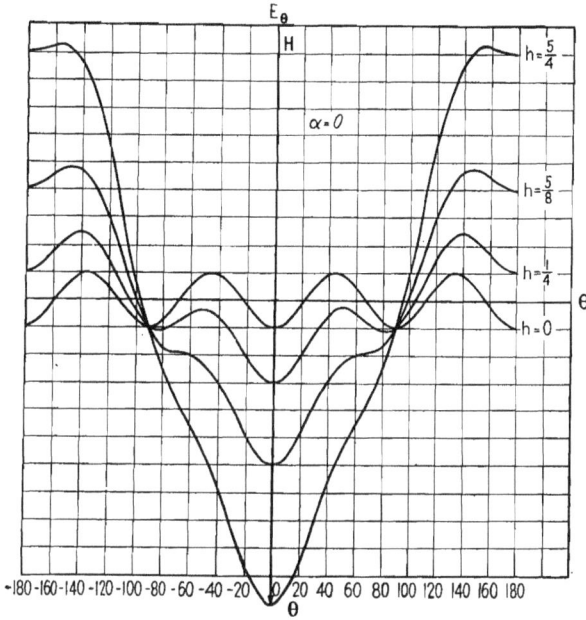

FIG. 100.—$E_{\theta+H}$ in iron in a (100) plane.

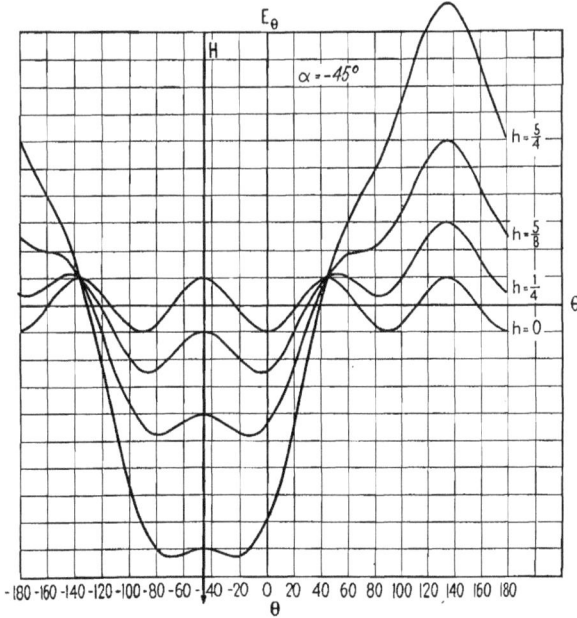

FIG. 101.—$E_{\theta+H}$ in iron in a (100) plane.

depth as the other minima at $\theta = \pm 90°$—$180°$, becomes lower than the rest when a field is applied. In this case we may expect translational magnetization until the entire crystal is magnetized parallel to the field, or $I = I_w$. In Fig. 101 the applied field is parallel to a [110] direction. In this case the minima at $\theta = -90°$

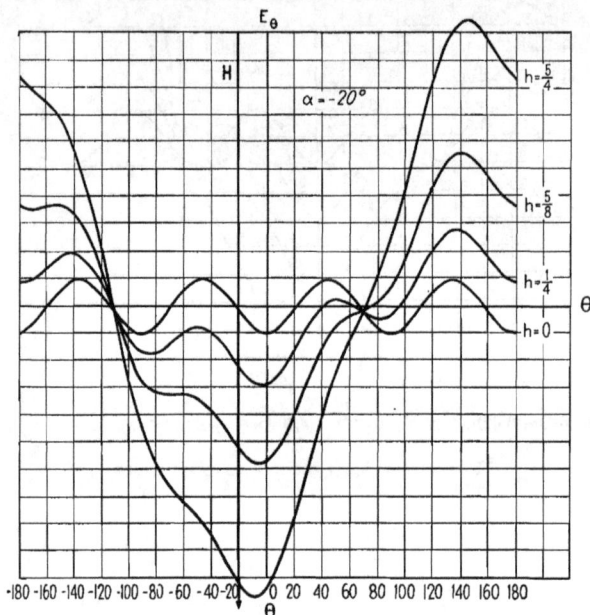

FIG. 102.—$E_{\theta+H}$ in iron in a (100) plane.

and $0°$ are lowered when a field is applied. The resulting translational magnetization will produce an intensity given by

$$I = I_w \cos \psi = \frac{I_w}{\sqrt{2}}$$

Small fields do not appreciably affect the angular position of the minima. Large fields, however, do, and so produce rotational magnetization. If equal volumes of the crystal are magnetized in the direction of each of the two minima in Fig. 101, we shall have $I_n = 0$. And finally in Fig. 102 the field is applied in a direction between [100] and [110]. There is only one absolute minimum, but this does not coincide with the direction of the applied field. We may therefore expect $I_n \neq 0$. The presence of such a perpendicular component of I is sometimes referred to as a deviation effect.

We shall now consider the (100) plane of a cubic lattice quantitatively. The minima of $E_{\theta+H}$, as given by Eq. 184, will be found for values of $\theta = \theta'$ which satisfy $\partial E_{\theta+H}/\partial\theta = 0$ or which satisfy

$$a_F \sin 4\theta' = I_w H \sin (\alpha - \theta') \tag{187}$$

For a comparison with experiment it is desired to know I_p and I_n as a function of α. In other words, as the crystal is rotated

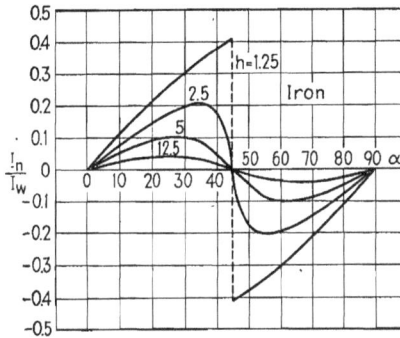

FIG. 103.—The component of magnetization normal to the applied field in a (100) plane in iron.

in a constant magnetic field, it is desired to know how the perpendicular component $I_n = I_w \sin (\alpha - \theta')$ and the parallel component $I_p = I_w \cos (\alpha - \theta')$ vary. Equation (187) may be written

$$a_F \sin 4\theta' = I_n H$$

which has a maximum for $\theta' = 22\frac{1}{2}$ deg. and for this value of θ' we have

$$H I_n]_{\max} = a_F \tag{188}$$

In sufficiently intense fields this maximum value is reached (as is shown above, for example, in the curves for $h = 2.5$, 5, and 12.5 but not for $h = 1.25$ in Fig. (103), and (188) is therefore a convenient method for determining a_F. With the previous definition of h in Eq. (186), Eq. (187) becomes

$$\sin 4\theta' = 2h \sin (\alpha - \theta') \tag{189}$$

The values of I_n and I_p, as calculated from this equation, are plotted in Figs. 103 and 104, a_F being assumed positive. The dotted part of the curve in Fig. 103 represents a translational

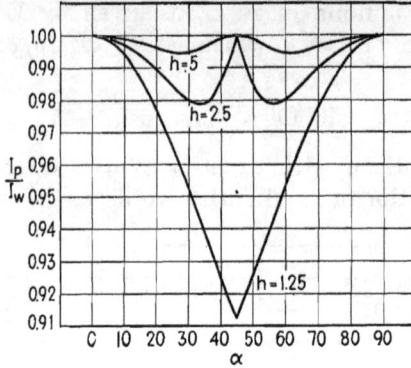

Fig. 104.—The component of magnetization parallel to the applied field in a (100) plane in iron.

change of magnetization which occurs when one of the minima of E_θ becomes lower than another. This occurs for $\alpha = 45$ deg., as may readily be seen from Figs. 101 and 102. In actual crystals

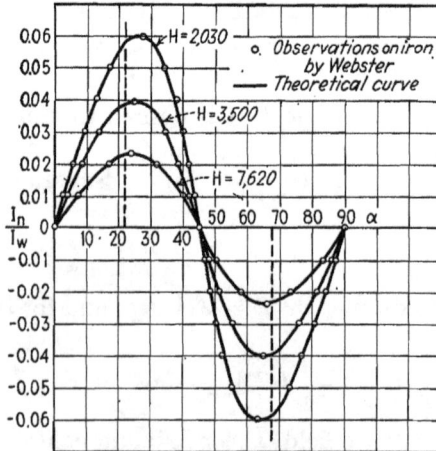

Fig. 105.—A comparison of the theoretical curves in Fig. 103 with experimental results.

this translational process does not take place at one definite angle but over a certain range of angles. In larger fields, however, there are no translational processes, and the agreement with experiment is more satisfactory. A comparison with experimental results obtained by Webster[1] on the deviation effect is given in Fig. 105. The values of a_F used to give the agreement shown on the three curves are

H	a_F
7620	2.63×10^5
3500	2.23×10^5
2030	1.95×10^5

This dependence of a_F on H is not in agreement with our assumption that a_F is a constant.

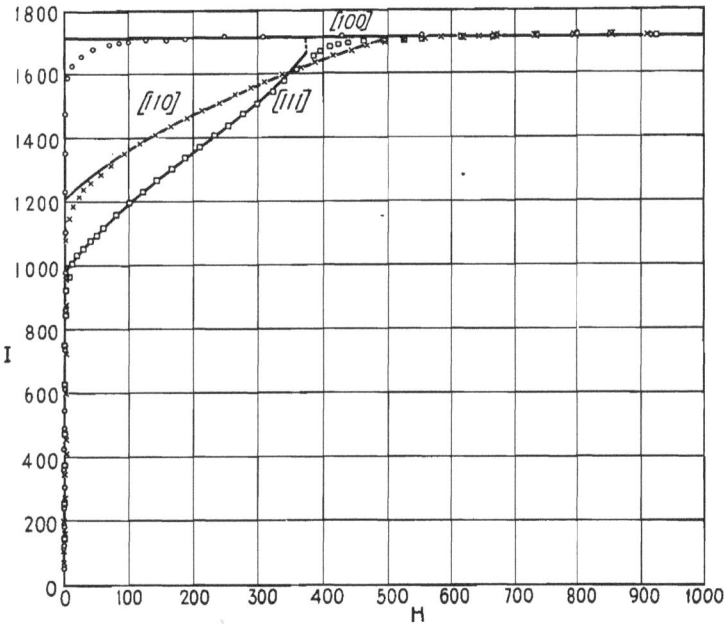

FIG. 106.—Magnetization curves for an iron crystal.

Magnetization curves may be calculated by essentially the same process as above. For magnetization parallel to a tetragonal axis we have translational magnetization up to saturation in infinitesimal fields, as shown in the curve marked [100] in Fig. 106. For magnetization parallel to a digonal axis, the deepest minima lie in a (100) plane, as may be seen from the plaster model in Fig. 96. We may therefore use $E_{\theta+H}$ for a (100) plane, as in

[1] W. WEBSTER, *Proc. Roy. Soc.*, **107**, 496, 1925.

Eq. (184) in making the calculation, putting $\alpha = \pi/4$, which leads to

$$a_F \sin 4\theta' = I_w H \sin \left(\frac{\pi}{4} - \theta' \right) \qquad (190)$$

as the condition to be satisfied by θ' in the rotational part of the magnetizing process. Putting $\psi = \frac{\pi}{4} - \theta'$, this may be written

$$a_F \sin 4\psi = I_w H \sin \psi$$
$$I_p = I = I_w \cos \psi \qquad (191)$$

which may be rewritten in the form

$$4 \sin \psi \cos \psi (2 \cos^2 \psi - 1) = \frac{I_w H}{a_F} \sin \psi$$

or simply

$$H = aI + bI^3$$
$$a = -\frac{4a_F}{I_w^2}; \qquad b = \frac{8a_F}{I_w^4} \qquad (192)$$

This function is represented by the curve marked [110] in Fig. 106. For $H = 0$ we have

$$0 = -\frac{4a_F I}{I_w^2} \left[1 - 2 \left(\frac{I}{I_w} \right)^2 \right]$$

which is satisfied for $I = \dfrac{I_w}{\sqrt{2}}$ in agreement with what has already been said regarding the extent of translational magnetization parallel to a digonal axis.

For magnetization along a trigonal axis, the minima of $E_{\theta+H}$ always lie on (110) or similar planes. One such is found by putting $\varphi = \pi/4$, which reduces Eq. (183) to

$$E_{\theta+H} = \frac{a_F}{4} \left(\frac{7}{4} - \cos 2\theta - \frac{3}{4} \cos 4\theta \right) - I_w H \cos (\alpha - \theta) \quad (193)$$

The minima are found for values of $\theta = \theta'$ satisfying

$$\frac{\partial E_{\theta+H}}{\partial \theta} = 0 = \frac{a_F}{4} (2 \sin 2\theta' + 3 \sin 4\theta') - I_w H \sin (\alpha - \theta')$$

or, in a more convenient form for computation,

$$\cos \psi - \cos (4\alpha - 3\psi) = \frac{2HI_w}{3a_F}$$

$$I = I_w \cos \psi$$

$$\cos \alpha = \frac{1}{\sqrt{3}} \qquad (194)$$

The parameter ψ may be eliminated from these equations, giving

$$\frac{I}{I_w}\left[7\left(\frac{I}{I_w}\right)^2 - 3\right] + \sqrt{2}\left[4\left(\frac{I}{I_w}\right)^2 - 1\right]\left[1 - \left(\frac{I}{I_w}\right)^2\right]^{\frac{1}{2}} = \frac{3HI_w}{2a_F} \qquad (195)$$

In this case the translational magnetization stops for $I/I_w = 1/\sqrt{3}$, which, substituted in the preceding equation, gives $H = 0$. Equation (195) is represented by the curve marked [111] in Fig. 106. The value of a_F used in plotting this figure is 2.14×10^5 ergs per cubic centimeter. For fields in the neighborhood of 375 gauss parallel to a [111] axis E_θ develops new minima which may give rise to translational processes near saturation. In any case, $E_{\theta+H}$ is very flat in this neighborhood, and the direction of magnetization is not very clearly defined energetically within considerable limits.

The points shown in the figure are observations published by Honda and Kaya.[1] The agreement is, on the whole, very good. Akulov[2] was the first to give the foregoing interpretation of the magnetization curves. More or less contemporaneous work by Mahajani,[3] Webster,[4] Powell,[5] and Fowler[6] was on the right track but was not carried so far. A very good discussion of the whole subject, including higher powered terms in E_θ, has been given by Gans and Czerlinski.[7] Also, Bozorth[8] has discussed the deviation effect from a point of view differing somewhat from that here adopted.

[1] K. HONDA and S. KAYA, Science Repts. Tôhoku Imp. Univ., 15, 721, 1926.

[2] N. S. AKULOV, Z. Physik, 57, 249, 1929; 67, 794, 1931; 69, 78, 1931.

[3] A. S. MAHAJANI, Phil. Trans. Roy. Soc., (a) 228, 63, 1929.

[4] W. L. WEBSTER, Proc. Phys. Soc. London, 42, 431, 1930.

[5] F. C. POWELL, Proc. Roy. Soc., 130, 167, 1930.

[6] F. C. POWELL and R. H. FOWLER, Proc. Camb. Phil. Soc., 27, 280, 1931.

[7] R. GANS and E. CZERLINSKI, Schriften Königsberger gelehrten Ges., 9, 1, 1932. R. GANS, Physik. Z., 33, 924, 1932.

[8] R. M. BOZORTH, Phys. Rev., 42, 882, 1932.

If $a_F < 0$, as in nickel, the deviation effect and magnetization curves may be derived by essentially the same argument as above. The results for the magnetization curves are, for H parallel to a digonal axis,

$$H = aI + bI^3$$
$$a = \frac{4a_F}{I_w^2}; \qquad b = \frac{-6a_F}{I_w^4} \tag{196}$$

and for H parallel to a tetragonal axis an equation of the preceding form with

$$a = \frac{2a_F}{I_w^2}; \qquad b = -\frac{6a_F}{I_w^4}$$

It is interesting to observe that the magnetization curves for cubic crystals may be put into the form of universal functions, so that the properties of different crystals differ only in the scale to be used for I and H. Putting $J = I/I_w$ so that $J = 1$ for saturation, and putting $h = I_w H/2a_F$, as above, we have, for $a_F > 0$,

$$H \parallel [100]$$

saturation in arbitrarily small fields;

$$H \parallel [110]$$
$$h = 2J(2J^2 - 1); \tag{197}$$
$$H \parallel [111]$$
$$h = \tfrac{1}{3}\{J(7J^2 - 3) + \sqrt{2}(4J^2 - 1)\sqrt{1 - J^2}\}; \tag{198}$$

and for $a_F < 0$,

$$H \parallel [100]$$
$$-h = J(3J^2 - 1); \tag{199}$$
$$H \parallel [110]$$
$$-h = J(3J^2 - 2); \tag{200}$$
$$H \parallel [111]$$

saturation in arbitrarily small fields.

All these equations are plotted for comparison on the same graph (Fig. 107). The agreement with experiment in the case of nickel is not so good as in the case of iron, chiefly because the translational magnetization does not proceed so readily in small fields. In a subsequent section we shall show that this is probably due to the fact that the nickel crystals so far investigated are relatively less perfect than the iron crystals, or, perhaps more correctly, that the imperfections present in nickel crystals are more disturbing than those present in iron crystals. The values of a_F and I_w for iron and nickel are

For Iron	For Nickel[1]
$a_F = 2.1$ to 2.2×10^5 ergs/cc.	$a_F = -1.8$ to -2.6×10^4 ergs/cc.
$I_w = 1720$	$I_w = 500$

In alloys having a cubic structure, results essentially similar to the above are obtained. Lichtenberger[2] has found that in

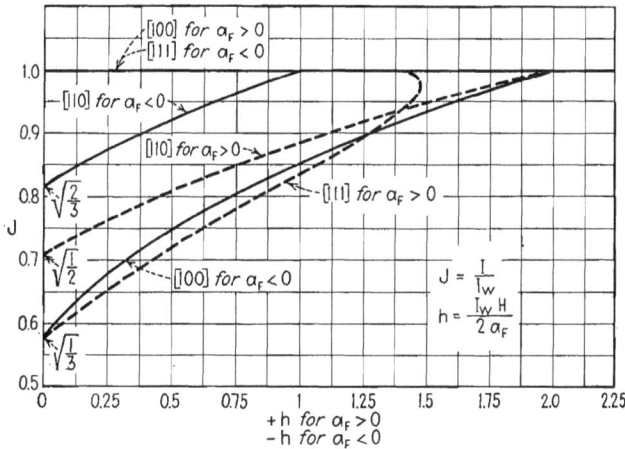

Fig. 107.—Magnetization curves for perfect cubic crystals, according to the theory of Akulov.

iron-nickel alloys $a_F > 0$ in the range 30 to 70 per cent Ni, and $a_F < 0$ in the range 70 to 100 per cent Ni. Similarly, Shih[3] found the following values for iron-cobalt alloys:

Per Cent Cobalt	a_F
30	0.57×10^5 ergs/cc.
40	0.16
50	−0.55
70	−2.1

The method of procedure in the foregoing calculations is sufficiently clear so that we shall merely indicate the results

[1] R. GANS and E. CZERLINSKI, *loc. cit.* F. BITTER, *Phys. Rev.*, **38**, 546, 1931.

[2] F. LICHTENBERGER, *Ann. Physik*, (5), **15**, 45, 1932.

[3] J. W. SHIH, *Phys. Rev.*, **46**, 139, 1934.

obtained for other crystals. For cobalt the expression for E_θ has been derived under the assumption of a rigid crystal. A similar expression may be derived for a free crystal:

$$E_{\theta+H} = a'_F \cos^4 \theta + a_F \cos^2 \theta - I_w H \cos(\alpha - \theta) \quad (201)$$

the constants a'_F, a_F being related to the constants a' and a of Eq. (149) through the elastic constants and the magnetostriction constants in a manner similar to the case of cubic crystals, worked out in Par. 57. θ is the angle between I_w and the hexagonal axis, and α is the angle between H and the hexagonal axis. The angle φ does not appear because to the preceding order of approximation hexagonal crystals are isotropic about the hexagonal axis. This is at least approximately borne out by experiment.

The deviation effect in cobalt crystals is essentially similar to that found in iron crystals in a (100) plane and illustrated in Figs. 103 and 104 except that the periodicity is 180 instead of 90 deg. This is so because a'_F, above, may to a first approximation be neglected, making E_θ essentially proportional to $\cos 2\theta$, instead of $\cos 4\theta$, as in iron (Eq. 185).

The directions of easy magnetization in hexagonal crystals may occur for the directions $\theta = \theta'$, satisfying the equation

$$\frac{\partial E_\theta}{\partial \theta} = 0 = -4a'_F \cos^3 \theta' \sin \theta' - 2a_F \cos \theta' \sin \theta'$$

which has solutions for

$$\theta' = 0$$

$$\theta' = \frac{\pi}{2}$$

$$\cos^2 \theta' = -\frac{a_F}{2a'_F}$$

In cobalt at room temperatures the constants have such values that the last solution is imaginary, the direction of easy magnetization is parallel to the hexagonal axis $\theta' = 0$, and the directions of most difficult magnetization are for $\theta' = \pi/2$.

The equation for the magnetization curve of cobalt in a direction perpendicular to the hexagonal axis is easily found to be[1]

---

[1] This expression was first applied to cobalt by Gans and Czerlinski, *loc. cit.*

$$4a'_F\left(\frac{I}{I_w}\right)^3 - 2(a_F + 2a'_F)\frac{I}{I_w} = I_wH \qquad (202)$$

This equation, with

$$a_F = -6.51 \times 10^6$$
$$a'_F = 1.18 \times 10^6$$
$$I_w = 1420$$

is plotted in Fig. 108, together with experimental points observed by Kaya.[1] The agreement is seen to be excellent. For a hexagonal crystal in which the directions of easy magnetization are in the plane perpendicular to the hexagonal axis, as in the case of cobalt at elevated temperatures (Par. 63), the formula for the magnetization curve is

$$4a'_F\left(\frac{I}{I_w}\right)^3 + 2a_F\frac{I}{I_w} = I_wH$$

$$(203)$$

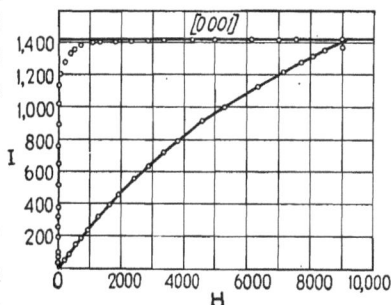

FIG. 108.—Magnetization curves for a cobalt crystal.

Pyrrhotite crystals behave in an interesting but rather complicated fashion. Various samples from different parts of the world differ considerably, but extensive observations have led to the following conclusions:[2] Although the crystals are generally considered to have hexagonal structure, the magnetic symmetry is not of this type. In the direction of the hexagonal axis the crystals are practically paramagnetic. Magnetization in the plane perpendicular to this axis is much easier. The magnetic symmetry in this plane differs from one sample to another and may in some crystals be altered by annealing in a magnetic field. Some crystals have a single direction of easy magnetization in this plane and have rhombic symmetry magnetically. Some behave as if they were composed of groups of crystals having their directions of easy magnetization displaced by 60 deg. with respect to each other. The magnetization curves of the crystals having

[1] S. KAYA, *Science Repts. Tôhoku Imp. Univ.*, **17**, 1157, 1928.

[2] P. WEISS, *J. phys.*, **4**, 49, 829, 1905. P. WEISS and J. KUNZ, *J. phys.*, **4**, 847, 1905. M. ZIEGLER, dissertation, Zurich, 1915.

rhombic symmetry may be derived from an energy function of the form

$$E_0 = a_1\alpha_1^2 + a_2\alpha_2^2 + a_3\alpha_3^2$$

Figure 109, taken from the International Critical Tables (page 413, vol. 6), shows the results obtained experimentally by Ziegler. I_z is for magnetization along the hexagonal axis; I_x and I_y, for two mutually perpendicular directions in the plane normal to the hexagonal axis.

63. Rotational Magnetization as a Function of T.—In the last section it was shown that the rotational magnetization of substances like iron and nickel could be expressed by means of universal functions [Eqs. (197) to (200)], the only arbitrarily disposable constants being those which determine the scale of I and H. As might be expected, the temperature affects both of these scales. The variation of I_w with T will be discussed in Par. 66. The variation of the scale of H is determined by the constants a_F and I_w in the relation

$$h = \frac{I_w H}{2a_F}$$

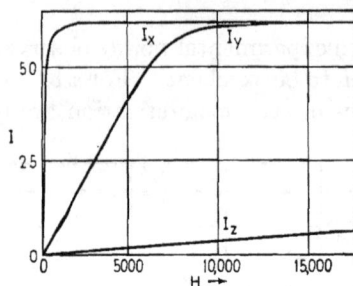

Fig. 109.—Magnetization curves for a pyrrhotite crystal.

Honda, Masumoto, and Kaya[1] have measured the magnetization curves of iron crystals in various directions over a considerable range in temperature. Using their experimentally determined values of I_w and a suitable value of a_F for every temperature, their results for magnetization in the [110] and [111] directions have been plotted in Figs. 110 and 111 as J vs. h. All the observations fall fairly well on the theoretical curves. The values of a_F used to obtain this agreement are shown in Fig. 112. It is interesting to note that the magnetic anisotropy of iron becomes very small considerably below the Curie temperature. There is at present no theory to account for this behavior.[2]

[1] K. Honda, H. Masumoto, and S. Kaya, *Science Repts. Tôhoku Imp. Univ.*, **17**, 111, 1928.

[2] A paper on this subject has recently appeared. N. S. Akulov, *Z. Physik*, **100**, 197, 1936.

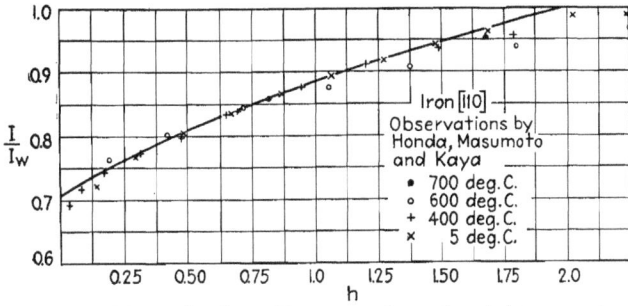

FIG. 110.—Magnetization of iron crystals at elevated temperatures.

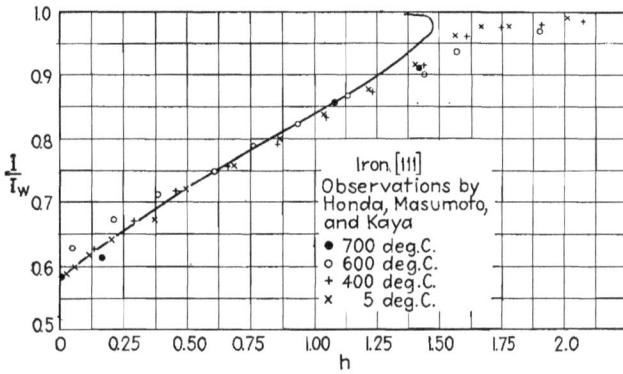

FIG. 111.—Magnetization of iron crystals at elevated temperatures.

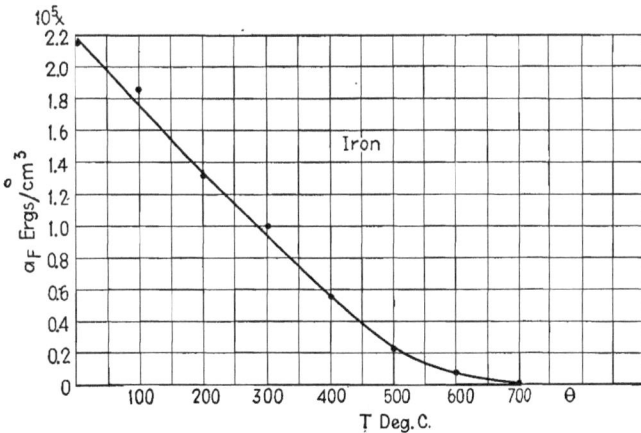

FIG. 112.—a_F in iron as a function of temperature.

Honda and Masumoto[1] have investigated the magnetization of cobalt crystals for temperatures ranging from -190 to $390°C$. Their results may be represented with considerable accuracy by curves derived from Eq. (201) with the following values for the constants:[2]

T, °C.	a_F	a'_F
-190	-12.8×10^6	3.1×10^6
12	-7.8	2.2
100	-4.7	1.4
200	-1.9	0.86
300	0	0.45
390	1.3	0.3

In order to determine the directions of easy magnetization, we must find the values of θ for which E_θ is a minimum or for which

$$\frac{dE_\theta}{d\theta} = 0 \quad \text{and} \quad \frac{d^2E_\theta}{d\theta^2} > 0$$

Values of θ satisfying both these conditions are readily found to be

$$\theta = \frac{\pi}{2} \quad \text{if} \quad a_F > 0$$
$$\theta = 0 \quad \text{if} \quad -2a'_F - a_F > 0$$

Every point on the diagram of Fig. 113 represents a possible set of values of a_F and a'_F, and those values of a_F and a'_F for which $\theta = \pi/2$ or $\theta = 0$ are directions of easy magnetization are represented by regions so marked on the diagram. In part of the diagram both of these directions are directions of easy magnetization, and in another part neither is a direction of easy magnetization. It may easily be verified that for values of a_F and a'_F falling in this latter part of the diagram the direction of easy magnetization is given by $\cos^2 \theta = -a_F/2a'_F$.

These values of a_F and a'_F found for cobalt at various temperatures are also plotted in Fig. 113. In the neighborhood of 250°C. we should expect to find that the direction of easy magnetization varies with temperature from $\theta = 0$ to $\theta = \pi/2$. The observations of Honda and Masumoto are not sufficiently extended to

---

[1] K. HONDA and H. MASUMOTO, *Science Repts. Tôhoku Imp. Univ.*, **20**, 323, 1931.

[2] These are taken from Gans and Czerlinski, *loc. cit.*, with slight alterations and corrections.

show this, but they do show that at 260°C. neither $\theta = 0$ nor $\theta = \pi/2$ is a direction of easy magnetization.

Recently, measurements have been made on nickel crystals over a wide range of temperatures.[1] Of especial interest is the fact that values of $a_F \sim -10^6$ have been observed at the temperature of liquid hydrogen

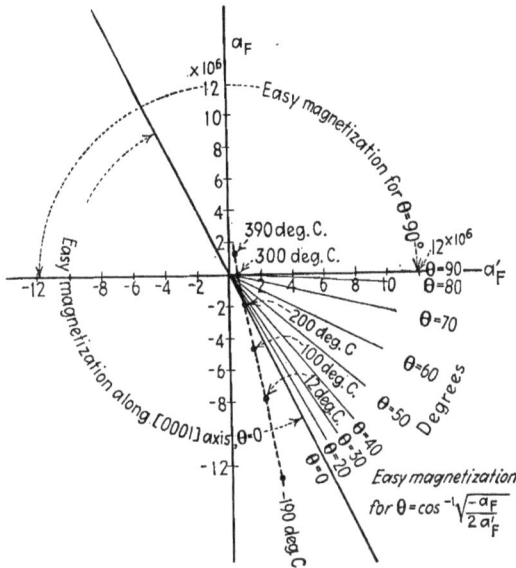

FIG. 113.—The anisotropy of cobalt as a function of temperature.

64. E in Polycrystalline Materials. Grain Orientation.—In polycrystals the lattice structure may be considerably distorted by internal stresses resulting from plastic deformation, and the magnetic properties may therefore be considerably changed. In well-annealed samples the internal strains may to a considerable extent be relieved but probably not often completely so. Furthermore, in polycrystals the internal strains will, in general, change with magnetization, the magnetostriction of grains having different orientations being of different magnitude or even of different sign. It appears to be true, however, that by suitable thermal treatment polycrystals can be produced having magnetic properties that are approximately the sum of the properties of the

[1] K. Honda, H. Masumoto, and Y. Shirakawa, *Science Repts. Tôhoku Imp. Univ.*, **24**, 391, 1935.

individual grains. Thus, for instance, the magnetization curve of annealed iron having a more or less random grain orientation is, roughly, at any rate, an average of the magnetization curves of all orientations, actually somewhat above the curve [110] in Fig. 106. If there is a preponderance of [100] axes in the direction of magnetization, the curve is higher; if there is a preponderance of [111] orientations, the curve is lower.[1]

This suggests the possibility of measuring preferred grain orientations, or fiber structures, magnetically. Such a magnetic

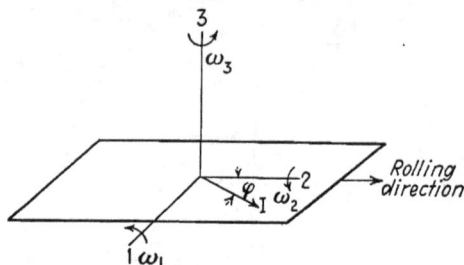

Fig. 114.

analysis might be undertaken in a variety of ways. A knowledge of I_n and I_p for all field strengths and all orientations of the sample in the field would make a fairly complete analysis possible. A convenient method for interpreting such results, however, has not yet been developed. We shall confine ourselves here to the interpretation of the deviation effect in rolled sheets of material whose crystals are cubic.

Figure 114 represents such a rolled sheet with a coordinate system fixed in the sheet. The 2-axis is in the rolling direction, and the 3-axis normal to the plane of the sheet. The orientation of any grain may be given by the angles ω_1, ω_2, and ω_3 through which it must be rotated from some standard orientation to bring it into its actual orientation. If $\Phi(\omega_1, \omega_2, \omega_3)d\omega_1 d\omega_2 d\omega_3$ represents the probability of finding an element of volume of the sample having an orientation between ω_1 and $\omega_1 + d\omega_1$, ω_2 and $\omega_2 + d\omega_2$, ω_3 and $\omega_3 + d\omega_3$, it follows that

[1] R. Gans, *Ann. Physik*, **15**, 28, 1932, has calculated the magnetization curves for polycrystalline materials having random grain orientation. The agreement with experiment is good for nickel, fair for iron, and poor for cobalt. The lack of agreement, when it occurs, is probably due to the anisotropy of the samples.

$$\int\int\int\Phi(\omega_1,\ \omega_2,\ \omega_3)d\omega_1 d\omega_2 d\omega_3\ =\ 1 \qquad (204)$$

$$\int\int\int E_\theta \Phi d\omega_1 d\omega_2 d\omega_3\ =\ \overline{E_\theta} \qquad (205)$$

the integration being taken over all possible orientations. $\overline{E_\theta}$ is the mean value of E_θ. If the material is isotropic, $\overline{E_\theta}$ is a constant; *i.e.*, the energy required to magnetize it to saturation is independent of the direction of magnetization. If the material is not isotropic, the form of $\overline{E_\theta}$ is determined by the distribution of grain orientations, and the problem is to find out as much as possible about Φ from a knowledge of $\overline{E_\theta}$.

For the sake of generality, we shall consider any physical property P which varies with orientation in a single crystal in a manner similar to E_θ, and we shall include in our considerations the effects of internal strains. We shall assume that P is additive in the sense that P as measured on an aggregate of units is equal to the sum of the corresponding measurements on the separate units. This would be true, for instance, for measurements of energy, or resistances coupled in series, but not for resistances coupled in parallel. According to (158), we may put

$$P\ =\ c\Sigma'\alpha_i^2\alpha_j^2 + k_1\Sigma A_{ii}\alpha_i^2 + k_2\Sigma'A_{ij}\alpha_i\alpha_j + c_0 \qquad (206)$$

the axes i, j, k being parallel to the cubic axes of the crystal. For the case $P \equiv E_\theta$, we should put $c = a_F$ or a, depending on whether the grains were free to execute their magnetostrictive changes in shape or not, and $k_1 = b_1$, $k_2 = b_2$. From the theory of elasticity of cubic crystals it follows that if E and G represent Young's modulus and the torsional modulus, respectively, measured in the direction α_i, α_j, α_k, then we may put

$$P = \frac{1}{G} \quad \text{if} \quad c_0 = s_{44}, \quad c = 2\left[(s_{11} - s_{12}) - \frac{1}{2}s_{44}\right],$$
$$k_1 = k_2 = 0$$

or

$$P = \frac{1}{E} \quad \text{if} \quad c_0 = s_{11}, \quad c = \left[(s_{11} - s_{12}) - \frac{1}{2}s_{44}\right],$$
$$k_1 = k_2 = 0$$

s_{11}, s_{12}, s_{44} being the elastic constants defined in Par. 55.

The first part of the problem is to express P in terms of the direction cosines α_1, α_2, α_3 measured in the coordinate system fixed in the sample instead of the direction cosines α_i, α_j, α_k

measured in the coordinate system fixed in the crystal grain. This transformation is most conveniently carried out in the matrix notation introduced in Par. 54. The first term of the expression for P in Eq. (206) may be put in the form

$$\Sigma c_{pqrs}\alpha_p\alpha_q\alpha_r\alpha_s$$

and the coefficients c_{pqrs} are transformed into the coefficients

$$c'_{klmn} = \Sigma\sigma_{kp}\sigma_{lq}\sigma_{mr}\sigma_{ns}c_{pqrs} \tag{207}$$

in a new frame of reference defined by the transformation matrix (σ), as in Eqs. (125) and (126). The transformation matrices for rotations ω_1, ω_2 and ω_3 around the 1-, 2-, and 3-axes are

$$\begin{pmatrix} 1 & 0 & 0 \\ 0 & \cos\omega_1 & -\sin\omega_1 \\ 0 & \sin\omega_1 & \cos\omega_1 \end{pmatrix}\begin{pmatrix} \cos\omega_2 & 0 & \sin\omega_2 \\ 0 & 1 & 0 \\ -\sin\omega_2 & 0 & \cos\omega_2 \end{pmatrix}\begin{pmatrix} \cos\omega_3 & -\sin\omega_3 & 0 \\ \sin\omega_3 & \cos\omega_3 & 0 \\ 0 & 0 & 1 \end{pmatrix}$$

respectively, and for the sum of the three rotations in the foregoing order, the resultant transformation matrix is their product as defined in (124):

$$\begin{pmatrix} \cos\omega_2\cos\omega_3 & -\cos\omega_2\sin\omega_3 & \sin\omega_2 \\ \sin\omega_1\sin\omega_2\cos\omega_3 + \cos\omega_1\sin\omega_3 & -\sin\omega_1\sin\omega_2\sin\omega_3 + \cos\omega_1\cos\omega_3 & -\sin\omega_1\cos\omega_2 \\ -\cos\omega_1\sin\omega_2\cos\omega_3 + \sin\omega_1\sin\omega_3 & \cos\omega_1\sin\omega_2\sin\omega_3 + \sin\omega_1\cos\omega_3 & \cos\omega_1\cos\omega_2 \end{pmatrix} \tag{208}$$

The coefficients c'_{klmn} may now be calculated by means of (207) and (208). They will be functions of ω_1, ω_2, and ω_3. From the definition of $\overline{P}$ it follows that there will be terms of the form

$$\bar{c}_{klmn}\alpha_k\alpha_l\alpha_m\alpha_n$$

where

$$\bar{c}_{klmn} = \int\int\int\Phi c'_{klmn}d\omega_1 d\omega_2 d\omega_3 \tag{209}$$

The coefficients $\bar{c}$ may be determined experimentally, and it is desired to use these experimental values in Eq. (209) to obtain information about Φ.

Simplifying assumptions must be made at this point in order to make the procedure outlined of practical importance. Akulov and Bruchatov[1] assumed that the actual distribution function Φ could be approximated by one having three groups of crystals, each group having a definite orientation. The solution of the problem then consisted in determining the relative size of these groups in such a way as to give the observed constants.

A solution for another set of simplifying assumptions is given below. The discussion is limited to rolled sheets and to observations in the plane of the metal. The assumptions made are

1. That the function Φ has the symmetry of the rolling process, or that the 1-2 and 2-3 planes are planes of symmetry. $\overline{P}$ in the rolling plane will therefore be an even function of φ, the angle between the direction in which P is measured and the rolling direction, as shown in Fig. 114.

2. That $\Phi(\omega_1,\omega_2,\omega_3)$ may be written in the form $\Phi_1(\omega_1)$ $\Phi_2(\omega_2)\Phi_3(\omega_3)$.

3. That the mean orientation of the grains is known. This mean orientation is to be chosen as the standard orientation from which deviations are measured. The mean orientation is defined by

$$\overline{\omega_1} = \int \omega_1 \Phi_1 d\omega_1$$
$$\overline{\omega_2} = \int \omega_2 \Phi_2 d\omega_2$$
$$\overline{\omega_3} = \int \omega_3 \Phi_3 d\omega_3$$

and the choice of this as the standard from which deviations are measured makes it possible to put

$$\overline{\omega_1} = \overline{\omega_2} = \overline{\omega_3} = 0$$

This assumption does not rob the analysis of its interest, because the mean orientations are generally known from X-ray analysis, and it is desired to obtain quantitative information about the departures from this mean in any given sample. Furthermore, as we shall see, it is possible under certain circumstances to recognize the mean orientation from an inspection of $\overline{P}$.

4. The coefficients c' in Eq. (209) may be expanded in powers of ω, which after integration will appear in $\overline{c}$ as $\overline{\omega_1}$, $\overline{\omega_1^2}$, $\overline{\omega_1^3}$, $\overline{\omega_1^4}$ . . . , etc. The previous assumptions have as a consequence that odd powers vanish, so that there remain only $\overline{\omega_1^2}$, $\overline{\omega_1^4}$, . . . , etc. We shall assume that all powers higher than the second are

[1] N. AKULOV and N. BRUCHATOV, *Ann. Physik*, **15**, 741, 1932.

negligibly small. This assumption becomes a better approximation as to the maximum of Φ as $\omega_1 = \omega_2 = \omega_3 = 0$ becomes
sharper. Special cases in which the foregoing is a poor approximation may be calculated by making other assumptions.

With these assumptions the transformation matrix (208),
simplified by putting

$$\sin \omega = \omega \qquad \cos \omega = 1 - \frac{\omega^2}{2}$$

and neglecting powers higher than the second throughout,
becomes

$$
\begin{pmatrix}
1 - \dfrac{\omega_2^2 + \omega_3^2}{2} & -\omega_3 & \omega_2 \\[2mm]
\omega_1\omega_2 + \omega_3 & 1 - \dfrac{\omega_3^2 + \omega_1^2}{2} & -\omega_1 \\[2mm]
-\omega_2 + \omega_3\omega_1 & \omega_2\omega_3 + \omega_1 & 1 - \dfrac{\omega_1^2 + \omega_2^2}{2}
\end{pmatrix}
\qquad (210)
$$

The procedure now is, first, to calculate the coefficients c_{pqrs}
for a crystal having the mean orientation $\omega_1 = \omega_2 = \omega_3 = 0$;
next, by means of (210) and (207) to calculate the coefficient c' as
functions of ω; and, finally, by means of (209) to calculate the
coefficients $\bar{c}$ as functions of $\overline{\omega_1^2}$, $\overline{\omega_2^2}$, $\overline{\omega_3^2}$ and the original c in Eq.
(206). The coefficients of the other terms in (206) may be
treated similarly. The results for a few special cases are given
below.

The expression for $\overline{P}$ in the rolling plane has the form

$$P = A_4 \cos 4\varphi + A_2 \cos 2\varphi + A_0 \qquad (211)$$

From experimental determinations of the constants A_4, A_2, and
A_0 and a knowledge of the mean orientation of the grains in the
sample and of the constants c_0, c, k_1, k_2 determining the properties of the individual grains, information concerning the mean
square deviations from the mean orientation may be obtained
from the following formulas:

Case 1.—The mean orientation has a [110] axis in the rolling
direction and a (100) plane in the rolling plane.

$$A_4 = \frac{c}{4}(1 - \overline{\omega_1^2} - \overline{\omega_2^2} - 8\overline{\omega_3^2})$$

$$A_2 = -\frac{c}{2}(\overline{\omega_2^2} - \overline{\omega_1^2}) - \frac{k_2}{2}(\overline{A_{11}} - \overline{A_{22}})$$

$$A_0 = \frac{c}{4}(1 + 3\overline{\omega_1^2} + 3\overline{\omega_2^2}) + \frac{k_1}{2}(\overline{A_{11}} + \overline{A_{22}}) + c_0 \qquad (212)$$

Case 2.—The mean orientation has a [100] axis in the rolling direction and a (100) plane in the rolling plane.

$$A_4 = -\frac{c}{4}(1 - \overline{\omega_1^2} - \overline{\omega_2^2} - 8\overline{\omega_3^2})$$

$$A_2 = -c(\overline{\omega_2^2} - \overline{\omega_3^2}) - \frac{k_1}{2}(\overline{A_{11}} - \overline{A_{22}})$$

$$A_0 = \frac{c}{4}(1 + 3\overline{\omega_1^2} + 3\overline{\omega_2^2}) + \frac{k_1}{2}(\overline{A_{11}} + \overline{A_{22}}) + c_0 \qquad (213)$$

Case 3.—The mean orientation has a [100] axis parallel to the rolling direction and a (110) plane parallel to the rolling plane.

$$A_4 = -\frac{c}{4}\left(\frac{3}{4} - \overline{\omega_1^2} + \overline{\omega_2^2} - 6\overline{\omega_3^2}\right)$$

$$A_2 = -\frac{c}{4}\left(1 - 4\overline{\omega_1^2} - 4\overline{\omega_2^2} - 2\overline{\omega_3^2}\right) - \frac{1}{4}(k_1 - k_2)\overline{A_{33}} + \frac{k_1}{2}\overline{A_{22}}$$

$$-\frac{1}{4}(k_1 + k_2)\overline{A_{11}}$$

$$A_0 = \frac{c}{4}\left(\frac{7}{4} + 3\overline{\omega_1^2} - 3\overline{\omega_2^2}\right) + \frac{1}{4}(k_1 - k_2)\overline{A_{33}} + \frac{k_1}{2}\overline{A_{22}} +$$

$$\frac{1}{4}(k_1 + k_2)\overline{A_{11}} + c_0 \qquad (214)$$

Case 4.—The mean orientation has a [100] axis parallel to the rolling direction and a random orientation around this axis.

This is an example of the modification of the procedure for cases not compatible with assumption 4 above. The steps are first to calculate rigorously the coefficients for the mean orientation, which can be done without difficulty even in this case of a random orientation about one axis, and then to proceed as in the other cases. Terms involving the deformation A_{ij} have been neglected.

$$A_4 = -\tfrac{7}{8}c(\tfrac{1}{4} - \tfrac{1}{2}\overline{\omega_1^2} - 2\overline{\omega_3^2})$$

$$A_2 = -c(\tfrac{1}{8} + \overline{\omega_1^2} + \tfrac{1}{4}\overline{\omega_3^2})$$

$$A_0 = \frac{c}{16}\left(\frac{11}{2} + 9\overline{\omega_1^2}\right) \tag{215}$$

If the terms involving the deformation A_{ij} in the expressions (211) to (215) may be neglected, the three equations in each case suffice precisely to determine the three unknowns $\overline{\omega_1^2}$, $\overline{\omega_2^2}$, $\overline{\omega_3^2}$.

The extent to which the preceding formulas are applicable in interpreting the results of various types of experiments remains to be determined by a detailed comparison with the results of X-ray analyses of grain orientations.   At present, no data are available for such a comparison.

Certainly, elastic experiments would not be ideal, because elasticities are not strictly additive in the sense defined earlier in this section.   Magnetic experiments on the deviation effect can give more reliable, though less complete, information.   For a disk cut out of a sheet and mounted in a magnetic field parallel to a diameter and strong enough to produce saturation, the torque component, parallel to the axis of the sample, exerted by the field is

$$T = -\frac{\partial \overline{E_\theta}}{\partial \varphi} = 4A_4 \sin 4\varphi + 2A_2 \sin 2\varphi \tag{216}$$

The directions of easiest magnetization are given by the conditions

$$T = 0; \qquad \frac{dT}{d\varphi} < 0$$

Measurements of this torque can determine only two of the three constants in Eqs. (212) to (216).

In spite of the limitations just mentioned, the methods of analysis described above have already proved their usefulness. Apparatus for measuring the deviation effect and apparatus for measuring the elasticity of disks cut from rolled sheets were constructed at the Westinghouse Laboratories.   The latter apparatus was capable of bending the disks around various diameters and gave readings of the deflection produced by a given force δ/F in various directions.   The results obtained with it are not very accurate but serve to show the large differences that can be produced in samples of identical chemical composition.

The results obtained on two samples of iron-silicon sheet are shown in Figs. (115) and (116). Sample A was produced by standard rolling practice, which is known from X-ray investigations to produce a fiber structure whose mean grain orientation has a [110] axis in the rolling direction and a (100) plane in the rolling plane, as in case 1 above. From Eqs. (212) and (216) we should, therefore, expect the torque curve to be

$$T = a_F(1 - \overline{\omega_1^2} - \overline{\omega_2^2} - 8\overline{\omega_3^2}) \sin 4\varphi - a_F(\overline{\omega_2^2} - \overline{\omega_1^2}) \sin 2\varphi$$
$$- b_2(\overline{A_{11}} - \overline{A_{22}}) \sin 2\varphi \quad (217)$$

For purposes of rough approximation the term containing $(\overline{A_{11}} - \overline{A_{22}})$ may be neglected, since the strains due to plastic

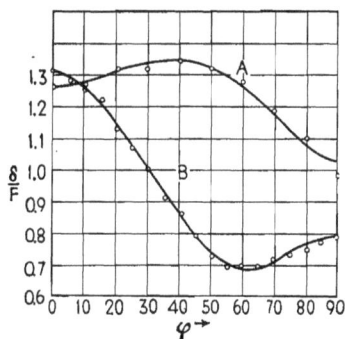

FIG. 115.—The elastic anisotropy of iron-silicon sheets.

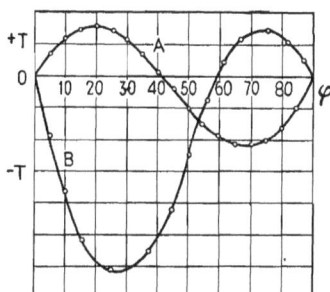

FIG. 116.—The magnetic anisotropy of iron-silicon sheets.

deformation probably cancel each other approximately in pairs, compressions occurring as frequently as extensions. This is convenient for the purposes of the present analysis but makes it necessary to look for effects depending on $\overline{A^2}$ if we want information concerning the distributions of strain orientations. We shall return to this subject in the next chapter.

The constant a_F for iron-silicon is not known, but the direction of easy magnetization of the crystal is [100], so that $a_F > 0$. It is also known from X-ray data that the chief deviation from the mean orientation is a tipping of the grains about the rolling direction, or that $\overline{\omega_2^2} > \overline{\omega_1^2}$. From this and Eq. (217) it follows that we should expect $T = 0$ for $\varphi = 0$, 90 deg., these being directions of difficult magnetization; $T < 0$ for $\varphi = 45$ deg.; and the direction of easy magnetization for $\varphi < 45$ deg. All these predictions are in agreement with curve A in Fig. 116, so that we may conclude that the magnetic data are to this extent consistent with the X-ray data.

Sample B was prepared by a special rolling technique giving a fiber structure in which a [100] axis is predominantly in the rolling direction. Curve B in Fig. 116 shows how clearly the difference between the structures of samples A and B is brought out by the deviation effect, and it is in showing up differences of this kind quickly and with simple apparatus that the magnetic method of analysis has been found most useful so far.

Finally, it is interesting to observe that the elastic measurements (δ/F in Fig. 115) are essentially proportional to $\bar{P}$, while the magnetic measurements are proportional to $dP/d\varphi$. The curves in Fig. 116 should therefore be proportional to the slope of the curves in Fig. 115, and this is at any rate approximately true; to this extent the results of the magnetic analysis are consistent with the results of the elastic analysis.

65. The Approach to Saturation.—The assumption that macroscopic magnetization in large fields is due to a rotation of spontaneously magnetized regions against the action of internal fields leads to a very simple expression for the approach to saturation. If ψ is the angle between the applied field and the direction of spontaneous magnetization at any point within a ferromagnetic medium, we have

$$I = I_w \cos \psi$$

If the material is nearly saturated, ψ must be small, and we may replace the preceding expression by

$$I = I_w\left(1 - \frac{\psi^2}{2}\right) \tag{218}$$

The torque exerted by the magnetic field on the spontaneous magnetization is

$$T_e = -I_w H \sin \psi = -I_w H \psi \tag{219}$$

The torque exerted by the crystalline field on I_w is

$$T_i = -\nabla E_\theta \tag{220}$$

For equilibrium we must have

$$T_i + T_e = 0$$

which, upon substitution of (219) and (220), leads to the following expression for ψ^2:

$$\psi^2 = \frac{(\nabla E_\theta)^2}{I_w^2 H^2}$$

Substituting this expression in (218) leads to

$$I = I_w\left(1 - \frac{c}{H^2}\right)$$
$$c = \frac{(\nabla E_\theta)^2}{2I_w^2}$$
$$(\nabla E_\theta)^2 = \left(\frac{\partial E_\theta}{\partial \theta}\right)^2 + \frac{1}{\sin^2 \theta}\left(\frac{\partial E_\theta}{\partial \varphi}\right)^2 \tag{221}$$

In polycrystalline material in which there are a random grain orientation and no strains, the constant c may be found by averaging over all possible orientations of the crystals with respect to the field:

$$c = \bar{c} = \frac{1}{4\pi}\int_0^{2\pi}\int_0^{\pi} c \sin\theta d\theta d\varphi$$

E_θ being given by Eq. (183). The result is[1]

$$\bar{c} = \frac{32a_F^2}{105I_w^2} \tag{222}$$

If strains are present, the complete expression for E_θ involving the strain tensor components must be used. The value of $\bar{c}$ given in (222) would then have to be modified even for a random distribution of grain orientations. We shall return to a discussion of this point in the next chapter.

E. Czerlinski[2] has reported some experiments undertaken to check Eq. (221). His conclusion is that although the results are adequately described in iron and nickel over a range of fields from 300 to 2000 oersteds, roughly, a modified expression of the form

$$I = I_w\left(1 - \frac{c}{H^2} - \frac{b}{H + a}\right)$$

would describe the results more accurately. The effect of the

[1] N. S. AKULOV, *Z. Physik*, **69**, 822, 1931.   R. GANS, *Ann. Physik*, **15**, 28, 1932.
[2] E. CZERLINSKI, *Ann. Physik*, **13**, 80, 1932.

extra term is to simulate an added magnetization which is observed for fields of the order of 2000 oersteds and more.

Other laws of approach to saturation have been suggested by various authors. For a further discussion of the whole subject the reader is referred to the papers cited on the previous page.

66. Saturation as a Function of T.—The curve in Fig. 117 represents the solution of the equation

$$\frac{I_w}{I_0} = \tanh\left(\frac{\theta_w}{T}\frac{I_w}{I_0}\right) \tag{223}$$

a simplified form of Eq. (69) for the spontaneous magnetization. The subscripts w are retained to indicate that the quantities

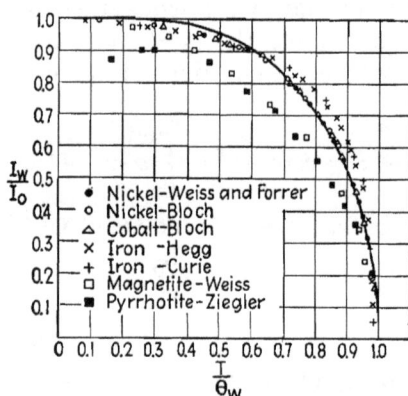

Fig. 117.—Saturation as a function of temperature.

refer to the theoretical spontaneous magnetization first introduced by Weiss. There is some difficulty about comparing Eq. (223) with experiment, because the definition of spontaneous magnetization and Curie temperature is, from an experimental point of view, somewhat ambiguous. For the purposes of this paragraph, however, we may correlate experimental values of the saturation intensity with I_w, neglecting the ambiguity in the definition of saturation, and similarly we may interpret the temperature near which ferromagnetization disappears as θ_w, neglecting the spread of temperature over which the magnetic changes take place. In Par. 68 we shall examine this range of temperatures more closely.

Experimental observations[1] on the variation of the saturation intensity with temperature are also plotted in Fig. 117. The results for the face-centered cubic crystals cobalt and nickel are in fair agreement with Eq. (223) for $T/\theta_w > 0.6$. The difference between these and the results for the body-centered cubic crystal iron for which $z = 8$ is that to be expected from the discussion of Par. 53 and illustrated in Fig. 76. A marked departure from the theoretical curve also occurs at low temperatures. Weiss and Forrer[2] made observations on the saturation intensity of various substances down to liquid air temperatures and found that the results could be well represented by an expression of the form

$$\frac{I_w}{I_0} = 1 - A\left(\frac{T}{\theta_w}\right)^2 \tag{224}$$

Their observations are plotted in Fig. 118. In addition, curve 1 in the figure represents the Weiss formula (50), and curve 2 represents the simplified Eq. (223). Bloch's $T^{\frac{3}{2}}$ law [Eq. (78)], which has more theoretical justification than any of the preceding expressions, is consistent with the data over a limited temperature range. In fact, more recent observations on iron and nickel by Fallot reported by Weiss[3] show that Bloch's expression is a better representation of the facts at very low temperatures (down to 20° abs.) than Eq. (224). The observations of Weiss and Forrer are nevertheless plotted as a function of $(T/\theta_w)^2$ in Fig. 118, because by so doing only two values of the constant A are required, one for the cubic crystals iron and nickel, and one for the othorhombic crystals magnetite (Fe_3O_4), cementite (Fe_3C), and Fe_2B. Recent experiments by Allen and Constant[4] on cubic

[1] Observations on iron, by F. HEGG, thesis, Zurich, 1910.   P. CURIE, *Ann. chim. phys.*, **5**, 289, 1875.

On nickel, by

O. BLOCH, thesis, Zurich, 1912.   P. WEISS and R. FORRER, *Ann. phys.*, **15**, 153, 1926.

On cobalt, by

O. BLOCH, thesis, Zurich, 1912.

On magnetite, by

P. WEISS, *J. phys.*, **6**, 661, 1907.

On pyrrhotite, by

M. ZIEGLER, thesis, Zurich, 1915.

[2] P. WEISS and R. FORRER, *Ann. phys.*, **12**, 279, 1928.

[3] P. WEISS, *Compt. rend.*, **198**, 1893, 1934.

[4] R. I. ALLEN and F. W. CONSTANT, *Phys. Rev.*, **44**, 228, 1933.

cobalt, which may be obtained at low temperatures by quenching, show that, in the cubic form, cobalt has the same value of A as iron and nickel. Further accurate experimental work is required to determine whether the law expressed in Eq. (224), A being the same for crystallographically similar crystals, has any real physical significance or whether the apparent agreement shown in Fig. 118 for the temperature range from liquid air to room temperature is merely fortuitous.

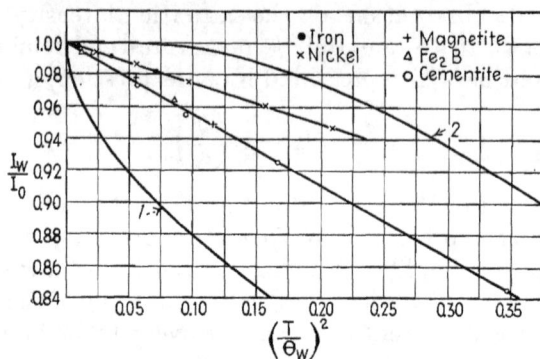

Fig. 118.—Saturation at low temperatures.

67. Saturation as a Function of Chemical Composition.—If an element goes into solution in a ferromagnetic substance, that element will, in general, affect all of the constants required to describe its behavior. Of these constants, the saturation intensity has been investigated extensively as a function of chemical composition.[1] The effect of the addition of a few per cent of a foreign element is, as a rule, to decrease the saturation intensity, but there are exceptions to this, as in the case of the addition of cobalt to iron or manganese to nickel.

68. The Neighborhood of the Curie Temperature.—Roughly, ferromagnetic materials are found to behave experimentally near the Curie point as predicted by the Weiss or Heisenberg theories. This behavior is characterized by the following phenomena: As the temperature is raised from below the Curie temperature, a rapid decrease occurs in the saturation intensity; as this decrease

---

[1] The effect of chemical composition on magnetic properties is reviewed in W. S. Messkin and A. Kussmann, "Die Ferromagnetischen Legierungen," Julius Springer, Berlin, 1932. See also C. Sadron, thesis, Strasbourg, 1932; and E. C. Stoner, *Phil. Mag.*, **15**, 1018, 1933. Also Fig. 51 of Chap. IV.

reaches completion, there is an anomaly in the specific heat, to be discussed further in Chap. IX; at still higher temperatures ferromagnetism has gone over to paramagnetism, the susceptibility being inversely proportional to $T - \theta$. According to the Weiss theory, there is only one critical temperature θ_w at which all the preceding transitions take place—the spontaneous magnetization vanishes, the specific heat drops, and the paramagnetic susceptibility inversely proportional to $T - \theta_w$ replaces the more complicated ferromagnetic behavior. Actually, the Curie temperature as measured by the disappearance of ferromagnetism, usually called the ferromagnetic Curie point θ_f, may differ by 10° or more from that found from extrapolation of paramagnetic susceptibilities and called the paramagnetic Curie point θ_p. It is probable, especially because of the specific-heat anomaly, that an abrupt change in physical properties at the Curie point is taking place at one definite temperature very much as changes of phase take place. The statistical part of the theory of ferromagnetism has not been sufficiently developed to give even a qualitative picture that is more than superficially satisfactory in describing the details of the transition from ferro- to paramagnetism. The references given below[1] contain experimental and theoretical work on the neighborhood of the Curie point and further references to other work on the subject.

69. Above the Curie Point.—The Weiss equation may be written in the form (45)

$$I = I_0 L(a) = I_0\left[\coth a - \frac{1}{a} \right]$$

$$a = \frac{\mu}{kT}(H + N_w I)$$

$$N_w = \frac{3k\theta_w}{\mu I_0} \tag{225}$$

or, if the elementary magnet is limited to positions parallel and antiparallel to the field, Eq. (225) becomes

$$I = I_0 \tanh a$$

$$N_w = \frac{k\theta_w}{\mu I_0} \tag{226}$$

[1] P. WEISS and R. FORRER, *Ann. phys.*, **15**, 153, 1926. R. FORRER, *J. phys.* **1**, 49, 1930; **2**, 312, 1931; **4**, 109, 186, 1933; **4**, 427, 501, 1933. L. F. BATES, *Proc. Phys. Soc.* **43**, 87, 1931. L. NÉEL, *J. phys.*, **5**, 104, 1934; **6**, 27, 1935.

where N_w is the molecular field constant. From either of these equations it follows that the initial susceptibility χ_0 above the

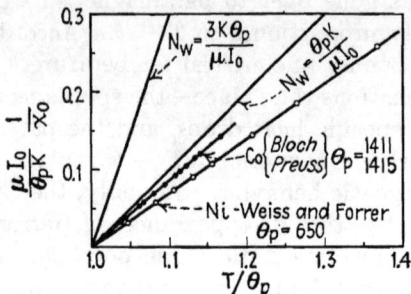

FIG. 119.—Susceptibilities above the Curie point.

Curie temperature is

$$\chi_0 = \frac{\theta_w/N_w}{T - \theta_w} \tag{227}$$

which may be put into the form

$$\frac{1}{N_w\chi_0} = \frac{T}{\theta_w} - 1 \tag{228}$$

which shows that above the Curie point $1/N_w\chi_0$ should be a universal function of the reduced temperature T/θ_w. The

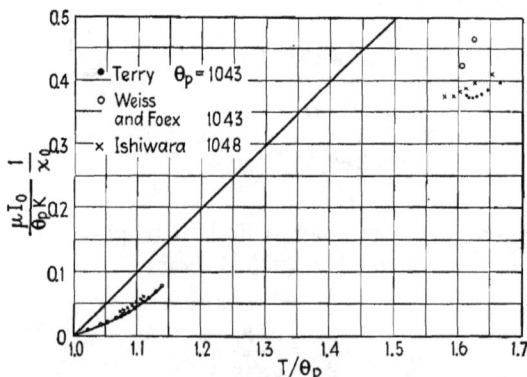

FIG. 120.—Susceptibilities above the Curie point.

definition of the Curie temperature in terms of the molecular field constant differs by a factor of 3 in Eqs. (225) and (226).

Data for nickel,[1] cobalt,[2] and iron[3] are plotted in Figs. 119 and 120. The experimental paramagnetic Curie point θ_p (Par. 68) is used in plotting the figures. The theoretical curves deduced from (225) and (226) are shown in addition to the experimental points. The gap in the experimental points for iron in Fig. 120 represents the temperature range for which the crystals are in the γ or face-centered phase.

[1] P. WEISS and R. FORRER, *Ann. phys.*, **15**, 153, 1926.

[2] O. BLOCH, thesis, Zurich, 1912. A. PREUSS, thesis, Zurich, 1912.

[3] E. M. TERRY, *Phys. Rev.*, **9**, 255, 394, 1917. T. ISHIWARA, *Science Repts. Tôhoku Imp. Univ.*, **6**, 133, 1917. P. WEISS and G. FOEX, *J. phys.*, **40**, 744, 1911.

CHAPTER VII

MECHANICAL DEFORMATION

A factor of outstanding importance in determining the behavior of ferromagnetic materials is the distortion of the crystal lattice. The mechanisms involved are probably of two kinds. Elastic deformations are shown to affect the directions of easy magnetization, or the coupling of the spontaneous magnetization to the lattice itself. This effect, and its converse, magnetostriction, or change of shape with magnetization, we shall discuss at some length in this chapter. In addition, local distortions may prevent translational magnetization from proceeding reversibly. Irreversible processes, giving rise to hysteresis, will be discussed in Chap. IX.

70. The Effect of Homogeneous Mechanical Deformation on Magnetization.—In Pars. 54 to 57 a convenient method was described for deriving the function E_θ, the energy of any crystal with any small homogeneous distortion, in its dependence on the direction of magnetization. To illustrate the significance of these results we shall discuss their application to iron, a cubic crystal, for which we have, from (150) and (151),

$$E_\theta = a\Sigma'\alpha_i^2\alpha_j^2 + b_1\Sigma\alpha_i^2 A_{ii} + b_2\Sigma'\alpha_i\alpha_j A_{ij} \qquad (229)$$

The constants have the following values for iron (see Par. 75):

$$a = 2.15 \times 10^5 \text{ ergs/cc.}$$
$$b_1 = -3.1 \times 10^7 \text{ ergs/cc.}$$
$$b_2 = 2.8 \times 10^7 \text{ ergs/cc.} \qquad (230)$$

The other symbols in Eq. (229) have the same meaning given them in Chap. V. The α's are the direction cosines of the spontaneous magnetization I_w with respect to the principal axes of the crystal, and the tensor components A_{ij} define the elastic distortion of the crystal. In the absence of distortions, $A_{ij} = 0$; the last two terms of (229) vanish; and E_θ reduces to the simple form

$$E_\theta = a\Sigma'\alpha_i^2\alpha_j^2$$

which is illustrated for iron in Fig. 94. The last two terms of
(229) may be shown to represent an ellipsoid whose shape and
orientation depend on the constants b_1 and b_2 and on the strain
tensor A_{ij}. This is described below for certain typical cases,
illustrated in Figs. 121 to 128. As in Figs. 93 to 97, the illustrations include a model of a cubic body-centered crystal standing
beside a plaster model. The energy of magnetization in any
direction in the crystal model is given by the length of a radius
parallel to this direction in the plaster model. Since the object

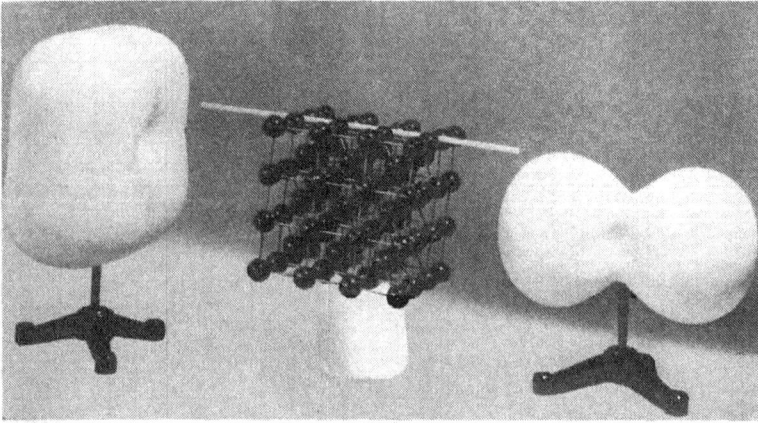

FIG. 121.—On the left, E_θ for an iron crystal elastically stretched 1 per cent
along a [100] axis. On the right, E_θ for an iron crystal elastically compressed
1 per cent along a [100] axis.

of this discussion is to illustrate qualitatively the types of effects
that can be produced, much larger deformations are included
than can be realized experimentally. The deformations chosen
for illustration are elongations accompanied by no change of
volume.

In Par. 62 a method for computing magnetization curves from
the function E_θ was outlined. The results of similar calculations
are given below, using, however, the more complete expression
for E_θ given in Eq. (229). These calculations may be expected
to give satisfactory results except when there are several directions of easy magnetization in the crystal which have equal or
almost equal energies. Under such conditions translational
magnetization will occur, and hysteresis effects are to be expected.
Since the behavior of a sample under such conditions will depend

primarily on the crystal imperfections, no exact calculations are possible, and the corresponding parts of the magnetization curves are not included in Figs. 122, 125 and 128.

Case 1. Elongation e Parallel to a Tetragonal Axis.—In this case we may put for the strain tensor

$$A_{ii} = e; \qquad A_{jj} = A_{kk} = -\frac{e}{2}; \qquad A_{ij} = A_{jk} = \cdot \cdot \cdot = 0$$

For positive values of e the addition to E_θ due to this distortion may be represented by an oblate ellipsoid of revolution having

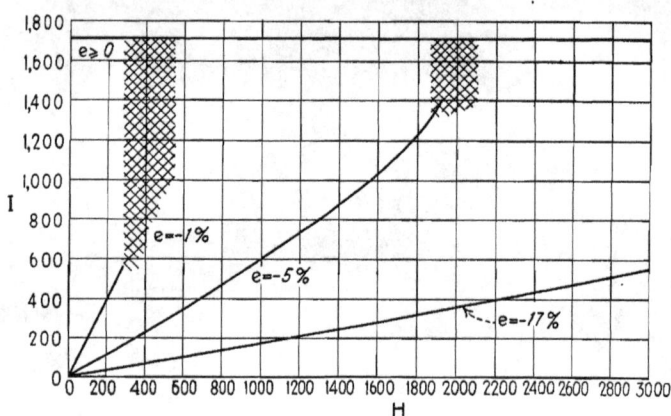

Fig. 122.—Magnetization curves for an iron crystal elastically stretched or compressed along a [100] axis by an amount e, the applied magnetic field being parallel to the elongation.

its minor axis in the direction of elongation. For negative values of e (compression) the ellipsoid is prolate having its major axis in the direction of compression. The eccentricity of this ellipsoid is determined by the constant b_1 alone. E_θ for $e = \pm 0.01$ is shown in Fig. 121. The magnetization curve for magnetization parallel to the elongation may be shown to be

$$H = \frac{3eb_1 + 4a}{I_w^2}I - \frac{8a}{I_w^4}I^3 \tag{231}$$

which is illustrated in Fig. 122. Compression leads to more difficult, elongation to easier, magnetization.

Case 2. Elongation e Parallel to a Digonal Axis.—In this case we may put for the strain tensor

$$A_{ii} = A_{jj} = \frac{e}{4}; \qquad A_{kk} = -\frac{e}{2}; \qquad A_{ij} = A_{ji} = \frac{3e}{4};$$

$$A_{jk} = A_{kj} = \cdots = 0$$

The addition to E_θ due to this distortion may be represented by an ellipsoid whose minor and major axes are both perpendicular

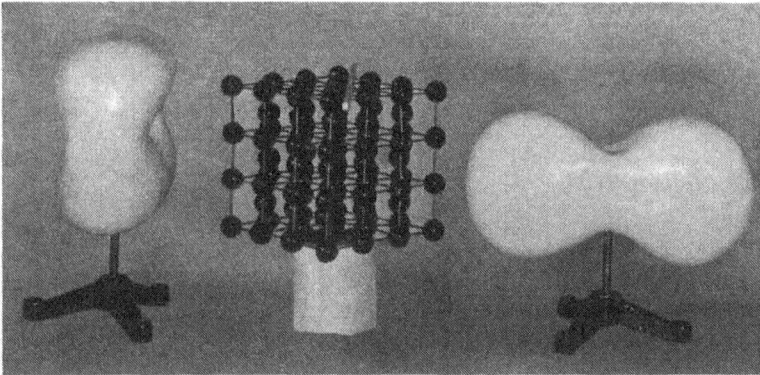

Fig. 123.—On the left, E_θ for an iron crystal elastically stretched 1 per cent along a [110] axis. On the right, E_θ for an iron crystal elastically compressed 1 per cent along a [110] axis.

Fig. 124.—On the left, E_θ for an iron crystal elastically stretched 1 per cent along a [110] axis. On the right, E_θ for an iron crystal elastically compressed 1 per cent along a [110] axis.

to the elongation. Both constants b_1 and b_2 enter into the expression. Two views of E_θ for $e = \pm 0.01$ are shown in Figs. 123 and 124. The magnetization curve for magnetization parallel to the elongation may be shown to be, for the upper parts of the curve,

$$H = \frac{3eb_2 - 4a}{I_w^2}I + \frac{8a}{I_w^4}I^3 \qquad (232)$$

for the lower parts of the curve,

$$H = \frac{\frac{1}{2}(b_1 + b_2)e + 4a}{I_w^2}I - \frac{6a}{I_w^4}I^3 \qquad (233)$$

which is illustrated in Fig. 125. It is interesting to observe that these curves cross each other, an effect often observed in iron

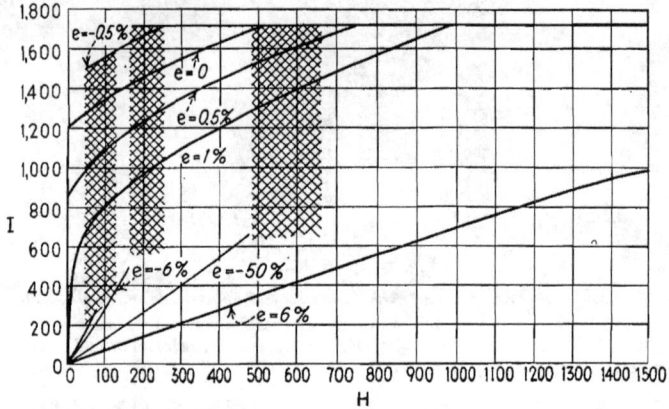

Fig. 125.—Magnetization curve for an iron crystal elastically stretched or compressed along a [110] axis by an amount e, the applied magnetic field being parallel to the elongation.

wires, which presumably had a fiber structure with preponderantly digonal axes parallel to the wire axis. In this case extension produces easier magnetization in small fields (not shown in Fig. 125 because of the superposition of translational effects) and more difficult magnetization in large fields. Compression produces more difficult magnetization in small and easier magnetization in large fields. This also is in qualitative agreement with experiments on polycrystalline wire.

Case 3. *Elongation e Parallel to a Trigonal Axis.*—In this case we may write for the strain tensor

$$A_{ii} = A_{jj} = A_{kk} = 0; \qquad A_{ij} = A_{ji} + A_{jk} = \cdots = \frac{e}{2}$$

For positive values of e the addition to E_θ due to the distortion may be represented by a prolate ellipsoid of revolution having its major axis in the direction of elongation. For negative values of e (compression) the ellipsoid is oblate, having its minor axis in the direction of compression.   The eccentricity of this ellipsoid is determined by the constant b_2 alone.   Two views of E_θ for $e = \pm 0.01$ are shown in Figs. 126 and 127.   The magnetization

Fɪɢ. 126.—On the left, E_θ for an iron crystal elastically stretched 1 per cent along a [111] axis.   On the right, E_θ for an iron crystal elastically compressed 1 per cent along a [111] axis.

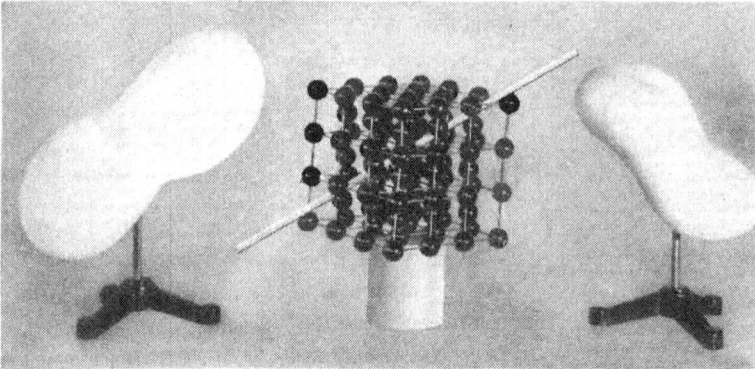

Fɪɢ. 127.—On the left, E_θ for an iron crystal elastically stretched 1 per cent along a [111] axis.   On the right, E_θ for an iron crystal elastically compressed 1 per cent along a [111] axis.

curve for magnetization parallel to the elongation may be put into the parametric form

$$H = \frac{\sqrt{3}}{I_w} \frac{2a \sin\theta \cos\theta[2\cos^2\theta - \sin^2\theta] + eb_2[\sin\theta\cos\theta + 2(\cos^2\theta - \sin^2\theta)]}{-\sin\theta + \sqrt{2}\cos\theta}$$

$$I = I_w\left[\frac{1}{\sqrt{3}}\cos\theta + \sqrt{\frac{2}{3}}\sin\theta\right] \qquad (234)$$

which is illustrated in Fig. 128. Compression leads to easier magnetization, elongation to more difficult magnetization.

A detailed comparison of the foregoing results with experiment is not at present possible, because no work has been done on deformed single crystals or well-oriented aggregates. Becker and Kersten, who first did considerable work on the preceding lines, concentrated on nickel, which is magnetically much more nearly isotropic than iron, so that grain-orientation effects could to a first approximation be neglected. Their theoretical and experimental results are in satisfactory agreement wherever

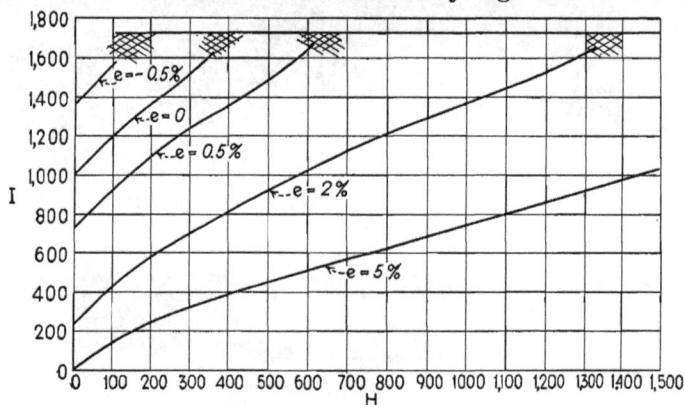

Fig. 128.—Magnetization curve for an iron crystal elastically stretched or compressed along a [111] axis by an amount e, the applied magnetic field being parallel to the elongation.

rotational magnetization alone is concerned. For a further account of this pioneering work the reader is referred to the original papers.[1]

71. The Effect of Small Randomly Oriented Distortions on Magnetization.—In previous descriptions of magnetization we have considered only homogeneous crystals which could be described by a single function E_θ which was independent of the space coordinates. The resulting magnetization curves, *e.g.*, as in Fig. 107, had sharp corners near $H = 0$ separating the translational from the rotational processes.

Actual crystals do not behave in this way. Experimental results for the magnetization of iron crystals in small fields, for

[1] R. Becker, Z. Physik, **62**, 253, 1930; Physik. Z., **33**, 905, 1932. R. Becker and M. Kersten, Z. Physik, **64**, 660, 1930. M. Kersten, Z. Physik, **71**, 553, 1931; **72**, 500, 1931; R. Gans, Ann. Physik, (5) **24**, 680, 1935.

instance, are shown in Fig. 129. It is not sufficient to say that hysteresis effects are excluded by the theoretical treatment and that as hysteresis effects are predominant in small fields, no agreement is to be expected. On the curve in question the hysteresis loop is approximately as wide as the size of the points on the diagram, so that we must account for considerable *reversible* departures from the curve suggested above for perfect crystals. Actual crystals are certainly not geometrically perfect. Because of impurities; because of strains produced by handling, machining, etc.; or, in the absence of such accidentally produced distortions, because of the thermal vibration of the lattice, small regions in some parts of the crystal will have slightly different symmetry from small regions in other parts. The effect of such lattice distortions can be calculated by applying the methods outlined in the previous paragraph. The exact calculations are very tedious, involving a great deal of graphical integration, and only a simplified approximation will be attempted below for iron and nickel.

For iron and nickel, which are cubic crystals, the function E_θ will have the form given in Eq. (229), the constants for iron having the values given in (230) and in nickel the values (see page 254)

$$a = -2.8 \times 10^4 \text{ ergs/cc.}$$
$$b_1 = 11. \times 10^7$$
$$b_2 = 3.5 \times 10^7 \qquad\qquad (235)$$

In a randomly distorted crystal the tensor A_{ij} will be a function of the space coordinates, and the magnetization curve of the whole crystal will be the average of the magnetization curves for all the small distorted regions. For small fields and small distortions, the positions of the minima of E_θ are given essentially by the first term in Eq. (229), so that for the initial part of the magnetization curve the only values of α_i, etc., to be considered are ± 1 or 0 for iron and $\pm 1/\sqrt{3}$ for nickel. In iron, for instance, E_θ for an undistorted single crystal in the absence of external fields has equal minima along the i-, j-, and k-axes. The effect of lattice distortions will be primarily to make, in some parts of the crystal, the minima along the i-axis deeper than those along the other axes, and similarly for the minima along the j- and k-axes in other parts of the crystal. Therefore, provided only that the distortions are distributed at random, their effect will be to limit the magnetization parallel to the i-axis in infinitesimal fields to $\frac{1}{3}I_w$, because, in two-thirds of the crystal, magnetization along the $\pm j$- and $\pm k$-axes will be energetically preferable, and infinitesimal fields will therefore be unable to change the direction of magnetization from $\pm j$ or $\pm k$ to $+i$. We may thus expect a first break in the magnetization curve for $I_1 = \frac{1}{3}I_w$, $H_1 = 0$. Similarly, if an infinitesimal magnetic field is applied along the digonal axis in the $j - k$ plane midway between the $+j$- and $+k$-axes, one-third of the crystal will be magnetized along the $+j$- and one-third along the $+k$-axes, the remaining third being magnetized along the $\pm i$-axis which is perpendicular to H. The resultant component of I_w in the direction of H for such a configuration is evidently $I_1 = \frac{2}{3}(1/\sqrt{2})I_w$, or $0.472I_w$. And similarly for a field parallel to a trigonal axis, we have $I_1 = (1\sqrt{3})I_w$. These results, together with others arrived at by similar reasoning for nickel, are given below.

Table III

Direction of magneti- zation	Iron				Nickel			
	H_1	I_1/I_w	cH_2	I_2/I_w	H_1	I_1/I_w	cH_2	I_2/I_w
[100]	0 0	$\frac{1}{3}$ 0.333	1 1	1 1	0 0	$1/\sqrt{3}$ 0.58	0 0	$1/\sqrt{3}$ 0.58
[110]	0 0	$\frac{2}{3}\sqrt{2}$ 0.472	$\sqrt{2}$ 1.41	$1/\sqrt{2}$ 0.71	0 0	$\frac{1}{2}\sqrt{\frac{2}{3}}$ 0.408	$\sqrt{\frac{6}{5}}$ 1.23	$\sqrt{\frac{2}{3}}$ 0.816
[111]	0 0	$1/\sqrt{3}$ 0.58	0 0	$1/\sqrt{3}$ 0.58	0 0	$\frac{1}{4}+\frac{3}{4}\cos\alpha$ 0.498	$1/(1-\cos\alpha)$ 1.5	1 1

α = angle between trigonal axes = $2 \cos^{-1}\sqrt{\frac{2}{3}}$.

A second break in the magnetization curve is to be expected when the difference in magnetic energy along two axes becomes greater than the energy difference due to strains. Assuming that the strains may produce a difference in energy for magnetization along two axes never exceeding ϵ, it follows that saturation, e.g., in iron along a [100] axis, will be reached when

$$I_w H_2 = \epsilon \qquad \text{or} \qquad cH_2 = 1$$

where $c = I_w/\epsilon$.

Similarly, when a field of intensity $H_2 = \sqrt{2}/c$ is applied along a digonal axis in the $j - k$ plane of an iron crystal, the whole of the crystal will be magnetized along the nearest directions of easy magnetization, the resultant intensity at this point being $I_2 = I_w/\sqrt{2}$. The results of similar calculations for the second breaks in the various magnetization curves are contained in the foregoing table. Briefly, the modifications of the magnetization curves of single crystals introduced by the assumption of lattice imperfections are the following:

In perfect crystals the magnetization of the entire crystal proceeds to saturation in infinitesimal fields in the direction of easy magnetization nearest the applied field.

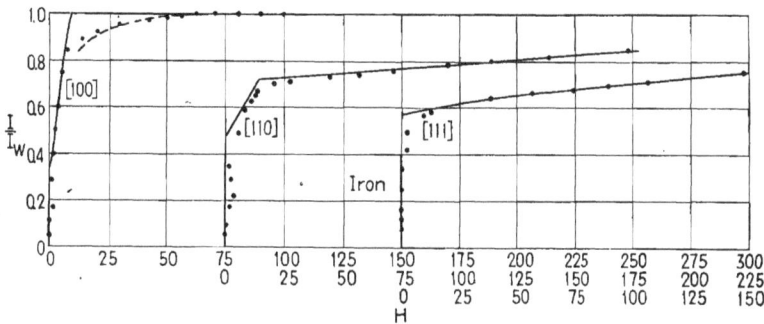

FIG. 129.—Magnetization curves of randomly distorted iron crystals.

In imperfect crystals having n directions of easy magnetization, a fraction $1/n$ of the total crystal will be magnetized to saturation in each of the n directions in the energetically most favorable sense in infinitesimal fields. A finite field, whose strength is dependent on the lattice distortion and the orientation of the crystal, is required to magnetize the entire crystal in that particular direction of easy magnetization nearest to the applied field.

The magnetization curve of imperfect crystals will, according to the preceding simplified calculations, proceed in infinitesimal fields to the first critical point at I_1, H_1, then at a different rate to the second critical point at I_2, H_2, and finally will approach saturation due to the rotation of the directions of easy magnetization in large fields, as in Par. 62. Such curves are plotted for iron and nickel in Figs. 129 and 130, respectively, the only disposable constant c being chosen $\frac{1}{10}$ for iron and $\frac{1}{12}$ for nickel. The two critical points have been arbitrarily connected by a straight line except for iron magnetized parallel to a tetragonal axis. In this case an actual calculation of the curve was carried out assuming $a = \infty$ and assuming that the terms in E_θ involving the distortion might be approximately represented by an oblate ellipsoid randomly oriented in the crystal. Representative magnetization curves for various orientations of the ellipsoid were plotted, and their average found by graphical methods. The experimental points in Figs. 129 and 130 were taken from papers by Honda and Kaya[1] and Kaya.[2] The experimental results for iron are not very accurate, and the best that can be said is that they are not in disagreement with the theoretical curves except as regards

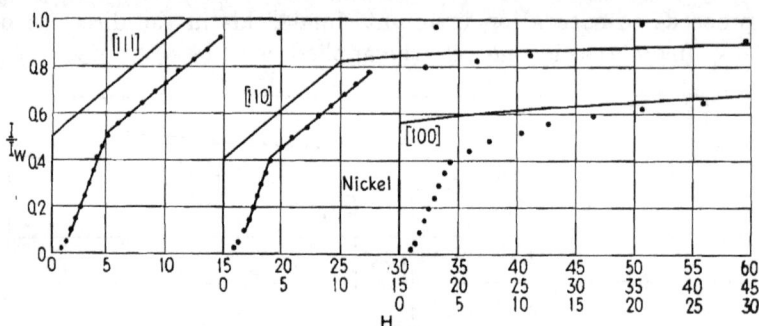

Fig. 130.—Magnetization curves of randomly distorted nickel crystals.

the corners at I_2, H_2. This will be discussed farther on. It should be remarked that steeper curves than those plotted have been observed both by Honda, Masumoto, and Kaya[3] and Dussler and Gerlach, which indicates that the strains responsible for the observations of Fig. 129 are accidentally produced in the preparation of the sample. The experimental results for nickel are much more accurate and could therefore be plotted on a larger scale, which, in turn, enlarges the hysteresis effects. The agreement between theory and experiment, such as it is, leaves little doubt that the suggested mechanisms do actually play a part in the magnetization of nickel crystals.

A similar comparison between theory and experiment should be made for the magnetostriction of single crystals as a function

[1] K. Honda and S. Kaya, *Science Repts. Tôhoku Imp. Univ.*, **15**, 721, 1926.

[2] S. Kaya, *Science Repts. Tôhoku Imp. Univ.*, **17**, 639, 1928.

[3] K. Honda, H. Masumoto, and S. Kaya, *Science Repts. Tôhoku Imp. Univ.*, **17**, 111, 1928.

[4] E. Dussler and W. Gerlach, *Z. Physik*, **44**, 284, 1927.

of the applied field, but the data at present available are too inaccurate to afford a reasonable check.

The sharp corners in the magnetization curves drawn in Figs. 129 and 130 at I_2, H_2 are a consequence of the assumption that α_i, etc., can have only discrete values, or, in other words, that a in Eq. (229) may be treated as infinite. The fact that in actual crystals a is finite means that, owing to the crystal imperfections, the magnetization will not be confined to certain crystallographic directions even in infinitesimal fields but that there will be a certain probability of finding regions within the crystal for which the directions of easy magnetization differ from the corresponding directions in perfect crystals. The amount of rounding off of the corners that this produces follows without further assumption from an exact computation of the curves in question, but these computations are, as has been said, rather involved, and only the simple case $a = 0$ has been worked out. The results so obtained are reasonably good approximations to the exact theory for magnetization near saturation and are given below for iron magnetized in a [100] direction.

For $a = 0$, Eq. (229) may be written, assuming the magnetic field parallel to the k-axis,

$$E_\theta = \epsilon \sin^2 (\psi - \theta) - I_w H \cos \theta \qquad (236)$$

where θ is the angle between the k-axis and the magnetization, and ψ the angle between the direction of easy magnetization produced by the strains and the k-axis, it being assumed that the strains produce at any point one direction of easy magnetization only and that the energy required to rotate the magnetization through 90 deg from the direction of easy magnetization is ϵ. The magnetization curve of a region having a distortion such as to produce the conditions described in Eq. (236) is

$$H = \frac{2\epsilon}{I_w} \frac{\sin (\psi - \theta) \cos (\psi - \theta)}{\sin \theta}$$

or, solving for $I_w \cos \theta = I$, we may write

$$I = f(H, \epsilon, \psi)$$

The probability that strains randomly oriented will produce a direction of easy magnetization between ψ and $\psi + d\psi$ is $\sin \psi\, d\psi$, so that we have, for the magnetization of a randomly distorted crystal,

$$I = \int_0^{\frac{\pi}{2}} f(H, \epsilon, \psi) \sin \psi d\psi \tag{237}$$

The curve representing Eq. (237) was calculated graphically and is shown as a broken line in Fig. 129, the same constant

$$\epsilon = \frac{I_w}{c} = 10I_w$$

being used as for the other curves for iron. The agreement is sufficiently good to indicate that randomly oriented imperfections are concerned in producing the observed approach to saturation.

A rough estimate of the order of magnitude of the strains necessary to account for the observed values of c in Figs. 129 and 130 indicates that for nickel these are larger than the magnetostrictive strains, being from 5 to 10×10^{-5}, and for iron from five to ten times larger.

In ferromagnetic materials having no magnetostriction the constants b_1 and b_2 in Eq. (229) vanish, so that the strains should have no effect on the magnetization curve. Observations on such materials should approach more closely the square curves of Chap. VI. In permalloy, an iron-nickel alloy containing roughly 20 per cent of iron, the constant a as well as b_1 and b_2 approaches zero, so that even a polycrystalline wire should show the characteristic behavior of a perfect single crystal in the direction of easy magnetization, as, in fact, it does. A curve published by Buckley and McKeehan[1] shows practically complete saturation in fields of 5 or 6 oersteds, whereas in iron and nickel crystals fields of about ten times this intensity are required.

72. Annealing in a Magnetic Field.—Every now and then for a good many years papers have appeared on changes in magnetic properties produced by annealing in a magnetic field. Most interesting results of this kind have been reported by Bozorth, Dillinger, and Kelsall.[2] These authors have shown that the

[1] O. E. BUCKLEY and L. W. McKEEHAN, *Phys. Rev.*, **26**, 261, 1925.

[2] R. M. BOZORTH, J. F. DILLINGER, and G. A. KELSALL, *Phys. Rev.*, **45**, 742, 1934. See also recent papers by O. DAHL and F. PAWLECK, *Z. Physik*, **94**, 504, 1935, and R. M. BOZORTH and J. F. DILLINGER, *Physics*, **6**, 279, 285, 1935.

maximum permeability of certain alloys of ferromagnetic materials can be greatly increased by a heat treatment below the Curie temperature in a magnetic field. For instance, a value of $\mu_{max} = 600,000$ is reported for an iron-nickel alloy containing 65 per cent nickel. Bozorth has suggested that the magnetic field produces these results by relieving internal strains. His argument is briefly the following: Above the Curie point every crystal grain is homogeneous and truly cubic. As the material is cooled to a temperature below the Curie point, small regions of spontaneous magnetization are formed, each of them no longer exactly cubic because of magnetostriction. Plastic flow will, therefore, take place to allow the crystal to accommodate itself to the magnetic state. If the regions of spontaneous magnetization are randomly oriented during this process of accommodation, the randomly oriented configuration will have the lowest energy, and work must be done to produce an ordered magnetized state. If, on the other hand, the accommodation takes place in the presence of a magnetic field, the ordered configuration will have the lowest energy, and magnetization will proceed more easily. It seems very reasonable to assume that this sort of thing may happen, but we know too little as yet to be certain that the presence of a magnetic field at high temperatures does not produce quite different changes as well.

73. Magnetic Strain Analysis.—Since distortions of the crystal lattice have such a marked effect on magnetization, it should be possible to obtain information about the strains from magnetic data. No methods have so far been found to determine just what the local disturbances in metals are, and as a result it is customary to speak only of the total amount of energy stored up in a metal in the form of self-supporting elastic strains. It seems very likely, however, that the nature of these strains as well as their extent can be controlled within considerable limits and that once we have learned how to observe them, we shall also be able to control them and so produce materials with new properties to study and use.

Magnetic strain analysis is a relatively unexplored field, and since only very little experimental work has been done on it so far, we cannot feel very certain of our predictions and interpretations. It seems best, therefore, to give only a few examples of the sort of application that might be made of the ideas described in this book and to leave a more exhaustive study of the possibilities to some future time when, with more experimental data available for check, we can proceed with more confidence.

In Par. 65 we found that the law of approach to saturation for a homogeneous ferromagnetic substance, in so far as rotational processes are concerned, is

$$I = I_w\left(1 - \frac{c}{H^2}\right)$$

$$c = \frac{(\nabla E_\theta)^2}{2I_w^2}$$

$$(\nabla E_\theta)^2 = \left(\frac{\partial E_\theta}{\partial \theta}\right)^2 + \frac{1}{\sin^2 \theta}\left(\frac{\partial E_\theta}{\partial \varphi}\right)^2 \tag{238}$$

and that in nonhomogeneous materials c must be replaced by an average taken over all the regions of the material which may each be considered homogeneous. In the absence of strains, c will depend on the orientation of the crystal grains only. We shall here neglect this part of the calculation and confine ourselves to isotropic material. In this case we may put

$$E_\theta = b_1 \Sigma \alpha_i^2 A_{ii} + b_2 \Sigma' \alpha_i \alpha_j A_{ij}$$
$$b_1 = b_2; \qquad a = 0 \tag{239}$$

The constant c at any point now may be calculated from the local value of the strain tensor and hence $\bar{c}$ for the whole material, which will depend on certain mean values of the strain tensor components.

For instance, if the sample to be investigated is in the form of a disk taken from a rolled sheet, we may measure the approach to saturation for magnetization in various directions in the plane of the disk and from this draw conclusions concerning the orientation and extent of the strains. Let i, j, k be axes fixed in the sample, and let φ measure the angle between the rolling direction and the applied field, as in Fig. 114. Assuming that the strains have the symmetry of the rolling process (see Par. 64), $\bar{c}$ may be shown to have the form

$$\bar{c} = \frac{1}{2I_w^2}[P \cos 4\varphi + Q \cos 2\varphi + R]$$
$$P = -\tfrac{1}{2}b_1^2\overline{(A_{11} - A_{22})^2} + 2b_2\overline{A_{12}^2}$$
$$Q = 2b_2^2\overline{(A_{23}^2 - A_{31}^2)}$$
$$R = \tfrac{1}{2}b_1^2\overline{(A_{11} - A_{22})^2} + 2b_2^2(\overline{A_{12}^2} + \overline{A_{23}^2} + \overline{A_{31}^2}) \tag{240}$$

The quantities P, Q, R are directly observable, and we there-fore have a possible experimental method for observing functions of the mean square value of the strain tensor components. It is, of course, not possible to evaluate all five of the unknowns appear-ing in Eq. (240), but interesting information can nevertheless be obtained by observations of $\bar{c}$ in the rolling plane. For instance, if the strains are preponderantly extensions and compressions in the direction of rolling, the coefficient of cos 4φ will be large, and this periodicity will predominate. If the strains are randomly oriented, the constant term will be most important. Similarly, a large coefficient of cos 2φ means a considerable difference in the distortions of the 1-3 and 2-3 planes.

Becker and Kersten have attacked the problem of measuring the mean value of strains in plastically deformed nickel, assuming isotropic material and randomly oriented strains.[1] This work was the first of its kind and was sufficiently successful to make the outlook for future developments look very promising. The difficulty is chiefly one of finding effects that can be observed under conditions compatible with the simplifying assumptions made in the calculations. Becker and Kersten studied the initial permeability μ_0, the reversible work

$$W = \int_0^{I_w} H dI$$

done on the sample during magnetization, and the remanence I_r (further discussed in Chap. IX) of plastically deformed nickel wires. The assumptions made in relating the foregoing observ-able quantities to the internal strains included, besides the isotropy of the material and the vanishing of the crystalline field ($a_F = 0$), the neglect of all but rotational magnetization processes. The consistency of their results indicates that for purposes of rough approximation, at any rate, their procedure was justified. The relationships used in determining the strains, as given by Kersten, are

$$\kappa_0 = \frac{\mu_0 - 1}{4\pi} = \frac{2}{9}\frac{I_w^2}{\lambda_\infty(\sigma_i)_{\kappa_0}}$$

$$W = \lambda_\infty(\sigma_i)_W$$

$$\left(\frac{\partial I_r}{\partial \sigma}\right)_{\sigma_0} = \frac{I_w}{4(\sigma_i)_{I_r}} \tag{241}$$

[1] M. KERSTEN, *Z. Physik*, **76**, 505, 1932; **82**, 723, 1933. Other references are given in these papers.

where σ is a homogeneous strain, λ_∞ is the magnetostrictive elongation at saturation, and (σ_i) is a measure of the internal strains produced by plastic deformation. Subscripts are added to this last quantity to indicate the method of observations, as all three values of σ_i are not identical owing to differences in the averaging process.

74. Magnetostriction. Saturated States.—In discussing this subject, we shall assume that a ferromagnetic crystal may be treated as an aggregate of regions of spontaneous magnetization, as before, and that each region is distorted in a manner determined by the direction of magnetization with respect to the crystallographic axes. The discussion may therefore be conveniently divided into two sections, treating, first, the local distortion of the regions, which can be directly observed by macroscopic measurements on saturated states when the directions of magnetization of all regions are parallel; and, second, the change in shape resulting from a variation of the intensity of the macroscopic magnetization rather than its orientation alone. It should be observed that measurements of magnetostriction can tell us more about the magnetization process than measurements of magnetization itself. For instance, if we observe a state of zero magnetization, we know only that the moments of the elementary magnets cancel each other but nothing of the nature of the distribution of orientations that brings this about. Magnetostriction measurements, however, can distinguish between different kinds of demagnetization, such as demagnetization resulting from having equal volumes of the crystal magnetized parallel and antiparallel to a given axis, and a random distribution of magnetization, and may therefore become a most important tool in further detailed studies of magnetization processes. On the other hand, in order to make measurements of magnetostriction, it is necessary to specify a standard state with respect to which changes in dimensions are measured, and great care should be taken in comparing observations that this standard state is the same.

In Par. 57 a method for describing the interaction between the external forces that can directly distort a crystal and the torques that can rotate its direction of (spontaneous) magnetization was discussed. As a result, it was possible to express the deformation of crystals as functions of the applied stresses and the direction of magnetization. For cubic crystals the result was (see Eq. 155)

$$A_{ii} = (s_{11} - s_{12})(F_{ii} - b_1\alpha_i^2) + s_{12}(\Sigma F_{ii} - b_1)$$
$$A_{ij} = \frac{s_{44}}{2}(F_{ij} - b_2\alpha_i\alpha_j) \tag{242}$$

Instead of defining the distortion by the strain tensor A_{ij}, it is often convenient to express it in terms of the change in length per unit length $\delta l/l$, as measured in a direction having direction cosines β_1, β_2, β_3 with respect to the cubic axes. These two representations of the distortion are related by the expression

$$\frac{\delta l}{l} = \sum A_{ii}\beta_i^2 + \sum{}' A_{ij}\beta_i\beta_j \tag{243}$$

From the form of (242) it follows that the total distortion is made up of three parts. One part depends only on the external forces and is unaffected by the direction of magnetization, since there are no terms involving products of F_{ij} and α_k. The second part depends on the direction of magnetization only and is unaffected by external forces. This is the magnetostrictive distortion in which we are interested. Finally, there is a change in shape which is independent both of the external forces and of the direction of magnetization and dependent only on the presence of the magnetization. This latter distortion is a change in volume given by the expression

$$\frac{\delta v}{v} = \sum A_{ii} = -(s_{11} + 2s_{12})b_1$$

and shows that the volume change produced by spontaneous magnetization is related to the directional magnetostrictive effects.[1] The preceding expression is not, however, the total change in volume produced by the magnetization.

[1] R. Becker, *Z. Physik*, **87**, 547, 1934, and M. Kornetzki, *Z. Physik*, **87**, 560, 1934, have found that experiments on the change in volume with magnetization of polycrystalline iron can best be explained by assuming an effect in single crystals of the form

$$\frac{\delta v}{v} = \text{const.} + \text{const.} \sum{}' \alpha_i^2\alpha_j^2$$

The presence of such an effect indicates that in order to describe E_θ in an iron crystal accurately it is necessary to include terms of the form $A_{ij}\alpha_k\alpha_l\alpha_m\alpha_n$ which is of higher order than the terms considered here. To

Substituting the expressions for A_{ij} given in Eq. (242) into (243) and retaining only terms involving α, we have, for the distortion in its dependence on the direction of spontaneous magnetization,

$$\frac{\delta l}{l} = \kappa_0 + \kappa_1 \sum \alpha_i^2 \beta_i^2 + \kappa_2 \sum{}' \alpha_i \alpha_j \beta_i \beta_j$$

$$\kappa_1 = -\frac{b_1}{c_{11} - c_{12}}; \qquad \kappa_2 = -\frac{b_2}{2c_{44}} \tag{244}$$

The constant κ_0 is an arbitrary constant defining the original state with respect to which changes are measured. In the special case of the longitudinal effect, where the measured change in length is parallel to the magnetostriction, we may put $\alpha_i = \beta_i$, etc.; and (244) reduces to

$$\frac{\delta l}{l} = \text{const.} + (\kappa_2 - \kappa_1) \sum{}' \alpha_i^2 \alpha_j^2 \tag{245}$$

which is illustrated in Figs. 93 and 94.

The only experiments available to check the correctness of Eq. (244) involve measurements of the change in shape produced by magnetizing crystals in various directions from 0 to saturation, and as this involves certain assumptions going beyond the discussion of this paragraph, a comparison with experiment will not be undertaken at this time. The best way to check Eq. (244) would be to mount a spherical- or disk-shaped crystal in an apparatus capable of measuring a diameter accurately and to observe the changes in length produced by rotating a field sufficiently strong to produce saturation. In this way only saturated states would be involved, and Eq. (244) could be checked without having to make further assumptions about demagnetization.

Similar considerations apply to other crystal classes. For hexagonal cobalt and pyrrhotite, which belong to the crystal

---

this order of approximation the constant a in $E_\theta = a\Sigma' \alpha_i^2 \alpha_j^2 + \cdots$ depends on lattice distortion. Kornetzki concludes from his experiments on iron that a would be reduced by about 12 per cent by a hydrostatic pressure of 10,000 atmospheres. R. Gans and J. von Harlem, *Ann. Physik,* **16,** 162, 1933, also conclude from an examination of experimental data on magnetostriction in single crystals of iron that the higher order terms should be included.

class C_6^v, we have, for the energy of the deformed crystal [see Eqs. (137) and (148)],

$$E = c_{1111}A_{11}^2/2 + c_{2222}(A_{22}^2 + A_{33}^2)/2 + c_{1122}(A_{11}A_{22} +$$
$$A_{11}A_{33}) + c_{2233}A_{22}A_{33} + (c_{2222} - c_{2233})A_{23}^2 + c_{1212}(A_{31}^2 + A_{12}^2)/2$$
$$+ [b_{1111}A_{11} + b_{1122}(A_{22} + A_{33})]\alpha_1^2 + (b_{2222}A_{22} + b_{2233}A_{33})\alpha_2^2 +$$
$$(b_{2233}A_{22} + b_{2222}A_{33})\alpha_3^2 + 2(b_{2222} - b_{2233})A_{23}\alpha_2\alpha_3 + b_{1212}(A_{31}\alpha_3\alpha_1$$
$$+ A_{12}\alpha_1\alpha_2) \quad (246)$$

In order to find the equilibrium configuration of such a crystal in the absence of external forces, we must solve for the strain tensor components A_{ij} satisfying the six equations:

$$\frac{\partial E}{\partial A_{ij}} = 0 \quad (247)$$

This may be done, and the result is

$$A_{11} = \kappa_1\alpha_1^2 + \lambda$$
$$A_{22} = \kappa_2\alpha_2^2 + \kappa_3\alpha_3^2 + \mu$$
$$A_{33} = \kappa_3\alpha_2^2 + \kappa_2\alpha_3^2 + \mu$$
$$A_{23} = (\kappa_2 - \kappa_3)\alpha_2\alpha_3$$
$$A_{31} = \kappa_4\alpha_3\alpha_1$$
$$A_{12} = \kappa_4\alpha_1\alpha_2 \quad (248)$$

$$\kappa_1 = \frac{c_{1122}(2b_{1122} - b_{2222} - b_{2233}) - (c_{2222} + c_{2233})b_{1111}}{c_{1111}(c_{2222} + c_{2233}) - 2c_{1122}^2}$$

$$\kappa_2 = \frac{(c_{2233}b_{2233} - c_{2222}b_{2222}) - (c_{2233} - c_{2222})(b_{1122} + c_{1122}\kappa_1)}{c_{2222}^2 - c_{2233}^2}$$

$$\kappa_3 = \frac{(c_{2233}b_{2222} - c_{2222}b_{2233}) - (c_{2233} - c_{2222})(b_{1122} + c_{1122}\kappa_1)}{c_{2222}^2 - c_{2233}^2}$$

$$\kappa_2 - \kappa_3 = -\frac{b_{2222} - b_{2233}}{c_{2222} - c_{2233}} \qquad \kappa_4 = -\frac{b_{1212}}{c_{1212}}$$

λ and μ are constants determining that part of the distortion which is not a function of the direction of magnetization and are consequently not directly observable. It should be noticed that the magnetostrictive distortions are determined by only four constants $\kappa_1 \ldots \kappa_4$, and that consequently a further experiment is required to determine all five of the constants b_{ijkl} appearing in Eq. (246).

From Eq. (248) it follows that there is a volume change

$$\frac{\delta v}{v} = \sum A_{ii} = (\kappa_1 - \kappa_2 - \kappa_3)\alpha_1^2 + \text{const.} \quad (249)$$

which depends only on the angle between the direction of magnetization and the hexagonal axis. Using Eq. (243), Eq. (248) may be rewritten in the more convenient form

$$\frac{\delta l}{l} = \kappa_0 + \kappa_1\alpha_1^2\beta_1^2 + \kappa_2(\alpha_2^2\beta_2^2 + \alpha_3^2\beta_3^2) + \kappa_3(\alpha_3^2\beta_2^2 + \alpha_2^2\beta_3^2) +$$
$$2(\kappa_2 - \kappa_3)\alpha_2\alpha_3\beta_2\beta_3 + 2\kappa_4\alpha_1\beta_1(\alpha_3\beta_3 + \alpha_2\beta_2) \quad (250)$$

κ_0 being again an arbitrary constant defining the standard configuration from which changes in shape are measured.

For the longitudinal effect we may put $\alpha_i = \beta_i$, and Eq. (250) reduces to

$$\frac{\delta l}{l} = \text{const.} + (\kappa_1 + \kappa_2 - 2\kappa_4)\alpha_1^4 - 2(\kappa_2 - \kappa_4)\alpha_1^2$$

or, putting $\alpha_1 = \cos\theta$,

$$\frac{\delta l}{l} = \text{const.} + \frac{\kappa_1 + \kappa_2 - 2\kappa_4}{8}\cos 4\theta + \frac{\kappa_1 - \kappa_2}{2}\cos 2\theta \quad (251)$$

75. Magnetostriction. Dependence on Magnetization.—In this paragraph we shall attempt to compare some of the theoretical results obtained with experimental results. One difficulty in doing this has already been mentioned, viz., the uncertainty regarding the exact reproducibility of the demagnetized state, with respect to which distortions are measured. There is the further difficulty that magnetostriction is dependent on the shape of the sample on which measurements are made and that this dependence has not been allowed for by most experimenters. The existence of such effects has been pointed out by various authors.[1] Becker's[2] calculations, which were experimentally checked by Kornetzki,[3] are based on very general assumptions and lead to the results given below.

For a prolate ellipsoid of revolution magnetized parallel to its major axis the magnetostriction is increased as a result of end effects by the following amounts:

In the longitudinal effect,

$$\frac{1}{2}I^2N\left(\frac{1}{3k} + \frac{a}{2G}\right)$$

[1] T. HAYASI, Z. Physik, **72**, 177, 1931. F. C. POWELL, Proc. Cambridge Phil. Soc., **27**, 561, 1931. L. W. McKEEHAN, Phys. Rev., **43**, 1022, 1933.

[2] R. BECKER, Z. Physik, **87**, 547, 1934.

[3] M. KORNETZKI, Z. Physik, **87**, 560, 1934.

In the transverse effect,

$$\frac{1}{2}I^2N\left(\frac{1}{3k} - \frac{a}{4G}\right)$$

In the volume effect,

$$\frac{1}{2}I^2N\frac{1}{k} \tag{252}$$

where I is the intensity of magnetization of the ellipsoid, k is the compressibility, G the torsional modulus, N the demagnetizing factor, and a a constant depending on the eccentricity of the ellipsoid. If e is the eccentricity of the ellipsoid, and R the axial ratio, then N is given by Eq. (163), and a by

$$a = \frac{2R^2 + 1}{R^2 - 1} - \frac{4\pi}{(R^2 - 1)N}$$

where

$$e^2 = 1 - \frac{1}{R^2} \tag{253}$$

Becker states that this formula holds for oblate $(R < 1)$ as well as prolate $(R > 1)$ ellipsoids and gives the following values of N and a for representative values of R.

TABLE IV.—THE CONSTANTS N and a AS FUNCTIONS OF THE AXIAL RATIO R

R	N	a
1	4.19	0.80
2	2.18	1.07
3	1.37	1.23
4	0.95	1.31
5	0.70	1.38
10	0.255	1.53
15	0.135	1.60
20	0.085	1.63
30	0.043	1.68

That the above-mentioned corrections are not trivial is shown in Table V, which gives experimental values for the magnetostric-

TABLE V.—MAGNETOSTRICTION AS A FUNCTION OF THE AXIAL RATIO R

R	1	2	3	4	5
$\delta l/l$	-3.15×10^{-6}	-3.95×10^{-6}	-4.5×10^{-6}	-5.0×10^{-6}	-5.8×10^{-6}

tion of samples of similar materials (iron) differing in shape only.

In order to evaluate the constants appearing in Eq. (244) we shall undertake a comparison with experiments by Honda and Masiyama[1] on iron and by Masiyama[2] on nickel. The samples used were in the shape of oblate ellipsoids which had an axial ratio, in the case of iron, of 50 and, in the case of nickel, of 20. For such samples the correction (252) is much smaller than the errors in measurement due to other sources, so that in the following discussion the form correction is omitted.

As we have said, the constant κ_0 depends upon the initial state which is chosen as a reference with respect to which distortions are measured. The state chosen for this purpose is the demagnetized state, and its precise nature need not be gone into further except that it should be structurally the same for any series of observations that are to be compared to each other. Nevertheless, it is interesting to calculate the value of κ_0 for the particular case in which demagnetization results from having equal volumes of a sample magnetized in each of the directions of easy magnetization. In iron there are three such directions, parallel to the tetragonal axes, and in nickel four, parallel to the trigonal axes, so that with the preceding assumption we may write, for iron,

$$\frac{\delta l}{l}\Bigg]\binom{\alpha_i,\ \alpha_j,\ \alpha_k}{\beta_i,\ \beta_j,\ \beta_k} - \frac{1}{3}\frac{\delta l}{l}\Bigg]\binom{1,\ 0,\ 0}{\beta_i,\ \beta_j,\ \beta_k} - \frac{1}{3}\frac{\delta l}{l}\Bigg]\binom{0,\ 1,\ 0}{\beta_i,\ \beta_j,\ \beta_k}$$
$$- \frac{1}{3}\frac{\delta l}{l}\Bigg]\binom{0,\ 0,\ 1}{\beta_i,\ \beta_j,\ \beta_k}$$

and for nickel,

$$\frac{\delta l}{l}\Bigg]\binom{\alpha_i,\ \alpha_j,\ \alpha_k}{\beta_i,\ \beta_j,\ \beta_k} - \frac{1}{4}\frac{\delta l}{l}\Bigg]\left(\frac{1}{\sqrt{3}},\ \frac{1}{\sqrt{3}},\ \frac{1}{\sqrt{3}} \atop \beta_i,\ \beta_j,\ \beta_k\right)$$
$$- \frac{1}{4}\frac{\delta l}{l}\Bigg]\left(-\frac{1}{\sqrt{3}},\ \frac{1}{\sqrt{3}},\ \frac{1}{\sqrt{3}} \atop \beta_i,\ \beta_j,\ \beta_k\right) - \frac{1}{4}\frac{\delta l}{l}\Bigg]\left(\frac{1}{\sqrt{3}},\ -\frac{1}{\sqrt{3}},\ \frac{1}{\sqrt{3}} \atop \beta_i,\ \beta_j,\ \beta_k\right)$$
$$- \frac{1}{4}\frac{\delta l}{l}\Bigg]\left(\frac{1}{\sqrt{3}},\ \frac{1}{\sqrt{3}},\ -\frac{1}{\sqrt{3}} \atop \beta_i,\ \beta_j,\ \beta_k\right)$$

[1] K. Honda and Y. Masiyama, *Science Repts. Tôhoku Imp. Univ.*, **15**, 757, 1926.

[2] Y. Masiyama, *op. cit.*, **17**, 945, 1928.

where the quantities in brackets indicate the direction of magnetization and observation, respectively. Upon substituting Eq. (244) in either of the preceding expressions, the result is

$$-\frac{\kappa_1}{3} + \kappa_1 \sum \alpha_i^2 \beta_i^2 + \kappa_2 {\sum}' \alpha_i \alpha_j \beta_i \beta_j$$

which is identical with (244) except that

$$\kappa_0 = -\frac{\kappa_1}{3} \qquad (254)$$

so that, if demagnetization actually proceeds according to the foregoing scheme, we should expect (254) to hold.

In Table VI are listed the directions of magnetization and observation for which we shall compare theory and experiment together with the values of $\delta l/l$ deduced from Eq. (244) for these special cases.

In Table VII are the experimental values for the foregoing six cases for iron and nickel, using the values for the constants κ listed in Table VIII.

In Table VIII are listed all the constants used in calculating the magnetomechanical properties of iron and nickel. The elastic constants are used in relating the behavior of rigidly held crystals to that of elastically deformable crystals showing magnetostriction (see Par. 57). No accurate values can be given for polycrystalline materials, as the constants have been

TABLE VI.—THEORETICAL MAGNETOSTRICTIONS

Case	Direction of magnetization	Direction of observation	$\delta l/l$
a	[100] axis $\alpha_i = 1, \alpha_j = 0, \alpha_k = 0$	$\beta_i = 1, \beta_j = 0, \beta_k = 0$	$\kappa_0 + \kappa_1$
b	[100] axis $\alpha_i = 1, \alpha_j = 0, \alpha_k = 0$	$\beta_i = 0, \beta_j = 1, \beta_k = 0$	κ_0
c	[100] axis $\alpha_i = 1, \alpha_j = 0, \alpha_k = 0$	$\beta_i = 0, \beta_j = 1/\sqrt{2}, \beta_k = 1/\sqrt{2}$	κ_0
d	[110] axis $\alpha_i = 1/\sqrt{2}, \alpha_j = 1/\sqrt{2}, \alpha_k = 0$	$\beta_i = 1/\sqrt{2}, \beta_j = 1/\sqrt{2}, \beta_k = 0$	$\kappa_0 + \frac{1}{2}(\kappa_1 + \kappa_2)$
e	[110] axis $\alpha_i = 1/\sqrt{2}, \alpha_j = 1/\sqrt{2}, \alpha_k = 0$	$\beta_i = 1/\sqrt{2}, \beta_j = -1/\sqrt{2}, \beta_k = 0$	$\kappa_0 + \frac{1}{2}(\kappa_1 - \kappa_2)$
f	[110] axis $\alpha_i = 1/\sqrt{2}, \alpha_j = 1/\sqrt{2}, \alpha_k = 0$	$\beta_i = 0, \beta_j = 0, \beta_k = 1$	κ_0
g	[111] axis $\alpha_i = 1/\sqrt{3}, \alpha_j = 1/\sqrt{3}, \alpha_k = 1/\sqrt{3}$	$\beta_i = 1/\sqrt{3}, \beta_j = 1/\sqrt{3}, \beta_k = 1/\sqrt{3}$	$\kappa_0 + \frac{1}{3}(\kappa_1 + 2\kappa_2)$
h	[111] axis $\alpha_i = 1/\sqrt{3}, \alpha_j = 1/\sqrt{3}, \alpha_k = 1/\sqrt{3}$	$\beta_i = 1/\sqrt{2}, \beta_j = -1/\sqrt{2}, \beta_k = 0$	$\kappa_0 + \frac{1}{3}(\kappa_1 - \kappa_2)$

found to vary considerably from sample to sample, depending partly on grain and strain orientation and possibly also on other

Table VII.—Experimental and Theoretical Magnetostrictions × 10^6

	Iron		Nickel	
Case	Experimental	Theoretical	Experimental	Theoretical
a	$\begin{cases} 17.1 \\ 15.3 \end{cases}$	17.0	$\begin{cases} -54.4 \\ -50.7 \end{cases}$	-52
b	-15.7	-15	21.1	21
c	-15.4	-15	24.0	21
d	$\begin{cases} -7.2 \\ -2.7 \end{cases}$	-5	$\begin{cases} -31.3 \\ -33.9 \end{cases}$	-29
e	14.0	7	14.5	-4
f	-9.1	-15	18.3	21
g	-12.9	-12	-27.1	-18
h	20.6	0	7.2	4

Table VIII.—Constants Describing the Magnetomechanical Properties of Iron and Nickel

	Iron	Nickel
c_{11}	2.37×10^{12} ergs/cc.	
c_{12}	1.41×10^{12} ergs/cc.	
c_{44}	1.16×10^{12} ergs/cc.	
G	0.75 to 0.85×10^{12} ergs/cc.	0.8×10^{12} ergs/cc.
E	1.9 to 2.2×10^{12} ergs/cc.	1.9 to 2.2×10^{12} ergs/cc.
k	1.5×10^{12} ergs/cc.	1.6×10^{12} ergs/cc.
a	2.15×10^5 ergs/cc.	-2.8×10^4 ergs/cc.
a_F	2.15×10^5 ergs/cc.	-2.4×10^4 ergs/cc.
b_1	-3.1×10^7 ergs/cc.	$11. \times 10^7$ ergs/cc.
b_2	2.8×10^7 ergs/cc.	3.5×10^7 ergs/cc.
κ_0	-1.5×10^{-5}	2.1×10^{-5}
κ_1	3.2×10^{-5}	-7.3×10^{-5}
κ_2	-1.2×10^{-5}	-2.3×10^{-5}
I_w	1720	500

factors. This is further discussed in Par. 77. The elastic constants for iron crystals c_{11}, c_{12}, and c_{44} are taken from Goens and Schmid.[1] Those for nickel crystals are not known. The values for the torsional modulus G, Young's modulus E, and the com-

[1] E. Goens and E. Schmid, *Naturwiss.*, **19**, 520, 1931.

pressibility k for polycrystalline materials are taken from the Landolt-Börnstein tables.   The difference between the constants a_F and a is the contribution of the magnetostrictive deformation to the magnetic anisotropy of crystals subject to no external forces.   This contribution is negligible in iron and small in nickel. The foregoing value of G for nickel is used to estimate a_F, b_1, and b_2 from κ_1 and κ_2, using the relations

$$a_F = a + \frac{b_1^2 - b_2^2}{4G}$$

$$\kappa_1 = -\frac{b_1}{2G}; \qquad \kappa_2 = -\frac{b_2}{2G} \tag{255}$$

which may be derived in the same manner as expressions (160), assuming isotropic elastic properties.

From Eq. (255) it follows that the relation

$$\kappa_1 - \kappa_2 = 0$$

must hold for material that is isotropic with respect to magnetostriction.   This condition is not satisfied for either iron or nickel.   Nickel is often considered more nearly isotropic than iron because the longitudinal effect has at least the same sign in all directions.

The agreement shown in Table VII is not very good, so that the values given for the constants κ_0, κ_1, κ_2, b_1, and b_2 are not to be relied on for more than order of magnitude.   Further experimental work, preferably along the lines suggested in the previous paragraph, is greatly to be desired.   Equation (254) is sufficiently well satisfied to indicate that demagnetization in these experiments tended, at any rate, to be that assumed in the derivation. Further work to check this more accurately and to investigate the factors determining the nature of demagnetization is also needed.   Until these further experimental data are available, we cannot be certain even that the number of constants given above is sufficient for an adequate description of iron and nickel.   However, with the understanding that changes in detail may be necessary, we shall use the foregoing for a starting point for a discussion of magnetostriction as a function of magnetization.

Assuming, then, the existence of small regions of spontaneous magnetization whose individual distortions are known, and that the macroscopic distortion of a crystal may be calculated addi-

tively from the distortions of these regions, we need only a knowledge of the distribution of the directions of spontaneous magnetization of the regions for a given magnetization in order to
calculate the resulting magnetostriction.   It may happen that in
any particular experiment, forces determining this distribution
are present.[1] The analysis of the magnetization curves in Par.
71, for instance, indicates that local strains in the crystals there
discussed played an important part in determining this distribution.   In fact, an elaboration of the statement made in Par. 71
concerning the magnetization of imperfect crystals leads, with
certain simplifying assumptions, to the magnetostriction *vs.*
intensity of magnetization curves first proposed by Akulov,[2]
and it is very likely that the behavior of some samples may be
more accurately described by Akulov's distribution function
than by that discussed below.

   If, however, there are no forces, we may expect translational
magnetization to proceed as described in Par. 50 and 60 without
any change in energy, and the distribution of orientations will,
in general, be simply the most probable of all possible distributions.   This idea was first proposed by Heisenberg,[3] and the calculation given below is taken from his paper.

   We shall consider first the distribution of magnetization in an
iron crystal magnetized parallel to a tetragonal axis.   Assuming
rectangular coordinates parallel to the cubic axes, we shall put the
external field H in the direction of the $+x$-axis.   As we have seen
(Par. 62), the crystal has six directions of easy magnetization, in the
directions of the $\pm x$-, $\pm y$-, $\pm z$-axes, and magnetization proceeds
without any change in energy by translational processes only.
The first part of the problem to be solved is to find the most
probable distribution of the directions of magnetization of N
regions of spontaneous magnetization of equal size among the
six possible orientations for any resultant value of I.   If N_1 is
the number of regions magnetized in the direction of the $+x$-axis,
N_3 the number magnetized in the direction of the $-x$-axis, and
N_2 the total number magnetized in the directions of the $\pm y$-
and $\pm z$-axes, we have

---

[1] In this connection see Par. 87 in which an effect due to the shape of
the sample is discussed.

[2] N. S. Akulov, *Z. Physik*, **69**, 78, 1931.

[3] W. Heisenberg, *Z. Physik*, **69**, 287, 1931.

$$N_1 + N_2 + N_3 = N \tag{256}$$

$$\frac{N_1 - N_3}{N} = \frac{I}{I_w} \tag{257}$$

The probability that any particular region be magnetized in any one of the six possible directions is clearly $\frac{1}{6}$, and since by definition the regions do not interact, the probability that all N regions be magnetized in specified directions simultaneously is simply the product of the probabilities that each region separately be magnetized in a given direction, or

$$\left(\tfrac{1}{6}\right)^{N_1}\left(\tfrac{4}{6}\right)^{N_2}\left(\tfrac{1}{6}\right)^{N_3}$$

But the number of ways in which the regions may be divided into three groups containing N_1, N_2, and N_3 regions, respectively, is

$$\frac{N!}{N_1!N_2!N_3!}$$

so that we have for the probability of finding any distribution of the type under consideration

$$W = \frac{N!}{N_1!N_2!N_3!}\left(\frac{1}{6}\right)^{N_1}\left(\frac{4}{6}\right)^{N_2}\left(\frac{1}{6}\right)^{N_3}$$

N_1, N_2, and N_3 may all be considered large enough to apply Stirling's formula (102). Neglecting small terms, this may be written

$$\log W = N \log N - N_1 \log N_1 - N_2 \log N_2 - N_3 \log N_3$$
$$+ N_1 \log \tfrac{1}{6} + N_2 \log \tfrac{2}{3} + N_3 \log \tfrac{1}{6} \tag{258}$$

The values of N_1, N_2, and N_3 satisfying Eqs. (256) and (257), for which this expression is a maximum, may be found by the method of Lagrangian multipliers. Add Eqs. (258), (256) multiplied by λ, and (257) multiplied by μ. For W to be a maximum, we must have

$$\frac{\partial}{\partial N_1}\left(\log W + \lambda N + \mu\frac{I}{I_w}\right) = 0$$

$$\frac{\partial}{\partial N_2}\left(\log W + \lambda N + \mu\frac{I}{I_w}\right) = 0$$

$$\frac{\partial}{\partial N_3}\left(\log W + \lambda N + \mu\frac{I}{I_w}\right) = 0$$

which leads to the equations

$$-\log N_1 - 1 + \log \tfrac{1}{6} + \lambda + \mu = 0 \tag{259}$$
$$-\log N_2 - 1 + \log \tfrac{2}{3} + \lambda \qquad = 0 \tag{260}$$
$$-\log N_3 - 1 + \log \tfrac{1}{6} + \lambda - \mu = 0 \tag{261}$$

λ and μ may be eliminated from these equations, and the relation

$$16 N_1 N_3 = N_2^2 \tag{262}$$

remains. Using (256) and (257), N_2 and N_3 may be eliminated from (262), and the following equation for N_1 is obtained:

$$\frac{N_1}{N} = \frac{3\dfrac{I}{I_w} - 1}{6} + \frac{1}{3}\sqrt{3\left(\frac{I}{I_w}\right)^2 + 1} \tag{263}$$

Similarly, the following expressions for N_2 and N_3 may be obtained:

$$\frac{N_2}{N} = \frac{4}{3} - \frac{2}{3}\sqrt{3\left(\frac{I}{I_w}\right)^2 + 1} \tag{264}$$

$$\frac{N_3}{N} = -\frac{3\dfrac{I}{I_w} + 1}{6} + \frac{1}{3}\sqrt{3\left(\frac{I}{I_w}\right)^2 + 1} \tag{265}$$

For $I = 0$, the preceding expressions reduce to

$$N_1 = \tfrac{1}{6}, \qquad N_2 = \tfrac{4}{6}, \qquad N_3 = \tfrac{1}{6}$$

or equal volumes in each of the six possible directions, so that the expression for magnetostriction reduces, as we have shown [see Eq. (254)] to

$$\frac{\delta l}{l} = \sum_{s=1,2,3} \frac{N_s}{N}\left[-\frac{\kappa_1}{3} + \kappa_1 \sum \alpha_i^2 \beta_i^2 + \kappa_2 \sum{}' \alpha_i \alpha_j \beta_i \beta_j \right] \tag{266}$$

where the summation over s means a summation over all the regions, taking account of the direction of spontaneous magnetization of each. Since we are considering longitudinal magneto-striction, or the change in length along the x-axis, we may put

$$\beta_i = \pm 1, \qquad \beta_j = \beta_k = 0$$

and (266) reduces to

$$\frac{\delta l}{l}\bigg]_{[100]} = \sum_s \frac{N_s}{N}\left[-\frac{\kappa_1}{3} + \kappa_1\alpha_z^2\right]$$

or, since

$$\begin{array}{lll} \alpha_z = 1 & \text{for} & s = 1 \\ \alpha_z = 0 & \text{for} & s = 2 \\ \alpha_z = -1 & \text{for} & s = 3 \end{array}$$

the foregoing may be written

$$\begin{aligned} \frac{\delta l}{l}\bigg]_{[100]} &= \left(-\frac{\kappa_1}{3} + \kappa_1\right)\frac{N_1}{N} - \frac{\kappa_1}{3}\frac{N_2}{N} + \left(-\frac{\kappa_1}{3} + \kappa_1\right)\frac{N_3}{N} \\ &= -\frac{\kappa_1}{3} + \kappa_1\frac{N_1 + N_3}{N} \end{aligned}$$

which, using (263) and (265), becomes

$$\frac{\delta l}{l}\bigg]_{[100]} = -\frac{2\kappa_1}{3}\left[1 - \sqrt{3\left(\frac{I}{I_w}\right)^2 + 1}\right] \tag{267}$$

Similarly, we have, for magnetization parallel to a trigonal axis, translational processes up to $I = I_w/\sqrt{3}$ giving rise to no change in length and, for more intense magnetizations, rotational processes which produce a contraction in the direction of magnetization. The result is

$$\frac{\delta l}{l}\bigg]_{[111]} = 0 \qquad 0 \leqslant I \leqslant \frac{I_w}{\sqrt{3}} \tag{268}$$

$$\frac{\delta l}{l}\bigg]_{[111]} = \frac{2}{3}\kappa_2\left(2x\sqrt{\frac{1 - x^2}{2}} + \frac{1 - x^2}{2}\right) \qquad \frac{I_w}{\sqrt{3}} \leqslant I \leqslant I_w$$

$$x = \frac{I}{I_w\sqrt{3}} + \sqrt{\frac{2}{3}\left[1 - \left(\frac{I}{I_w}\right)^2\right]}$$

For magnetization parallel to a digonal axis the result is

$$\frac{\delta l}{l}\bigg]_{[110]} = \frac{\kappa_1}{6}\left[2 - \sqrt{4 - 6\left(\frac{I}{I_w}\right)^2}\right] \qquad 0 \leqslant I \leqslant \frac{I_w}{2}$$

$$\frac{\delta l}{l}\bigg]_{[110]} = \frac{\kappa_1}{6} + \frac{\kappa_2}{2}\left[2\left(\frac{I}{I_w}\right)^2 - 1\right] \qquad \frac{I_w}{\sqrt{2}} \leqslant I \leqslant I_w \tag{269}$$

The foregoing results may be compared with the experiments of Webster.[1] His observations may best be represented, if we choose

$$\kappa_0 = -\frac{\kappa_1}{3}$$

as above, by assuming

$$\kappa_1 = 2.93 \times 10^{-5}$$
$$\kappa_2 = -2.55 \times 10^{-5} \tag{270}$$

values that are in poor agreement with those deduced from the experiments of Honda and Masiyama and listed in Table VIII.

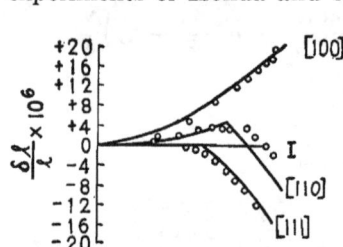

Fig. 131.—Longitudinal magneto-striction of an iron crystal.

However, using the values (270) in the preceding formulas, the curves shown in Fig. 131 are obtained. On the same figure are plotted Webster's experimental data. The agreement is not too good, but it does not seem desirable to modify the theory to fit the facts until the facts themselves are more surely established. A detailed discussion of the magnetostriction of iron and nickel crystals is to be found in a paper by Gans and von Harlem.[2]

In very intense fields there is a change in volume of ferromagnetic materials that is a linear function of the magnetizing field. This effect has been discussed by Becker[3] and observed by Masiyama,[4] Von Auwers,[5] and Kornetzki.[6] Masiyama's and von Auwers' results on Fe-Ni, Ni-Co, and Co-Fe alloys are especially interesting because of the very pronounced maxima and minima that they find in the $\delta v/v$ vs. composition curves.

76. The Effect of Mechanical Deformation on Magneto-striction.—Equation (242) shows that the deformation of a cubic crystal depends both on the externally applied stresses and on

---

[1] W. L. Webster, *Proc. Roy. Soc.*, (A) **109**, 570, 1925.

[2] R. Gans and J. von Harlem, *Ann. Physik*, **16**, 162, 1933.

[3] R. Becker, *Z. Physik*, **87**, 547, 1934.

[4] Y. Masiyama, *Science Repts. Tôhoku Imp. Univ.*, **20**, 574, 1931; **21**, 394, 1932; **22**, 338, 1933.

[5] O. von Auwers, *Physik. Z.*, **34**, 824, 1933.

[6] M. Kornetzki, *Z. Physik*, **87**, 560, 1934.

the direction of magnetization but that the change in shape produced by either of these factors is independent of the other. In other words, a change in the direction of spontaneous magnetization produces a certain change in shape which is the same regardless of whether external forces are present or not. Magnetostriction regarded as a function of the direction of spontaneous magnetization is independent of external forces and is describable by a function of the form of (244). Conversely, a change in external forces produces a change in shape which is the same for any fixed direction of spontaneous magnetization. The elastic constants are independent of the direction of spontaneous magnetization.

However, in experiments in which only the average macroscopic magnetization is observed instead of the spontaneous magnetization mentioned above, both of the foregoing statements no longer hold. The change in shape accompanying a certain change in macroscopic magnetization from I to $I + \delta I$ will not be the same in the presence of external forces as without them, because the orientation of the regions of spontaneous magnetization giving a certain I is dependent on external forces. We shall discuss this phenomenon below. Likewise, since external forces produce a reorientation of the directions of spontaneous magnetization within a sample, the elastic constants of a crystal will be affected by the magnetization, even under conditions in which the macroscopic magnetization is constant. This latter aspect of the problem will be discussed in the next section.

We shall consider first the total change in length in the direction of magnetization produced by magnetization of crystals distorted by extension or compression and, moreover, confine ourselves to the case of magnetization parallel to the elongation or compression. An equation of the form (244) still holds; but if we chose the shape of the crystal in the demagnetized state as the standard with respect to which deformations are measured, we must evaluate the constant κ_0 accordingly. We shall assume that demagnetization results from having equal volumes of a crystal magnetized in each of the directions of easy magnetization, an assumption that for undistorted crystals led to Eq. (254):

$$\kappa_0 = -\frac{\kappa_1}{3} \tag{271}$$

Mechanical deformations, however, change the directions of easy magnetization, as is illustrated by the plaster models shown in the illustrations of Par. 70. For instance, for iron under sufficient compression parallel to the x-axis, the directions of easy magnetization are $\pm y$ and $\pm z$, so that we should have to put for the total change in length in the direction β_i, β_j, β_k resulting from magnetization to saturation in the direction α_i, α_j, α_k

$$\frac{\delta l}{l}\begin{pmatrix}\alpha_x, & \alpha_y, & \alpha_z \\ \beta_x, & \beta_y, & \beta_z\end{pmatrix} - \frac{1}{2}\frac{\delta l}{l}\begin{pmatrix}0, & 1, & 0 \\ \beta_x, & \beta_y, & \beta_z\end{pmatrix} - \frac{1}{2}\frac{\delta l}{l}\begin{pmatrix}0, & 0, & 1 \\ \beta_x, & \beta_y, & \beta_z\end{pmatrix}$$

which reduces to Eq. (244), except that

$$\kappa_0 = -\tfrac{1}{2}\kappa_1(\beta_y^2 + \beta_z^2)$$

and we therefore have for the total change in length in the direction of magnetization

$$\beta_x = 1, \qquad \beta_y = 0, \qquad \beta_z = 0$$

$$\frac{\delta l}{l}\bigg]_{\substack{[100]\\ \text{compression}}} = \kappa_1$$

Similar calculations for other cases lead to the results given in the Table IX. If the tension or compression is sufficient, the direc-

TABLE IX.—Longitudinal Magnetostriction in Crystals with and without Tension or Compression in the Direction of Magnetization

Material	a	b_1	b_2	$b_1 + b_2$	Direction of magnetization	$\delta l/l$	$\delta l/l$ with tension	$\delta l/l$ with compression
Fe	+	−	+	−	[100]	$\frac{2}{3}\kappa_1$	0	κ_1
					[110]	$\frac{1}{2}\left(\frac{\kappa_1}{3} + \kappa_2\right)$	κ_2	$\frac{1}{2}(\kappa_1 + \kappa_2)$
					[111]	$\frac{2}{3}\kappa_2$	κ_2	0
Ni	−	+	+	+	[100]	$\frac{2}{3}\kappa_1$	κ_1	0
					[110]	$\frac{1}{2}\left(\frac{\kappa_1}{3} + \kappa_2\right)$	$\frac{1}{2}(\kappa_1 + \kappa_2)$	0
					[111]	$\frac{2}{3}\kappa_2$	κ_2	0
80% Ni 20% Fe			0		[111]	0	0	0
45% Ni 55% Fe			−		[111]	$\frac{2}{3}\kappa_2$	0	?

tions of easy magnetization are given by the sign of a, b_1, b_2, and $b_1 + b_2$, and the signs assumed for these quantities are also listed.

The sign of b_2 for the alloys containing 80 and 45 per cent Ni, respectively, is taken from data by F. Lichtenberger.[1] Furthermore, McKeehan and Cioffi[2] found that the magnetostriction of a wire of the 80 per cent Ni alloy with and without tension is zero, while Honda and Shimizu[3] found that for a wire of the alloy containing 45 per cent Ni the magnetostriction under tension is zero. In nickel and iron wires, the last-named authors find the magnetostriction with and without tension as shown in Table X.

TABLE X.—MAGNETOSTRICTION OF WIRES

Without Tension		With Tension
$- 4 \times 10^{-6}$	in iron	$< - 9 \times 10^{-6}$
-30×10^{-6}	in nickel	$\sim -42 \times 10^{-6}$

All these results are in general agreement with the predictions of the Table IX provided we assume the iron wires to be fibered with a digonal axis parallel to the wire axis and all the other wires to be fibered with a trigonal axis parallel to the wire axis.

The calculation of magnetostriction under tension as a function of H may be carried out as in Par. 75. We shall here be content with pointing out that for both iron and nickel fibered wires under sufficient tension, I is proportional to H up to saturation, and the magnetostriction is proportional to I^2. This is of especial interest for iron, in that it predicts the disappearance of the change in sign of the magnetostriction in wires and single crystals magnetized in a [110] direction. This result is confirmed by the experiments of Honda and Shimizu,[3] and the proportionality to I^2 has been found in nickel by Heaps.[4]

77. The Elasticity of Ferromagnetic Materials.—To illustrate the effect of ferromagnetism on elastic properties we shall consider the special case of tension or compression parallel to a tetragonal axis in cubic crystals. Accordingly, all components of the stress tensor may be put equal to zero except one, say F_{11}, which represents tension when positive and compression when negative.

[1] F. LICHTENBERGER, *Ann. Physik*, (5), **15**, 45, 1932.
[2] L. W. McKEEHAN and P. P. CIOFFI, *Phys. Rev.*, **28**, 146, 1926.
[3] K. HONDA and S. SHIMIZU, *Phil. Mag.*, **4**, 338, 1902.
[4] C. W. HEAPS, *Phys. Rev.*, **42**, 108, 1932.

Equation (242) then reduces to

$$A_{11} = s_{11}F_{11} + \kappa_1\alpha_1^2 - \frac{\kappa_1}{3} \qquad (272)$$

in so far as the deformation in the direction of the applied force is concerned. In the preceding expression κ_1 is put for $-(s_{11} - s_{12})b_1$, a relation that was established in Pars. 55 and 57, and the constant independent of F and α is so chosen that the deformation is zero in a free crystal demagnetized by having equal volumes magnetized in each of the directions of easy magnetization. The direction of spontaneous magnetization in a crystal subject to the type of force under consideration and in an arbitrary field is given by values of the direction cosines α which make $E_\theta - W$ [see Eq. (159)]

$$E_\theta - W = a_F \Sigma' \alpha_i^2 \alpha_j^2 - \kappa_1 F_{11}\alpha_1^2 - \mathbf{I} \cdot \mathbf{H} \qquad (273)$$

a minimum. The values of α_1 so determined substituted in (272) determine the distortion A_{11}.

The distribution of directions of spontaneous magnetization may change as the result of two different types of processes, translational processes requiring, we have assumed, no energy for their completion, and rotational processes requiring an amount of energy that may be calculated from (273). The effect of these processes on the elastic behavior of iron and nickel is given below.

In iron, a_F being positive, $E_\theta - W$ has minima for $\alpha_i = \pm 1$, 0, *i.e.*, for magnetization parallel to the cubic axes, provided H is not too large. For H parallel to F_{11},

$$\begin{aligned} E_\theta - W &= -\kappa_1 F_{11} - I_w H &&\text{for} && \alpha_1 = \pm 1 \\ &= 0 &&\text{for} && \alpha_1 = 0 \end{aligned}$$

so that

$$\begin{aligned} A_{11} &= s_{11}F_{11} + \tfrac{2}{3}\kappa_1 &&\text{for} && -\kappa_1 F_{11} - I_w H < 0 \\ A_{11} &= s_{11}F_{11} - \tfrac{1}{3}\kappa_1 &&\text{for} && -\kappa_1 F_{11} - I_w H > 0 \end{aligned}$$

A similar calculation may be made for the case $H \perp F$. The resulting stress-strain diagrams are illustrated in Fig. 132, assuming values for the constants as given in Table VIII (Par. 75). s_{11} may be evaluated by using Eq. (140). In the absence of a field any tension makes magnetization in the direction of the tension energetically preferable. The change of magnetization from α_2 or $\alpha_3 = \pm 1$ to $\alpha_1 = \pm 1$ takes place as a result of translational processes; and if no energy changes are involved, as we have assumed, the crystal is entirely inelastic for

$$-\frac{\kappa_1}{3} \leqslant A_{11} \leqslant \frac{2\kappa_1}{3}$$

The effect of the magnetic field is merely to shift the inelastic region along the stress-strain curve. Once the direction of

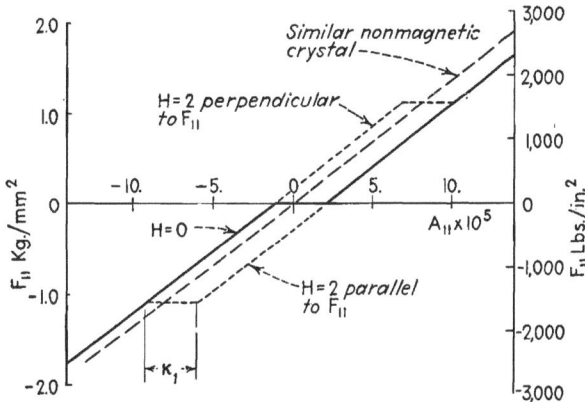

FIG. 132.—Stress-strain diagram for an ideal iron crystal for extension or compression parallel to a tetragonal axis.

magnetization is fixed, the crystal behaves normally. Actually, we know that translational processes do not proceed as in the foregoing idealized case. In order to estimate how this would alter Fig. 132, we shall take the sample whose properties are illustrated in Fig. 129 as an example. Fields of the order of 10 oersteds are needed to bring the translational magnetization even approximately to completion. This means that energies of the order of $I_w H$, or $1720 \times 10 = 1.7 \times 10^4$ ergs/cc., are needed. Similar energy differences are established by external forces when

$$\kappa_1 F_{11} = 1.7 \times 10^4$$

or for

$$F_{11} = \frac{1.7 \times 10^4}{3.2 \times 10^{-5}} \sim 5 \times 10^8 \text{ dynes/cm.}^2 \sim 5 \text{ kg./mm.}^2$$

In such a crystal the effects illustrated could not possibly be observed; but in a crystal that is so nearly perfect and free from impurities that translational magnetization can be brought approximately to completion for $H < 1$, the diagram in Fig. 132 should be a reasonably good approximation.

In addition to altering the shape of the stress-strain diagram, ferromagnetism also has an effect on elastic hysteresis, which will be discussed in Chap. IX.

In nickel, a_F being negative, $E_\theta - W$ has minima in a digonal plane for F and H parallel to a tetragonal axis. We may therefore put

$$\alpha_2 = \alpha_3 = \frac{1}{\sqrt{2}}\sqrt{1 - \alpha_1^2}$$

which, substituted into (273), gives

$$E_\theta - W = 2a_F[\tfrac{1}{4} + \tfrac{1}{2}\alpha_1^2 - \tfrac{3}{4}\alpha_1^4] - \kappa_1 F_{11}\alpha_1^2 - I_w H \alpha_1$$

an expression that has minima for values of α_1 satisfying

$$\alpha_1(6a_F\alpha_1^2 + 2\kappa_1 F_{11} - 2a_F) = -I_w H \qquad (274)$$

For the case $H = 0$ this reduces to

$$\alpha_1^2 = \frac{a_F - \kappa_1 F_{11}}{3a_F}$$

which, substituted into (272), gives

$$A_{11} = \left(s_{11} - \frac{\kappa_1^2}{3a_F}\right)F_{11} \qquad \text{for} \qquad 0 \leqslant \alpha_1 \leqslant 1 \qquad \text{or}$$

$$\text{for} \qquad \frac{-2a_F}{\kappa_1} \leqslant F_{11} \leqslant \frac{a_F}{\kappa_1}$$

$$A_{11} = s_{11}F_{11} - \frac{\kappa_1}{3} \qquad \text{for} \qquad F_{11} > \frac{a_F}{\kappa_1}$$

$$A_{11} = s_{11}F_{11} + \frac{2\kappa_1}{3} \qquad \text{for} \qquad F_{11} < -\frac{2a_F}{\kappa_1}$$

This function, using the values of the constants given in Table VIII of Par. 75 and putting $s_{11} = 1/E$ for lack of more adequate information, is shown in Fig. 133. Rotational magnetization alone is involved, so that good agreement with experiment is to be expected except near the points on the diagram where sharp breaks in the curve are shown. Also, since reversible rotational processes alone are involved, the ferromagnetism should make no contribution to the elastic hysteresis in this particular experiment.

The foregoing illustrates the processes that would take place if it were possible to distort a nickel crystal sufficiently to produce them. An application of tension or compression parallel to a tetragonal axis produces a deformation that rotates the direction of spontaneous magnetization. When this rotation has been accomplished, and the maximum magnetostrictive elongation is in the direction of applied tension or the maximum magneto-strictive shrinkage is in the direction of applied compression,

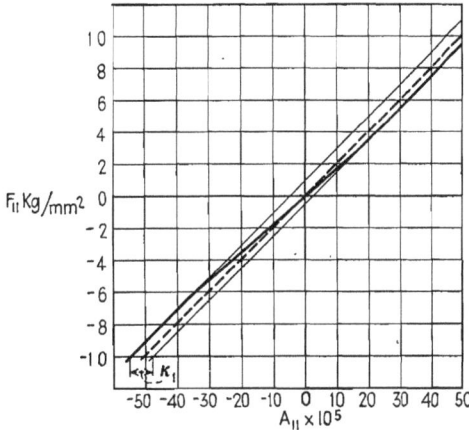

Fig. 133.—Stress-strain diagram for an ideal nickel crystal for extension or compression parallel to a tetragonal axis.

further deformation proceeds normally, as if the crystal were not ferromagnetic. The foregoing anomalies due to ferromagnetism may also be illustrated in a manner susceptible to experimental verification by considering the behavior of Young's modulus $E = dF_{11}/dA_{11}$ for small deformations in the presence of a field H parallel to the applied force. Differentiating (272) with respect to F_{11}, we have

$$\frac{1}{E} = s_{11} + 2\kappa_1\alpha_1\frac{d\alpha_1}{dF_{11}} \tag{275}$$

and differentiating (274) at the point $F_{11} = 0$,

$$(18a_F\alpha_1^2 - 2a_F)\frac{d\alpha_1}{dF_{11}} + 2\kappa_1\alpha_1 = 0 \tag{276}$$

Substituting the value of $d\alpha_1/dF_{11}$ given by (276) into (275), one obtains

$$\frac{1}{E} = s_{11} - \frac{\frac{2}{3}\frac{\kappa_1^2}{a_F}}{3 - 1/3\alpha_1^2} \qquad \text{for} \qquad \frac{1}{\sqrt{3}} \leqslant \alpha_1 \leqslant 1 \qquad (277)$$

α_1 being given as a function of H by

$$H = \frac{2a_F}{I_w}(1 - 3\alpha_1^2)\alpha_1 \qquad (278)$$

These equations giving $1/E$ as a function of H are plotted in Fig. 134. The discontinuity for $H = 192$ comes from the fact

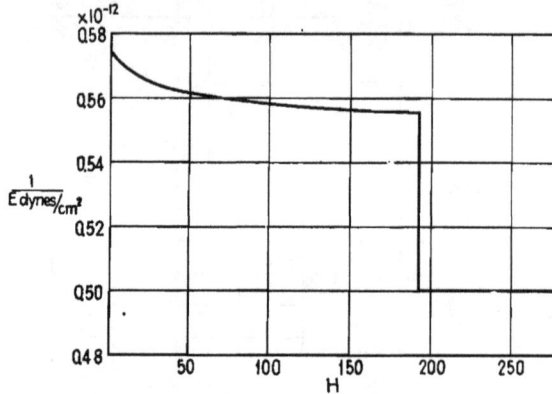

Fig. 134.—Young's modulus as a function of H parallel to the applied force for small compressions or elongations, parallel to a tetragonal axis in nickel.

that theoretically magnetization parallel to a [100] axis in nickel is abruptly reached in a field of this strength. Crystals so far investigated show a gradual approach to saturation, which would change the foregoing discontinuity to a gradual transition. It should further be pointed out that since small fields in the preceding experiment would produce translational processes, elastic hysteresis in this experiment may be increased by the application of such fields.

The foregoing discussion shows how the theory of ferromagnetism may be applied to problems concerning elastic behavior. For further details regarding special problems and materials, the reader is referred to original papers on the subject.[1]

[1] N. Akulov and E. Kondorsky, Z. Physik, **78**, 801, 1932; **85**, 661, 1933. M. Kersten, Z. Physik, **85**, 708, 1933. R. Becker and M. Kornetzki, Z. Physik, **88**, 634, 1934. W. Möbius, Physik. Z., **35**, 806, 1934. J. Zacharias, Phys. Rev., **44**, 116, 1933. E. Giebe and E. Blechschmidt, Ann. Physik, **11**, 905, 1931.

CHAPTER VIII

ELECTRICAL PHENOMENA

The electrical properties of ferromagnetic materials have as yet received relatively little attention from a theoretical point of view, and it is therefore not possible to do much more than describe the various experiments that have been performed. We shall here attempt only a very superficial survey of the subject, since no noteworthy simplification of the original papers is possible. Nevertheless, readers should bear in mind that the connection between ferromagnetism and electrical properties may be very intimate and that further contributions to the subject are greatly to be desired.

78. Discussion of Symmetry Relations.—The general discussion of symmetry relations of Chap. V may be applied to the electrical properties by considerations involving the rate at which a current dissipates energy in a lattice instead of the energy of the lattice itself. If W represents this rate of dissipation of energy produced by a current i having components parallel to a rectangular coordinate system i_i, i_j, i_k, and if this current is maintained by an e.m.f. $\mathbf{E}$ having components E_i, E_j, and E_k, we may put

$$W = \sum_i E_i i_i \tag{279}$$

Assuming Ohm's law, that the current is a linear vector function of the e.m.f., we may put

$$E_i = \sum_j \rho_{ij} i_j \tag{280}$$

which, substituted in (279), gives

$$W = \sum_{ij} \rho_{ij} i_i i_j \tag{281}$$

The coefficients ρ_{ij} describe the properties of the material in which the current is flowing, and we shall assume that they are dependent on the orientation of the spontaneous magnetization I_w, given by the direction cosines α_i, α_j, α_k. Proceeding as in Eq. (119), we may expand W, or, more simply, ρ_{ij}, as functions of α_i and obtain

$$\rho_{ij} = \rho_{ij}^0 + \sum_k \rho_{ijk}\alpha_k + \sum_{kl}\rho_{ijkl}\alpha_k\alpha_l + \cdots \qquad (282)$$

The limitations that any particular crystallographic symmetry puts on the coefficients of the preceding expansion may be calculated by the methods outlined in Par. 54. The problem is slightly complicated by the fact that in treating the interaction between a current and magnetic field, care must be taken to distinguish between right- and left-handed coordinate systems and that reflection in a plane changes one to the other.

For cubic crystals the calculations lead to the following results:

$$\rho_{123} = \rho_{231} = \rho_{312} = -\rho_{321} = -\rho_{132} = -\rho_{213} \qquad (283)$$

For the four-index coefficients one obtains, just as in the case of magnetostriction,

$$\rho_{1111} = \rho_{2222} = \rho_{3333}$$
$$\rho_{1212} = \rho_{2323} = \rho_{3131} = \rho_{2121} = \rho_{3232} = \rho_{1313} \qquad (284)$$

and similar expressions may be found for the coefficients of further terms in Eq. (282), should the foregoing prove insufficient. A detailed discussion of the coefficients of Eq. (282) for various types of crystals has been published by M. Kohler.[1] In his papers the theory is developed for nonferromagnetic substances, but it is applicable to ferromagnetic substances by substituting the spontaneous magnetization I_w for the magnetic field H, provided H is not too large.

79. The Hall Effect.—If a current is passed through a conductor in a magnetic field in a direction at right angles to the field, an e.m.f. is developed at right angles to both the field and the current. This phenomenon is known as the Hall effect. Recent investigations by Pugh[2] and by Pugh and Lippert[3] have shown that the Hall e.m.f. in a variety of ferromagnetic materials is accurately a linear function of the intensity of magnetization. The analysis

---

[1] M. Kohler, *Ann. Physik*, **20**, 878, 891, 1934.
[2] E. M. Pugh, *Phys. Rev.*, **36**, 1503, 1930.
[3] E. M. Pugh and T. W. Lippert, *Phys. Rev.*, **42**, 709, 1932.

of the previous section is therefore applicable, and we need only the second term on the right side of Eq. (282), since that alone is a linear function of the magnetization. Putting ρ_H for the single coefficient in (283) needed to describe the Hall effect in cubic crystals, Eq. (280) reduces to

$$E_i = \rho_H(i_j\alpha_k - i_k\alpha_j)$$

or, in vector notation, $\mathbf{E}_H$ being the Hall e.m.f.,

$$\mathbf{E}_H = \frac{\rho_H}{I_w}[\mathbf{i} \times \mathbf{I}_w] \qquad \qquad (285)$$

This equation states that $\mathbf{E}_H$ is perpendicular to the current and the spontaneous magnetization and independent of crystallographic orientation in cubic crystals. No experimental results on single crystals are available to check this. Furthermore, since $\mathbf{E}_H$ is perpendicular to the current, it will make no contribution to the change of resistance with magnetization which is discussed in the next paragraph.

80. Resistance as a Function of the Orientation of I_w.—The change of resistance with direction of magnetization predicted by Eq. (281) may conveniently be expressed as

$$\frac{\delta R}{R} = \frac{W - \sum_{ij}'\rho_{ij}^0 i_i i_j}{i^2 R} \qquad (286)$$

where ρ_{ij}^0 describes that part of the resistance in Eq. (282) which is independent of α_i, etc., and R is the resistance of a sample in a standard condition, which may be chosen arbitrarily. Introducing the constants ρ_1 and ρ_2 instead of the more complicated expressions in (284), and putting $\beta_i, \ldots$ for the direction cosines of the current with respect to the axes of a cubic crystal, the substitution of (281) in (286) gives

$$\frac{\delta R}{R} = \rho_0 + \rho_1\sum \alpha_i^2\beta_i^2 + \rho_2\sum{}' \alpha_i\alpha_j\beta_i\beta_j \qquad (287)$$

where $\rho_0 =$ an arbitrary constant defining the state of the crystal for which $\delta R = 0$. This equation is exactly equivalent to the expression (266) for magnetostriction, and, as was shown in that discussion,

$$\rho_0 = -\tfrac{1}{3}\rho_1$$

if a demagnetized state with equal volumes of the crystal magnetized in each of the directions of easy magnetization is chosen for $\delta R = 0$. The preceding expression was first proposed by Akulov.[1] It expresses a relationship between the resistance and the direction of spontaneous magnetization, and in order to apply it to crystals with varying total magnetization we must introduce the further assumptions of Chap. VI concerning the reorientation of the regions of spontaneous magnetization by the field. The considerations are similar to those of Par. 75 and lead to the following expressions for the change in resistance parallel to the magnetization in cubic crystals like iron having easy magnetization parallel to a tetragonal axis:

$$\frac{\delta R}{R}\bigg]_{[100]} = -\frac{2}{3}\rho_1(1 - \sqrt{3J^2 + 1}) \tag{288}$$

$$\frac{\delta R}{R}\bigg]_{[110]} = \frac{\rho_1}{6}(2 - \sqrt{4 - 6J^2}) \quad \text{for} \quad 0 \leqslant J \leqslant \frac{1}{\sqrt{2}}$$

$$= \frac{\rho_1}{6} + \frac{\rho_2}{2}(2J^2 - 1) \quad \text{for} \quad \frac{1}{\sqrt{2}} \leqslant J \leqslant 1 \tag{289}$$

$$\frac{\delta R}{R}\bigg]_{[111]} = 0 \quad \text{for} \quad 0 \leqslant J \leqslant \frac{1}{\sqrt{3}}$$

$$= \frac{2}{3}\rho_2\left(2x\sqrt{\frac{1 - x^2}{2}} + \frac{1 - x^2}{2}\right) \quad \text{for} \quad \frac{1}{\sqrt{3}} \leqslant J \leqslant 1 \tag{290}$$

$$x = \frac{J}{\sqrt{3}} + \sqrt{\frac{2}{3}(1 - J^2)} \qquad J = \frac{I}{I_w}$$

These expressions correspond to Eqs. (267) to (269) for magnetostriction. Observations by Webster[2] on the change of resistance of iron crystals are plotted in Fig. 135 together with curves representing the preceding equations, using the following values for the constants:

$$\rho_1 = 0.07 \times 10^{-2} \qquad \rho_2 = 0.6 \times 10^{-2}$$

The agreement is not very good and can be improved by using higher order terms in Eq. (282), as has been shown by Gans and Von Harlem,[3] but the experimental results seem as yet too uncertain to guarantee the correctness of such a procedure.

[1] N. S. Akulov, *Z. Physik*, **59**, 254, 1930.
[2] W. L. Webster, *Proc. Roy. Soc.*, **113**, 196, 1926.
[3] R. Gans and J. von Harlem, *Ann. Physik*, **15**, 516, 1932.

In nickel, however, the expression (287) must surely be amplified. Kaya[1] has investigated the transverse effect by measuring the variation of resistance of nickel rods as a strong field is rotated in a plane perpendicular to the axis of the rod. For a

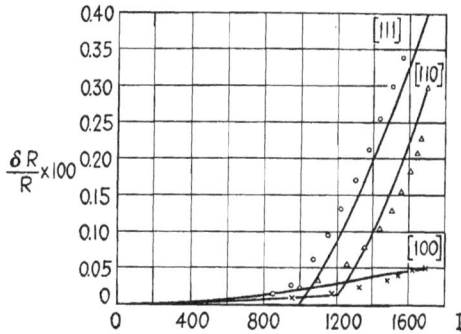

FIG. 135.—The change of resistance with magnetization in an iron crystal.

rod having a tetragonal axis parallel to the axis of the rod, the conditions are described by putting

$$\beta_1 = 1 \qquad \beta_2 = 0 \qquad \beta_3 = 0$$
$$\alpha_1 = 0 \qquad \alpha_2 = \sqrt{1 - \alpha_3^2}$$

in Eq. (287), which reduces to

$$\frac{\delta R}{R} = \rho_0 \tag{291}$$

Kaya finds a strong 90-deg. periodicity, which is incompatible with (291). Gans and von Harlem discuss these results of Kaya's at considerable length in the paper cited above.

Gerlach[2] and his collaborators have done a great deal of work on the change of resistance related to the subject of this paragraph and the next, and Matuyama[3] has investigated polycrystalline iron, nickel, cobalt, and Heusler alloys in fields up to 1800 oersteds at low and high temperatures.

Since lattice distortion reorients the directions of easy magnetization, it alters the resistance and the change of resistance in

[1] S. KAYA, *Science Repts. Tôhoku Imp. Univ.*, **17**, 1027, 1928.

[2] W. GERLACH, *Physik. Z.*, **33**, 953, 1932, gives further references.

[3] Y. MATUYAMA, *Science Repts. Tôhoku Imp. Univ.*, **23**, 537, 1934.

a magnetic field.   A discussion of this effect is to be found in an article by McKeehan,[1] with extensive references and a summary of experimental data, and more recently in papers by Steinberg and Miroschnitschenko[2] and by Gnesotto[3] and Drigo.[4]

81. Resistance as a Function of the Magnitude of I_w.—It has been found that the resistance of ferromagnetic materials depends on the magnitude as well as on the orientation of the spontaneous magnetization, and it further seems to be fairly generally true that an increase in spontaneous magnetization decreases the resistance.   The work of Gerlach[5] and his collaborators and of Potter[6] indicates that the change in resistance is proportional to the square of the spontaneous magnetization, or to the internal energy of magnetization.   Thus, when a ferromagnetic substance is cooled through the Curie point there is an anomalous decrease in resistance which is proportional to I_w^2; or if in the neighborhood of the Curie point the spontaneous magnetization be increased by an external field, a similar decrease in resistance is found.   Potter has taken the change in temperature accompanying a change in magnetization as a measure of the change in internal energy and has shown that in the neighborhood of the Curie point the change in resistance with field is accurately proportional to the change in energy so measured.

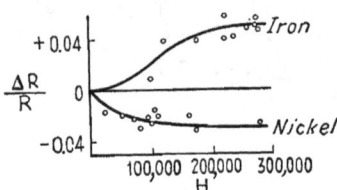

Fig. 136.—The change of resistance of iron and nickel in intense fields.   (*According to Kapitza.*)

The measurements of Kapitza[7] on the change of resistance of iron and nickel in fields up to 300,000 oersteds are shown in Fig. 136.   In the light of the foregoing one is tempted to say that because an increase in resistance is found for iron, the mechanism producing it is not the increase in I_w that is produced even at room temperature by such powerful fields.

[1] L. W. McKeehan, *Phys. Rev.*, **36**, 948, 1930.

[2] D. S. Steinberg and F. D. Miroschnitschenko, *Physik. Z. Sowjetunion*, **5**, 241, 1934.

[3] T. Gnesotto, *Atti ist. Veneto*, **91**, 697, 1932.

[4] A. Drigo, *Nuovo cimento*, **10**, 172, 1933, also containing references to earlier work on the resistance of ferromagnetic materials.

[5] References are given in W. Gerlach, *Physik. Z.*, **33**, 953, 1932.

[6] H. H. Potter, *Proc. Roy. Soc.*, **132**, 560, 1931; *Phil. Mag.*, **13**, 233, 1932.

[7] P. Kapitza, *Proc. Roy. Soc.*, **123**, 334, 1929.

82. Thermoelectric Properties.—Ferromagnetic materials have unusual thermoelectric properties. It is not at present certain, however, whether these properties are directly related to ferromagnetism or only indirectly related—through the magnetostrictive lattice distortion, for instance. The thermoelectric properties at any given temperature depend on the magnetization. A recent paper by Seass[1] describes this and gives references to earlier work. Of considerable interest is also the anomalous behavior in the neighborhood of the Curie point. This has been investigated by a number of people.[2] The thermoelectric properties depend primarily on the energy of the conduction electrons, and any anomaly may consequently be described in terms of peculiarities in the specific heat of the electrons. Dorfman suggested that the anomaly in the specific heat of the electron gas as calculated from thermoelectric observations be compared to the total specific heat anomaly observed calorimetrically at the Curie point, with the idea that if these two were equal, the identity of the electrons responsible for conduction and ferromagnetism could be shown. The results, however, are not such as to confirm this interesting suggestion, at any rate in its present simple forms.

[1] S. SEASS, *Phys. Rev.*, **38**, 1254, 1931.

[2] J. DORFMAN, R. JAANUS, and I. KIKOIN, *Z. Physik*, **54**, 277, 289, 1929. J. DORFMAN, R. JAANUS, K. GRIGOROW, and M. CZERNICHOWSKI, **70**, 796, 1931. K. E. GREW, *Phys. Rev.*, **41**, 356, 1932. L. F. BATES, *Phil. Mag.*, **13**, 393, 1932. A. SCHULZE, *Z. Metallkunde*, **22**, 194, 308, 1930. A. FOSTER, *Proc. Leeds Phil. Soc.*, **2**, 401, 1933. A. DRIGO, *Atti accad. Padova*, **46**, 7, 1930; **47**, 3, 1931. E. C. STONER, *Proc. Leeds Phil. Soc.*, **2**, 149, 1931; *Phil. Mag.*, **12**, 737, 1931.

CHAPTER IX

THE ABSORPTION AND EVOLUTION OF THERMAL ENERGY

A· ferromagnetic substance is capable of storing energy in a variety of ways, as, for instance, in mechanical deformations produced by external mechanical forces or by magnetostriction, as discussed in Chap. VII; in the internal fields, of which we have discussed that producing spontaneous magnetization, the crystalline field, and the internal magnetic field; or in the form of thermal energy. In this last chapter we shall complete the discussion of the distribution of the energy of a ferromagnetic substance among its various energy reservoirs by considering the thermal energy in some detail. The theoretical approach to the subject is very limited. The Weiss theory and its statistical elaboration in Chap. V make it possible to systematize some of the observations concerning reversible thermal changes. But in the main, and especially in so far as irreversible processes such as hysteresis are concerned, we shall have to be satisfied for the present with an account of the empirical facts and a qualitative interpretation.

83. Thermal Expansion.—When a ferromagnetic substance is heated, the spontaneous magnetization is decreased, as discussed in Par. 66; and since spontaneous magnetization is accompanied by magnetostriction, the thermal expansion will have, in addition to its normal behavior, a part that is due to the variation of magnetostriction with temperature. This additional part will further be most pronounced just below the Curie point where the spontaneous magnetization changes most rapidly with temperature (Fig. 117).

The anomaly in the coefficient of linear expansion α will, in general, be made up of two parts, one resulting from the change in shape of the crystal grains due to the change in the magnetostriction constants of Chap. VII (κ_1 and κ_2 for cubic crystals); the other due to a change of volume. It can be shown for cubic crystals that if every crystal of an aggregate is demagnetized by having equal volumes magnetized in each of the directions of easy magnetization, the variation of κ_1 and κ_2 with temperature will have no influence on α, and, the total anomaly will result from changes of volume. It is, in general, difficult to know just how a

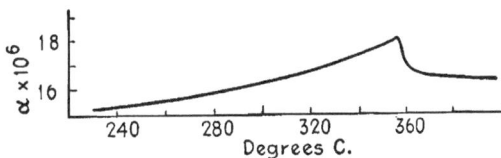

Fig. 137.—The coefficient of thermal expansion of nickel in the neighborhood of its Curie point. (*According to Williams.*)

sample is demagnetized, and this uncertainty introduces a corresponding uncertainty in the interpretation of observations of the linear thermal expansion.

The results for iron[1] indicate that ferromagnetism produces an anomalous expansion. This has been discussed at some length by Fowler and Kapitza[2] and more recently by Powell.[3] In nickel, on the other hand, ferromagnetism produces contraction. The observations of Williams[4] on the coefficient of expansion

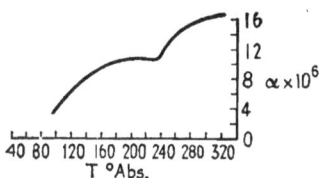

Fig. 138.—The coefficient of thermal expansion of iron at low temperatures. (*According to Simon and Bergmann.*)

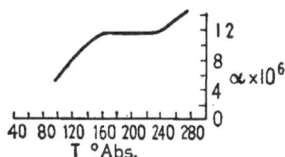

Fig. 139.—The coefficient of thermal expansion of nickel at low temperatures. (*According to Simon and Bergmann.*)

near the Curie point are shown in Fig. 137. Similar observations have been made by Uffelmann,[5] whose observations extend to somewhat higher temperatures.

The temperature range below room temperature has been investigated by Simon and Bergmann,[6] and their results are reproduced in Figs. 138 and 139. The cause of this peculiar

[1] C. BENEDICKS, *J. Iron Steel Inst.*, **89**, 407, 1914.

[2] R. H. FOWLER and P. KAPITZA, *Roy. Soc. Proc.*, **124**, 1, 1929.

[3] F. C. POWELL, *Proc. Phys. Soc. London*, **42**, 390, 1930.

[4] C. WILLIAMS, *Phys. Rev.*, **46**, 1011, 1934.

[5] F. L. UFFELMANN, *Phil. Mag.*, **10**, 633, 1930.

[6] F. SIMON and R. BERGMANN; *Z. physik. Chem.*, B, **8**, 255, 1930.

behavior is not known. It is, however, probably connected with ferromagnetism, as none of the other materials investigated showed peculiarities of this sort.

84. Specific Heats.—The thermal expansion and magnetization of ferromagnetic materials show that internal changes take place with temperature. These changes are also revealed by the specific heat, which is a measure of the energy required to produce them. A most interesting change is that from a ferromagnetic state at low temperature to a paramagnetic state at high temperature. This change was discussed at some length in Chap. V. In linear chains of atoms (Par. 51) there is no abrupt change in properties at any temperature, and the magnetic energy E and magnetic specific heat σ_m vary continuously with the temperature. The case of a three-dimensional model could unfortunately not be calculated rigorously, but it was shown that with various additional assumptions (Par. 50, 52, and 53) models having properties comparable to those of the common ferromagnetic materials and having discontinuities in the specific heat of the order of $\frac{3}{2}k$ per dipole at the Curie point, as shown in Fig. 78, could be set up. Expressed in calories per gram atom, the preceding jump in specific heat may be written $\frac{3}{2}nR$, n being the number of dipoles (Bohr magnetons) per atom. Data on iron, nickel, and cobalt are listed in Table XI.

Table XI.—The Jump in the Specific Heat at the Curie Point

	n	$\frac{3}{2}nR$	Obs., calories per degree per gram atom
Iron..................................	2.2	6.6	5—7
Cobalt................................	1.7	5.1	5.5
Nickel................................	0.6	1.8	1.7—2.2

The observations vary considerably, and the exact shape of the specific heat *vs.* temperature curves is not yet certain. The observations of Lapp[1] on nickel are reproduced in Fig. 140. These observations are probably as precise as any that have been made, and they agree with those of other investigators in the following important points:

[1] E. Lapp, *Ann. Phys.*, **12**, 442, 1929.

1. As the temperature is raised from below the Curie point, the specific heat increases more rapidly than might be expected on the basis of Eq. (109).

.2. The sudden decrease near the Curie temperature is not discontinuous but covers a range of temperatures. Observations differ, especially on the extent of this temperature range. The magnitude of the decrease is given approximately by $\frac{3}{2}nR$.

3. Above the Curie temperature there is still an excess specific heat of the order $\frac{1}{2}R$ per gram atom.

References to other investigations of the specific heats of ferromagnetic substances near their transformation points are given below.[1]

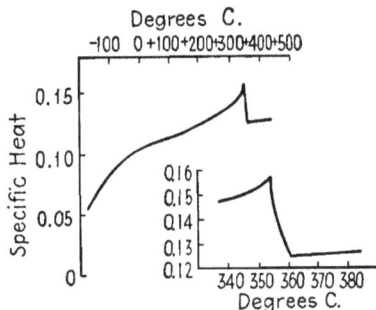

Fig. 140.—The specific heat of nickel. (*According to Lapp.*)

85. The Thermodynamics of Magnetization.[2]

—The thermodynamic treatment of magnetic processes is formally very similar to that of systems whose coordinates are p, v, and T instead of I, H, and T. The discussion given below follows along the lines developed by Goodenough in his "Principles of Thermodynamics."

We shall assume that the properties of the material under discussion may be represented by an equation of the form

[1] Co. Göbl, Diss. Zurich, 1911.

Fe, Ni, Fe₃O₄. P. Weiss, A. Piccard, and A. Carrard, *Arch. sci. phys. nat.*, **42**, 378; **43**, 22, 113, 199, 1917.

Heussler Alloys and Ni. W. Sucksmith and H. H. Potter, *Proc. Roy. Soc.*, **112**, 157, 1926.

Steel, Fe, Ni, Co. S. Umino, *Science Repts. Tôhoku Imp. Univ.*, **15**, 331, 597, 1926; **16**, 593, 1009, 1927; **18**, 91, 1929.

Fe, Ni, Fe-Mn. H. Klinkhardt, *Ann. Physik*, **84**, 167, 1927.

Mn-As. L. F. Bates, *Proc. Roy. Soc.*, **117**, 680, 1928; *Proc. Phys. Soc.*, **42**, 441, 1930.

Mn-P. B. G. Whitmore, *Phil. Mag.*, **7**, 125, 1929.

Ni, Ni-Cu. K. E. Grew, *Proc. Roy. Soc.*, **145**, 509, 1934.

Ni-Cr. A. W. Foster, *Phil. Mag.*, **18**, 470, 1934.

Ni. E. Ahrens, *Ann. Physik*, **21**, 169, 1934.

[2] A very complete discussion of this subject is given by E. A. Guggenheim, *Proc. Roy. Soc.*, **155**, 49, 70, 1936.

$$I = f(H, T)$$

and that, of the three variables, any two may be taken as independent. If q represents the heat absorbed per unit volume of the magnetizable substance under discussion, we define the thermal capacities as follows:

$$\left(\frac{\partial q}{\partial T}\right)_I = s_I = \rho\sigma_I \qquad \left(\frac{\partial q}{\partial I}\right)_T = l_I$$

$$\left(\frac{\partial q}{\partial T}\right)_H = s_H = \rho\sigma_H \qquad \left(\frac{\partial q}{\partial H}\right)_T = l_H$$

ρ being the density, and σ_I and σ_H the specific heats measured at constant magnetization and constant field, respectively.

The heat absorbed in an infinitesimal change of state may be written in any of the following three forms:

$$dq = l_I dI + s_I dT \quad = \left(\frac{\partial q}{\partial I}\right)_T dI + \left(\frac{\partial q}{\partial T}\right)_I dT \qquad (292)$$

$$dq = s_H dT + l_H dH = \left(\frac{\partial q}{\partial T}\right)_H dT + \left(\frac{\partial q}{\partial H}\right)_T dH \qquad (293)$$

$$dq = \left(\frac{\partial q}{\partial H}\right)_I dH + \left(\frac{\partial q}{\partial I}\right)_H dI \qquad (294)$$

and the change of magnetization

$$dI = \frac{\partial I}{\partial T}dT + \frac{\partial I}{\partial H}dH \qquad (295)$$

Substituting (295) in (292), we have

$$dq = l_I\frac{\partial I}{\partial H}dH + \left(s_I + l_I\frac{\partial I}{\partial T}\right)dT \qquad (296)$$

and comparing the coefficients of (293) and (296),

$$l_H = l_I\frac{\partial I}{\partial H} \qquad (297)$$

$$s_H - s_I = l_I\frac{\partial I}{\partial T} \qquad (298)$$

and similarly, putting

$$dH = \frac{\partial H}{\partial I}dI + \frac{\partial H}{\partial T}dT$$

$$l_I = l_H\frac{\partial H}{\partial T} \tag{299}$$

$$s_H - s_I = -l_H\frac{\partial H}{\partial T} \tag{300}$$

In Par. 5 we saw that the change in internal energy in any adiabatic magnetization process may be written HdI per unit volume. If, in addition, an amount of heat dq is added to the magnetizable substance, the total change in internal energy is[1]

$$du = dq + HdI \tag{301}$$

Furthermore, the entropy φ is defined by

$$dq = Td\varphi \tag{302}$$

In addition, we shall introduce the thermodynamic potential i defined by

$$i = u - IH \tag{303}$$
$$di = du - IdH - HdI$$
$$di = dq - IdH \tag{304}$$

dq may be eliminated by combining (301), (302), and (304) with (292) and (293), giving

$$du = (l_I + H)dI + s_IdT \tag{305}$$
$$di = (l_H - I)dH + s_HdT \tag{306}$$

$$d\varphi = \frac{l_I}{T}dT + \frac{s_I}{T}dT \tag{307}$$

$$d\varphi = \frac{l_H}{T}dH + \frac{s_H}{T}dT \tag{308}$$

---

[1] This equation refers to processes in which the configuration of the system does not change. In so far as magnetostriction may be neglected, however, the equation is applicable to systems at constant pressure also. It should be noted that HdI in Eq. (301) is not the total work done in producing magnetization but only that part which has gone to increasing the internal energy u of the sample. By the internal energy u is meant that energy which results from the interaction of the various parts of the sample with each other only.

From these relations it follows that

$$l_I + H = \frac{\partial u}{\partial I}\bigg)_T \qquad s_I = \frac{\partial u}{\partial T}\bigg)_I$$

$$l_H - I = \frac{\partial i}{\partial H}\bigg)_T \qquad s_H = \frac{\partial i}{\partial T}\bigg)_H$$

$$\frac{l_I}{T} = \frac{\partial \varphi}{\partial I}\bigg)_T \qquad \frac{s_I}{T} = \frac{\partial \varphi}{\partial T}\bigg)_I$$

$$\frac{l_H}{T} = \frac{\partial \varphi}{\partial H}\bigg)_T \qquad \frac{s_H}{T} = \frac{\partial \varphi}{\partial T}\bigg)_H$$

Further, since

$$\frac{\partial}{\partial T}\frac{\partial u}{\partial I} = \frac{\partial}{\partial I}\frac{\partial u}{\partial T}$$

we have

$$\frac{\partial l_I}{\partial T} + \frac{\partial H}{\partial T} = \frac{\partial s_I}{\partial I} \qquad (309)$$

$$\frac{\partial l_H}{\partial T} - \frac{\partial I}{\partial T} = \frac{\partial s_H}{\partial H} \qquad (310)$$

$$\frac{\partial l_I}{\partial T} - \frac{l_I}{T} = \frac{\partial s_I}{\partial I} \qquad (311)$$

$$\frac{\partial l_H}{\partial T} - \frac{l_H}{T} = \frac{\partial s_H}{\partial H} \qquad (312)$$

Combining (309) and (311)

$$l_I = -T\frac{\partial H}{\partial T} \qquad (313)$$

and similarly, combining (310) and (312),

$$l_H = T\frac{\partial I}{\partial T} \qquad (314)$$

For adiabatic processes, $dq = 0$, we have two expressions of particular importance, to which we shall return later, derived by substituting the foregoing expressions for l_I and l_H into (292) and
(293).

$$dT = \frac{T}{s_I}\frac{\partial H}{\partial T}dI \qquad (315)$$

$$dT = -\frac{T}{s_H}\frac{\partial I}{\partial T}dH \qquad (316)$$

The complete expressions for $dq \neq 0$ are

$$dq = s_I dT - T\frac{\partial H}{\partial T}dI \tag{317}$$

$$dq = s_H dT + T\frac{\partial I}{\partial T}dH \tag{318}$$

Furthermore, by substituting (313) and (314) into (305) and (306), we obtain

$$du = s_I dT - \left(T\frac{\partial H}{\partial T} - H\right)dI \tag{319}$$

$$di = s_H dT + \left(T\frac{\partial I}{\partial T} - I\right)dH \tag{320}$$

From (311) and (313) we have

$$\left.\frac{\partial s_I}{\partial I}\right)_T = -T\left.\left(\frac{\partial^2 H}{\partial T^2}\right)\right)_I \tag{321}$$

and similarly, from (314),

$$\left.\frac{\partial s_H}{\partial H}\right)_T = T\left.\left(\frac{\partial^2 I}{\partial T^2}\right)\right)_H \tag{322}$$

and substituting l_H from (314) into (300),

$$s_H - s_I = -T\frac{\partial H}{\partial T}\frac{\partial I}{\partial T} \tag{323}$$

All these relationships apply independently of the particular properties of any given material, subject, of course, to the usual conditions required to make the equations meaningful, such as, for instance, that the functions used be single valued. Further progress may be made by making use of the equations of state of particular substances. This is briefly illustrated below for the case of an ideal paramagnetic obeying the Curie law:

$$I = \frac{BH}{T} \tag{324}$$

where B is a constant.
From this equation it follows that

$$\left.\frac{\partial H}{\partial T}\right)_I = \frac{I}{B} \qquad \left.\frac{\partial I}{\partial T}\right)_H = -\frac{BH}{T^2}$$

Inserting these expressions into (319), we have

$$du = s_I dT - \left(\frac{TI}{B} - H\right) dI = s_I dT \qquad (325)$$

which shows that s_I is a function of T only and independent of H and I, just as in the case of the specific heat at constant volume in a perfect gas.

Further, from (323),

$$s_H - s_I = -T\frac{I}{B}\left(-\frac{BH}{T^2}\right) = \frac{IH}{T} = \frac{I^2}{B} \qquad (326)$$

and (315) and (316) reduce to

$$dT = \frac{T}{s_I}\frac{I}{B}dI = \frac{HdI}{s_I} \qquad (327)$$

$$dT = \frac{-T}{s_H}\left(\frac{-BH}{T^2}\right)dH = \frac{IdH}{s_H} \qquad (328)$$

That these equations are compatible with each other may readily be seen by comparison with the equations governing adiabatic magnetization, derived below.

From (301) and (325) we have

$$dq = s_I dT - HdI \qquad (329)$$

and from (324) we find, by differentiation,

$$dT = \frac{BdH}{I} - \frac{BHdI}{I^2} = \frac{B}{I^2}(IdH - HdI)$$

and using (326),

$$dT = \frac{IdH - HdI}{s_H - s_I}$$

Substituting this in (329) and putting $dq = 0$ for adiabatic processes, we have

$$HdI = \frac{s_I}{s_H - s_I}(IdH - HdI) \qquad (330)$$

or, putting $K = s_H/s_I$,

$$\frac{dH}{H} - K\frac{dI}{I} = 0 \qquad (331)$$

which, integrated, becomes

$$H = \text{const. } I^K \qquad (332)$$

86. The Magnetocaloric Effect.—Equations (315) and (316) state that adiabatic magnetization is accompanied by reversible temperature changes and make it possible to calculate the extent of this temperature change if the magnetic equation of state is known.

Assuming only that the total field acting on the magnetized substance is $H + N_w I_w$, as in the Weiss theory (45), and that

$$I_w = f\left(\frac{H + N_w I_w}{T}\right) \tag{333}$$

regardless of the form of f, we find that

$$\left(\frac{\partial H}{\partial T}\right)_I = \frac{H + N_w I_w}{T}$$

$$\left(\frac{\partial^2 H}{\partial T^2}\right)_I = \frac{1}{T}\frac{\partial H}{\partial T} - \frac{H + N_w I_w}{T^2} = 0 \tag{334}$$

from which it follows, from (317), that

$$dq = s_I dT - (H + N_w I_w) dI_w \tag{335}$$

and, from (319) and (321), that

$$du = s_I dT - N_w I_w dI_w$$

$$\frac{\partial s_I}{\partial I} = 0 \tag{336}$$

The last two equations show that as in the case of a paramagnetic, s_I is a function of T only. From (335) it follows that for adiabatic magnetization

$$dT = \frac{H + N_w I_w}{s_I} dI_w \tag{337}$$

The subscript w has been used in order to emphasize that in the preceding equations we are dealing with changes in the spontaneous magnetization and not the average total magnetization. Furthermore, since Eq. (301) involves the average magnetization I and not the spontaneous magnetization I_w, the foregoing considerations will apply only under conditions for which I and I_w are equal. Such is approximately the case near saturation in intense fields.

From Eq. (316) it is apparent that large magnetocaloric temperature changes are to be expected when $\partial I/\partial T$ is large, and from the discussion in Par. 66 and Fig. 79 it follows that this is to be expected near the Curie temperature. In Fig. 141 the experimental results of Weiss and Forrer[1] on nickel are plotted, and the expected maximum near the Curie temperature appears. It would be interesting to compare the observations directly with such a theoretical expression as (337), but the calculations have not been carried out, both because of their complexity and because the comparisons of experiment with theory in regard to specific heat and magnetization effectively check the same points. Weiss and Forrer measured magnetization as well as the magnetocaloric effect and conclude from their investigation that no major corrections are needed in the theory.

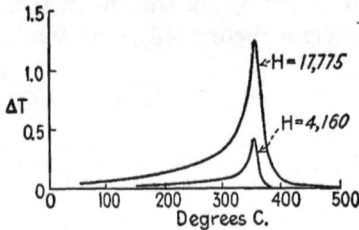

Fig. 141.—The magnetocaloric effect in nickel. (*According to Weiss and Forrer.*)

Observations of the magnetocaloric effect near the Curie point in iron and in Heussler alloys have been carried out by Potter.[2]

Most interesting observations of the change of temperature with magnetization at room temperature have been made at

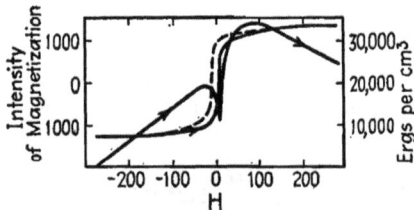

Fig. 142.—Temperature changes, expressed in ergs per cubic centimeter, accompanying magnetization in carbon steel. (*According to Ellwood.*)

Columbia University by the students of S. L. Quimby. The experiments have been confined to much smaller fields than those used by other investigators, and the temperature changes are consequently very small—of the order of a few times 10^{-4}°C. In Figs. 142 and 143 representative results on carbon steel and

[1] P. Weiss and R. Forrer, *Ann. phys.*, **15**, 153, 1926.

[2] H. H. Potter, *Proc. Roy. Soc.*, **132**, 560, 1931; **146**, 362, 1934; *Phil. Mag.*, **13**, 233, 1932.

hard-drawn nickel by Ellwood[1] and Townsend[2] are shown, together with a hysteresis loop of the material. These observations are sufficiently accurate to show the irreversible increase in temperature[3] due to hysteresis, to be discussed in the next section. One is tempted to consider the results for nickel as confirming the formulas developed in the last section, which predict reversible heating with magnetization and cooling with demagnetization, but Ellwood's results on steel are not at all in accordance with such an explanation.[4]

87. Hysteresis.—The discussion of Par. 5 and 7 showed that the work done in taking a sample through a magnetic cycle is equal to the area of the hysteresis loop. This amount of work is converted into heat

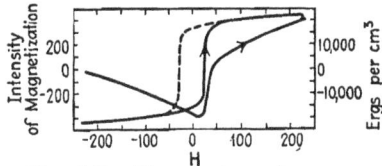

FIG. 143.—Temperature changes, expressed in ergs per cubic centimeter, accompanying magnetization in nickel. (*According to Townsend.*)

and raises the temperature of the sample. Figures 142 and 143 illustrate the experimental verification of this point and indicate, moreover, that most of the heat produced by irreversible processes is liberated in the steep part of the hysteresis loop. A close examination of this part of the loop shows that magnetization proceeds discontinuously, or in jumps, and a discussion of the mechanism of hysteresis will have to take these discontinuities, known as the Barkhausen effect, into account. In this present section we shall describe some of the more general facts and ideas about magnetic hysteresis, leaving the Barkhausen effect to be treated in the next section.

Magnetic hysteresis may be observed either in alternating fields varying in intensity but fixed in direction or in rotating fields of fixed intensity varying in direction. The usual hysteresis

---

[1] W. B. Ellwood, *Phys. Rev.*, **36**, 1066, 1930.

[2] A. Townsend, *Phys. Rev.*, **47**, 306, 1935.

[3] See also experiments reported by U. Adelsberger, *Ann. Physik*, **83**, 184, 1927. F. W. Constant, *Phys. Rev.*, **32**, 486, 1928. K. Honda, J. Okubo, and T. Hirone, *Science Repts. Tôhoku Imp. Univ.*, **18**, 409, 1929. A. Guilbert, *Bull. Soc. Fr. El*, **1**, 175, 1931; **2**, 417, 1932.

[4] Professor Quimby has informed the author that the results obtained by Ellwood are probably affected by the fact that the specimens did external work as a result of magnetostriction combined with the manner of clamping used in the experiments.

loop refers to the alternating type of field and becomes larger as the limits of the loop increase. The energy loss due to a rotational cycle at first increases as the field increases but reaches a maximum and diminishes again as the field becomes strong enough to produce saturation. Results by Perrier[1] on nickel are shown in Fig. 144. More recent observations by von Harlem[2] and others confirm the observations.

In addition to the hysteresis losses mentioned above, which are independent of the frequency with which a magnetizing cycle is accomplished, eddy currents produced by the changing magnetization give rise to losses which must be taken into account when alternating current is used. The separation of eddy-current and hysteresis losses may be carried out by making use of the fact that the eddy-current loss per cycle is proportional to the frequency. For further discussion of this point see Spooner's book "Properties and Testing of Magnetic Materials."

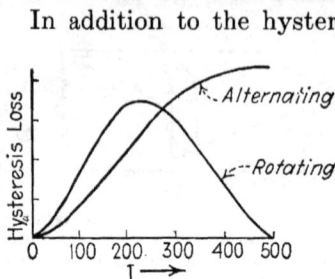

Fig. 144.—Alternating and rotating hysteresis in nickel. (*According to Perrier.*) The data are taken from vol. IV of the International Critical Tables.

Two empirical laws concerning magnetization are frequently referred to.

Steinmetz' Law.—Hysteresis loss is proportional to B_{max}^x where x has values in the neighborhood of 1.6.

Rayleigh's Law.—For small fields, the magnetization curve has the form

$$I = aH + bH^2$$

It seems unlikely that the particular form of either of these expressions has any special significance, and they should be treated as simplified expressions having limited applicability.

Two quantities determined by a hysteresis loop are the remanence and the coercive force (see Fig. 82). The coercive force seems to depend primarily on inhomogeneous strains. In very carefully annealed and purified materials it has its lowest values. In materials used for permanent magnets large coercive

---

[1] A. Perrier, thesis, Zurich, 1909.

[2] J. von Harlem, *Ann. Physik*, **14**, 667, 1932.

forces are desired, and these are obtained by treating super-saturated solid solutions in such a way that finely divided pre-cipitates, causing as much lattice distortion as possible, are produced.

The remanence is determined by the orientation of the regions of spontaneous magnetization in zero applied field. Kaya[1] has shown that the remanence (or at least a measured quantity which closely approximates the remanence) of single crystals of iron is given by the expression

$$I_r = \frac{I_s}{l + m + n} \tag{338}$$

The observations were made on crystals in the shape of rods magnetized longitudinally. l, m, and n are the direction cosines of the rod axis (or of the applied field) with respect to the cubic axes of the crystal. I_s is the saturation intensity. As Kaya points out, this result is compatible with the assumption that the remanent magnetization is in the direction of the axis of the rod, for if I_x, I_y, and I_z are the components of I_r in the directions of the cubic axes, we have

$$I_x = lI_r \qquad I_y = mI_r \qquad I_z = nI_r$$

and if all the regions of spontaneous magnetization are magnetized in the same sense along these three axes, we must have

$$I_s = I_x + I_y + I_z = I_r(l + m + n)$$

which is equivalent to (338).

The following conclusions may be drawn from Kaya's experiments:

1. That demagnetization involves, first, rotational processes and that not until these are sensibly complete do translational processes occur. This is quite in agreement with the assumptions and development of the theory of magnetization in Chap. V.

2. The remanent magnetization of a rod, and probably also, in general, the magnetization in small fields involving translational processes only, will be such that there is no resultant component perpendicular to the axis of the rod. This seems quite reasonable, since magnetization perpendicular to a rod axis

[1] S. KAYA, *Z. Physik*, **84**, 705, 1933.

requires more energy in view of the greater demagnetizing factor in such directions.

A theoretical discussion of magnetization including hysteresis is to be found in papers by Bloch[1] and Gentile.[2]

88. The Barkhausen Effect.—As has been stated, the steep part of the magnetization curve of ferromagnetic materials is not a smooth curve, and the discontinuities that are observed may be interpreted as resulting from abrupt reorientations of the regions of spontaneous magnetization. An enormous amount of work has been done on the investigation of this effect since its discovery in 1919, but it has not been possible to incorporate the results more than qualitatively into the theory of ferromagnetism. A few references[3] which cover some of the more important aspects of the problem are given below. The established facts are briefly the following:

1. In general, changes in magnetization produced by a magnetic field proceed discontinuously.

2. Changes in magnetization produced by changes of temperature proceed without such abrupt changes.

3. The discontinuities may involve the reversal of the magnetization of an arbitrarily large part of a sample under special conditions.

4. In Armco iron, single crystals of iron, nickel, and permalloy the largest volume found to reverse its magnetization abruptly

---

[1] F. Bloch, *Z. Physik*, **74**, 295, 1932.

[2] G. Gentile, *Nuovo cimento*, **11**, 20, 1934.

[3] Discovery of the effect. H. Barkhausen, *Physik. Z.*, **20**, 401, 1919.

Discovery of large discontinuities. R. Forrer, *J. physique*, **7**, 109, 1926.

Estimate of size of regions and transverse effect. R. M. Bozorth, *Phys. Rev.*, **34**, 772, 1929; **39**, 353, 1932; R. M. Bozorth and J. F. Dillinger, *Phys. Rev.*, **35**, 733, 1930; **41**, 345, 1932.

Directional effect in single crystals and references to earlier work. R. F. Clark, Jr., and F. J. Beck, Jr., *Phys. Rev.*, **47**, 158, 1935.

Effect of temperature. B. del Nunzio, *Lincei rend.*, **12**, 125, 1930.

Effect of alternating current. S. Procopiu, *J. phys.*, **1**, 306, 1930.

Change in length. C. W. Heaps and A. B. Bryan, *Phys. Rev.*, 326, 1930.

Change in resistance. C. W. Heaps, *Phys. Rev.*, **46**, 1108, 1934.

Thorough general survey. F. Preisach, *Ann. Physik*, **3**, 737, 1929.

Discovery of propagation. K. J. Sixtus and L. Tonks, *Phys. Rev.*, **37**, 930, 1931; **42**, 419, 1932; **43**, 70, 931, 1933.

Recent work on propagation, R. E. Reinhart, *Phys. Rev.*, **45**, 420, 1934; **46**, 483, 1934. F. Hülster, *Z. tech. Physik*, **15**, 387, 1934.

is of the order of $10^{-8} - 10^{-9}$ cm.[3] according to Bozorth and Dillinger.

5. On the steep part of the hysteresis loop only a very small number of atoms reverse their magnetization in groups of less than 10^{10} atoms (10^{-13} cc.), according to Bozorth.

6. Barkhausen discontinuities have been studied in single crystals and rotating fields, and directional effects have been found.

7. Abrupt changes in length and electrical resistance, resulting from Barkhausen discontinuities, have been found.

8. Large discontinuities are found in special cases, *e.g.*, in wires whose direction of easy magnetization is artificially made to lie along the length of the wire by the application of external forces.

9. The large discontinuities start as local reversals at certain points and spread with a finite velocity as a result of the movement of the boundary of the reversed regions.

89. Elastic Hysteresis.—In Par. 77 the relationship between magnetism and elastic properties was discussed, and it was shown that elastic deformations may produce both rotational and translational processes. Since translational processes in imperfect crystals are generally not reversible, one may expect elastic hysteresis of magnetic origin wherever such processes are involved and, conversely, a decrease of elastic hysteresis when such translational processes are avoided. That such is the case is beautifully shown in an experiment performed by Becker and Kornetzki.[1] A well-annealed iron wire is suspended in a solenoid and is caused to perform torsional oscillations by means of a weight at its lower end. A spot of light reflected from a mirror attached to the weight records the oscillations on a photographic plate. The results obtained with no field and with a field of 100 oersteds are shown in Fig. 145. The effect of the field is to prevent the magnetization of the regions of spontaneous magnetization from wiggling about irreversibly. It is interesting to note that the foregoing type of elastic hysteresis varies with the type of deformation and the crystal orientation. For instance, extension and compression in nickel parallel to a tetragonal axis, discussed in some detail in Par. 77, produce rotational processes only and should therefore be relatively free from elastic hysteresis.

[1] R. BECKER and M. KORNETZKI, *Z. Physik,* **88,** 634, 1934.

The foregoing considerations apply essentially to slow changes in shape for which eddy currents can be neglected. For rapid

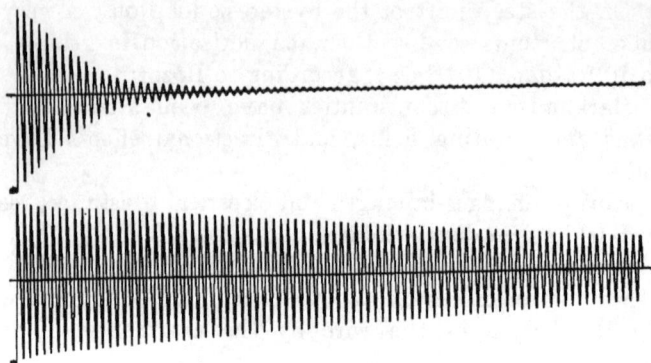

Fig. 145.—Torsional oscillations of an iron wire, above, with no field and, below, with a longitudinal field of 100 oersteds.

oscillations of magnetized samples the damping due to eddy currents is to be expected when conditions are such that the oscillations produce changes in magnetization. Kersten[1] has discussed the experiments of von Auwers[2] and others and finds that

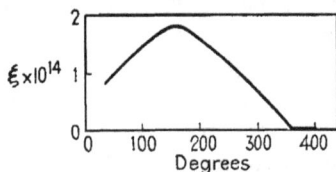

Fig. 146.—The internal friction of nickel as a function of temperature. (*According to Zacharias.*)

the results can be nicely interpreted by taking the eddy currents into account.

The elastic hysteresis of nickel crystals has been measured by Zacharias[3] over a range of temperatures extending to above the Curie point. His results are shown in Fig. 146. ξ is the coefficient of internal friction defined by the relation

$$W = \xi S_0^2$$

where W is the energy loss per cycle, and S_0 the amplitude of the elastic stress. The fact that ξ is very small above the Curie point indicates that the major part of the elastic hysteresis of nickel at room temperature is of ferromagnetic origin.

[1] M. Kersten, *Z. Tech. Phys.*, **15**, 463, 1934.
[2] O. von Auwers, *Ann. Physik*, **17**, 83, 1933.
[3] J. Zacharias, *Phys. Rev.*, **44**, 116, 1933.

APPENDIX

COOPERATIVE PHENOMENA*

By

F. Zwicky

A. Introduction.—A few of the most characteristic properties of matter in the solid state may briefly be described as follows:

a. In a solid body, shearing stresses can be set up by the application of purely static loads. In a liquid, shearing stresses are produced only if various parts of this liquid are in relative motion.

b. On heating at constant pressure, the transition from the solid to the liquid or gaseous state takes place almost discontinuously in a very narrow range of temperature.

c. Microscopically, solids are conglomerates of crystals. The building stones (atoms, ions, molecules) of individual crystals are, on the average, located in discrete sets of points which, in general, constitute fairly regular geometrical lattices.

One important problem of the physics of the solid state is to investigate how the interactions between the atoms produce the *long-distance order* such as is found in crystals and how the existence of *sharp transition* points from one phase into another can be explained. In the following we shall give a few considerations which suggest that the problems of the sharp transition points and of long-distance order can be solved only after a detailed study of certain *cooperative phenomena* which are characteristic of systems containing many particles.

In addition, the study of cooperative phenomena leads to the conclusion that in many cases even the most perfect crystals cannot geometrically be completely described as ideal lattices

---

* The term "cooperative phenomena" was proposed by Zwicky[1,2] on the occasion of a study of various types of interactions involving great numbers of particles. More recently R. H. Fowler[3] has introduced the term "cooperative states" for any stable configuration of matter whose equilibrium is essentially characterized by cooperative actions between many particles.

whose elementary cells have linear dimensions of the order of Bohr's atomic-length prototype $d = h^2/4\pi me^2$. It has been shown theoretically and verified experimentally that the presence of cooperative actions often results in a subdivision of single crystals into cells whose characteristic dimensions D are large as compared with the ordinary lattice constants $(D \gg d)$. Some crystalline properties which involve great characteristic lengths will be discussed later.

B. Types of Cooperative Phenomena. 1. *Cooperative Phenomena Related to Special Laws of Force Which Govern the Interactions between the Elementary Particles of a System.*—Suppose that u_{ik} is the energy of interaction between two elementary particles i and k of a given system. If u_{ik} is entirely determined by the relative position of the particles i and k, i.e., if u_{ik} is not influenced by the presence of additional particles, then the total energy U, corresponding to the interactions of all the N particles of our system, is simply

$$U = \frac{1}{2}\sum_{i=1}^{N} u_i \tag{339}$$

where

$$u_i = \sum_{k=1}^{N} u_{ik} \qquad (k \neq i) \tag{340}$$

u_i is the energy necessary to remove the particle i from the system. In all of the cases that interest us here, u_{ik}, in terms of the mutual distance r_{ik} of the two particles, may be expanded as follows:

$$u_{ik} = \left[\frac{a_p}{r^p} + \frac{a_{p+1}}{r^{p+1}} + \cdots\right]_{ik} \tag{341}$$

The coefficients a_p, a_{p+1}, etc., are functions of certain angles which must be given in order to fix in space the directional characteristics (dipoles, quadrupoles, etc.) of the particles i and k. The exponent p is some positive whole number. For values of r which are very large compared with the average mutual distance of the particles the sum in (340) may be replaced by an integral. The contribution δu_i to u_i from particles at great distances from i (after summation over all the angles involved) takes on the form

$$\delta u_i = \int \Phi_i(r) 4\pi r^2 dr \qquad (342)$$

with

$$\Phi(r) = \frac{A_p}{r^p} + \frac{A_{p+1}}{r^{p+1}} + \cdots \qquad (343)$$

From these relations it is evident that $p = 3$ represents a critical exponent, inasmuch as for an infinitely extended system the integral

$$\int A_p 4\pi r^2 \frac{dr}{r^p} \qquad (344)$$

possesses a finite value only if

$$p > 3 \qquad (345)$$

It may, of course, happen that $A_p = 0$, in spite of the fact that terms of the type a_p/r^p appear in u_{ik}. One such case will be mentioned later. In general, however, if $p \leq 3$, the energy u_i for an infinitely extended system will be infinite. For systems of finite dimensions, u_i will depend very essentially on the geometrical boundaries of the system. Therefore no equation of state in the ordinary sense exists for such a system, inasmuch as the relation among pressure, density, and temperature will not be the same for every point of the system. For $p > 3$ an equation of state in the sense of ordinary thermodynamics exists.

From the foregoing considerations it follows that for $p > 3$ the *individual interactions* between small groups of neighboring particles play the most important role in determining the total energy of the system. For $p < 3$ the *cooperative interactions* between many or all of the particles become very important. A few special examples perhaps serve best to illustrate these statements.

Case $p = 1$.—A system that is built up of particles carrying charges e_i of one sign only, such as a space charge of electrons, belongs to this class. We have

$$u_{ik} = \frac{e_i e_k}{r_{ik}} \qquad (346)$$

It is well known that no equation of state exists in this case. The pressure in a given point depends not only on the local density and the temperature but also on the position of the point considered, relative to the geometrical boundary of the system.

There is another case for which $p = 1$. Indeed, the mutual gravitational energy of two masses i and k in the relative distance r_{ik} is equal to

$$u_{ik} = -\frac{\Gamma m_i m_k}{r_{ik}} \tag{347}$$

where Γ = universal gravitational constant. For a sphere of radius R and of uniform density ρ, the total gravitational potential energy is

$$U_g = -\frac{3\Gamma M^2}{5R} \tag{348}$$

where

$$M = \frac{4\pi\rho R^3}{3} \tag{349}$$

From this we see that the average energy W per unit mass of the sphere is

$$W = \frac{U_g}{M} = -\frac{3\Gamma M}{5R} \tag{350}$$

The *specific* quantity W therefore depends on the *total mass* of the system.

Case $p = 3$.—We consider a system whose particles carry permanent and rigid electric or magnetic dipoles μ. The relative potential energy of the two dipoles μ_i and μ_k at the distance r_{ik} is

$$u_{ik} = \frac{a_{ik}\mu_i\mu_k}{r_{ik}^3} \tag{351}$$

where a_{ik} depends on the relative orientation of the dipoles. If a volume V is uniformly covered with equal dipoles, the energy of a given dipole relative to all others, according to (344), would contain terms of the order $\log V$, which for infinite V are infinite. However, a_{ik} is not a constant but depends on the relative orientation of the dipole vectors. The contributions of the distant dipoles to the potential energy of a given dipole are therefore partly positive and partly negative. Consequently, the convergence of the sum (340) is, in most practical cases, either absolute or at least conditional.

Let us, for instance, consider a substance whose molecules possess electric dipoles μ. In the gaseous state, at sufficiently high temperatures, thermal agitation will produce a random distribution of the dipole vectors. Their mutual potential energy, on the average, will be zero. At lower temperatures dipoles that are far away from one another will still show a random distribution $(A = 0)$, whereas neighboring dipoles will have a tendency to associate and hence contribute a certain negative amount of potential energy to the total energy of the gas, thus causing deviations from the ideal gas laws. Since, in this case, the whole interaction is confined to neighboring dipoles, the expression (339) for the total energy of interaction will be an *absolutely convergent* sum. If we go to still lower temperatures, the association between the dipoles, under certain circumstances, will extend throughout the whole system in such a way that at the absolute zero point all of the dipoles might be lined up parallel to one another and thus produce a configuration of minimum energy. In this case the total energy of interaction u_i of one dipole with the rest will be expressed by a *conditionally convergent sum*. In other words, u_i will have a finite value, no matter how extended the system is, but this value will depend on whether the boundary up to which we carry out the summation is a sphere, an ellipsoid, or some other surface. This becomes clear if we consider the two special cases of a very long cylinder and a sphere which are cut out of a cubic lattice in whose lattice points (n per cm.^{3}) electric dipoles μ are located. We assume that all of the dipoles are parallel to one another and, in the case of the cylinder, parallel to its axis. The average electric field $\bar{E}$ inside the cylinder (and of course also outside) is zero. However, the local electric field E_l in a lattice point is equal to the so-called Lorentz force F:

$$E_l = F = \frac{4\pi n\mu}{3} \tag{352}$$

The work necessary to remove an individual dipole from the lattice is

$$w = \mu E_l = \mu F \neq 0 \tag{353}$$

In case of the sphere, the average electric field inside is

$$\bar{E} = -\frac{4\pi n\mu}{3} \tag{354}$$

We have again the Lorentz force $F = 4\pi n\mu/3$, so that the local electric field in each lattice point becomes

$$E_l = \bar{E} + F = 0 \tag{355}$$

This result can also be derived by a direct calculation of the local field in a lattice point by summing up the contributions from all the other dipoles. The work necessary to remove a dipole is, in this case,

$$w = E_l\mu = 0 \tag{356}$$

The value of w therefore depends on the external boundary of the system, and no equation of state in the ordinary sense exists. This, we may also say, is a consequence of the well-known fact that the so-called *depolarizing*, or *demagnetizing*, *factors* of different geometrical bodies are different (zero for a needle, $4\pi/3$ for a sphere, 4π for an infinitely extended plate which is polarized normal to the two boundary surfaces, etc.).

Using the preceding example, we now illustrate our previous assertion that cooperative phenomena may play an important role in determining certain fundamental properties of the solid state.

a. The fact that at low temperatures not only are the individual interactions of a given dipole with its immediate neighbors important but also the cooperative interactions with distant dipoles leads to an understanding of the long-distance order (all the dipole vectors are lined up parallel to one another).

b. The transition from the ordered state, which is characterized by a permanent polarization $P = n\mu$, to a state in which the individual dipoles are directionally distributed at random takes place abruptly $(dP/dT = -\infty)$ at the Curie point, whose temperature, as Weiss has first shown, is

$$\theta = \frac{4\pi n\mu^2}{9k} \tag{357}$$

where $k = 1.37 \times 10^{-16}$ erg is Boltzmann's constant.

c. In order to demonstrate how cooperative phenomena may lead to a *subdivision* of a crystal into cells that are large compared with the ordinary elementary cells, we may argue as follows.

Consider a crystal whose building stones, in addition to other physical characteristics, are endowed with permanent electric or magnetic dipoles. As we have seen, these dipoles may be lined up parallel to one another at sufficiently low temperatures. It is to be noticed, however, that an assembly of parallel dipoles results in a state of lowest (free) energy only if our crystal has the shape of a very long thin cylinder. In all other cases the depolarizing factors will be different from zero. A configuration of low and perhaps of lowest energy can then be obtained only if the crystal is subdivided into bundles of thin cylinders which are alternately polarized in opposite directions. Any such *subdivision* which is fundamentally related to atomic properties of the crystal may be called a *secondary structure*, in contradistinction to the ordinary *primary* lattice *structure*.

The expectation of large subdivisions or the existence of secondary structures is actually borne out by various observations on *ferromagnetic crystals*. These crystals, in the absence of external magnetic fields, are known to be permanently magnetized. However, the total magnetic moment of a good crystal of macroscopic dimensions is always zero. This means that the crystal is subdivided into regions whose magnetic moments compensate one another.

A direct proof of the existence of subdivisions was given by Bitter in a series of experiments using the sedimentation method of colloidal Fe_2O_3 particles. The beautiful sedimentation patterns which he obtained on surfaces of ferromagnetic crystals in the presence of external magnetic fields furnish particularly strong support for the view that crystals may exhibit fundamental periodicities characterized by lengths D which are large compared with the ordinary lattice constants.

2. *Cooperative Phenomena Which Are Related to Self-perpetuating Electric Fields.*—In the preceding section we have considered the case where the mutual potential energy u_{ik} of two particles i and k is not influenced by the presence of additional particles. This is an assumption that for atoms, ions, and molecules is never rigorously true. If an atom or a molecule is placed into an electric field E, a dipole of strength $\mu = \alpha E$ will be induced in it, where α is the polarizability of the particle. If we consider three particles i, k, and m, the energy u_{ik} will depend on the magnitude of the electric dipoles induced in the particles i and k by the electric field due to m.

How the dielectric properties of atoms give rise to the existence of important cooperative actions is perhaps easiest demonstrated by discussing briefly Herzfeld's *criterion* of the *metallic state*.[4]

Consider a simple cubic lattice which is occupied by atoms whose polarizability is α (see Fig. 147). Suppose that every atom except A is endowed with an infinitely small electric dipole μ whose orientation is parallel to the axis of a long cylinder which we have cut out of our lattice. According to equation (352),

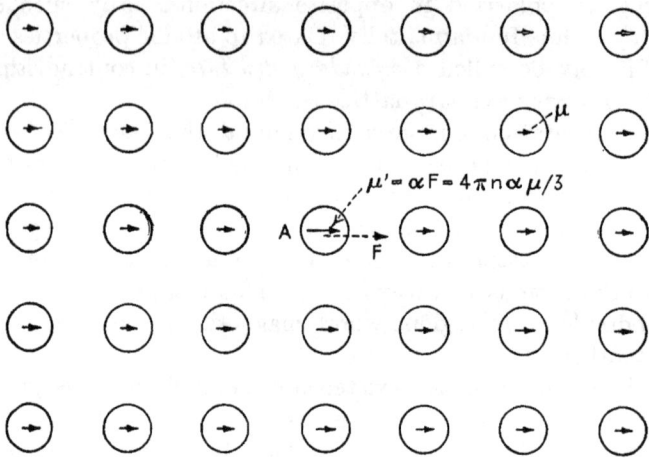

$$\mu' = \alpha F = 4\pi n \alpha \mu/3$$

Fig. 147.

the local field in A is equal to the Lorentz force $F = 4\pi n\mu/3$. This field will induce in the atom A a dipole μ'.

$$\mu' = \alpha F = \frac{4\pi n \alpha \mu}{3} \tag{358}$$

Suppose, now, that

$$\frac{4\pi n \alpha}{3} = \frac{4\pi N \alpha \rho}{3M} = \frac{P\rho}{M} > 1 \tag{359}$$

where P is the molar refractivity, ρ the density, M the molecular weight, and $N = 6.06 \times 10^{23}$ is Loschmidt's number. It then follows that

$$\mu' > \mu \tag{360}$$

This means that the induced dipoles form a cooperative assembly whose total electric moment is ever increasing by self-perpetuating interaction. Consequently, all of the atoms will be stripped of their loosest electrons. The remaining ions have polariz-- abilities that are considerably smaller than those of the neutral atoms. A state of equilibrium will, therefore, be reached after a certain number of electrons have been set free and the substance has assumed the character of a metal.

The condition, derived from classical theory, for a cubic lattice to be a metal is

$$\frac{P\rho}{M} > 1 \qquad (361)$$

In deriving Herzfeld's criterion for the metallic state we have made use of cooperative actions between all of the dipoles of the system. According to the preceding section, this leads to conditionally convergent sums; and we should seem to arrive at the paradoxial conclusion that the criterion for the metallic state would be different for different external shapes of the material considered. In reality this is, of course, not the case. The theoretical justification for the unambiguity of Herzfeld's criterion can be obtained by *subdividing* an arbitrarily shaped crystal into cylindrical columns with alternating directions of the polarization vectors. The preceding considerations have been partly reformulated and refined by the use of quantum mechanics.

Calculations similar to those given by Herzfeld were used by Zwicky[5] and Evjen[6] in order to show that ideal ionic lattices of the NaCl type are often dynamically unstable. The simplest and so far perhaps the most important result of these calculations is the following:

If the mutual energy ϵ between two ions of charge $\pm e$ is assumed to be of the form

$$\epsilon = \pm\frac{e^2}{r} + \frac{C}{r^q} \qquad (362)$$

the equilibrium condition of an ideal lattice of the NaCl type relative to a uniform compression requires C to be a certain function of q and the lattice constant $2a$ of the crystal. In addition, q may be determined from the compressibility. With the values of C and q thus chosen, ideal lattices of the alkali-halides are, in general, stable relative to compression, extension, and shearing. But Zwicky and Evjen[6] obtained the surprising result that these lattices are unstable against small displacements of the partial lattices of positive and negative ions relative to one another, provided that

$$Q = \mathfrak{M}(q - 2)\left(1 - \frac{4\pi\bar{\alpha}}{3a^3}\right) < 4\pi \qquad (363)$$

where $\bar{\alpha}$ is the average polarizability of the two types of ions, and $\mathfrak{M} = 3.49$ is the so-called Madelung constant for a lattice of the NaCl type. For LiCl, LiBr, AgCl, and AgBr the constant Q is found to satisfy the inequality (363). Since only small displacements are considered, this result remains unaltered if any other mathematical functions for the second term in the expression for ϵ are used, provided that these functions lead to correct values for the elastic constants of the lattice.

Considerations of the type given have suggested the conclusion that not only ferromagnetic lattices but most crystals in thermal equilibrium cannot geometrically be completely described as ideal lattices. Zwicky[7] suggested that the deviations from the ideal lattice result in the formation of *secondary structures*. Just what the detailed characteristics of these structures are constitutes a very difficult problem which probably can be solved only by persistent cooperation of theory and experiment.* A few ideas which may prove important for the determination of the characteristic dimensions D of the large-scale subdivisions are as follows:

3. *Normal Modes and Retarded Potentials.*—Consider, again, a *uniform* relative displacement r of the partial positive and negative lattices in a heteropolar crystal. The oscillation $r = r_0 \times \sin 2\pi\nu t$ is that *normal oscillation* of the crystal as a whole which determines the characteristic *residual rays* whose frequencies are of the order $\nu = 10^{13}$ sec^{-1}. Because of the conditional convergence related to assemblies of parallel electric dipoles, this frequency would depend strongly on the external shape of the crystal, provided that the interactions between the dipoles were

---

* Zwicky has made tentative suggestions regarding possible types of secondary structures. *Qualitative* objections against these suggestions were raised by various authors.[8] These objections must be regarded as of doubtful value as long as no *quantitative calculations* are forthcoming proving the incorrectness of such perfectly definite instability criteria as (363) and (361) used by Zwicky and Evjen.

transmitted with infinite speed. If, however, we take into account that electromagnetic actions cannot travel faster than light, retardation effects become important. Retardation effects cause the actions of the faraway oscillating dipoles to cancel one another so that ν will be expressed by an absolutely convergent sum and will become independent of the macroscopic boundaries. In addition, the constant amplitude r_0 of the *classical* normal mode (velocity of light $c \rightarrow \infty$) will become a periodic function of the space coordinates with a characteristic period D of the order

$$D = c/n\nu \sim \frac{[M_1 M_2/m_e(M_1 + M_2)]^{\frac{1}{2}}}{nR} \tag{364}$$

where n is a dimensionless constant of the type of a refractive index, R is Rydberg's constant, and m_e, M_1, and M_2 are the masses of the electron and of the two ions, respectively.

For an electron lattice the period would be of the order of

$$D' = \frac{1}{nR} \tag{365}$$

Because of the existence of a zero-point energy, it would seem that even at the absolute zero these fundamental lengths D and D' must play an essential role in determining the character of secondary subdivisions of crystals. These lengths must be especially important in all those cases where the ideal lattice is unstable with respect to r-displacements [criteria (361) and (363)].

The relation between normal modes and retarded potentials can, of course, be treated correctly only on the basis of the quantum mechanics, inasmuch as the classical theory always leads to strong damping of the optical normal modes because of radiation losses. Such a treatment so far has not been given.

Summarizing, we draw the conclusion that the fundamental lengths D and D' are essential not only in the theory of spectra but also in the physics of solids, in which they play an important role.

In passing, we mention that recent theories[9] of superconductivity also make use of a length that is equal in order of magnitude to the reciprocal of Rydberg's constant, *viz.*, $D = ch^3/2\pi^2me^4$. This is of interest because of the fact that superconduction exhibits all the earmarks of a cooperative state, such as sharp transition point, long-distance order, etc.

4. *Other Cooperative Phenomena.*—We call attention to a few more phenomena which are important for the theory of solids. For detailed information we must refer to the literature.

From the examples that we have given it follows that the character of cooperative phenomena is dependent on two factors: The *energy* of *interaction* between the individual particles that constitute the system and the *geometrical characteristics* of the system are equally essential.

For instance, the expression for the total energy of interaction of a great number of dipoles can be conditionally convergent only if the dipoles occupy a *three-dimensional* region. For one- and two-dimensional assemblies it is always absolutely convergent.

The fundamental importance of geometrical probabilities for the determination of thermodynamic equilibria becomes apparent if we remember the *canonical equation* of state (relation among the free energy per mol F, the density ρ, and the temperatures T) as it is obtained from statistical mechanics:

$$F = -NkT \log \sum_i \gamma_i e^{\frac{-\epsilon_i}{kT}} \tag{366}$$

where the sum is to be extended over all possible configurations of the system. Each configuration is characterized by a definite energy ϵ_i and a geometrical a priori probability γ_i.

High energy states with correspondingly small Boltzmann factors may possess large values of γ so that a free energy results equal to that of configurations of low energy and small a priori probability. As a result, our system may contain two or more *phases* which are in thermal equilibrium.

A good quantitative illustration for the existence of sharp transition points and long-distance order in crystals resulting from the cooperation of many atoms is to be found in Bethe's theory of *superlattices* in metallic alloys.[10]

The simultaneous (cooperative) proximity of many molecules results in configurations of small a priori probability and of low energy which are to be identified with the liquid and the solid states of matter.

An example for cooperation in a *linear* chain of atoms has been discussed quantitatively by Dehlinger[11] in his theory of "dislocations." This theory seems to be of some importance for the understanding of recrystallization phenomena.

Finally, we mention the exclusion principle as an example of a cooperative phenomenon whose great importance for the theory of metals is well known.

C. Great Characteristic Lengths in Crystals.—The study of cooperative phenomena suggests that many crystals in the thermally stable state are subdivided into physically distinct regions (block structure, secondary structure) whose linear dimensions D are large compared with the ordinary lattice constants. It must be emphasized that secondary structures may be either *geometrically regular* or *irregular*. For instance, subdivisions caused by the superposition of normal oscillations of incommensurable wave lengths will seem to be irregular. It must also be kept in mind that secondary structures are much more *sensitive* to external disturbances than are primary structures. Real crystals consequently exhibit often slightly irregular block structures (mosaic structures).

Some types of secondary structures may be present at the absolute zero of temperature, whereas others appear only at higher temperatures, depending on whether they correspond to deviations from the ideal atomic lattices which lead to absolute or relative minima of the total energy.

The prediction of the existence of great fundamental lengths D in crystals has been verified experimentally in a number of cases. Without going into any details, we mention briefly a few observations which prove that lengths of the order of 0.1 to 10μ and more often play an important role in the physics of crystals.

Subdivisions of the kind mentioned have been found under the microscope on certain surfaces of good single crystals of $KClO_3$, Cu, Bi, Zn, Cd, and other substances.[7,12,13,14]

The block structure of single crystals can be brought out clearly by etching or partial evaporation. This indicates that the binding energy of atoms in the interior of the blocks is different from the binding energy of the atoms between the blocks.

The planes that separate the secondary blocks from one another often act as slip planes during the process of plastic deformation.[15] This result provides a satisfactory explanation of the formerly puzzling fact that slipping does not take place on all equivalent planes, as one would expect from the theory of ideal lattices.

Certain impurities have a tendency to segregate along the distinguished planes which define the large-scale subdivisions of crystals. In this connection the interesting experiments of Focke[16] on the appearance of discrete sets of ranges of α particles from small amounts of polonium in bismuth single crystals are particularly important. They make possible the determination of the spatial characteristics of secondary structures without necessitating any disturbances of the crystals investigated.

Abrupt changes of the magnetic susceptibility[17] of single crystals whose dimensions become smaller than certain critical lengths $D \gg d$ also prove that these lengths are of fundamental importance.

The theory has predicted further that some crystals, grown and held in electric or magnetic fields, must show secondary structures whose characteristics depend on the applied field.[18] For the electric field this prediction has not yet been verified. Bitter has shown that in the case of magnetism it is not even necessary to grow the crystals in the field. Very regular and reproducible patterns of stray fields appear on the surfaces of ferromagnetic crystals (Fe, Ni, Co, etc.) immediately on application of external fields. This proves that great lengths are intrinsic characteristics of the thermally stable states of crystals.

All experiments on the secondary structure, however, must be executed with great care, since certain great lengths also appear as a consequence of particular boundary conditions during the growth of crystals. It is indeed well known that temperature gradients near the surfaces of growing crystals may cause the formation of slip bands,[19] the discontinuous segregation of impurities, and the freezing in of columnar vortices (hexagonal basalt columns). Concentration changes of impurities in solutions and in melts may result in the formation of Liesegang figures, lineage, and so on. All of these phenomena lead to deviations from the ideal lattice structures which are characterized by great lengths. However, these lengths, in contradistinction to secondary lattice constants, are *accidental* in character, and their magnitudes therefore can be changed by changing the conditions of growth of crystals.

References

1. F. Zwicky, *Proc. Nat. Acad. Sci.*, **17**, 524, 1931.
2. F. Zwicky, *Phys. Rev.*, **43**, 270, 1933.

3. R. H. FOWLER, *Proc. Roy. Soc.*, **149A**, 1, 1935.
4. K. F. HERZFELD, *Phys. Rev.*, **29**, 701, 1926.
5. F. ZWICKY, *Phys. Rev.*, **38**, 1772, 1931.
6. H. M. EVJEN, *Phys. Rev.*, **44**, 491, 1933; and **44**, 501, 1933.
7. F. ZWICKY, *Proc. Nat. Acad. Sci.*, **15**, 816 1929; and **15**, 253, 1929.
8. International Conference on Physics, vol. 2, London, 1934.
9. H. G. SMITH and J. O. WILHELM, *Rev. Mod. Phys.*, **7**, 263, 1935.
10. H. A. BETHE, *Proc. Roy. Soc.*, **150A**, 552, 1935.
11. U. DEHLINGER, *Ann. Physik*, **2**, 786, 1929.
12. LORD RAYLEIGH, *Proc. Roy. Soc.*, **102**, 668, 1923.
13. A. GOETZ, *Proc. Nat. Acad. Sci.*, **16**, 99, 1930.
14. M. STRAUMANIS, *Z. physik. Chem.*, **13B**, 316, 1931.
15. M. STRAUMANIS, *Z. Kryst.*, **83**, 29, 1932.
16. A. B. FOCKE, *Phys. Rev.*, **46**, 623, 1934.
17. S. R. RAO, *Phys. Rev.*, **44**, 850, 1933.
18. F. ZWICKY, *Helvetica Phys. Acta*, III, 292, 1930.
19. F. ZWICKY, *Phys. Rev.*, **40**, 73, 1932.

INDEX